D1553198

LABOR AND EMPLOYMENT

RELATIONS ASSOCIATION SERIES

Transforming the U.S. Workforce Development System:

Lessons from Research and Practice

EDITED BY

David Finegold, Mary Gatta, Hal Salzman,

and Susan J. Schurman

First Edition

ISBN 978-0-913447-01-7

Price: $24.95

LABOR AND EMPLOYMENT RELATIONS ASSOCIATION SERIES
Proceedings of the Annual Meeting (published electronically beginning in 2009)
Annual Research Volume (published in the fall)
LERA Online Membership Directory (updated daily, member access only)
LERA Newsletter (published electronically 3-4 times a year)
Perspectives on Work (published once a year in the summer/fall)
Perspectives on Work Online Companion (published twice a year as a supplement)

Information regarding membership, subscriptions, meetings, publications, and general affairs of the LERA can be found at the Association website at www.lera.illinois.edu. Members can make changes to their member records, including contact information, affiliations and preferences, by accessing the online directory at the website or by contacting the LERA national office.

LABOR AND EMPLOYMENT RELATIONS ASSOCIATION
University of Illinois at Urbana-Champaign
School of Labor and Employment Relations
121 Labor and Industrial Relations Building
504 East Armory Ave.
Champaign, IL 61820
Telephone: 217/333-0072   Fax: 217/265-5130
Internet: www.lera.illinois.edu   E-mail: leraoffice@illinois.edu

CONTENTS

CHAPTER 1

Introduction: Meeting America's Skills Challenge

MARY GATTA
DAVID FINEGOLD
Rutgers University

Introduction

If there was ever a time when the United States needed a national skills strategy, it is today. The nation shed jobs at an alarming rate during the deep recession of 2007 to 2009, and despite major government stimulus spending, no leading economist expects the job losses to be restored for many years. Individuals need help coping with this crisis—identifying where the current and new job opportunities are likely to be and how to develop the skills for them—and the current system is not up to the task.

The skills crisis, however, goes much deeper than the current economic crisis. Geopolitical changes, ranging from the fall of the Soviet Union to the integration of China as well as other emerging economies into the global economy, have occurred alongside new technology that provides greater integration and exchange across a great swath of the globe. These changes, in combination with global, regional, and bilateral trade agreements, have facilitated new corporate strategies for the global distribution of work and new markets for sales.

The workforce challenges these realities present for current generations differ dramatically from the range of challenges and opportunities of the past century. The once unique, or at least comparative, advantages of the U.S. workforce provide much less advantage or protection in the face of these global changes and the emerging corporate competitive strategies. It is no longer just low-skill manufacturing work that can be located offshore, but rather work across the entire skill spectrum—and increasingly high skill-service work—that can be done by workers in low-wage countries.

1

In the face of these challenges, workforce development has not kept pace with the needs of current workers or of students preparing to enter the workforce. The "loosely coupled" education and workforce development systems of the United States can no longer provide the global advantages they once did. Although the United States has historically achieved the highest rates of college graduation and provided high mobility for career changes and business start-ups, increasingly workers in other nations have advantages that erode the edge held by workers in the United States. The problem begins with inadequate investment in early childhood development, particularly for children in disadvantaged families, where both program evaluation and the latest scientific research suggest the rate of return is highest by helping to improve labor market outcomes for the rest of individuals' lives (Heckman 2010). The skills issue is compounded by poorly performing urban public schools, the lack of rigorous language education or knowledge about how the global economy functions, the loss of leadership in mass higher education that was a foundation for U.S. economic leadership in the postwar period, and the absence of a lifelong learning system. Together these factors have left our population ill-prepared to compete in this new global order. The governments in both the United Kingdom and Australia, the countries that are the United States' main competitors for attracting the best postsecondary students from around the world, have recently undertaken major efforts to develop concrete national skills strategies through to the year 2020. The United States has no similar process under way.

To paraphrase Rahm Emanuel, we should not waste a good crisis. In this case, the crisis means that millions of highly educated workers who have never heard of, much less thought of using the services of, a workforce investment board (WIB) or a One-Stop Career Center are out of work or soon will be. In some states, including New Jersey, we're losing thousands of our best jobs as Wall Street refugees and scientists and managers who have been displaced from the high-tech, knowledge intensive industries such as pharmaceuticals struggle to find new work. Although the short-term opportunities for work depend more on the economy than on worker skills, we are in danger of underinvesting, or even disinvesting, in workforce development during the crisis and thus being ill-prepared to have the workforce needed when the economy recovers. In fact, without a workforce better educated and trained than when we entered the crisis, the country will be at a disadvantage in accelerating the growth opportunities that do develop. New jobs, new technologies, new scientific discoveries will flow to the countries that are best prepared to take advantage of them rather than just reappear or expand in areas that had historical claims to them. Whether the arena is automobile production or pharmaceutical research, the recovery will witness a global reallocation of work to those places that provide the best conditions for growth—and a skilled, educated, and trained workforce will be a key component.

We need a workforce development system that can help workers at all levels locate new opportunities, whether joining a high-tech start-up or retraining to fill the need for strong primary and secondary teachers. In addition, we have millions of lower-skilled workers who are either stuck in low-wage jobs or unable to secure any work at all. These workers need skill upgrades and literacy and other education and training to qualify for jobs that can offer them routes out of poverty. Our workforce system, which was already ill-equipped to deal with the massive challenges faced by workers at all rungs of the skill ladder, will require greater investment and development, not less, during the current crisis.

The Current Skills Challenge

For politicians and policy makers, enhancing education and training has long been seen as the answer to a wide range of social and economic problems. Every decade has faced particular challenges relative to skills and the best ways to develop them for U.S. citizens (see Figure 1). After World War II, in order to help returning veterans secure good jobs, the federal government passed the GI Bill of 1944—a major catalyst for the mass higher education system. In the 1960s we competed in the race for space—investing in science, engineering, math, and technology to catch up with Soviet advances after the Sputnik launch. The 1970s saw a concern for "the over-educated American" (Freeman 1976), when an oversupply of college graduates saw a decline in their wage premiums. Just as

FIGURE 1
Skills Challenges over the Decades.

1940s—GI Bill: Tuition assistance and supportive services are provided for returning veterans to attend college.

1960s—The Race for Space: A drive begins to improve science and math education to catch up with Russia after Sputnik.

1970s—The Over-Educated American: There is a decline (ultimately short-lived) in the wage premium earned by those with college education, attributed to an oversupply of college graduates struggling to find good jobs.

1980s—A Nation at Risk: Concern erupts that the United States lacks the skills needed to compete with Japan and Germany in global manufacturing.

1990s—The War for Talent: The dot-com boom combined with the looming retirement of Baby Boomers creates fear of major skill shortages, particularly of top leadership talent.

Today and Tomorrow—The Flat World: The Internet and effective integration of over two billion new workers into the global economy allow knowledge work to flow wherever best talent can be found at the best price.

policy makers began to focus on the risk of too many college graduates, the situation reversed dramatically, with the earnings for college graduates rising significantly, while the wages of high school graduates and dropouts stagnated or fell in real terms over the next several decades.

By the 1980s a headline-grabbing report, *A Nation at Risk* (National Commission on Education and the Economy 1983), made the bold claims that the country's poor state of education imperiled the U.S. economy. This appeared during an era when the Japanese incursion into the U.S. automobile market was recognized as a serious challenge to the dominance of the "Big Three" car makers, and other firms shifted their competitive strategies by shedding low-value-added activities, a period that marked the beginning of a decades-long march toward downsizing and outsourcing. Surveying the changing landscape, the report, using Cold War rhetoric, identified poor education as its focal point:

> Our once unchallenged preeminence in commerce, industry, science, and technological innovation is being overtaken by competitors throughout the world. . . . If an unfriendly foreign power had attempted to impose on America the mediocre educational performance that exists today, we might have viewed it as an act of war. As it stands, we have allowed this to happen to ourselves. . . . We have in effect, been committing an act of *unthinking, unilateral educational disarmament*" (authors' emphasis; p. 5).

In an effort to maintain international economic competitiveness, the report mobilized policy makers to focus on improving education as a way of providing U.S. workers the skills needed to compete with Japan and Germany in global manufacturing. The Department of Energy "declared education to be a 'matter of mission' for the DOE laboratories" and tasked a group at Sandia Laboratories to conduct a study to "elucidate key issues in education and thereby help focus our laboratories' attention on the most pressing challenges" (Carson, Huelskamp, and Woodall 1993:259). Conducting an extensive review of the data, interviews, and other research, the Sandia group found that the indicators pointed to a quite different outcome than that proclaimed by *A Nation at Risk*: Rather than portraying a nation in educational decline, the evidence indicated steady improvements in nearly all measures, from drop-out rates to test scores. Though the Sandia group found an education system in great need of improvement, it was not comparatively worse than those of other countries, although the distribution of educational spending and outcomes were more unequal. And it was producing a supply of workers sufficient to meet employer demands in the U.S. economy.

Despite this subsequent research, the core message of *A Nation at Risk* served as a focal point for spurring on educational reform as part of a changing ideology about factors responsible for economic performance and corporate strategy. This perceived loss of U.S. firm competitiveness attributed to the education and training system prompted decades of education reform, from the National Association of Educational Progress to School to Work to No Child Left Behind to the current Race to the Top. Billions of dollars were devoted to these reforms, and whether as a consequence of or incidental to them, educational performance continued its slow but steady improvement over the decades that followed (see, for example, Lowell and Salzman 2007 and Salzman and Lowell 2008 for reviews). At the same time the U.S. economy managed to restore its global leadership position through strength in services and high-tech sectors, while Japan entered a 20-year slump brought on by its financial and real estate crash, and West Germany was slowed by the major task and costs of reintegration with East Germany (despite providing its industry a highly educated and lower-cost workforce).

By the 1990s the concern for America's global competitiveness and its workers' skill shortages took a new direction with the War for Talent (Chambers et al. 1998). The combination of dot-com boom, tight labor market, and looming retirement of Baby Boomers created fear of major skill shortages, particularly top leadership talent. The response centered on strategies for attracting, retaining, and retraining managers and employers—in particular leadership training, along with attention to marginal groups, particularly women and people of color.

The War for Talent was in turn brought to an abrupt end by 9/11 and the dot-com crash. The slowdown in demand precipitated by these events coincided with a dramatic expansion in global labor supply. The Internet and effective integration of over one billion new workers into the global labor market allow firms to move their knowledge work to wherever the best talent can be found at the best price. This huge increase in the global labor supply must now factor into our workforce and economic development policies. Chinese firms and workers have become leaders in providing not just low-cost manufacturing but increasingly highly engineered products, while India has emerged rapidly as a growing source for talent in high-skill services. While U.S. multinational corporations have been taking advantage of these new low-cost sources of suppliers and talent to increase their profitability and focus on growth in emerging markets, policy makers and others are concerned about the ability of the U.S. economy to create good jobs for American workers.

Indeed, a college degree is no longer insurance that one will have a good job. Alan Blinder (2007) has estimated that 30 to 40 million information processing jobs are vulnerable to offshoring in our new economy. At the same time, U.S. private sector job growth has declined, and more recently the public sector has been forced to cut back on employment to try to deal with major structural budget deficits. While the 1990s saw a growth of 19.3 million private sector jobs, the first decade of the 2000s saw negative growth, with a decline of 1.47 million private sector jobs (Britt 2009).

The long-term structural problems with the U.S. skill development system were greatly exacerbated by the global recession of 2007 to 2009 and the accompanying financial crisis. There is a negative economic return to investments in retraining if there are no jobs available for individuals afterward to use their new skills (Lafer 2002). And in the case of this recession—by many indicators the deepest since the Great Depression—the rate of job loss relative to new job creation has been particularly high. This resulted in a record level of individuals out of work relative to job vacancies, as well as lengthening of the duration of unemployment to record levels: a peak median length of 17.9 weeks in June 2010, nearly 50% longer than the previous peak over the prior 50 years of just over 12 weeks in the 1983 recession (Hughes and Seneca 2009). With these factors taken together, we are facing a workforce and economic crisis of epic proportions, and the rapid and effective response of our public workforce system is more critical than ever.

There are two key challenges in particular for workforce development and the economy. The depth and breadth of the current economic crisis has overshadowed any underlying weaknesses in the supply of skilled workers. There is no shortage of skilled workers at the moment, nor can workforce development investments be expected to provide any immediate solutions to the crisis. In this climate, with severe budget crises at every level of government and many firms, we risk underinvesting in workforce development and thus not having the skills needed during the recovery.

The second challenge, we would argue, is fostering a new strategic direction for the U.S. workforce development system. The need for more skills in many jobs, coupled with the long-standing structure of the U.S. system, has led policy makers to focus on "college for all" as a necessary prerequisite for nearly all jobs. Less consideration has been given to a more fundamental restructuring of the system, creating new high schools that blend a strong education foundation with technical and vocational options that connect academic content to real occupations and developing multiple high-status postsecondary education and training pathways leading to well-recognized qualifications as well as to informed citizens. A perspective that our secondary education system should be developed to enable direct entry into the workforce for the segment of the population that is either unprepared for or uninterested in a traditional college degree does not have much currency among education and workforce policy makers. Considering such an alternative raises a series of research and policy questions: Do we integrate education and workforce development? How do we provide both a broad liberal arts education and skill development? How do we address the structure of a system that has, to date, resisted such changes? Could there be a U.S. version of effective skill development systems as exists in Germany? To explore these questions and others in the chapters that follow, it is important to first consider how the U.S. system has evolved over the past two thirds of a century.

A Quick History of the Evolution of the U.S. Public Workforce Development System

While a comprehensive history of the workforce development system is beyond the scope of this introduction, it is helpful to review the key features of past U.S. government employment and training programs, as they shed a great deal of light on how we got to where we are now (see Figure 2). Our current public workforce system first emerged out of the economic challenges of the Great Depression. During the 1930s, President Roosevelt created a series of employment and training programs as part of the New Deal. Through programs including the Works Progress Administration, the Civilian Conservation Corps, the National Youth Authority, and the Civil Works Administration, hundreds of thousands of unemployed workers received targeted training to qualify for subsidized employment in the public sector. While the focus of these programs was job creation, and education and train-

FIGURE 2
Timeline of Major U.S. Federal Workforce Development Programs.

1962—Manpower Development Training Act (MDTA): Short-term training courses to prepare recipients for entry-level jobs.

1960s—Work Incentive Program (WIN): Supplement to welfare policy providing job training.

1973—Comprehensive Employment and Training Act (CETA): Public-service job creation program targeting unskilled and semiskilled jobs and training.

1982—Job Training Partnership (JTPA): Replaces CETA and takes a new approach to employment policy, with a focus on training and skills building rather than public job creation.

1996—Personal Responsibility and Work Opportunities Reconciliation Act (PRWORA): "Workfirst" model of welfare removes any notion that welfare is a social entitlement and severely restricts access to education and skills training.

1998—Workforce Investment Act (WIA): Replaces JTPA and focuses on short-term training for immediate placement in the private sector. Includes a three-tiered system of core, intensive, and training services, which becomes more of an employment policy than a training policy.

ing were only a small part of the policy response, the implementation structure of the training programs was unique for the time. Specifically, as Shaw, Goldrick-Rab, Mazzeo, and Jacobs (2006) have noted, as a result of the Roosevelt Administration's distrust of the current educational system, the New Deal training programs were administered not through the Department of Education or local schools, but instead through community-based organizations.

As the country entered World War II, the focus on the public workforce development system diminished, but it quickly reemerged after the war via one of the country's most significant training programs—the GI Bill of 1944. This legislation provided returning veterans with tuition assistance and supportive services to attend college. As Shaw, Goldrick-Rab, Mazzeo, and Jacobs note (2006:22), "This was perhaps the federal government's biggest intervention into education ever, and it opened doors to college for millions of men who otherwise would never been able to afford it." While the GI Bill was a policy intervention that focused on traditional postsecondary education as a route out of poverty, job training as an option became part of the policy response in 1962 with the Manpower Development Training Act (MDTA). Under MDTA, recipients received short-term training courses (10–15 weeks) to prepare them for entry-level jobs. Several years later the Work Incentive Program (WIN) was created as a supplement to welfare policy (Aid to Families with Dependent Children). Through WIN, job training was provided to welfare recipients (along with a subset of recipients who were mandated into work). The GI Bill, WIN, and MDTA were some indicators that education and training were becoming a preferred solution to unemployment (Shaw, Goldrick-Rab, Mazzeo, and Jacobs 2006).

The coupling of MDTA and WIN also points to a significant historical moment that was beginning to take shape in federal workforce development policy: "education and training were soon reframed as a means through which to reduce welfare dependency and work emerged as a legitimate component of welfare" (Shaw, Goldrick-Rab, Mazzeo, and Jacobs 2006:23). However, during this period, education and training were still a relatively small aspect of the policy response, and when used they were directed to low-skill workers. Over the ensuing decades, training programs began to be matched with a comprehensive public employment and services program. Grubb and Lazerson (2004) trace the growth of "services" strategy in public workforce policy. Education and training were part of a larger strategy—including supports such as child care, transportation, and Medicaid—to help individuals work their way out of poverty. A key milestone in this policy evolution was the passage of the Comprehensive Employment and Training Act (CETA) in 1973.

CETA was a public service jobs program that created unskilled and semiskilled jobs and provided training for individuals to succeed in those jobs (Shaw, Goldrick-Rab, Mazzeo, and Jacobs 2006; Katz 2001). CETA programs were targeted to disadvantaged adults and youth, and similarly to the original New Deal employment programs, CETA was administered locally; states were generally not involved in the administrative structure. Again, similarly to New Deal programs, community-based organizations were often responsible for the development and implementation of CETA programs. As Lafer (2002) has noted, these organizations were often aligned with the interests of the workers and not the employers. Accountability was measured by the number of people served, not using outcome performance measures, and no funding was tied to actual performance. Yet CETA was quite successful in providing jobs for disadvantaged workers. "At its height in 1978, CETA had provided nearly three-quarters of a million jobs for adults, and an additional million summer jobs for teenagers" (Lafer 2002:21). While CETA focused on creating public service jobs, education and training were seen as secondary but important tools to reduce unemployment and poverty (Shaw, Goldrick-Rab, Mazzeo, and Jacobs 2006).

However, as we proceeded through the early 1980s, the political winds began to shift in ways that significantly impacted the goals of employment and training policy. With the ascent of Ronald Reagan in the United States and Margaret Thatcher in Britain, a neoliberal perspective on the economy and role of government emerged, with different views of both poverty and employment policy. At the center of this policy shift was a more individualized conceptualization of poverty, along with the potential for "transformation through job training. The rising popularity of skills-building strategies served to undermine the support for public service jobs" (Shaw, Goldrick-Rab, Mazzeo, and Jacobs 2006:24). The problem of poverty was conceived not as a lack of jobs, but as a lack of skills on the part of the worker. Job training, not job creation, was heralded as the appropriate policy response. In 1982 the United States took a new approach to employment policy—a move away from public jobs and a focus on training and skills building as the legitimate way to reduce poverty—and CETA was replaced by the Job Training Partnership Act (JTPA) (Lafer 2002; Shaw, Goldrick-Rab, Mazzeo, and Jacobs 2006).

JTPA was enacted with a good deal of bipartisan support, and indeed it was "a radical realignment of CETA, in response to specific concerns about how workforce services were structured and delivered" (Gatta 2005). First, the job creation of CETA was eliminated, shifting JTPA's focus from "directly alleviating poverty and employment toward providing the means through which individuals could rise out of poverty" (Shaw,

Goldrick-Rab, Mazzeo, and Jacobs 2006:100). JTPA had a focus on the poor, and eligibility for services was determined by a means test. In addition, budget authority was no longer held at the local level, but instead was given to the states. Implementation of training programs was moved away from community-based organizations and centralized in private industry councils (PICS)—indicating a movement away from the worker to the employer as the "client." Finally, 6% of JTPA funds were allocated to provide incentives to meet performance standards, setting the stage for a movement away from program implementation and toward program outcomes (Lafer 2002; Shaw, Goldrick-Rab, Mazzeo, and Jacobs 2006).

JTPA was quite successful in providing training for low-income adults, although the evaluations of how well the training translated into jobs and increased earnings were less than impressive (Lafer 2002). Criticisms of mismanagement and poorly coordinated services in the JTPA system abound, causing many to demand changes to the public employment and training system.

Occurring alongside the skills policy arena were changes to welfare policy. In 1996 President Clinton signed the Personal Responsibility and Work Opportunities Reconciliation Act (PRWORA). This newly designed "work-first" model of welfare removed any notion that welfare was a social entitlement and severely restricted access to education and skills training. PRWORA's assistance program, Temporary Aid to Needy Families (TANF), set a two-year limit to find paid work and a five-year lifetime limit on the receipt of federally funded cash benefits by individuals. TANF was based on the idea that paid work was better than welfare, education, or job training. This reframing of poverty as one of "inadequate workforce attachment and dependency on government" led to a new workforce policy where "the human capital notion at the root of JTPA was quickly replaced with a work-first idea that held rapid job placement and reduction of welfare rolls as its primary goals" (Shaw, Goldrick-Rab, Mazzeo, and Jacobs 2006:25). As such, the definition of "client" continued to shift away from workers and toward employers.

In 1998, JTPA was replaced with the Workforce Investment Act (WIA). Sharply departing from the country's history of job creation and education to address workforce needs, WIA focused on short-term training for immediate placement in the private sector. To accomplish this, One-Stop Career Centers—a mix of privately and publicly managed local agencies—were established across the country to organize delivery of workforce development programs under the responsibility of Workforce Investment Boards (WIBs). In this system, the WIBs—representing both the public and private sector—coordinate and oversee education and job training at the state and local level.

In addition to the administrative overhaul of the workforce system, WIA was developed to encourage universal access, not just services targeted to the poor. The legislation was organized around a three-tiered system of core, intensive, and training services. Core services, the most basic form, include informational resources, self-services, and job search and job research assistance. These services are available to all workers, regardless of income, job, or educational level. The next level—intensive services—includes short-term assistance to provide individuals job opportunities given their existing skills. This level is reserved for unemployed or underemployed individuals determined by the One-Stop operator to need more services to obtain or retain employment that would lead to self-sufficiency. The highest level, training services, includes on-the-job training and classroom skills development leading to a credential and/or occupation-specific skills. Participants are supplied with an Individualized Training Account (ITA) that serves as a voucher that the individual can use to "purchase" training from an eligible provider. As with intensive services, eligibility for training services is determined by the One-Stop operator. In order to advance through the tiers, an individual must demonstrate that her or his employment objectives cannot be met at the lower tier.

Within WIA, funding is tied to performance and incentive measures of job placement. "Some of these measures—namely, newly entered employment levels and earnings gains—provide disincentives to serving individuals who are already working and instead favor the unemployed or other groups" (Miller, Molina, Grossman, and Golonka 2004). As a result, fewer individuals have received skills training through the One-Stop system under WIA than under its predecessor, JTPA. According to the U.S. Department of Labor, in 2000, at the peak of the economic boom, approximately 50,000 adults received training under WIA, compared with 150,000 annually in the final years of JTPA (Chicago Jobs Council 2003). These trends continued through subsequent WIA program years. The Center for Law and Social Policy (2005) noted that single parents in particular have experienced a decline of training services under WIA. For example, in 1998 (the last program year of JTPA), 43.7% of individuals receiving adult training were single parents. By 2000 (the first full year of WIA data), that percentage had fallen to 34.5, and it has continued to decline subsequently, falling to 24.6% in 2003.

The decline in the numbers of individuals who receive training is directly related to the three-tiered levels of service. Indeed, WIA appears to be primarily an employment policy (particularly for private sector jobs) rather than a training policy. Individuals must pass through core and intensive services before they can access new training on occupation-specific skills, and a client who can be employed without training is typically denied access to training. In addition, while WIA encourages collaboration and co-location of services, it still maintains separate performance measures and funding streams (Gatta 2005), making coordination quite difficult to achieve. Lafer (2002) has further noted that One-Stop Centers serve more as a central office to refer individuals to training services (performed by different agencies) as opposed to a cohesive employment and training program.

While the work-first policies of WIA have succeeded in providing the immediate mobilization of groups of people to work, they do not provide the next step of lifelong learning and training for entry-level workers (Gatta 2005), nor can they meet the needs of the growing dislocated workers in this current economic recession—professional skilled and educated workers who need retraining into new and growing jobs in our economy. Addressing the unemployment and underemployment experienced by workers at all levels in our economy requires ensuring that workforce development be more than a sole focus on on-the-job placement of low-skilled individuals. Instead we need a system aimed at ensuring that all workers have up-to-date skills training and at creating the right incentives for firms to pursue strategies that create jobs that demand high levels of skill. Moreover, we must do so in ways that are flexible and acknowledge individuals' work and family demands.

Overview of the Book

To address these multiple challenges, we have brought together a leading group of researchers, policy makers, and practitioners to synthesize the latest research and innovative practices that can be used to improve the U.S. workforce development system. This volume, intended as an update to the 1990 LERA Research Volume devoted to workforce development two decades ago (Ferman, Hoyman, Cutcher-Gershenfeld, and Savoie 1991), will explore the primary changes in skill issues since that time. An underlying premise for the book is that the guiding vision for workforce development policies should be shared prosperity—that U.S. competitiveness ought to be based primarily on added value (productivity and quality) rather than wage or cost competition. Achieving this vision, we argue, requires a radical rethinking of the workforce development system. The central thesis is that the public U.S. workforce development system—to the extent that a system exists—can no longer focus almost exclusively on economically disadvantaged groups. The majority of the population, including people with college degrees, may find access to good jobs threatened at some point during their working lives if their skills are not kept on the cutting edge and if U.S. employers do not invest in innovation and the design of high-performance organizations that can make the most effective use of these skills. And the willingness of companies to make this investment voluntarily may be diminished with the erosion of the traditional employment relationship and access to global labor markets. We examine the state of the U.S. workforce development system in comparative perspective along with the major changes that are required to help better prepare U.S. workers for the challenges of competing in the decades ahead. The book is divided into two main parts. Chapters 2 through 4 discuss the particular challenges of this economic context and the skills that are in demand and will be in demand in the future. David Finegold and Alexis Spencer Notabartolo review literature from a variety of disciplines on the competencies required for the 21st-century workforce. They find a large degree of consensus across countries on the general skills needed for success by all levels of workers—from entry-level to managers and professionals—but uncovered surprisingly few studies demonstrating that these competencies are associated with positive individual and/or organizational outcomes. Leonard Lynn and Hal Salzman, in Chapter 3, address the impact of globalization on skill development strategies and policies for the United States. They criticize the dominant 20th-century perspective of U.S. global hegemony and college-education-for-all as strategies geared toward "top of the pyramid" jobs. Instead, they suggest, policies for U.S. prosperity in "third-generation globalization" require workforce development throughout the skills spectrum, with renewed emphasis on noncollege pathways and on developing science and engineering capacities through global collaboration rather than technonationalism. In Chapter 4, George Benson and Edward Lawler examine the demand side of the skill equation, looking at the changing nature of organizational and work requirements. They review several decades of evidence on the benefits of high-skill, high-performance organizations and the reasons why the systemic adoption of these practices has been limited, even among the world's largest companies.

We dedicate the remainder of the volume to studies of different key dimensions of workforce development and options for enhancing their operation. A workforce development system for the 21st-century needs to reflect the use of technology in the wider society. Estimates for the United States project much faster growth in occupations requiring postsecondary education and training; the fastest growth will be of occupations that require an associate's degree or a postsecondary vocational award. But among the estimated 150 million adults in the labor force, more than 18 million lack high school diplomas, and more than 51 million have high school diplomas but no postsecondary education. Despite this gap between labor force qualification and skill demand, less than 10% of the more than 80 million adults who need additional education either to improve literacy, obtain a high school degree, or pursue post-secondary education and training are served by the public and private sector systems in place to serve them. Technology alone cannot solve these issues, but it can expand access to learning in ways that benefit adults in need and simultaneously teach adults to use computers and the Internet—the "ICT literacy" necessary to get and keep jobs in today's economy. In Chapter 5 Mary McCain describes the challenges of ensuring that adults are prepared for the jobs of today and tomorrow and examines options for meeting these challenges, illustrated with cutting-edge examples.

Susan Schurman and Louis Soares concentrate their analysis in Chapter 6 on the variety of postsecondary institutions in the United States, showing how most have failed to adapt to either the curriculum needs of knowledge-based firms or to an increasingly adult, part-time student population. As a consequence, the United States has lost its global lead in providing degrees for its citizens and suffers from very high attrition of people entering the higher education system but not completing a degree. They outline what would be required to reform the system to improve articulation and attainment, including recent experiments that allow for transfer of credit between apprenticeships and community colleges.

It is important to recognize that the dominant workforce development actors for adults in the United States are employers, who invest 10 to 20 times the amount spent on public-sponsored training and produce higher rates of return since the skills developed are more closely related to job needs. Yet, as Robert Lerman shows in Chapter 7, the country lacks reliable information on the scale and impact of employer-led training. In analyzing recent data from national household surveys, he finds that the annual incidence of formal employer-led training varies widely, from 57% of all workers in one survey to about 20% in another. Lerman argues that employer-led training can play a bigger and more effective role in helping American workers and firms by making better use of employer tuition subsidies, expanding apprenticeship training, and treating employer-led training costs as investment outlays.

In Chapter 8, David Finegold and John McCarthy make the case that regional clusters of related industries are a key to success in the global economy and that the U.S. workforce development system is poorly designed to support the development of clusters, with the specialized skills they require. The authors review a range of leading international examples and recent U.S. experiments with sector-skill initiatives that provide lessons on how to cost-effectively build a sectoral dimension into the reauthorization of WIA and the benefits that this change could produce.

Joint union–management training programs have proven to be resilient institutions with the capacity to respond to the great need for ongoing worker education for employed and laid-off workers. In Chapter 9, Dan Marschall and Ellen Scully-Russ argue that the involvement of joint union–management partnerships in internal and external labor markets not only strengthens the joint training program model but also helps improve the broader workforce development system in those industries and regions where joint programs exist.

The rapid rate of change in technology, corporate strategy, and market conditions combined with intensifying pressure to control costs to remain competitive globally has led many organizations to respond by reducing the size of their core workforce. Firms following this predominant corporate strategy have downsized, outsourced, and grown their cadres of contingent workers—temps, consultants, contractors, and part-timers—without permanent attachment to particular companies. These workers need services like training and insurance that cannot be provided very effectively on an individual basis, leading to the creation of new organizational forms like the Freelancers Union, discussed by Charles Heckscher, Sara Horowitz, and Althea Erickson in Chapter 10.

It is also important to understand the systemic effects of this system on different groups. As Mary Gatta and Luisa Deprez point out in Chapter 11, the only way family incomes have been sustained is by dramatic increases in women's working time, an outcome that not only is self-limiting, but also is not accommodated very well by existing labor market institutions and training policies. The authors propose ways that the workforce development system can address the lived experiences of women by helping connect them to meaningful work and education while acknowledging the vital role they continue to play as the prime family caretaker.

Finally, Henry Plotkin and Ray Marshall, two eminent state and national policy makers in this field, close by synthesizing findings from the different chapters to suggest ways to move our workforce development system forward to meet the needs of the 21st century.

Taken together, these diverse perspectives both update the Ferman, Hoyman, Cutcher-Gershenfeld, and Savoie (1991) volume from two decades ago and provide a comprehensive analysis that can guide future policy and program development. They provide a clear call for developing a new vision and goals for a more coherent and comprehensive workforce development system and key signposts for the direction in which the system needs to evolve.

References

Blinder, A. 2009. "How Many U.S. Jobs Might Be Offshorable." *World Economics*, Vol. 10, no. 2 (April–June), pp. 41–78.

Britt, Ross. 2009. "Lost Decade for Job Growth." *Marketwatch*, September 4. <http://www.marketwatch.com/story/lost-decade-for-job-growth-2009-09-04>. [July 30, 2010].

Carson, C.C., R.M. Huelskamp, and R.D. Woodall. 1993. "Perspectives on Education in America." *Journal of Educational Research*, Vol. 86 (May/June), pp. 259–310.

Center for Law and Social Policy. 2005. *Declining Share of Adults Receiving Training Under WIA Are Low-income or Disadvantaged.* <http://clasp.org/publications/decline_in_wia_training.pdf>. [March 1, 2010]

Chambers, Elizabeth, Mark Foulon, Helen Handfield-Jones, Steven M. Hankin, and Edward G. Michaels III. 1998. "The War for Talent," *McKinsey Quarterly*, Vol. 45, no. 3, pp. 44–57.

Chicago Jobs Council. 2003. *Improving Our Response to Work Needs: Recommendations for Reauthorization of the Workforce Investment Act of 1998.* Chicago: Chicago Jobs Council. <http://www.cjc.net/publications/files/2_Workforce_Investment_Act_PDFs/wia_improving_response_rpt.pdf>. [May 1, 2010].

Ferman, Louis, Michele Hoyman, Joel Cutcher-Gershenfeld, and Ernest Savoie, eds., 1991. *New Developments in Worker Training: A Legacy for the 1990's.* Madison, WI: Industrial Relations Research Association.

Freeman, Richard. 1976. *The Over-Educated American.* New York. Academic Press.

Gatta, Mary. 2005. *Not Just Getting By: The New Era of Flexible Workforce Development.* Lanham, MA: Lexington Books.

Grubb, W. Norton, and Marvin Lazerson. 2004. *The Education Gospel.* Cambridge, MA: Harvard University Press.

Heckman, James J. 2010. *The Linkage between Early Childhood Investment and Later Labor Market Outcomes.* Keynote address at the Tenth China Forum on the Humanities and Social Science, Renmin University, Beijing, June 12.

Hughes, James, and Joseph Seneca. 2009. *America's New Post-Recession Employment Arithmetic.* New Brunswick, NJ: Advance and Rutgers Report.

Katz, Michael. 2001. *The Price of Citizenship: Redefining the American Welfare State.* New York: Metropolitan Books.

Lafer, Gordon. 2002. *The Job Training Charade.* Ithaca, NY: Cornell University Press.

Lowell, B. Lindsay, and Harold Salzman. 2007. *Into the Eye of the Storm: Assessing the Evidence on Science and Engineering Education, Quality, and Workforce Demand.* Paper presented at the annual meeting of the Association for Public Policy Analysis and Management, Washington, DC, November 8–10. <http://policy.rutgers.edu/faculty/salzman/411562_Salzman_Science.pdf>. [May 1, 2010].

Miller, Jennifer, Frieda Molina, Lisa Grossman, and Susan Golonka. 2004. *Building Bridges to Self Sufficiency: Improving Services for Low-Income Working Families.* New York: MDRC.

National Commission on Education and the Economy. 1983. *A Nation at Risk.* Washington, DC: National Commission on Education and the Economy. <www2.ed.gov/pubs/NatAtRisk/risk.html>. [March 1, 2010].

Salzman, Hal, and Lindsay Lowell. 2008. "Making the Grade." *Nature*, Vol. 453, no. 7191, pp. 28–30.

Shaw, Kathleen, Sara Goldrick-Rab, Christopher Mazzeo, and Jerry Jacobs. 2006. *Putting Poor People to Work: How the Work-First Idea Eroded College Access for the Poor.* New York City: Russell Sage.

CHAPTER 2

21st-Century Competencies and Their Impact: An Interdisciplinary Literature Review

DAVID FINEGOLD
Rutgers University

ALEXIS SPENCER NOTABARTOLO
Writers Guild of America, West

Executive Summary

What worker competencies are most important for the 21st century? And can it be shown that to possess them makes a difference in educational or economic outcomes for individuals and organizations? This chapter summarizes key insights and empirical findings from a wide range of literature on these questions. It looks at 16 general competency areas reviewed under five broad categories: analytic skills, interpersonal skills, ability to execute, information processing, and capacity for change/learning.

We find widespread consensus among policy makers and researchers across the Organisation for Economic Co-operation and Development (OECD) that all five of these competency areas are important for workers in the 21st century; however, there is surprisingly little evidence of the relationship between these competencies and individual or organizational outcomes. In contrast with the large literature on the economic returns to education, few studies directly assess the effects of competencies on outcomes, in part because of the lack of common measures of the competencies.

The clearest evidence for the growing importance of these competencies in the OECD countries comes from long-term shifts in the occupational structure. There has been a decline in lower-skilled, manual labor and a growth in knowledge work and service occupations where these broad competencies are in greater demand. In these occupations, possession of general competencies becomes a prerequisite for securing employment. It is important to note, however, that many of the largest service occupations, as currently defined in the United States (e.g., home health care worker, cashier), are considered low-skill jobs, where there is limited opportunity or reward for skill development.

Future research is needed to demonstrate the relationship between these competencies and outcomes and to explore what mechanisms are most effective in developing generic skills. Our review provides guidance on core elements for this future research and policy agenda:

1. Focus on the demand side of the skill equation, looking at how the design of organizations and jobs impacts skill requirements and performance.

2. Recognize that general competencies should not be studied in isolation from occupation-specific contexts—problem solving in engineering, for example, may entail skills very different from those needed to solve problems in social work.

3. Treat some competencies—problem solving, capacity for change—as advanced stages of development within a range of specific skill areas, rather than as discrete competencies.

4. Explore inclusion of other competencies—cross-cultural fluency, systems thinking, financial literacy—that appear to be growing in importance in today's global economy.

5. Expand research in the United States in comparative perspective—a great deal of the work directly measuring competencies has been done in the United Kingdom and Australia/New Zealand, where they have national competency frameworks and regular, nationally representative workplace and skill surveys. It would be useful to compare U.S. skill levels with these and other nations.

Clarification of which competencies enhance performance, and how best to enable their development, benefits both companies and their workers. There is value to being able to "unpack, at various levels, the skills often simply called communication, prioritizing or problem-solving" (New Zealand Department of Labour 2009:25). "This allows the creation of job families and sequences linked by the development of proficiency in key under-recognized areas, broadening the options for internal sourcing of skills."

Introduction

While it is not the business of education to prove every statement made, any more than to teach every possible item of information, it is the business to cultivate deep-seated and effective habits of discriminating tested beliefs from mere assertions, guesses, and opinions; to develop a lively, sincere, and open-minded preference for conclusions that are properly grounded, and to ingrain into the individual's working habits methods of inquiry and reasoning appropriate to the problems that present themselves.

John Dewey, *How We Think,* pp. 27–8, 1910

What competencies will enable individuals, firms, and nations to compete successfully in the global economy of the 21st century? As the quotation from John Dewey illustrates, the debate about the role education and training should play in preparing individuals to succeed as citizens and economic actors is not new. This chapter will distill, from a variety of literatures, the findings on what competencies are believed to be most important for the 21st century and what evidence exists that possessing these competencies makes a difference in educational or economic outcomes for individuals and organizations.

We adopt the OECD's usage, in its *Definition and Selection of Competencies (DeSeCo) Project,* of "competency." A competency is

more than just knowledge and skills. It involves the ability to meet complex demands, by drawing on and mobilizing psychosocial resources (including skills and attitudes) in a particular context. For example, the ability to communicate effectively is a competency that may draw on an individual's knowledge of language, practical IT skills and attitudes towards those with whom he or she is communicating (Organisation for Economic Co-operation and Development 2005:4).

This definition of competency avoids "the narrow perspective of competencies embedded in most interpretations of human capital, [which has] led to a growing dissatisfaction, primarily because so much of what people need to do to succeed in work and life goes beyond this interpretation" (Schuller and Desjardins 2007:40). An important facet of the OECD's definition is the assertion that "despite the fact that competencies comprise more than just taught knowledge, . . . a competency can itself be learned within a favorable learning environment" (Organisation for Economic Co-operation and Development 2005:85).

What is the difference between a competency and a skill? The short answer is, in an economy that demands flexibility from its workers, not much. The concept of skill has changed from the "technical knowledge and skills required of a particular job or occupation, to one that includes an array of general and personal capacities and attitudes" (Chappell, Hawke, Rhodes, and Solomon 2003:5). Many terms are now used to describe the ability to read, write, undertake basic arithmetic, and communicate effectively: examples are "foundation skills," "core skills," "transferable skills," and "key competencies." For the purpose of this chapter, the terms "skill" and "competency" will be used interchangeably. It is important to note, however, that the current construction of "skill" in much of the literature is "a distinctly 'Anglo' concept—individualistic, defined by employers, and not contested by (or embedded in) other social forces" (Hampson and Junor 2009:3).

We review a wide range of literatures that discuss the development, measurement, and outcomes of 21st-century competencies. We start with the literature on human capital, where economists measure the rates of return to investments in different skills. Unfortunately, they typically rely on proxies—most often, time spent in education and training or possession of a formal qualification—because standardized, direct measures of competencies are not available. Closely associated with this are labor market projections regarding the changing occupational structure and what skills the future will demand. Then we examine the literature on work readiness and literacy from a number of vantage points, including research on the effectiveness of vocational education and training, the levels of literacy of the working population, and the extent to which individuals use their skills at work.[1] As part of the broader discussion on vocational education and training, we pay special attention to both career technical education (CTE) and the apprenticeship model of learning. The apprenticeship model will be important for tracing the relationship between what is known and what is able to be performed in the workplace, and how capabilities may positively impact employment training (which in turn should produce improved work outcomes). We also discuss the sociology of work and management literatures as it relates to the use of competencies in the workplace.

Increasingly, national bodies have begun to look at the larger trends in the world of work and to craft national frameworks of competence-based, sectoral-skill qualification to help guide the workforce development efforts of individuals, firms, and governments. The United States is notable for the lack of a common qualifications framework. The implications of this for the United States will be discussed in an appendix, since it does not relate directly to outcomes.

What Are 21st-Century Competencies?

The U.S. Department of Labor's influential 1991 Secretary's Commission on Achieving Necessary Skills (SCANS) report *What Work*

Requires from Schools defined the agenda for much of the subsequent work on what general competencies are required for work. The commission spoke with a wide range of managers and workers: "Their message to us was the same across the country and in every kind of job: good jobs depend on people who can put knowledge to work" (1991:i). The SCANS report identified a five-competency framework that built on a three-part set of foundation skills and personal qualities for success in the modern workplace. Individuals in the workplace should be able to productively use 1) resources, 2) interpersonal skills, 3) information, 4) systems, and 5) technology. These competencies require an underpinning of a) the basic skills of reading, writing, arithmetic, speaking, and listening; b) the thinking skills of solving problems and reasoning (among others); and c) the personal qualities of individual responsibility, sociability, self-management, self-esteem, and integrity.

A great deal of subsequent international research has confirmed the importance of the initial SCANS list and identified a range of other related competencies that appear relevant for 21st-century work. For the purposes of this review, a list of the following 16 competencies, focusing on the five most commonly found in international and national skills assessment, is the focus: Critical thinking, problem solving, communication, collaboration, and flexibility and adaptability (see Figure 1). Based on an examination of the cross-national literature, and in an attempt to regroup some often discussed competencies based on common

FIGURE 1
21st-Century Competencies.

Original SCANS List

• Creativity/innovation	• **Flexibility and adaptability;** **learning to learn**	• Leadership and responsibility
• **Critical thinking**		
• Information literacy	• Research and inquiry	• **Collaboration**
• **Problem solving**	• **Communication**	• ICT operations and concepts
• Decision making	• Initiative and self-direction	• Digital citizenship
	• Productivity	• Media literacy

Revised Groupings

• **Analytic skills**	• **Ability to execute**	• **Capacity for change**
Critical thinking	Initiative and self-direction	Creativity/innovation
Problem solving	Productivity	Adaptive learning/
Decision making	• **Information processing**	learning to learn
Research and inquiry	Information literacy	Flexibility
• **Interpersonal skills**	Media literacy	
Communication	Digital citizenship	
Collaboration	ICT operations and concepts	
Leadership and responsibility		

underlying attributes, this chapter offers an alternative approach to grouping the set of 21st-century competencies. This accords, for example, with the approach of OECD's DeSeCo Project (2005:5), which integrates many of the separate competencies defined above into a broader construct: "individuals need to be able to use a wide range of tools for interacting effectively with the environment: both physical ones such as information technology and socio-cultural ones such as the use of language. They need to understand such tools well enough to adapt them for their own purposes—to use tools interactively." Our proposed framework groups the 16 competencies under five broad categories: analytic skills, interpersonal skills, ability to execute, information processing, and capacity for change/learning (see Figure 1).

Our discussion of 21st-century competencies will define each broad competency and examine available evidence of the outcomes associated with greater competence in this area.

Analytic Skills

One of the most common competencies mentioned in the literature surveyed was problem solving. The description offered by Murray, Owen, and McGaw (2005) in their examination of the Adult Literacy and Life (ALL) Skills Survey speaks to the role that analysis plays in that competency:

> *Problem solving*—Problem solving involves goal-directed thinking and action in situations for which no routine solution procedure is available. The problem solver has a more or less well-defined goal, but does not immediately know how to reach it. The incongruence of goals and admissible operators constitutes a problem. The understanding of the problem situation and its step-by-step transformation, based on planning and reasoning, constitute the process of problem solving (p. 16).

Problem solving has become a key component for workplace success in an economy that demands flexibility and innovation instead of repetitive manufacturing tasks. In their analysis of the ALL Skills survey, Murray, Owen, and McGaw (2005) highlight the importance of profiling and comparing problem-solving skills.[2] A number of skill domain assessments were built into the survey, but "only the problem-solving domain was shown to meet the high empirical standards set for directly assessing skills in the ALL study" (p. 26). Osterman's study (2006) of the positive wage effects of high-performance work organization (HPWO) suggests that as the elements of HPWO become more diffuse, including "self-managed teams, quality programs and job rotations" (p. 188), "soft skills such as problem solving or interaction skills may become increasingly important in HPWO settings" (p. 189). For example, in their study of 1,066 trainee truckers at a large U.S. trucking firm, Burks, Carpenter, Goette, and Rustichini (2009) found that a greater ability to problem-solve[3] had a clear positive correlation to job retention, performance, and satisfaction. And in a survey of 2,765 Dutch workers, Groot and Maassen van den Brink (2000) found a wage premium for problem solving among male workers but not for female workers. Specifically, male workers who "have to ask for help from colleagues to solve problems earn 4% less, while workers who need instructions from a supervisor earn 7% less" (p. 581) than those who can problem-solve on their own. Notably, they also found that "a year of education increases the probability of solving problems on your own by .8%" (p. 579).

A second area of often-discussed, desirable analytical skills is critical thinking. The Society for Human Resource Management (SHRM) and WSJ.com/careers (2008) undertook a study of critical skill needs and resources for the changing workforce. The two organizations surveyed 407 HR professionals and 334 employees (contacted through the *Wall Street Journal* Careers website) and found that "overall, employers placed the greatest weight on employee adaptability and critical thinking skills. HR professionals and employees both reported that adaptability/flexibility and critical thinking/problem-solving skills were of greatest importance now compared with two years ago" (p. 6). Notably, the study also found that "fewer than one out of ten organizations did not provide or pay for skills training or professional development for their US workforce" (p. 6). Johanna Martinsson (2009), writing on behalf of the World Bank, also argues that critical thinking skills be made a feature of education systems the world over, as those skills are increasingly in demand in the global labor market. We could find no direct studies showing the outcomes of enhanced critical thinking skills, although proponents of liberal arts education have long argued that one of its greatest strengths is developing graduates who can think critically, a competency that enables success in a wide range of occupations and leadership roles.

Interpersonal Skills

Competency in the realm of communication is seen as a necessity for success in the job market, regardless of level of education or type of work. As noted, the DeSeCo project's first key competency is

the effective use of spoken and written language skills, computation and other mathematical skills, in multiple situations. It is an essential tool for functioning well in society and the workplace and participating in an effective dialogue with others. Terms such as 'communication competence' or 'literacies' are associated with this key competency (Organisation for Economic Co-operation and Development 2005:10).

The importance of communication competency was echoed in every national framework we surveyed.

Communication skills are seen as vitally important in the growing service sector. In the high-end retail service sector, for example, Gatta (2010) found that communication manifests in both the ability of workers to interact with customers and how they communicated via their appearance—what is referred to as aesthetic skills. While employers were willing to train workers in the practical knowledge needed to function in the context of the store, they "were less likely to provide training on the . . . basic customer service, aesthetic and emotional work demanded of retail work. [Employers] instead viewed this as something the prospective worker had or did not have, and was a prerequisite to hiring" (p. 16). Drawing on the work of Nickson, Warhurst, and Dutton (2004) on retail in Glasgow, Gatta (2010) argues that in the service sector, "indeed the right appearance and personality took precedence over technical qualifications of staff. Such work requires more than just technical and social skills, but also aesthetic skills—forcing workers to look good and sound right" (p. 9).

Not possessing the correct communication competency, especially as related to the previously discussed aesthetic skills, may have a direct, negative economic outcome that further supports their importance. As discussed by Hampson and Junor (2009), aesthetic skills "[cede] the definition of 'aesthetic' (beautiful) to employers, with real dangers of employment discrimination based on body shape and age . . . The concept of aesthetics goes beyond (or should go beyond) mere visual or aural aesthetics to include a sense of 'situational appropriateness,' even ethical responsiveness (cf. Bolton and Houlihan 2005)" (p. 6).

Communication skills are equally vital to effective operation within knowledge-based manufacturing enterprises. In their survey of ten organizations in the high-tech, pharmaceutical, and medical devices sectors, the Expert Group on Future Skills Needs (Ireland) found that communication skills in those areas were of "ever-increasing importance in the workplace" (2003:v), but that such "soft" skills were more difficult to train.

Collaboration can be viewed as a broader concept that requires both effective communication skills and also a greater sensitivity to co-workers: "In an increasingly interdependent world," DeSeCo notes (Organisation for Economic Co-operation and Development 2005:5), "individuals need to be able to engage with others, and since they will encounter people from a range of backgrounds, it is important that they are able to interact in heterogeneous groups." A survey of Australian undergraduate students echoes the value of engagement with others to developing communication and collaboration skills (Crebert et al. 2004). Respondents to the survey noted that "group work was their preferred option for the development of oral communication, problem solving, teamwork, leadership, assuming responsibility and making decisions and [developing] high ethical standards" (p. 153). Several studies and surveys (Gordon 1992; Cohen and Bailey 1997; Peterson, Mitchell, Thompson, and Burr 2000; Solansky 2008) have noted the growth in the use of teams in the workplace, with some estimates showing that more than 80% of companies with 100 or more employees use teams as part of their work structure (Gordon 1992; Cohen and Bailey 1997). This chapter has previously discussed that certain areas of competency support self-directed or autonomous group work, which Wall, Kemp, Jackson, and Clegg (1986) note require "a high degree of self-determination by employees in the management of their day-to-day work" (p. 280). In their study of two sites within a large, nonunionized British confectionary company, these authors found that in a manufacturing environment "productivity benefits [were] possible because autonomous workgroups reduced indirect labor costs; a side effect was increased dismissals" (p. 298) as some workers did not readily fit into the new structure, in terms of attitudes about the new system. As Gittell (2001) outlines, this finding is in line with the larger body of work on postbureaucracy theory and that "with high levels of task interdependence, performance is expected to benefit significantly from strong group process" (p. 468). She offers an extensive discussion of "the management of task interdependencies—carried out in the context of relationships with other group members" (p. 471):

> Relational coordination includes a communication component, reflecting the frequency and timeliness of communication among group members. In addition, it includes a relational component, reflecting the strength of problem solving, helping, mutual respect, shared goals, and shared knowledge among group members involved in the same work process (p. 471).

Ability to Execute

The third of the DeSeCo Project's key competencies speaks to the importance of initiative: "Individuals need to be able to take responsibility for managing their own lives and situate their lives in the broader social context and act autonomously" (Organisation for Economic Cooperation and Development 2005:5). Like many of the competencies discussed, initiative, as defined above, readily connects and interacts with other competency areas. Hampson and Junor (2009) discuss the related concept of "articulation work skills" as "'supra' or 'second order' skills needed to manage the exercise of other skills. They are of two types: those used to organize and manage one's own work in time, and those used to integrate a particular 'line of work' with others, in order to create a coordinated workflow" (p. 17).

Information Processing

The role of information processing in skill frameworks has grown with recent international survey work. Both the ALL skills survey examined by Murray, Owen, and McGaw (2005) and the IALS report (Organisation for Economic Co-operation and Development and Statistics Canada 2000) discuss literacy as a function of processing information: "The ability to understand and employ printed information in daily activities, at home, at work and in the community—to achieve one's goals, and to develop one's knowledge and potential" (Organisation for Economic Co-operation and Development and Statistics Canada 2000:x). The ALL survey aimed to go beyond the IALS results to measure "foundation skills"—the prose and document literacy and numeracy, but also the skills of problem solving and an indirect measure of "familiarity and use of information and communication technologies" (Murray, Owen, and McGaw 2005:15). Bishop and Mañe (2004) found that computer skills were valuable even for those in noncomputer career–technical education: Students who took one computer course earned $828 (3.1%) more annually and 1.4% more per hour than their peers who took none. Dickerson and Green (2002) also found a wage premium existed for computing skills[4] in the United Kingdom and that it was greatest for the highest level of computing skills (26% for programming), while the premium for straightforward usage (such as utilizing email) was a much lower 11%.

Likewise, for unemployed workers, "the results clearly indicate that persons with higher proficiency in document literacy are capable of finding employment sooner" (Murray, Owen, and McGaw, 2005:114), and that document and numeracy skills were rewarded more than others for workers of all ages across all seven ALL countries. Using the Armed Services Vocational Aptitude Battery (ASVAB), Bishop (1995) found that one standard deviation increase in mathematical ability increased productivity by 5.3% in all nonclerical military occupations and raised compensation by $1,906 (in 1993 dollars), and it raised productivity and wages for clerical workers by 10.8% and $3,277, respectively (also in 1993 dollars). Smaller effects were seen in related academic categories, including verbal ability, scientific knowledge, and computational speed.

Both the IALS and the ALL skills survey are crucial to understanding the central role that information processing plays and will continue to play in the formation of 21st-century competencies. As Kirsch et al. (2002) note, the 23 countries and territories surveyed in the IALS found that higher levels of information processing ability (*prose, document,* and *quantitative*) on real-world problems are significant predictors of not only success in education, employment, and earnings, but also lower crime rates and higher levels of participation in community activities. The United States ranks in the middle of the IALS results.

Media literacy, as defined by Tornero (2008) and cited by Martinsson (2009), is "the ability to access, analyze, evaluate, and create media content" (Martinsson 2009:3). Both authors argue that media literacy is vital in assisting in the acquisition of other skills, including "critical thinking, problem solving, personal autonomy, and social and communicative skills" (Martinsson 2009:3), as well as its role in encouraging "informed discussion in the public sphere [that] can engage citizens as active stakeholders in governance reforms" (p. 3). Given the volume of media now available in digital form, Martinsson notes that "physical access is only one aspect of technology adoption; perhaps more important is access to quality content and ability to analyze, evaluate, and apply it" (p. 6). An individual's exposure to information and computer technology (ICT) operations and concepts varies by country and socioeconomic status, as evidenced by the 26% of Americans who reported not using the Internet in 2009 (Pew Internet and American Life Project 2010). The ALL skills survey was designed to offer a first attempt at measuring the impact of ICT at the individual level across countries. These results illustrate how many 21st-century competencies directly impact one another. The ALL skills survey found that "as prose, document, numeracy and problem solving levels increase, adults' perceived usefulness and attitude toward computers, Internet use, and use of computers for various tasks also increase. In most countries, respondents with medium to high literacy have between two and three times the odds of being a high-intensity computer user" (Murray, Owen, and McGaw 2005:182).[5] Mossberger, Tolbert, and McNeal (2008) were able to use national U.S. data to show that the likelihood of voting and civic engagement increases as use of the Internet increases and that "for workers who are lower paid and less educated, computer and Internet skills may be one factor needed for mobility into better-paying jobs, with greater job security, health insurance benefits, and full-time hours. For those who are seeking new or better jobs, Web sites have become a tool for finding job openings and researching employers" (p. 5). These benefits are especially pronounced for African Americans and Latinos.

Capacity for Change

Given the rate of technological innovation and frequency of organizational restructuring, work process knowledge theory argues that the ability of individuals to adapt and innovate is now vital at all levels of the economy. For example, Chappell, Hawke, Rhodes, and Solomon (2003) found that "workers in the contemporary economy are now expected to use their technical and generic knowledge and skills to contribute to the production of new knowledge within the workplace on an ongoing basis, rather than merely applying existing knowledge to workplace activities" (p. 7), and as a consequence, they must understand the "wider societal concerns that impact on the work of the business such as sustainability and environmental damage" (p. 7; see also Boreham, Samurcay, and Fischer 2002). This is an example of the broader competence of "adaptive learning" or "reflectiveness: the ability to apply routinely a formula or method for confronting a situation, but also the ability to deal with change, learn from experience and think and act with a critical stance" (Organisation for Economic Co-operation and Development 2005:5).

If workers are to be adaptive, then they must also be flexible. This is important not only when considering the skills a worker needs for success but also what firms need for success. The discussion of employee flexibility as a soft-skills asset runs prominently through the human resources literature, with discussion of businesses' need to be more flexible in light of the ever-shifting consumer market. With this increased need for flexible business, from an employer or human resources perspective, the need for workers who are also flexible—in terms of skills and availability—is substantial. The human resources literature views flexibility in a fashion subtly different from other fields, as it argues that "organizations must be occupationally flexible, enabling workers to become mobile between different tasks, in particular by helping them to shift from less to more productive occupations" (Philpott 2002:10).

Determining the Right Competencies and Relationships Among Them

Given this broad overview of the general competencies needed for labor market success in the 21st century, a crucial question becomes how to measure the acquisition of these competencies and how they relate to each other. Several major studies, including the ALL skills survey and its predecessor, the IALS, measured literacy skills along a continuum of proficiency rather than a binary of "literate" or "illiterate." Using the same measurement scale as IALS, the ALL survey's spectrum of measurement comprises five levels of proficiency for document and prose literacy. For problem solving, four levels of proficiency were developed;

each rests on respondents' being at a static numeric value in the ability scale. Hampson and Junor (2009) offer a compelling alternative view. Rather than separating out the concept of "learning" as an individual skill, they see "learning as fundamental to the conceptualization of skill levels" (p. 18). In their taxonomy, based on extensive fieldwork in the New Zealand service sector and developed as the New Zealand Department of Labour (2009) Spotlight framework, two of the five priority 21st-century competencies—problem solving and critical analysis—are viewed as levels of development of many competencies in specific occupational settings rather than standalone traits (see Figure 2).[6,7]

The review of the literature also suggests some competencies that may be vital for the 21st century that were not on the original list. *Systems thinking* is seen to be growing in importance as disciplines become more integrated, organizations shift from vertically integrated to more network-based, and more work within them is performed in cross-functional projects. This is supported by the emergence of new professional science master's degrees to develop "T-shaped," or hybrid, professionals (Institute for Manufacturing at the University of Cambridge and IBM 2008; Palmer 1990). Systems thinking corresponds closely to the highest level in the New Zealand Spotlight framework (New Zealand Department of Labour 2009).

Another general skill area of growing importance appears to be *financial literacy,* as laid out by Lusardi and Mitchell (2007), which may be distinctly important from general literacy and numeracy, especially as it relates to long-term and retirement planning. Many households, the study notes, lack the basic financial literacy skills to make appropriate financial decisions, and the result is a negative impact on long-term economic outcomes.

Cross-cultural fluency and global acumen are seen to be more salient as the economy has become more global, but defining this competency has proven to be difficult. The Australian Education Council's Mayer Committee (1992), tasked with developing a set of "key competencies," for example, failed to come to a consensus on how to define this competence.

Emotional intelligence and emotional labor, as articulated by Goleman (1998)—"managing feelings so that they are expressed appropriately and effectively, enabling people to work together smoothly towards their common goals" (p. 7)—has been recognized as a key competence for an increasingly knowledge- and service-based economy since Goleman's seminal work. Philpott (2002) notes that in order to remain competitive, organizations need to "guarantee to customers the personal touch, whether in terms of a 'can do' approach to service delivery, a friendly voice on the customer service phone line, or a helpful or caring attitude

FIGURE 2
New Zealand Spotlight Competence Framework.

Skill Elements

A. *Shaping awareness*
    Capacity to develop, focus, and shape your own and other participants' awareness, by
A1 Sensing contexts or situations
A2 Monitoring and guiding reactions
A3 Judging impacts

B. *Interacting and relating*
    Capacity to negotiate interpersonal, organizational, and intercultural relationships by
B1 Negotiating boundaries
B2 Communicating verbally and nonverbally
B3 Connecting across cultures

C. *Coordinating*
    Capacity to organize your own work, link it into the overall workflow and deal with obstacles and disruptions by
C1 Sequencing and combining activities
C2 Interweaving your activities with others'
C3 Maintaining and/or restoring workflow

Learning Levels: Definitions and Basis

Descriptor	Capacity to	Basis
Familiarization	Build experience through practice, reflection, and learning from others	Participating as a novice, by building expertise through observation, practice, and reflection
Automatic fluency	Apply experience automatically and independently	Participating as a practiced performer, independently applying operational knowledge to the point where activity is automatic
Proficient problem solving	Use automatic proficiency while solving new problems	Participating as an experienced problem solver, able to carry out operations already learned, while applying widening knowledge and experience to creating new solutions
Creative solution sharing	Help create new approaches by exchanging solutions	Participating as a sharer of practical knowledge, in the exchange of "local knowledge" through stories or notes about trial-and-error solutions
Expert system shaping	Embed expertise in an ongoing work system	Participating as a knowledge creator or system innovator, helping to spread or change systems of practical knowledge (and possibly also its theoretical basis)

Source: New Zealand Department of Labour 2009; Hampson and Junor 2009.

in the shop, restaurant, railway, post office or hospital" (p. 9). Hochschild (1983), Bolton and Houlihan (2005), and Hampson and Junor (2009) offer an alternative to Goleman's perspective, arguing that "the terms 'appropriately' and 'effectively' embody corporate value judgments" (Hampson and Junor 2009:6) and that workers in front-line service jobs are now often compelled to display certain emotions as part of their "emotional labor," causing stress and job dissatisfaction.

Are Competencies Universal and Equally Valuable?

Recent research on business strategy challenges the basic premise of focusing on the value of a set of generic competencies. Becker, Huselid, and Beatty (2009), for example, drawing on data from more than 3,000 firms over more than a decade, argue that a business should not value all talent equally but should differentiate the value (and thus compensation level) of skills among its workforce in relation to the key elements of its firm strategy that differentiate it among competitors. By definition, generic capabilities cannot create a sustainable competitive advantage versus competitors (Prahalad and Hamel 1990). Becker, Huselid, and Beatty (2009) cite Porter (1996) and endorse the idea that an effective strategy "means performing *different* activities from rivals or performing similar activities in *different* ways" (p. 31). In terms of competency development, this suggests that, depending on the situational context, not all competencies are created equal. Becker, Huselid, and Beatty's taxonomy, intended for firms to use to better prioritize workforce needs, offers four stages of differentiation and value of competencies: 1) one size fits all; 2) generic fit; 3) differentiation by strategic capability; and 4) differentiation by jobs within strategic capabilities (Becker, Huselid, and Beatty 2009). For some organizations, the workforce strategy might reflect elements from several stages simultaneously.

What's the Relationship Between Education and Training, Competencies and Outcomes?

The relationship between worker competencies and individual and organizational outcomes is complex and contested. There is wide agreement among policy makers about the need for basic skills and competencies, but much less evidence about where such skills are best acquired. Additionally, blanket statements about labor market outcomes are difficult to make because of the inconsistent measures of competencies from one survey to another. Murray, Owen, and McGaw (2005) found that skills and education were rewarded at different levels in terms of pay in the different countries surveyed in the ALL. For example, in Bermuda and Italy, returns to skill are far higher[8] than the returns to education,[9] suggesting that "skills are highly valued on the labour market and that education is rewarded only in so far as it is associated with these skills" (p. 167).

The research suggests that the way in which competencies are developed—in particular, whether employers are cooperating with educational institutions—may be as important as the competencies themselves. Crebert et al. (2004) found that undergraduate students felt that, while a university setting was the best place to develop the competencies of "oral and written communication skills, critical analysis and evaluation, problem solving and teamwork skills" (p. 153), their experiences in employment-based learning opportunities were the most beneficial for subsequent success in the job market. Bishop, Mañe, and Ruiz-Quintanilla (2001) found in their analysis of data from the National Education Longitudinal Study of 1988 (NELS-88) that school–business collaborations "significantly reduce unemployment in the two years after leaving high school and significantly increase employment, annual earnings and hourly wage rates" (p. 14). These programs may achieve this by signaling to employers involved in their design and implementation "that the school is doing a good job of preparing young people for work" (p. 10). These findings are supported by Mason, Williams, and Cranmer (2006), who studied efforts to foster "employability skills" for 3,589 graduates from eight UK universities. They found that participation in structured work experience was associated with a 29% increase in the probability that graduates would find employment appropriate to their level of education ("graduate-level") within six months of graduation, while explicit teaching and assessment of so-called employability skills was not found to have a clear impact on graduate labor market outcomes.

The effects of general skills may also be cumulative, because they increase the likelihood that individuals will receive and benefit from subsequent training in the workplace. Research has shown consistently that more qualified people receive most employer-provided training that is on offer (e.g., Philpott 2002). As Murray, Owen, and McGaw (2005:118) note, "for many, the link between foundation skills and employability is not necessarily direct. Employability also depends on the willingness and capacity of workers to participate in training. . . . Many lack the basic skills to engage in training that maintains their employability, including younger and older workers." Likewise, Bertschy, Cattaneo, and Wolter (2009) found that, among the upper-secondary vocational students they examined,[10] higher scores on the academic PISA assessment[11] were "associated with more intellectually demanding vocational training, and that at the same time students who pursued vocational training with higher intellectual demands [were] more likely to have a smoother education-to-work transition, meaning that they [had] a higher probability of finding an adequate job" (p. 129).

Training design and assessment design are also important. In formal workplace training scenarios, the Kirkpatrick model of training evaluation (cf. Kirkpatrick 1959) is still a generally accepted standard. Kirkpatrick and Kirkpatrick (2009:23) note that "learning leaders still try to demonstrate their value to the[ir] business by using attendance [Kirkpatrick model] Level 1 reaction data and [Kirkpatrick model] Level 2 testing scores." The authors go on to argue that a narrow focus on immediate reactions to a learning event is not indicative of a worker processing or critically assessing new knowledge, required elements of workers progressing to effective application of new training or skills (Level 3 of the Kirkpatrick model) or reaching the final, desired outcome (Level 4). Phillips (1996) built on the original Kirkpatrick framework by adding a fifth level: measuring return on investment (ROI). Using this five-level framework, the Skillnets pilot project (Impact Management Center 2005), funded by the Irish National Training Fund, found that among 18 different firms operating in Ireland, use of the Kirkpatrick/Phillips training evaluation system "greatly improved the quality, efficiency, and effectiveness of training" (p. 1). For example, at Braun Oral B Ireland (Skillnets, Ltd. 2005), the manufacturing employees who underwent training designed to facilitate development of problem-solving skills and the sharing of ideas[12] discovered "a significant variation in stock take [inventory] that would not have been noted without the higher levels of engagement of the trained employees" (p. 12).

Bishop (1988) found that training-related employment is key to benefiting from occupation-specific education. If a training-related job is not obtained, then there are no economic benefits of such vocational training. Bishop found that, though occupation-specific skills obtained through vocational education are not a substitute for basic skills (the ability to read, write, speak, compute, and reason), there were positive impacts on graduation rates and "monthly earnings [were] 7–8% greater" (p. 2) when training-related employment is secured.[13]

Emerging trends in education support the idea that industry needs have an increasingly important role in the success of individuals in the labor market, reinforcing the benefits of on-the-job training. Taking into account the previously discussed positive labor market outcomes for UK graduates who took part in courses designed in cooperation with employers (Mason, Williams, and Cranmer 2006), MacCluer and Seitelman (2005:2) note that industry pressures to do more with less favor programs that offer "a strong technical background together with a knowledge of business practices [that] will equip students for substantial roles in both product development and organizational management." Employers require "T-shaped professionals" who possess both "'contributory knowledge' (deep learning in the science) as well as

'interactional/articulatory expertise' (breadth of workplace skills)"
(National Research Council 2008:14). The call for professionals with T-
shaped competencies is supported by industry players like IBM, who
offer products to help develop T-shaped employees and note on their
websites that "it's no longer enough for a programmer to be just a programmer" (IBM 2010). This sentiment is reinforced by industry's work
with academia (see Institute for Manufacturing at the University of
Cambridge and IBM 2008).

The relationship between skill, education, and earnings is further
fleshed out in the ALL survey report, which notes that certified "skills
have a large effect on earnings in the majority of countries. The extent to
which economic rewards are attributable to either skill or education is
mixed and varies by country. . . . In Canada and the United States, the
labor market appears to separately reward both the skills measured in
ALL [prose literacy, document literacy, numeracy and problem solving]
and additional schooling" (Murray, Owen, and McGaw 2005:165). In
Canada, "each additional year of schooling is on average associated with
about five percent higher weekly earnings even after adjusting for
directly observed skills" (p. 167). The United States saw similar results,
with returns ranging from 6% to 9%. This can be compared to the previously discussed results in Italy and Bermuda, where skills are rewarded
but there are no discernible returns to additional education.

Individual Outcomes—Obtaining a Job

A major reason for the focus on 21st-century competencies is that
the majority of recent and future job growth in OECD nations has been,
and is projected to continue to be, in services and knowledge work occupations, jobs that are thought to require higher levels of these general
skills than manual work. The UK National Skills Surveys of 1997 and
2001[14] show a growth in demand for and actual use of generic skills
(Dickerson and Green 2002). In the United States, the Bureau of Labor
Statistics (2009) projects that, between 2008 and 2018, "more than half
of the new jobs will be in professional and related occupations and service occupations" (p. 1). BLS also projects that "occupations where a
postsecondary degree or award is usually required are expected to
account for one third of total job openings during the projection period."
Increasing levels of education is a complex component of skills analysis,
because "although education and skills are strongly related, exclusive
reliance on measures of educational attainment to predict adult skills
will lead to considerable error" (Murray, Owen, and McGaw 2005:61).
These trends toward higher skill demands are being magnified by globalization, as not only lower-skilled jobs, but even the highest levels of

research and development work in the United States—for example, jobs performed by Ph.D.-level chemists and biologists—may now be off-shored (Finegold, Earhart, and Sako 2009).

The changing nature of what competencies workers require is also being shaped by technological developments. Drawing on the UK Labour Force Survey, Kirby and Riley (2006) estimated the impact of information and computer technology (ICT) on general and occupational-specific skill returns in different industries in the United Kingdom between 1994 and 2001. Using schooling and potential work experience as proxies for general skills and job tenure as a proxy for job-specific experience for 16 industry groups in the UK data, the study's results

> lend support to the notion that ICT is biased towards general skills, which are useful in acquiring new skills and in performing a broad range of activities, and biased against skills that are less transferable between jobs. The findings reported here are consistent with the interpretation that recent technical change, although skill-biased, renders some job-specific skills obsolete (p. 7).

Using data from O*NET, Elliott (2007) projects that advances in a range of technologies (computers, artificial intelligence, optics, robotics) could combine to substitute for human abilities in nearly 60% of the jobs currently held by the U.S. workforce.

The pressure for increasing levels of skill is not limited to jobs requiring high levels of education for entry. Drawing on a data set from the Bay Area Longitudinal Study, Maxwell (2006) found that there was a strong argument to be made that even low-skilled jobs require English, math, communication, and problem-solving skills, along with certain job-specific skill sets (like physical and mechanical ability). Maxwell did not find, however, a conclusive link that computer skills "are an identifiable skill set widely used in low-skilled jobs, at least at entry level" (p. 53). Likewise, in a West German study, Spitz-Oener (2006) showed that service tasks are also increasing in complexity, with analytical and interactive tasks overtaking routine and manual ones. Spitz-Oener builds on the model for assessing needs for changing skills proposed by Autor, Levy, and Murnane (2003), which drew on analysis of the Current Population Survey job titles in light of data from the Dictionary of Occupational Titles (DOT). Spitz-Oener's main concern with Autor, Levy, and Murnane's approach is that it "precludes, to a large extent, a discussion of task changes within occupations" (p. 236) in part because the DOT underestimates "true changes in job content" (p. 242).

Many of the largest categories of service workers—for example, cashiers and home health workers—are in low-wage, low-skilled areas that get little skill development. Lloyd and Payne (2008) challenge the assertion that the jobs offered in call centers[15] are skilled based on the need for workers to be adept in emotional or articulation work skills. Echoing an earlier study by Appelbaum, Bernhardt, and Murnane (2003) of low-wage service work in the United States, Lloyd and Payne note that "there is a worrying trend within these discourses to equate 'skill' with the ability to cope with badly designed jobs and stressful working conditions" (2008:21). In other cases, differences in national institutional contexts can result in those in jobs with similar titles—childcare and home health workers—being treated as skilled professionals requiring recognized qualifications and paid a living wage (France/Scandinavia) versus being treated as low-skilled workers whose competencies are generally unrecognized and unrewarded (the United States).

Wage Premiums

Technological and economic changes appear to be increasing the returns to certain types of general skills. Murnane, Willett, and Levy's 1995 analysis of the National Longitudinal Study of the High School Class of 1972[16] and the High School and Beyond survey of 1980[17] found that the increasing wage premiums between 1972 and 1980 were tied to "the increase in return to cognitive skills" (p. 259). Looking at the returns to completing higher education, the study showed that by the time 1972 high school graduates reached age 24 in 1978, each year of college completed carried a 2.2% wage premium for men and a 5.5% wage premium for women (as compared to those graduates who had only a high school education). For the class of 1980, by age 24 in 1986 there was a 4.5% wage premium for men and a 6.7% wage premium for women for each year of college completed.

Ananiadou, Jenkins, and Wolf (2004) undertook an expansive literature review of work derived from the United Kingdom on the effects of so-called "basic skills" of literacy and numeracy on individual workers' wages and employment probability. Based on analysis of IALS and the longitudinal National Child Development Study,[18] they found "that the wage effects of higher numeracy skills are greater for men than for women, and that the reverse is true for literacy, while, in terms of employment, higher numeracy skills seem to have more impact on women's employment chances than men's"[19] (p. 295). Results of the UK's Skills for Life Survey[20] confirm that "those with lower-level numeracy (Level 3 or below) earned £8,000 less than those with Level 2 numeracy or above"[21] (Williams, Clemens, Oleinikova, and Tarvin 2003:22).

In terms of the return on specific skills, De Anda and Hernandez (2008) utilize data from the 1992 National Adult Literacy Survey[22] to show that different races and genders benefit differently from levels of literacy. They find "the effect of literacy skills on the earnings of black males [in the United States] is bifurcated: literacy skills seem to be more significant for less-educated black males than those with college degrees" (p. 241). Black males are seen to benefit most from literacy competency, which is accompanied by a weekly earnings increase of 18%. This is compared to the return on literacy skills for white females (13% increase), white males (12% increase), and black females (9.8% increase).

Dearden, McIntosh, Myck, and Vignoles (2000) found in their survey of three major UK data sets[23] that labor market returns associated with academic qualifications are generally higher than those associated with vocational qualifications of the same level. When time required to obtain these qualifications was factored in, however, the returns per year on vocational qualifications "move closer on average to those accruing to academic qualifications" (p. 3). For males, there is a labor market return of 10% to 28% for holding an academic degree and a return of 6% to 9% for a vocational qualification like the National Vocational Qualification (NVQ) at Levels 3 to 5. For women, an academic degree saw labor market returns of 21% to 26%, while NVQs at Levels 3 to 5 saw a return of 1% to 5%, with the NVQ return for women so small in the IALS sample as to be statistically insignificant.

Organizational Outcomes, Skill Shortages, and the Demand for Skills

A review of the literature on employer benefits from enhanced basic workforce skills finds that research showing direct firm outcomes is scant and that what research there is often suffers from significant weaknesses (Ananiadou, Jenkins, and Wolf 2003). The authors examine Gallup's 1992 effort (Adult Literacy and Basic Skills Unit 1993) to quantify the economic losses of UK employers caused by deficiencies in workers' basic skills.[24] The study, focusing on companies with over 50 employees, found firms on average lost £166,000 per year in 1993 figures due to skill deficiencies (£208,000 in 2002 prices), with the losses of large firms (over 1,000 workers) over five times that of smaller firms (51–100 workers). Ananiadou, Jenkins, and Wolf (2003) note, however, that these estimates have come under heavy criticism for both the methodology employed and the approach taken in extrapolating the figures from the small sample (cf. Robinson 1997).

The impact of skill shortages varies by skill type and industry. Utilizing firm interviews and "information from an ICT benchmarking survey of British enterprises with post-survey financial data for the same enterprises," Forth and Mason (2006:2) "found strong evidence that internal ICT skill shortages—skill gaps among existing employees—have negative indirect effects on firm-level performance because of the ways in which such skill deficiencies restrict companies both in terms of ICT adoption and the intensity of use of ICTs once they have been installed" (p. 27). But the study did not find support for a direct link between skill constraints, ICT training, and financial performance. Stevens (2004) found considerable heterogeneity across industries in how skill shortages affect employment practices. Some industries experience only intermittent skill shortages in the workforce, while others, like the metal manufacture and metal products sector, experience "pro-cyclical skill shortages." This heterogeneity suggests that "industry-specific skills play a part in explaining labor market behavior" (2004:9) and influence firms' employment practices. Shury, Winterbotham, Davies, and Oldfield (2010) found that one in five UK employers reported a skills gap for some portion of their workforce. Of these skills gaps, 7 in 10 can be attributed to "a lack of experience and staff having been recently recruited" (p. 30). The same survey also found that the effects of skill mismatch can include "an increased workload for other staff . . . increased operating costs, difficulties meeting quality standards, and difficulties introducing new working practices" (p. 31).

An influential series of studies, largely published by the UK's National Institute of Economic and Social Research (NIESR), used an innovative matched establishment methodology to explore the relationship of skills supply, firm strategy, work organization, and uses of technology to productivity and other measures of performance in many manufacturing and service industries.[25] Across multiple sectors, German firms seemed to be able to secure higher-value-added niches in global markets because their front-line skilled workers were highly productive and flexible thanks to the mix of strong general and occupation-specific skills they had developed through the apprenticeship system. Mason and Finegold (1997) examined the linkage between productivity and intermediate or sub-baccalaureate skill levels by comparing the relatively low-skilled yet highly productive manufacturing sector of the United States with matched samples from Dutch and British metal working firms[26] and food manufacturers in Britain, the Netherlands, Germany, and France.[27] They attributed the U.S. lead in labor productivity to scale economies of production, while Western European firms used greater supplies of skilled workers, especially in the case of Germany, to produce smaller batches of higher-value-added products.

Carr's work (1992) compared skills and productivity in vehicle component manufacturing in Japan, the United States, Britain, and Germany, finding a large Japanese performance advantage. Japan trailed Germany in terms of the initial technical qualifications of shop-floor workers and trailed all three countries in the technical skills of graduates, but it more than made up for those shortcomings by subsequent in-company training based around a team-based organization. Workers at various levels were able to move between jobs to gain experience in different production and technical fields, providing a general skill set that helped foster quality and flexibility.

The skills present in the workforce may impact the organization of the work engaged in, along with the outcome for the firm. In their discussion of high-involvement workplace strategies, Benson and Lawler (Chapter 4, this volume) note that high-involvement practices, which include "teams, employee development, gain sharing plans, and participative leadership . . . are correlated with a variety of organizational performance measures including return on assets, sales, entrepreneurial growth, customer satisfaction, and productivity." Combs, Liu, Hall, and Ketchen (2006) conducted a meta-analysis of 92 studies that included relevant statistics on the link between high-performance work practices (HPWP) and organizational outcomes. The researchers found a pronounced (.20) correlation between HPWP and organizational outcomes, but with varying impact depending on the type of firm and conditions in which the practices are implemented. Benson and Lawler (Chapter 4, this volume) note that "taken together this research shows that employee involvement increases individual, team, and unit productivity in industries as diverse as professional services, steel manufacturing, apparel, medical imaging, and semiconductor fabrication." Adoption of these practices, however, is uneven, occurring in only a relatively small percent of all U.S. employers. Benson and Lawler also point out that in the service sector, where costs must be aggressively kept down for firms to compete, employee involvement may not make short-term economic sense.

Investing in improving individuals' general capabilities is unlikely to yield a positive return if jobs are not designed to use them. As Murray, Owen, and McGaw (2005) note in their examination of the ALL survey, this can create the problem of skills mismatch: "despite the strong associations between skill and economic outcomes . . . there are significant proportions of workers who have medium to high levels of skill but who nevertheless occupy low-paying jobs. Naturally the opposite is also true. There are low- to medium-skilled workers who are nevertheless well paid" (p. 166). Individuals who are overeducated for the positions they occupy suffer a wage penalty (as compared with those with a match of skills, education level, and occupational need), and women suffer a greater penalty when mismatch occurs (Green, McIntosh, and Vignoles 2002; Williams, Clemens, Oleinikova, and Tarvin 2003). To illustrate this issue, Green, McIntosh, and Vignoles (2002:795) offer the example of a university graduate in a secretarial role, where "that graduate may be no more productive than a less educated secretary. The graduate's skills will be under-utilized, and he or she will be less productive and earn less than s/he would in a graduate job." The scale of this problem is reaching alarming proportions in the United Kingdom, where two out of every five workers report they are overqualified for their jobs, up 10% over the last two decades, reflecting a large increase in the supply of graduates, but also casting doubt on the extent to which employers have created jobs that demand high skill levels (Felstead, Gallie, Green, and Zhou 2007).[28]

Drawing on a much simpler one-question questionnaire and a smaller sample size[29] in each country, Bevan and Cowling (2007) compared the United Kingdom to other European countries; they found that, in both 1996 and 2000, the United Kingdom had the worst rate of job matching in the EU-15, although a much lower level of overqualification (8%) than Felstead, Gallie, Green, and Zhou (2007) found. Bevan and Cowling found an overall reduction in the rate of overskilling among the EU-15 between 1996 and 2000 (from 8.8% to 7.4%, respectively). The difference in education systems among the EU-15 is cited as a possible factor in the difference in overskilling, specifically "differences in

FIGURE 3
Growth in Overqualified UK Workers.

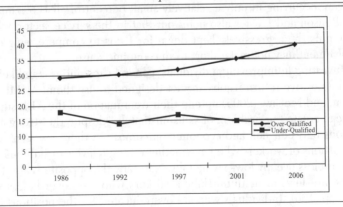

Source: Felstead, Gallie, Green, and Zhou (2007).

the degree to which individuals can stay voluntarily in education" (Bevan and Cowling 2007:22), as well as in the success in reforms to decrease such a skill mismatch.

The problem of skill mismatch cuts both ways, however. As Williams, Clemens, Oleinikova, and Tarvin (2003) note, one third of those surveyed as holding high managerial or professional occupations did not test at the highest level of literacy (Level 2 or above). Their study suggests that these respondents "successfully worked around their weaknesses or that the level of literacy demanded at Level 2 or above is not essential for their work" (p. 82). This concern is likely to decline as the supply of graduates to fill these positions increases across OECD nations (Felstead, Gallie, Green, and Zhou 2007).

National Outcomes

Evidence also suggests that skills have a major effect on national economic performance. Hanushek et al. (2010:6) "relate cognitive skills—as measured by PISA and other international instruments—to economic growth. The relationship indicates that relatively small improvements in the skills of a nation's labor force can have very large impacts on future well-being. Moreover, the gains, put in terms of current Gross Domestic Product (GDP), far outstrip the value of the short-run business-cycle management. This is not to say that efforts should not be directed at issues of economic recession, but it is to say that the long-run issues should not be neglected."

Conclusions and Areas for Future Research

This review of the literature suggests that there is widespread consensus among policy makers and researchers across the OECD on the key competencies that workers require in the 21st century, yet surprisingly little evidence of the relationship between these competencies and individual or organizational outcomes. In contrast with the large literature on the economic returns on education, few studies directly assess the effects of competencies on outcomes, in part because of the lack of common measures of these competencies.

This reality suggests a strong need for future research to demonstrate the relationship between these competencies and outcomes and to explore what mechanisms are most effective in developing these generic skills. Our review provides guidance on core elements for this future research and policy agenda:

- Focus on the demand side of the skill equation, looking at how the design of organizations and jobs impacts skill requirements and performance.

- Recognize that general competencies should not be studied in isolation from occupation-specific contexts—for example, problem solving in engineering may entail skills very different from those used in social work.

- Treat some of these competencies—problem solving, capacity for change—as more advanced stages of development within a range of specific skill areas, rather than as discrete competencies.

- Be open to including other competencies—cross-cultural fluency, systems thinking, financial literacy—that appear to be growing in importance in today's global economy.

- Research these issues in the U.S. context. To date, a great deal of the best work directly measuring competencies has been done in the United Kingdom and Australia/New Zealand, which have both national competency frameworks and regular, nationally representative workplace and skill surveys.

Companies and their workers benefit from a clarification of what competencies enhance performance and how best to develop them. There is a value to human resource professionals of being able to "unpack, at various levels, the skills often simply called communication, prioritizing or problem-solving" (New Zealand Department of Labour 2009:25). Drilling down to the essence of skills "allows the creation of job families and sequences linked by the development of proficiency in key under-recognized areas, broadening the options for internal sourcing of skills . . . [which] is likely to enhance staff retention" (p. 25).

Endnotes

[1] The literature on measurement of competencies within firms is outside the scope of this chapter.

[2] The Adult Literacy and Life (ALL) Skills Survey is a large-scale cooperative effort undertaken by governments, national statistics agencies, research institutions, and multilateral agencies to build on the International Adult Literacy Survey. Seven countries or regions took part in the first round of the ALL survey in 2003: Bermuda, Canada, Italy, Norway, Switzerland, the United States, and the Mexican state of Nuevo Leon.

[3] Burks, Carpenter, Goette, and Rustichini (2009) employ the term "planning" to describe the "ability of the individual to effectively reason backward from a goal about how to reach it" (p. 4). This is remarkably similar to the definition of problem solving offered by the ALL survey and will thus be discussed as problem solving.

[4] These returns are measured through Dickerson and Green's use of "two specially designed surveys which deploy a job analysis approach that has been borrowed and adapted from commercial psychology" (2004:1), like those used by commercial firms such as Hay and Novations designed to examine the "changes in skill utilisation and their association with pay" (p. 1).

[5] It is important to note that digital competency depends not only on skills, but also on access to relevant technology; the issue of unequal access of low-income groups to ICT, or "the digital divide," can exacerbate inequality (Mossberger, Tolbert, and McNeal 2008).

[6] Concerned with the underrecognition of so-called soft skills, a research team led by Junor and Hampson conducted 57 in-depth interviews over three waves of site visits in New Zealand in 2006. This information was analyzed in light of relevant skills literature and 94 position descriptions "in which managers had clearly sought specific employee input" (Hampson and Junor, 2009:17) to develop a taxonomy where workers are "able to build a base of experience through practice and reflection . . . in which 'supra' work wields 'lower level' skills" (p. 19). The goal of this framework is to assist in identifying and valuing often-overlooked skill areas by mapping three central skill sets onto five learning levels.

[7] New Zealand Department of Labour. 2009. *Spotlight: A Skills Recognition Tool*, Wellington: New Zealand Department of Labour. Available on request on CD from http://www.dol.govt.nz/services/PayAndEmploymentEquity/spotlight.asp.

[8] Murray, Owen, and McGaw (2005) note that in Bermuda and Italy "every increase of 10 percentiles in the ranking of the distribution of prose, document, numeracy or problem solving skills is associated with between 15 to 55 per cent higher weekly earnings, depending on the skill domain considered" (p. 167).

[9] In Bermuda and Italy, Murray, Owen, and McGaw (2005) found that, "returns to education that are not statistically different from zero or are negative imply that if additional years of schooling are not associated with higher skill proficiencies, then those extra years of schooling are not rewarded on the labour market" (p. 167).

[10] Bertschy, Cattaneo, and Wolter (2009) drew on a longitudinal data set that followed a group of 642 vocational students and apprentices in Switzerland. This data set came from the "PISA [Programme for International Student Assessment] survey 2000, and from five waves of the Transitions from Education to Employment Survey (TREE). The TREE data come from a longitudinal survey of all participants of the PISA 2000 survey and they contain information on educational and occupational choices and outcomes during the post-compulsory school period up to the age of 22" (p. 117).

[11] The Programme for International Student Assessment (PISA) is an international effort of member-countries of the OECD to survey their population of 15-year-old students as they approach the end of their compulsory schooling. PISA includes measures of competency in reading, mathematical, and scientific literacy. In 2003, PISA added a problem-solving domain. See Hanushek et al. (2010).

[12] The full list of training goals were "Ownership and understanding of KPIs [key performance indicators] and business needs; Enhanced engagement/involvement; Increased commitment; Appreciation of Departmental functions; Cross fertilization of ideas; Understanding Business needs and the 'bigger picture'; Improved employee relations; Problem Solving skills; Conduct effective meetings" (Skillnets, Ltd. 2005:11).

[13] In subsequent work, Kang and Bishop (1989:143) found that there "[are] decreasing returns from specialization and that a complementarity exists between academic and vocational education" and illustrated what mix of courses would maximize earnings for males and females. For males who took a total of 12 full-year

courses, "earnings in the calendar year after high school are maximized when approximately 36% of academic and vocational courses are vocational" (p. 143). For females, 48% of academic and vocational courses should be vocational to maximize earnings the year after graduation. The study also shows, however, that there are diminishing returns to increasing the number of vocational courses in relation to academic courses.

[14] The UK National Skills Surveys were "large-scale cross-sectional representative survey[s] of individuals aged between 20 and 60 in Britain in paid work at the time of interview. . . . Interviews were conducted face to face in respondents' homes, and the achieved samples of 2467 and 4470 respectively were each representative of the British population" (Dickerson and Green 2002:4–5). These are different assessments than the UK National Employment Skills Surveys.

[15] In their survey, Lloyd and Payne (2008) conducted "44 face-to-face interviews with senior managers, team leaders and call centre operators across the two call centres, which we label C1 and C2. The interviews were recorded and ranged in length from one to two hours with managers and team leaders to 30 to 45 minutes with individual agents" (p. 8).

[16] Survey included information on the labor market experiences of 22,652 students first surveyed as high school seniors in 1972.

[17] Survey included information on the labor market experiences of 11,500 students first surveyed as high school seniors in 1980.

[18] The National Child Development Study is "one of the major longitudinal surveys of people living in Great Britain who were born at a particular point in time: in this case, between 3 and 9 March 1958" (Ananiadou, Jenkins, and Wolf 2004:292). The sample discussed in Ananiadou, Jenkins, and Wolf (2004) includes 1,714 respondents (or 10% of the cohort) who were 37 years old in 1995. Respondents were "assessed using a specially developed literacy and numeracy test that provided a direct measure of their basic skills as adults" (p. 292).

[19] Ananiadou, Jenkins, and Wolf (2004) find that 42% of men with very low and low literacy fell in the low-income group (less than £200 per week) compared with 24% for those with good literacy. The figures for women were 53% (low or very low literacy) in the low-income group (less than £150 per week) compared with 39% of those with good literacy. An even more marked effect was found with respect to numeracy skills for men: 49% of men and 52% of women with very low numeracy fell in the low-income group, compared with 19% of men and 30% of women with good numeracy skills.

[20] The UK Skills for Life survey "was carried out between June 2002 and May 2003. The survey was commissioned by the Department for Education and Skills. The aim was to produce a national profile of adult literacy, numeracy, ESOL, and information and communications technology (ICT) skills over five broad levels of competence" (Williams, Clemens, Oleinikova, and Tarvin 2003:12). The surveyed population "was all adults aged between 16 and 65 and normally resident in England. Residents of institutions were excluded for practical reasons. BMRB completed 8,730 first interviews although, in some cases, respondents did not fully complete tests and, in others, previously unidentified problems with the test programmes prevented final scores from being computed. In total, 7,873 respondents completed the literacy test and 8,041 respondents completed the numeracy test. 7,517 completed both. A total

of 4,656 took part in the second interview, with 4,464 assigned levels in both ICT assessments" (p. 13).

[21] Numeracy at "Level 2 or above" in the UK Skills for Life survey is defined as "Understands mathematical information used for different purposes and can independently select and compare relevant information from a variety of graphical, numerical and written material" (Williams, Clemens, Oleinikova, and Tarvin 2003:11).

[22] The National Adult Literacy Survey (NALS) is a representative random sample of 26,000 adults in the United States. Respondents are asked to complete "background items (e.g., demographic characteristics, education, and labor force participation) and . . . a series of diverse literacy tasks measuring their prose, document, and quantitative skills. Each group of tasks was scored separately, so that respondents received scores along a prose scale, a document scale, and a quantitative scale. The tasks were designed to measure a person's ability to succeed in common, practical, and analytical problems encountered in daily life or at work" (De Anda and Hernandez 2008:235).

[23] Dearden, McIntosh, Myck, and Vignoles (2000) drew on "the 1991 sweep of the National Child Development Study (NCDS), the British data from the 1995 International Adult Literacy Survey (IALS), and the 1998 Labour Force Survey (LFS)" (p. 7) for their study. The Labour Force Survey is "a quarterly survey of representative households, which asks respondents about their personal circumstances and labour market status. The LFS covers about 120,000 individuals, in around 60,000 British households and is carried out by the Office for National Statistics" (p. 13).

[24] Gallup undertook 400 interviews with employer representatives (usually a human resources or training manager) from a random sample of companies employing 51 or more employees in the United Kingdom. The interviews were intended to assess the level of their employees' reading, writing, numeracy, and oral communication skills. The total cost to industry of poor basic skills among employees was estimated by asking employers "a series of questions relating to specific aspects of their company's business. Specifically, they were first asked to indicate how many customer orders were cancelled per year because of errors/problems, how many orders were dispatched/produced incorrectly and the number of customers lost per year through problems or misunderstandings" (Ananiadou, Jenkins, and Wolf 2003:19).

[25] See Mason and Finegold (1997), Finegold and Wagner (1998), Prais (1981), Prais and Wagner (1983), and Prais and Wagner (1988).

[26] This sample included visits to 12 British plants and nine Dutch plants during 1991 (see Mason and van Ark 1993).

[27] This sample included 29 visits to European biscuit factories between 1989 and 1991: 10 in Britain, eight in Germany, six in France, and five in the Netherlands (see Mason, van Ark, and Wagner 1994).

[28] The UK's 2006 Skills Survey is designed to measure a wide range of skills used in the workplace by individuals in Britain between the ages of 20 and 65. It utilizes "survey-based measures of job skills adapted from the general principles of job analysis" (Felstead, Gallie, Green, and Zhou 2007:8) carried out over seven months and involving "4,800 productive interviews with individuals aged 20–65 years old and in work" (p. 15). For greater detail, see pp. 5–15.

[29] Bevan and Cowling (2007) drew on the European Working Conditions Survey, which covers respondents who are 15 years or older in each EU member-state. In the 1996 survey, "around 1,000 workers were interviewed in each Member State, a total of 15,800. For the 2000 Survey, around 1,500 workers were interviewed in each Member State, a total of 21,703 interviews [the EU had expanded its membership between 1996 and 2000]. Luxembourg has a reduced sampling requirement due to its smaller population size" (pp. 16–17).

[30] See Forfás's (2009) publications *Future Skills Requirements of the Food and Beverage Sector*, *Skills in Creativity, Design and Innovation*, and *Monitoring Ireland's Skills Supply—Trends in Education and Training Outputs*.

[31] The study comprised responses to individual questionnaires and recordings of group conversations of "a 10% sample (40) of second year Advanced GNVQ students in five further education colleges [studying in 9 of the 13 GNVQ areas] . . . and a 17% sample (20) of former GNVQ students in Sheffield Hallam University" (Smith 1998:58).

[32] Those factors were "Union collusion, works councils and restricted mobility; Unobserved heterogeneity in worker's costs of mobility; Firing costs, uncertainty and option value" (Harhoff and Kane 1997:178). A fourth, less verifiable factor identified by German human resources professionals interviewed by the authors was a social expectation that such apprenticeship programs would be offered.

[33] District of Columbia, Florida, New Jersey, New York, Rhode Island, Washington.

Acknowledgment

An earlier version of this chapter was prepared for a study of the National Academy of Sciences, commissioned by the Hewlett Foundation. We would like to thank them for their permission to include the chapter in this volume.

Appendix
Implications for the U.S.: National Qualification and Training Systems

Assessing and providing for skill needs in the workforce is, by several measures, directly tied to the health of a country's broader economy. Hanushek et al. (2010:10) argue that "the human capital influence on growth is best characterized by the relationship between direct measures of cognitive skills and long-term economic development. The evidence suggests that differences in cognitive skills are an explanation of a majority of the differences in economic growth rates across OECD countries." Through the OECD's (2005:19) DeSeCo Project, international experts came together "to identify an agreed set of fundamental ideals with which a framework of key competencies needs to be compatible. This reflects a commonality of aspiration while accepting a diversity of application." Building on the OECD's work, the European Qualifications Framework (EQF; European Parliament and European Council 2008) defines "skills" as "the ability to apply knowledge and use know-how to complete tasks and solve problems[;] skills are described as cognitive (involving the use of logical, intuitive and creative thinking) or practical (involving manual dexterity and the use of methods, materials, tools and instruments)" (p. 4) and defines "competence" as "the proven ability to use knowledge, skills and personal, social and/or methodological abilities, in work or study situations and in professional and personal development . . . described in terms of responsibility and autonomy" (p. 4). Some scholars, including Hampson and Junor (2009), have questioned the conceptual clarity and challenges of implementing these distinctions.

Many countries have instituted programs and systems to assist in the acquisition and assessment of the skills that they identify as critical to the economy. England, Australia, and Ireland have created qualification frameworks and begun assessing future skill requirements in key economic sectors (food and beverage; creativity, design, and innovation; education and training outputs; etc.).[30] Government efforts to align individual skills and the needs of business through national competence frameworks have not been without their difficulties. The vocational education and training (VET) policies Australia has developed, after much policy frustration and failure (cf. Hampson 2002), are intended to "integrate all forms of work-related learning into a coherent and unified system of recognition" (Chappell, Hawke, Rhodes, and Solomon 2003:vi) based on collaboration between industry groups and institutions of higher education. These Australian Training Packages represent "nationally endorsed industry standards against which training can be developed and flexibly delivered to meet particular local, individual, industry and enterprise requirements" (Service Skills Australia 2007). VET policies in this context take on a much broader role than in other discussions of skills development. These policies include the commonly discussed problem solving and communication, but also encompass "curiosity, motivation and risk taking. This suggests that contemporary vocational learning should be as much in the business of constructing new worker identities as providing workers with vocational knowledge and skills as traditionally understood" (Chappell, Hawke, Rhodes, and Solomon 2003:4). Schofield and McDonald (2004:4) note that "the Training Package model has the potential, with improvements, to facilitate good labor market and educational outcomes for enterprises, industries, individuals and communities." Problems may arise, however, when training policy is subsumed in employment policy. As Hampson (2002) argues, the goal of training policy is to create a pool of skills, while employment policy focuses on lowering unemployment; the combination of the two (as Hampson describes for Australia, but has also occurred in the United Kingdom and the United States) may generate tensions.

The General National Vocational Qualification (GNVQ) and the older National Vocational Qualification (NVQ) in the United Kingdom were designed to recognize the "core skills to support vocational competence" (Smith 1998:538). The NVQs range from Level 1, which certified introductory knowledge of a discipline, to Level 5, which measured an advanced professional understanding of the discipline (Futuremorph.org 2008). In the case of the GNVQ, students "should have developed the generic skills and competencies needed for both employment and for higher education" (Smith 1998:538). The GNVQ framework "covers six core skills; application of number, communication, information technology, working with others, improving own learning and performance, and problem solving." In Smith's (1998:547) small-scale[31] study of the perceptions of the GNVQ in relation to its better-known counterpart, the Advanced Level General Certificate in Education (A-level), GNVQs were found to only marginally achieve their goals of increasing student autonomy, fostering teamwork skills and encouraging "deep and reflective learning." Smith posits that the bureaucratic structure of the GNVQ assessment procedures detracts from the student autonomy goals, as "assessment procedures may be one reason for . . . continuing dependence, as only the teacher can explain and demystify their use" (p. 544).

Germany, Austria, and Switzerland each have strong sectoral skill frameworks and apprenticeship traditions that offer insight into vocational education and training systems that have succeeded in developing a strong foundation of general skills combined with an occupational focus. Harhoff and Kane (1997) examined whether the German apprenticeship model would be appropriate for the United States, concluding that "German apprentices occupy roughly the same place relative to unskilled workers and college graduates as that held by high school graduates in the United States. Further, the age-earnings profiles for German apprentices and US high school graduates are quite similar" (p. 173). The study concludes that several factors found in Germany but not the United States influence employer willingness to offer apprenticeships[32] and that absent "other inducements (such as a 'training tax' or similar public subsidy)" (p. 186), apprenticeships are unlikely to extend beyond their relatively narrow niche in the American context.

In contrast, the United States has limited and spotty implementation of competency standards and associated workforce development efforts to build core generic skills. Most public workforce development efforts focus on getting unemployed individuals into jobs as quickly as possible, with relatively narrow training programs. The National Work Readiness Credential for low- and entry-level skills assessment was launched in 2006 to recognize the "foundational skills of value-creating relationships" (National Work Readiness Credential 2010). It features online assessments of four competencies: situational judgment, oral language, reading with understanding, and using math to solve problems. A relatively new program, it currently serves six states[33]; it appears too early to tell if it will adequately serve as a way to recognize skills at entry level.

Why the United States lags in developing a national competency system and to what extent this absence has affected actual individuals' attainment of general competencies remain major questions. In part, this appears to be due to the relatively limited role that the U.S. federal government has historically played in education and training. According to the Forfas report (2006:12) "the US adopted at an earlier stage a broader, more holistic set of generic skills, including basic skills and personal attributes to be applied across the whole spectrum of 21st century living, whereas the Anglo/Australian approach was initially more narrowly focused on workplace requirements and excluded personal attributes and value."

References

Adult Literacy and Basic Skills Unit. 1993. *The Cost to British Industry: Basic Skills and the Workforce.* London: Adult Literacy and Basic Skills Unit.

Ananiadou, Katerina, Andrew Jenkins, and Alison Wolf. 2003. *The Benefits to Employers of Raising Workforce Basic Skills Levels: A Literature Review.* London: National Research and Development Centre.

Ananiadou, Katerina, Andrew Jenkins, and Alison Wolf. 2004. "Basic Skills and Workplace Learning: What Do We Actually Know About Their Benefits?" *Studies in Continuing Education*, Vol. 26, no. 2 (July), pp. 289–308.

Appelbaum, Eileen, Annette Bernhardt, and Richard J. Murnane, eds. 2003. *Low-Wage America: How Employers Are Reshaping Opportunity in the Workplace.* New York: Russell Sage Foundation.

Australian Education Council, Mayer Committee. 1992. *Key Competencies.* Report of the Committee to Advise the Australian Education Council and Ministers of Vocational Education, Employment and Training on Employment-related Key Competencies for Postcompulsory Education and Training. Canberra: Australian Education Council and Ministers of Vocational Education, Employment, and Training.

Autor, David H., Frank Levy, and Richard J. Murnane. 2003. "The Skill Content of Recent Technological Change: An Empirical Exploration." *Quarterly Journal of Economics*, Vol. 118, no. 4 (November), pp. 1279–334.

Becker, Brian, Mark Huselid, and Richard Beatty. 2009. *The Differentiated Workforce: Turning Talent into Strategic Impact.* Cambridge, MA: Harvard Business Press.

Bertschy, Kathrin, M. Alejandra Cattaneo, and Stefan C. Wolter. 2009. "PISA and the Transition into the Labour Market." *LABOUR: Review of Labour Economics and Industrial Relations*, Vol. 23, no. 1, pp. 111–37.

Bevan, Stephen, and Marc Cowling. 2007. *Job Matching in the UK and Europe.* London: The Work Foundation/UK Commission for Employment and Skills.

Bishop, John. 1988. *Occupational Training in High School: When Does It Pay Off?* Cornell University Working Paper #88-09. Ithaca, NY: New York State School of Industrial and Labor Relations, Cornell University.

Bishop, John. 1995. *Expertise and Excellence.* Cornell University Working Paper #95-13. Ithaca, NY: Center on the Educational Quality of the Workforce, Cornell's Program on Youth and Work, and the New York State School of Industrial and Labor Relations, Cornell University.

Bishop, John H., and Ferran Mañe. 2004. "The Impacts of Career-Technical Education on High School Labor Market Success." *Economics of Education Review*, Vol. 23, pp. 381–402.

Bishop, John H., Ferran Mañe, and S. Antonio Ruiz-Quintanilla. 2001. *STW in the 1990s: School–Employer Partnerships and Student Outcomes.* <http://digital commons.ilr.cornell.edu/cgi/viewcontent.cgi?article=1033&context=articles>. [October 11, 2010].

Bolton, Sharon C., and Maeve Houlihan. 2005. "The (Mis)representation of Customer Service." *Work, Employment, and Society*, Vol. 19, no. 4, pp. 685–703.

Boreham, Nick, Renan Samurcay, and Martin Fischer. 2002. *Work Process Knowledge*. London: Routledge.

Bureau of Labor Statistics. 2009. *Employment Projections: 2008–2018 Summary*. Washington, DC: U.S. Department of Labor. <http://www.bls.gov/news.release/ecopro.nr0.htm>. [March 15, 2010].

Burks, Stephen V., Jeffery P. Carpenter, Lorenz Goette, and Aldo Rustichini. 2009. "Cognitive Skills Affect Economic Preferences, Strategic Behavior, and Job Attachment." *Proceedings of the National Academy of Sciences of the United States of America, Early Edition,* Vol. 106, no. 19, pp. 7745–50.

Carr, Christopher. 1992. "Productivity and Skills in Vehicle Component Manufacturers in Britain, Germany, the USA and Japan." *National Institute Economic Review*, Vol. 139, no. 1, pp. 79–87.

Chappell, Clive, Geof Hawke, Carl Rhodes, and Nicky Solomon. 2003. *High Level Review of Training Packages Phase 1 Report: An Analysis of the Current and Future Context in Which Training Packages Will Need to Operate*. Brisbane: Australian National Training Authority.

Cohen, Susan G., and Diane E. Bailey. 1997. "What Makes Teams Work: Group Effectiveness Research from the Shop Floor to the Executive Suite." *Journal of Management*, Vol. 23, no. 3, pp. 239–90.

Combs, James, Yongmei Liu, Angela Hall, and David Ketchen. 2006. "How Much Do High Performance Work Practices Matter? A Meta-Analysis of Their Effects on Organizational Performance." *Personnel Psychology*, Vol. 59, pp. 501–28.

Crebert, Gay, Merrelyn Bates, Barry Bell, Carol-Joy Patrick, and Vanda Cragnolini. 2004. "Developing Generic Skills at University During Work Placement and in Employment: Graduates' Perceptions." *Higher Education Research and Development*, Vol. 23, no. 2, pp. 147–65.

De Anda, Roberto M., and Pedro M. Hernandez. 2008. "Literacy Skills and Earnings: Race and Gender Differences." *Review of Black Political Economy,* Vol. 34, no. 3, pp. 231–43.

Dearden, Lorraine, Steven McIntosh, Michal Myck, and Anna Vignoles. 2000. *The Returns to Academic and Vocational Qualifications in Britain*. London: Centre for the Economics of Education London School of Economics and Political Science.

Dewey, John. 1910. *How We Think*. Boston: D.C. Heath, pp. 27–8.

Dickerson, Andrew, and Francis Green. 2002. "The Growth and Valuation of Generic Skills." SKOPE Research Paper No. 26, Spring 2002. Oxford: Centre on Skills Knowledge and Organizational Performance, Oxford and Warwick Universities.

Dickerson, Andrew, and Francis Green. 2004. "The Growth and Valuation of Computing and Other Generic Skills." *Oxford Economic Papers*, Vol. 56, no. 3, pp. 371–406.

Elliott, Stuart. 2007. *Projecting the Impact of Computers on Work in 2030*. <http://www7.nationalacademies.org/cfe/Future_Skill_Demands_Presentations. html>. [March 27, 2010].

European Parliament and European Council. 2008. "Recommendation of the European Parliament and of the Council of 23 April 2008, on the Establishment of the European Qualifications Framework for Lifelong Learning." *Official Journal of the European Union*, Vol. 51, no. C111 (May), pp. 1–7.

Expert Group on Future Skills Needs (Ireland). 2003. *Soft Skills for Organizational Success, Fourth Report of the Expert Group on Future Skills Needs.* <http://www.skillsireland.ie/publication/egfsnSearch.jsp?ft=/publications/2003/title,2581,en.php> [March 20, 2010].

Felstead, Alan, Duncan Gallie, Francis Green, and Ying Zhou. 2007. *Skills at Work, 1986–2006.* Oxford: ESRC Centre on Skills, Knowledge and Organizational Performance.

Finegold, David, Niclas Erhardt, and Mari Sako. 2009. "Offshoring Knowledge Work: How Far Can It Go? Evidence from Drug R and D." In Karl E. Carettas, ed., *Outsourcing, Teamwork and Business Management.* Hauppauge, NY: Nova Science Publishers.

Finegold, David, and Karin Wagner. 1998. "The Search for Flexibility: Skills and Workplace Innovation in the German Pump Industry." *British Journal of Industrial Relations*, Vol. 36, no. 3, pp. 469–87.

Forfás. 2006. *The Changing Nature of Generic Skills.* <http://www.skillsstrategy.ie/pdfs/TheChangingNatureofGenericSkills.pdf>. [March 20, 2010].

Forfás. 2009. *Future Skills Requirements of the Food and Beverage Sector.* <http://www.forfas.ie/media/egfsn091120_skills_food_beverage.pdf>. [October 11, 2010].

Forfás. 2009. *Monitoring Ireland's Skills Supply—Trends in Education and Training Outputs.* <http://www.forfas.ie/media/egfsn-091102-monitoring-skills-supply.pdf>. [October 11, 2010].

Forfás. 2009. *Skills in Creativity, Design and Innovation.* <http://www.forfas.ie/media/egfsn-091104-cdi.pdf>. [October 11, 2010].

Forth, John, and Geoff Mason. 2006. *Do ICT Skill Shortages Hamper Firms' Performance? Evidence from UK Benchmarking Surveys.* Discussion paper 281. London: National Institute of Economic and Social Research.

Futuremorph.org. 2008. "Qualification Routes." <http://www.futuremorph.org/_db/_documents/QualificationRoutesOct08.pdf>. [April 16, 2010].

Gatta, Mary. 2010. *In the 'Blink' of an Eye—American High-End Small Retail Businesses and the Public Workforce System.* Unpublished paper. New Brunswick, NJ: Rutgers University.

Gittell, Jody Hoffer. 2001. "Supervisory Span, Relational Coordination, and Flight Departure Performance: A Reassessment of Postbureaucracy Theory." *Organization Science*, Vol. 12, no. 4 (July–August), pp. 468–83.

Goleman, Daniel. 1998. *Working with Emotional Intelligence.* New York: Bantam Dell.

Gordon, J. 1992. "Work Teams: How Far Have They Come?" *Training*, Vol. 29, no. 10, pp. 59–65.

Green, Francis, Steven McIntosh, and Anna Vignoles. 2002. "The Utilization of Education and Skills: Evidence from Britain." *The Manchester School*, Vol. 70, no. 6, pp. 782–811.

Groot, Wim, and Henriette Maassen van den Brink. 2000. "Education, Training and Employability." *Applied Economics*, Vol. 32, no. 5, pp. 573–81.

Hampson, Ian. 2002. "Training Reform: Back to Square One?" *Economic and Industrial Relations Review*, Vol. 13, no. 2, pp. 149–74.

Hampson, Ian, and Anne Junor. 2009. *Employability and the Substance of Soft Skills.* Paper presented at the 27th Annual International Labour Process Conference, Edinburgh, April 6–8.

Hanushek, Eric A., Ludger Woessmann, Andreas Schleicher, Romain Duval, and Maciej Jakubowski. 2010. *The High Cost of Low Educational Performance: The*

Long-Run Economic Impact of Improving PISA Outcomes. Paris: Organisation for Economic Co-operation and Development.

Harhoff, Dietmar, and Thomas J. Kane. 1997. "Is the German Apprenticeship System a Panacea for the U.S. Labor Market?" *Journal of Population Economics,* Vol. 10, no. 2, pp. 171–96.

Hochschild, Arlie Russell. 1983. *The Managed Heart: Commercialization of Human Feeling.* Berkeley: University of California Press.

IBM. 2010. *Business Skills for IT Professionals.* <http://www-01.ibm.com/software/websphere/education/business_skills_for_IT_professionals/curriculum.html>. [March 15, 2010].

Impact Management Center. 2005. *Measuring the Impact of Training and Development in the Workplace.* <http://www.skillnets.ie/sites/skillnets.ie/files/pdf/Measuring_the_Impact_-_Final_Report.pdf>. [August 19, 2010].

Institute for Manufacturing at the University of Cambridge and IBM. 2008. *Succeeding Through Service Innovation: A Service Perspective for Education, Research, Business and Government.* <http://www.ifm.eng.cam.ac.uk/ssme/documents/080428ssi_us_letter.pdf>. [April 4, 2010].

Kang, Suk, and John Bishop. 1989. *Vocational and Academic Education in High School: Complements or Substitutes?* Cornell University, ILR Reprints No. 624. Ithaca, NY: New York State School of Industrial and Labor Relations, Cornell University.

Kirby, Simon, and Rebecca Riley. 2006. *The Returns to General versus Job-Specific Skills: The Role of Information and Communication Technology.* Discussion paper no. 274. London: National Institute for Economic and Social Research.

Kirkpatrick, Donald L. 1959. "Techniques for Evaluating Training Programs." *Journal of American Society for Training and Development,* Vol. 13, no. 11–12.

Kirkpatrick, Jim, and Wendy Kirkpatrick. 2009. "The Kirkpatrick Model: Past, Present and Future." *Chief Learning Officer,* Vol. 8, no. 11, pp. 20–55.

Kirsch, Irwin, John de Jong, Dominique LaFontaine, Joy McQueen, Juliette Mendelovits, and Christian Monseur. 2002. *Reading for Change: Performance and Engagement Across Countries, Results from PISA 2000.* Paris: Organisation for Economic Co-operation and Development.

Lloyd, Caroline, and Jonathan Payne. 2008. *What Is a Skilled Job? Exploring Worker Perceptions of Skill in Two UK Call Centres.* Oxford. Centre on Skills Knowledge and Organizational Performance, Oxford and Cardiff Universities.

Lusardi, Annamaria, and Olivia S. Mitchell. 2007. "Financial Literacy and Retirement Preparedness: Evidence and Implications for Financial Education." *Business Economics,* Vol. 42, no. 1, pp. 35–44.

MacCluer, Charles R., and Leon H. Seitelman. 2005. *Helpful Hints for Establishing Professional Science Masters Programs.* <http://www.sciencemasters.com/portals/0/pdfs/Establish_Sustain_PSM_Programs.pdf>. [March 28, 2010].

Martinsson, Johanna. 2009. *The Role of Media Literacy in the Governance Reform Agenda.* Washington, DC: World Bank Communication for Governance and Accountability Program.

Mason, Geoff, and David Finegold. 1997. "Productivity, Machinery and Skills in the United States and Western Europe." *National Institute Economic Review,* Vol. 162, no. 1, pp. 85–98.

Mason, Geoff, and Bart van Ark. 1993. "Productivity, Machinery and Skills in Engineering: An Anglo–Dutch Comparison." National Institute Discussion Paper no. 36. In David Mayes, ed., *Sources of Productivity Growth.* Cambridge: Cambridge University Press, pp. 97–117.

Mason, Geoff, Bart van Ark, and Karin Wagner. 1994. "Productivity, Product Quality and Workforce Skills: Food Processing in Four European Countries." *National Institute Economic Review,* Vol. 147, no. 1, pp. 62–83.

Mason, Geoff, Gareth Williams, and Sue Cranmer. 2006. *Employability Skills Initiatives in Higher Education: What Effects Do They Have on Graduate Labour Market Outcomes?* Discussion paper 280. London: National Institute of Economic and Social Research.

Maxwell, Nan L. 2006. *The Working Life: The Labor Market for Workers in Low Skilled Jobs.* Kalamazoo, MI: W.E. Upjohn Institute for Employment Research.

Mossberger, Karen, Caroline J. Tolbert, and Ramona S. McNeal. 2008. *Digital Citizenship: The Internet, Society and Participation.* Cambridge, MA: MIT Press.

Murnane, Richard J., John B. Willett, and Frank Levy. 1995. "The Growing Importance of Cognitive Skills in Wage Determination." *Review of Economics and Statistics*, Vol. 77, no. 2, pp. 251–66.

Murray, T. Scott, Eugene Owen, and Barry McGaw. 2005. *Learning a Living: First Results of the Adult Literacy and Life Skills Survey.* Paris and Ottawa: Organisation for Economic Co-operation and Development and Statistics Canada.

National Research Council, Committee on Enhancing the Master's Degree in the Natural Sciences. 2008. *Science Professionals: Master's Education for a Competitive World.* Washington, DC: National Academy of Sciences.

National Work Readiness Credential. 2010. *National Work Readiness Credential.* <http://www.workreadiness.com/nwrcred.html>. [April 10, 2010].

New Zealand Department of Labour. 2009. *Spotlight: A Skills Recognition Tool.* Wellington, NZ: Department of Labour, Te Mari Mahi.

Nickson, Dennis, Chris Warhurst, and Eli Dutton. 2004. *Aesthetic Labour and the Policy-making Agenda: Time for a Reappraisal of Skills?* Research Paper 48. Coventry, England: SKOPE Publications, Warwick Business School.

Organisation for Economic Co-operation and Development. 2005. *Definition and Selection of Key Competencies: Executive Summary.* Paris: OECD Publishing.

Organisation for Co-operation and Development and Statistics Canada. 2000. *Literacy in the Information Age: Final Report of the International Adult Literacy Survey (IALS).* Paris and Ottawa: OECD Publishing.

Osterman, Paul. 2006. "The Wage Effects of High Performance Work Organization in Manufacturing." *Industrial and Labor Relations Review*, Vol. 59, no. 2 (January), pp. 187–204.

Palmer, Colin. 1990. "'Hybrids'—A Critical Force in the Application of Information Technology in the Nineties." *Journal of Information Technology*, Vol. 5, pp. 232–35.

Peterson, Erika, Terence R. Mitchell, Leigh Thompson, and Renu Burr. 2000. "Collective Efficacy and Aspects of Shared Mental Models as Predictors of Performance Over Time in Work Groups." *Group Processes & Intergroup Relations*, Vol. 3, no. 3, pp. 296–316.

Pew Internet and American Life Project. 2010. *Trend Data—Online Activities, Total.* <http://www.pewinternet.org/Trend-Data/Online-Activites-Total.aspx>. [April 1, 2010].

Phillips, Jack J. 1996. "Measuring ROI: The Fifth Level of Evaluation." *Technical and Skills Training*, Vol. 7, no. 3, pp. 10–3.

Philpott, John. 2002. *Perspectives: Productivity and People Management.* London: Chartered Institute for Personnel and Development.

Porter, Michael E. 1996. "What Is Strategy?" *Harvard Business Review* (November–December), pp. 61–78.

Prahalad, C.K., and Gary Hamel. 1990. "The Core Competence of the Corporation." *Harvard Business Review*, Vol. 68, no. 3, pp. 79–91.

Prais, S.J. 1981. "Vocational Qualifications of the Labour Force in Britain and Germany." *National Institute Economic Review*, Vol. 98, no. 1, pp. 47–59.

Prais, S.J., and Karin Wagner. 1983. "Some Practical Aspects of Human Capital Investment: Training Standards in Five Occupations in Britain and Germany." *National Institute Economic Review*, Vol. 105, no. 1, pp. 46–65.

Prais, S.J., and Karin Wagner. 1988. "Productivity and Management: The Training of Foremen in Britain and Germany." *National Institute Economic Review*, Vol. 123, no. 1, pp. 34–46.

Robinson, Peter. 1997. *Literacy, Numeracy and Economic Performance*. CEP Special report CEPSP08. London: Centre for Economic Performance, London School of Economics.

Schofield, Kaye, and Rod McDonald. 2004. *Moving On: Report of the High Level Review of Training Packages*. Melbourne: Australian National Training Authority.

Schuller, Tom, and Richard Desjardins. 2007. *Understanding the Social Outcomes of Learning*. Paris: OECD Publishing.

Service Skills Australia. 2007. *What Is a Training Package?* <http://www.serviceskills.com.au/index.php?option=com_content&task=view&id=946>. [April 3, 2010].

Shury, Jan, Mark Winterbotham, Ben Davies, and Katie Oldfield. 2010. *National Employer Skills Survey for England 2009: Key Findings Report*. London: UK Commission for Employment and Skills.

Skillnets, Ltd. 2005. *Case Studies from the Skillnets Pilot Project: Measuring the Impact of Training and Development in the Workplace*. <http://www.skillnets.ie/sites/skillnets.ie/files/pdf/Measuring_the_Impact_-_Case_Studies.pdf>. [August 20, 2010].

Smith, Jan. 1998. "Beyond the Rhetoric: Are General National Vocational Qualifications (GNVQs) Doing Students Any Good?" *Journal of Vocational and Educational Training*, Vol. 50, no. 4, pp. 537–48.

Society for Human Resource Management and the *Wall Street Journal* Career Journal. 2008. *Critical Skills Needs and Resources for the Changing Workforce: Keeping Skills Competitive*. <http://californiaworkforceassociation.pbworks.com/f/Critical%20Skills%20Needs%20and%20Resources%20for%20the%20Changing%20Workforce%20Survey%20Report.pdf>. [April 3, 2010].

Solansky, Stephanie T. 2008. "Leadership Style and Team Processes in Self-Managed Teams." *Journal of Leadership and Organizational Studies*, Vol. 14, no. 4, pp. 332–41.

Spitz-Oener, Alexandra. 2006. "Technical Change, Job Tasks, and Rising Educational Demands: Looking Outside the Wage Structure." *Journal of Labor Economics*, Vol. 24, no. 2 (April), pp. 235–70.

Stevens, Philip A. 2004. *Skill Shortages and Firms' Employment Behavior*. Discussion paper 240. London: National Institute of Social and Economic Research.

Tornero, José Manuel Pérez. 2008. "Media Literacy—New Conceptualisation, New Approach." In Ulla Carlsson, Samy Tayie, Genevieve Jauinot-Delaunay, and José Manuel Pérez Tornero, eds., *Empowerment through Media Education—An Intercultural Dialogue*. Goteborg, Sweden: Nordicom, pp. 106–8.

United States Department of Labor, Secretary's Commission on Achieving Necessary Skills. 1991. *What Work Requires of Schools: A SCANS Report for America 2000*. <http://wdr.doleta.gov/SCANS/whatwork/whatwork.pdf>. [August 18, 2010].

Wall, Toby D., Nigel J. Kemp, Paul R. Jackson, and Chris W. Clegg. 1986. "Outcomes of Autonomous Work Groups: A Long-Term Field Experiment." *Academy of Management Journal*, Vol. 29, no. 2, pp. 280–304.

Williams, Joel, Sam Clemens, Karin Oleinikova, and Karen Tarvin. 2003. *The Skills for Life Survey: A National Needs and Impact Survey of Literacy, Numeracy and ICT Skills*. London: UK Department for Education and Skills.

CHAPTER 3

The Globalization of Technology Development: Implications for U.S. Skills Policy

LEONARD LYNN
Case Western Reserve University

HAL SALZMAN
Rutgers University

Throughout most of the 20th century, the U.S. "skills system" was a model in many ways for the rest of the world. Primary and secondary schools offered mass education to provide industry with a large supply of literate and numerate workers. Land-grant and other universities trained people in practical skills such as engineering, medicine, and agriculture, and they also created new knowledge useful in these and other fields. American firms drew on these skills to develop new technologies and to gain global leadership. Government supported the enterprise by funding K–12 schools, universities, pure research projects, and U.S. firms. The "best and the brightest" from around the world were drawn to the United States by the quality of its education system and career opportunities. The elements of a good government skills and innovation policy seemed clear: Support K–12 education. Support universities. Support basic and applied R&D. Support U.S. business firms. Allow the global brain drain to continually enrich the U.S. pool of human resources. And underwrite the development of leading-edge technology through space and military programs.

At the same time, a number of structural weaknesses were noted in the U.S. system, especially as compared to other industrial countries. Unlike Germany, for example, the United States has a very weak and miniscule apprenticeship system. Vocational education in general, and craft skills in particular, have not been seen as part of the core public educational mission. Apprenticeship programs are largely the province of unions, and vocational education is considered a "second-class" educational track within high schools. Career tracks are not well articulated, and U.S. youth generally have not had clear career pathways other than preparing for college entry (Hamilton 1994; Lerman 2008). Noncollege pathways have remained weak and relatively overlooked in educational policy despite the fact that less than 30% of the U.S. population has a four-year degree as of 2008 (the proportion of those 25 to 29 with a bachelor's degree reached just 30.8% in 2008 [U.S. Department of Education 2008], with little increase in the past three decades, while other Triad nations [United States, European Union, and Japan] have been expanding their populations attaining college degrees). Thus, for the vast majority of Americans, the United States is not developing an education system that is linked to career pathways.

Despite these weaknesses, the U.S. education and skills system histori-cally supported overall economic growth by offering multiple paths of achievement, including nontraditional career pathways and widely avail-able opportunities for entrepreneurship. Quite importantly, the United States also benefited from earlier massive expansion of higher education through the GI Bill and land-grant colleges. The openness of the American system to career mobility, business start-ups, immigration, and creativity led to an innovative, high-productivity economy, even if the individual costs were high to those disenfranchised because of low skills, poor educa-tion, discrimination, poverty, or other factors. The overall economic per-formance of the United States thus muted any pressure for major changes in the skill development systems, particularly for noncollege careers.

In the late 20th century a confluence of trends such as reductions in barriers to international travel, communications, collaborative activity, and trade introduced a number of changes in the demands on the U.S. science and technology (S&T) workforce. While each of these trends has been widely commented on, we believe there is still an insufficient understanding of how the various trends interact, and how in that inter-action they change the nature of skills policies needed for the 21st cen-tury. This lack of understanding leads American policy makers to believe they can restore the superiority the United States enjoyed in earlier stages of globalization by recreating or expanding the U.S. advantages of those earlier periods. Thus, for example, we see national "competitive-ness" strategies placing "college for all" approaches at the top of their lists of policy priorities (e.g., Council on Competitiveness 2004; National Academy of Sciences 2007; Lederman 2009). The notion is that the United States will maintain its leadership position and economic vitality by dominating global innovation, by having an economy that focuses pri-marily on the "top of the pyramid" jobs and activities (e.g., National Center on Education and the Economy 2007), and by developing poli-cies to attract and sequester the best global talent within the national borders of the United States.

Although these approaches worked well in supporting economic growth and national security over the past half century, they are woefully inadequate and misguided for this century. In this chapter we argue that not only are such efforts unlikely to succeed, but they may deflect us from developing the skills policies most likely to be beneficial to Americans. The first need for policy makers is to come to a clearer understanding of how S&T human resources can and should fit into 21st-century globalization. Such an understanding can only come by looking at the collective and interactive impacts of the various widely noted trends. We have elsewhere (Lynn and Salzman 2004, 2009) sought to provide a historical perspective on the emerging global environment for knowledge work, concluding that the current environment differs sharply from that of two previous periods following World War II and is thus placing very different demands on national skill formation policies. We call this new environment the "third-generation globalization of knowledge work." In this chapter we examine its implications for skill development needs and policies.

To assess what a skills policy should be for this new era of globalization, we first consider the nature of third-generation globalization, to understand its drivers, structure, and dynamics. Then we assess the commonly proposed responses. We offer a critical focus on five interrelated assumptions and tactics that underlie many current skill development and education proposals: 1) that U.S. "competitiveness" vis-à-vis other countries is best judged by readily available metrics on test scores or numbers of engineering graduates and that they provide a helpful benchmark by which to set our goals for S&T and workforce development policy; 2) that creating a sense of crisis in which the United States is depicted as losing a Sputnik-style race with formidable adversaries will spur policy makers to take beneficial actions, such as improving our education system; 3) that national boundaries can "contain" innovation and that just increasing our strength in basic science and innovation will lead to a new period of U.S. dominance in the world (or at least keep us "ahead" of others); 4) that since China, India, and other countries are crafting strategies to build up their S&T workforces and capabilities, the United States would be well-advised to follow similar strategies; and 5) that restoring U.S. global "dominance" in S&T is the most direct approach to ensuring U.S. economic and social vitality.

After a brief discussion of "third-generation globalization," we examine the evidence supporting these assumptions in the context of recent patterns of globalization. Based on this analysis, we conclude the chapter by discussing the implications for what skills policies should and should not be.

Third-Generation Globalization of Knowledge Work

The new era of globalization is often characterized as being different from those of the past. A common interpretation points out that globalization is bringing countries into more direct competition with each other, and that more countries, particularly emerging economies, are being brought into the competitive pool. Many argue that in this new "flat world," countries have become direct competitors in a zero-sum game in which the successes of one country imply losses for all other countries.

One aspect of this zero-sum game is the location of the "best jobs." There are widespread fears that the United States is losing in a competition to retain and grow the highest-value-added, highest-paid jobs. Some observers point out that U.S. multinational enterprises (MNEs) are being driven by global competitive pressures to lower their labor costs by locating their S&T jobs in the emerging economies. Others argue that U.S. firms are increasingly being forced to go offshore to find scientists and engineers because of shortages within the United States. According to a report by Duke University's Offshoring Research Network, in 2009 more than half of U.S. firms had corporate-wide initiatives to move innovation activities offshore, more than double the number of firms that had such initiatives in 2005 (Wadhwa 2009). A National Science Board report (2010b) found that the U.S. share of worldwide R&D expenditures has been dropping in recent years, while the share of the Asia/Pacific region has been growing rapidly. The report also suggests that, on balance, the United States has benefited less from the globalization of R&D than have other nations.

In a zero-sum world this would imply that the United States and other members of the Triad are fated to lose the high-paid jobs associated with S&T, the other economic and social benefits that stem from S&T, and the overall economic and strategic competitiveness that rests largely on the strength of the country's workforce. In this model of the new globalization, the ability of a country to keep or grow firms located within its borders is linked to the level of education and the size of its science and engineering workforce. This, in turn, suggests that U.S. skills policy is vital to stemming an economic crisis and loss of competitiveness to other countries: If only we had more engineers, U.S. MNEs wouldn't locate their technology development activities offshore. Or, though no one seems to want to state it this baldly, if we trained enough engineers and scientists in the United States, then salaries would be driven down, reducing the motivation of U.S. MNEs to go offshore.

While parts of this picture may be rooted in reality, in our view the overall picture being presented is distorted and incomplete. We believe it is useful to draw contrasts among three distinct eras of the globalization of S&T work in the last half of the 20th century and the early 21st century. Each era posed particular challenges and opportunities for policy makers and corporate strategists. Policies and strategies suited to one era may be misguided and even disastrous for another, and this is particularly true of skills policies based on misconceptions of how firms and national economies are globalizing.

One aspect of the globalization of technology development in the decades immediately after World War II was the rise of MNEs. Indeed, a highly influential argument was that MNEs exist because they are the most efficient mechanism for transferring knowledge across national borders (Coase 1937; Hymer 1960; Kogut and Zander 1993). In the case of MNE activities in the emerging economies during this first generation of product development globalization, the transfer of knowledge was generally unidirectional. Triad MNEs did not view themselves as having much to learn from the emerging economies. The central strategy was based on the concept of the "international product life cycle" (Vernon 1966, 1971; Wells 1968). In essence, Triad MNEs squeezed out extra profits by transferring obsolescent technologies to less demanding markets. If development work was done at all in the emerging economies, it was generally to "dumb down" technology to make it usable by less skilled workforces, simpler so as to be more robust to withstand harsher environments, and cheaper so as to be affordable for less affluent consumers. Central R&D laboratories were highly valued by the Triad MNEs, and goals of technological autonomy led to a tendency to undervalue "NIH" (not invented here) technology.

The S&T policies of the emerging economies in that era were often guided by dependency theories in which these countries were advised to restrict MNE investment because reliance on foreign companies was seen as forestalling the development of indigenous S&T and other capabilities. In-bound technology transfers were discouraged (see, for example, Frank 1967 on dependency theory and Reddy and Zhao 1991; Correa 1995; and Bruton 1998 on specific policies). Policy makers in the newly postcolonial emerging economies were also concerned about "brain drains," particularly to the United States. If a newly independent country was still dependent on the Triad for technology and if it sent its most talented people, its "best and brightest," to the Triad, was the country any more independent than it had been as a Triad colony?

On the other hand, U.S. government policy makers were far more concerned with the strategic and military implications of technology development and transfer than with the economic implications. It was important to lead in basic science because that might lead to breakthroughs that would facilitate the rapid development of new missile systems or nuclear weapons, but technology transfer agreements that may not have been favorable for U.S. commercial interests were promoted if they helped solidify the anticommunist stance of our trade partners. Those in the education community used the perceived military threats posed by the USSR in the 1950s and 1960s and the perceived economic threats posed by the Japanese in the 1970s and 1980s to advocate much of what they advocate today—stronger math and science education and the training of more scientists and engineers. But the science and engineering workforce increases that actually occurred were driven more by strong demand, largely from government spending, than by a reliance on supply-driven factors such as provision of more math and science education. It might also be noted in passing that it is not clear how much any ramping up of the U.S. skill development system that resulted was a factor in overcoming the Soviet and Japanese threats. Russia and Japan may have won the race to train more engineers, but in the longer term the United States did better than Russia militarily and Japan economically.

In the 1980s and early 1990s, the environment shifted as we moved to the second generation of knowledge work. Under competitive pressures from lower-cost products from East Asia, more and more U.S. MNEs moved operations to lower-cost offshore sites. Influential management thinkers pointed to the advantages of outsourcing and offshoring. The MNEs sought to retain their core competencies in the development of technology, but influential management gurus like Bartlett and Ghoshal (e.g., 1989, 1998) were beginning to advise firms to locate particular R&D activities in areas where relevant resources and activities were located. Still, most cutting-edge R&D continued to be carried out in the Triad.

The location of manufacturing activities in low-cost emerging economies by the MNEs led to widespread concern in the United States, Europe, and Japan that key manufacturing capabilities were being lost—that the Triad economies were being "hollowed out." Overall, however, the conventional wisdom was that the richer countries would continually replace low-paid jobs with higher-paid ones. Policy makers in Japan and the EU sought to create comparative advantage in high-tech industries because these were seen as offering higher salaries and a variety of spillover benefits (Tyson 1992). Many countries pursued policies to develop their indigenous industrial base in these new technologies. The emerging economies started to encourage the introduction of technology through import agreements. While foreign direct investment may not have been welcome, original equipment manufacturer (OEM) agreements that allowed the emergence of internationally competitive domestic firms were strongly encouraged.

Then the policy environment changed further in the mid-1990s, initiating the third generation of globalized knowledge work. The World Trade Organization was formed in 1994, and with other organizations it led in establishing the suite of policies commonly termed "the Washington Consensus." The international movement of MNEs was greatly facilitated. To gain the benefits of trade, emerging economies had to dismantle barriers and extend more protection to foreign businesses and investors. Between 1991 and 2000, nearly 1,000 changes were made in laws worldwide to facilitate foreign direct investment. Policy changes permitting joint ventures in India in 1994, for example, encouraged the inflow of Triad investment and technology, though domestic ownership requirements maintained some local control. The Chinese began to welcome foreign firms, often pressuring them to form local joint ventures in exchange for market access and requiring them to share some of their core/proprietary technology as a further cost of doing business in China. As the 1990s drew to a close, Triad firms sought help from software engineers in India to cope with widely feared Y2K problems (Salzman 2000; Salzman and Biswas 2000).

The Internet, new collaborative technologies, and reduced travel and communications costs made it possible for globally distributed teams to work together on technology projects. These changes reached the threshold of maturity and acceptance in firms in the early 2000s. By the middle of the decade, firms had created globally distributed teams that regularly interacted in projects (Flecker and Meil, forthcoming). A group of managers at a U.S. MNE in the electronics industry told us during interviews in 2005 that ten years before, they and their offshore teams had barely known each other. By 2005 they were in telephone contact several times a week. A vice president at a chemical firm told us in 2004 how engineers could be sent offshore on six-month projects while continuing to participate in their U.S.-based product development teams. Earlier they had been sent overseas on three-year assignments and had only sporadic relationships with the firm's engineers based in the United States.

Other changes have also taken place that make this third generation of the globalization of knowledge work different from its predecessors. Centers of technological excellence began to develop in some of the emerging economies. Some MNEs found it useful to seek new sources of S&T human resources and knowledge near these centers. In our interviews, we were repeatedly told about highly valued Chinese or Indian engineering or R&D managers working at a U.S. MNE who were now reaching later stages of their careers and wanted to go home. It was typically these managers who made a persuasive business case for the MNE to locate R&D or product development activities in the manager's home country. Moving these core activities to an emerging economy would have been unthinkable in the first- or second-generation eras.

In parallel, and related to these changes, Triad MNEs were moving from an avoidance of NIH technology to trying to find ways to outsource technology development. The conventional wisdom was that outsourcing saved money, and financial analysts liked to hear corporate managers describe aggressive outsourcing targets (Lynn and Salzman 2009). In some industries, new models of modular production led to an increased reliance on OEM and original design manufacturer (ODM) firms in emerging economies. Technologies increasingly crossed traditional boundaries of industrial expertise, and it seemed that no firm, no matter how large, could possibly master every relevant technology. In fact, it became a management truism that large firms could not keep pace with innovation that, it was thought, increasingly came from start-ups and small firms. With the increased mobility of people and companies and radically improved means of storing and moving information, knowledge flowed far more rapidly and supported collaborations more tightly linked but globally dispersed.

Not surprisingly, as Triad MNEs took on increasing numbers of foreign sites of operation, foreign senior managers and other key employees, and foreign investors, they began to identify less and less with their country of origin. It may make sense to speak of an MNE as being American if its key stakeholders (investors, employees, managers, communities, customers, and suppliers) are all American, but what if only a minority in some or all of these groups is American? As Baumol and Gomory (1998) point out, Americans (and their government) have not yet realized that the interests of large global corporations based in the United States can diverge from the interests of the country (see also Gomory and Baumol 2000). The divergence of corporate and national interests is also manifest in the new character of individual identities by employees the world over. We were struck in interviews in China with the degree to which Chinese managers identified with the U.S. multinational they worked for, seeing their futures as intertwined with the U.S. firm and hoping to rise into its top management. When they discussed cultural issues within the firm, aspects of national culture were largely irrelevant to them—it was the culture of the firm that defined how they did business—and, within each company, national culture had minimal impact on operations from one global location to another.

In the wake of these changes, the leading emerging economies have clear and common policy goals for skill development. They want to radically improve their K–12 education systems, build great universities, train large numbers of S&T personnel, support domestic firms in their technology development activities, and entice, or compel if necessary, foreign MNEs to share technology as well as develop new technology within their borders. In addition, emerging economies are increasingly recruiting back home their nationals who have S&T education and experience in the Triad. But what should the U.S. response be? Should we assume that policies that may be good for the emerging economies are equally applicable to the United States? Putting aside for the moment the issue of whether there really is a new problem that threatens the well-being of Americans, let us look briefly at the proposals that have surfaced in the current debate. We will critically examine these proposals in the light of the assumptions and data supporting them and in how well suited they seem to the current era of third-generation globalization of knowledge work.

The K–12 "Problem"

Although the American education system is perennially portrayed as being in crisis (e.g., National Commission on Excellence in Education 1983; National Association of Manufacturers 2005), the nature of the crisis has taken a new turn in the past decade. A host of business associations and related committees flooded the policy arena with reports, including an influential report issued through the National Academy of Sciences (2007), all arguing that student test scores are integrally linked to economic outcomes. In so doing, they have linked the education problem to the perceived crisis in national competitiveness. Policy makers and commentators have focused on the quality of K–12 education, apparently as measured by comparative test scores, as one of the more important issues determining the future of the American economy vis-à-vis the emerging economies and even as the means of addressing the recent financial crisis.

In a bit of loose reasoning, some of those pointing with alarm to comparative test scores cite the fact that students in a number of mostly small countries, such as Finland and Estonia, score better than their American counterparts. No one identifies these countries as economic or military threats to the United States. Strangely enough, the threats that critics worry most about come from China and India. Yet neither China nor India participates in the international tests; if they did on a nationwide basis, they would no doubt score quite low, given the problems these countries have had in extending their education systems to poorer and more remote areas. Indeed, in India more than a third of the population is illiterate (United Nations Development Program 2009). The countries leading in literacy rates are all former Soviet Bloc countries, with Cuba and Georgia leading the list, the United States 19th, and China and India placing 80th and 147th, respectively. Similarly, the UN education index (using a composite of several education achievement factors) provides a similar ranking, with the United States ranking below Iceland, Cuba, Slovenia, and Barbados (United Nations Development Program 2009). Clearly, the educational rankings list appears quite unrelated to rankings of economic performance. Since no one would suggest that these nations are economic or political models for the United States, it is not clear what significance high test scores have for outcomes other than the test performance itself.

There are broader problems with arguments based on relative U.S. student performance on tests such as the Programme for International Student Assessment (PISA) or Trends in International Mathematics and Science Study (TIMSS), the two major international education tests. The tests do *not* actually show the United States to be seriously lagging the world. On average, the United States scores in a solid second-place group of countries on some subjects and in the first tier on others. It is one of only a few nations that show consistent improvements or stability in performance from year to year and over all grades and subjects. In fact, a number of states within the United States that are similar in size to the "leading" countries, such as Singapore and Finland, do as well as or even better than these countries (Lowell and Salzman 2007; Salzman 2007; Salzman and Lowell 2008). Moreover, even if we accept the notion that it is the absolute size of the top-performing student pool that is important for the size and output of the S&T workforce, then it is important to recognize that the United States currently produces a group of highest-performing students in science as well as in reading many times greater than that of any other nation, and in math second only to Japan (Salzman and Lowell 2008; see Figures 1A, 1B, and 1C). Overall, in terms of level, quantity, and consistency across all subjects, the top-performing U.S. students are second to those of no other country. The United States achieves this performance level despite having a population that is economically and socially much more diverse than that of any other country. The proportion of top-performing math and science students has not wavered over the past three decades and, with a growing population, this has resulted in ever-greater numbers of top-performing math and science graduates, far exceeding the employment opportunities in the science and engineering fields each year (Lowell and Salzman 2007; Salzman 2007; Salzman and Lowell 2008; also see Walker 2010, reporting that only 42% of 2009 engineering graduates found jobs, a decline from prior years in which 70% of engineering graduates found engineering jobs).

FIGURE 1A
Percentage of All OECD High-Performing Students in Science.

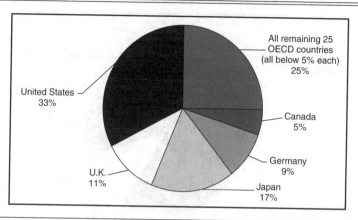

Source: OECD–Science and Math, 2006 PISA. Tabulations: Salzman and Lowell 2008.

FIGURE 1B
Percentage of All OECD High-Performing Students in Math.

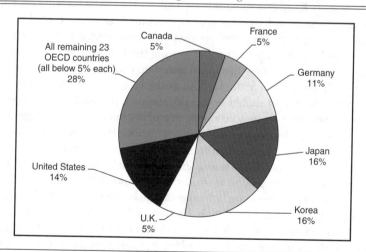

Source: OECD–Science and Math, 2006 PISA. Tabulations: Salzman and Lowell 2008.

FIGURE 1C
Percentage of All OECD High-Performing Students in Reading.

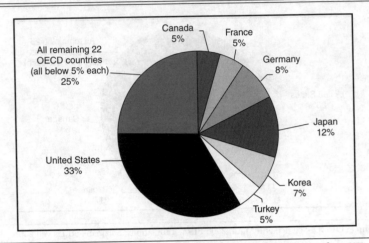

Source: OECD–Reading, 2003 PISA (U.S. did not have results for 2006 in reading; UK did not have results for 2003 in reading). Tabulations: Salzman and Lowell 2008.

Certainly K–12 education is important, and we do not wish to encourage complacency with the U.S. system, particularly since the United States also has a large group of very poorly performing students. Yet it is misguided to base the argument for improving the U.S. education system on exaggerated views of how this might speed up economic growth or how it might help the United States to close imagined gaps with other countries. Of course the nation should make education a top priority for a range of reasons, including not only economic prosperity but also civic engagement and the overall development of our population. However, even when it comes to the role of education in supporting economic competitiveness, the use of narrow criteria of uncertain validity, such as K–12 math and science test scores, may lead us to overlook the demands for a broad range of skills or the need to improve basic skills at the bottom of the distribution.

In the third-generation globalization of technology development, people are more and more likely to work and live in other countries, and more likely to find themselves working in cross-national teams. In this world, might not training in foreign culture and languages be as important as skills in math and science? Might not design, humanities, and social sciences be important to understanding consumer needs and developing innovative consumer products, such as various Apple products that are distinguished by far more than their technical engineering? An examination of the full portfolio of needed skills should also focus us on the need to create high-quality pathways to develop those skills, such as apprenticeship and other noncollege routes into the workforce (e.g., Lerman 2008; also see Rothstein 1998; Rothstein, Jacobsen, and Wilder 2006; and Ravitch 2010 for related critiques).

Finally, it seems questionable to define the U.S. education system as being in a "race" against other countries with systems that we want to emulate because of their test performance. Some countries may have education systems that are part of and reflect political systems inimical to American values, such as those operating under autocratic or authoritarian rule. Many countries have not been able to translate high test scores into any tangible innovative or economic performance (e.g., Latvia or Moldavia today, or the other Communist Bloc countries during the Cold War, or educationally top-scoring Finland, with over a quarter of its youth unemployed, which is also in the top unemployment group [Statistics Finland 2010]). More importantly, as we will discuss, it is the overall "competitiveness" strategy that the United States develops as a roadmap for economic and social well-being in the global economy that should guide the workforce development component of education and training programs.

In the next section we examine the supply of and demand for engineers, one of the more important technology workforces, and the role of engineering in a nation's economy. Here again we consider the evidence underlying some commonplace assumptions.

The Engineer Race

Concerns that the United States may be losing a test-score race with other countries often lead to concerns that the United States is losing a race for developing enough competent engineers. Numerous reports point with alarm to statistics that show rapid increases in the number of engineers being trained in India, China, and other countries. The proposed solution to this "problem" is to train more Americans to be engineers (partly by increasing Americans' interest in science and engineering and by improving science and math education in grades K–12). Although increasing the numbers of educated workers is intrinsically a laudable goal, we would argue that citing global competition and workforce size in other countries does not provide useful guidance for U.S. workforce development policy; such comparisons do not actually provide an analysis of what the United States would achieve by increasing the numbers of its own engineers.

Let us first consider what most engineers actually do. Engineers make up just over 1% of the civilian workforce, and just under half of all engineers are civil, mechanical, and industrial engineers, with 56% of all engineers working in either manufacturing or construction. Not quite 5% (4.8%, or just over 75,000) are in "scientific research and development services," and probably only a few percent more are involved in key innovation activities. So most engineers are not creating new technology or developing new products or industrial processes. They are busy designing bridges, roads, power plants, factories, and buildings and running manufacturing operations (Bureau of Labor Statistics 2008).

China is rapidly developing, and its engineers are doing what a developing country needs engineers to do: building new manufacturing facilities and power plants, expanding cities, and constructing new bridges, railways, and highways. In comparison to the more than 30,000 miles of new interstate highway China built in the past decade, for example, the United States added only 608 additional miles. While China is building thousands of miles of additional rail and waterway transit, the United States has actually seen a decline in total mileage of both. As a proxy of construction and manufacturing activities, it is illustrative to compare the national consumption of cement and steel, two key inputs for construction and manufacturing. As Table 1 and Figure 2 show, China is ravenously consuming these inputs while U.S. consumption has remained flat.

Consequently, we should expect parallel trends in the production and employment of human resources used for that building and manufacturing. In China, it is the remarkable growth of the domestic economy and its global expansion that are generating the demand for engineers. Thus, it hardly seems remarkable that in 2008 China graduated approximately 660,000 engineers from a population of 1.3 billion people to add to a total workforce of over 780 million. The vast increase of engineers in China is focused on meeting rather basic domestic and international infrastructure and natural resource needs, not on an engineering arms race that threatens the U.S. ability to innovate or to compete.

Nor are most of the new Chinese engineers qualified to the same level as American engineers. McKinsey finds that only 10% of China's engineering graduates are considered employable in global firms, compared to over 80% of U.S. engineering graduates (as cited in Farrell and Grant 2005). Adjusting for quality, then, China is graduating fewer internation-

TABLE 1
Growth of Infrastructure from 1997 to 2007.

Length (miles)	U.S.	China
Interstate/expressway	608	30,519
Navigable channels	(680)	8,510
Rail	(4,030)	7,436

Sources: U.S.—National Transport Statistics, 2009, Bureau of Transport Statistics, U.S. Department of Transportation; China—China Statistical Yearbook, 2008, National Bureau of Statistics of China.

FIGURE 2
Steel and Cement Consumption° in the United States and China, 1997–2007.

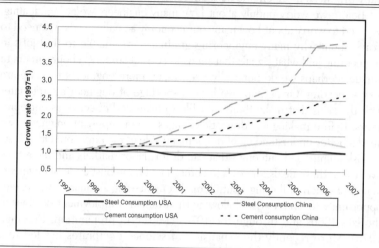

°U.S. cement consumption = production (excluding clinker) + import for consumption (excluding clinker) – exports.
°China cement consumption = production – export.
°Steel consumption = steel shipments + imports – exports + adjustment for industry stock changes + adjustments for import of semi-finished steel products (USGS).

Sources:
U.S. Steel: USGS Mineral Commodity Summaries, Iron and Steel.
China Steel (1998–2005): OECD, Recent Steel Market Developments, 28 June 2004.
China Steel (1997): OECD, The Steel Market in 1997 and the Outlook for 1998 and 1999.
China Steel (2006): OECD, News Brief of Steel Committee Meeting, 2007.
China Steel (2007): OECD, News Brief of Steel Committee Meeting, 2008.
U.S. Cement: USGS Mineral Commodity Summaries, Cement.
China Cement: China Statistical Yearbook.

ally qualified engineers than the United States (66,000 qualified Chinese engineering graduates versus more than 80,000 American bachelor's and master's engineering graduates [National Science Board 2010a]).

The single-minded discussion of the supply of engineers can blind us to thinking about how many engineers are actually needed for the U.S. economy. What if, for example, the United States were to expand its current engineering workforce by a third, adding another half million engineers? What would we do with them? Typically, about a third of each year's engineering graduates do not find jobs in an engineering field, and following the financial meltdown, more than half of new U.S. graduates did not find engineering jobs in 2009 (Walker 2010). While engineering provides a fine technical education and many transferrable skills, there is little evidence of any unique advantage provided to a country that artificially produces more engineers than it has jobs for in engineering. Before we worry unduly about how many engineers we are graduating, we need to worry about how many our economy actually needs. We need to worry about why many engineering graduates are unable to find jobs in engineering and what signals that sends to current students about careers to pursue. Perhaps we do not really need many more engineers than we are now educating. Or perhaps we have a shortage of engineering graduates with the skills that make them valuable to firms and effective as entrepreneurs. Before making any dramatic changes in our supply of engineers, we need a better understanding of the demand side of the equation. Otherwise, we risk unintended outcomes that can distort labor markets and the attractiveness of these fields for years to come. The boom–bust cycle of engineering employment following Sputnik made engineering an unattractive career opportunity for many years following the dramatic employment declines in the late 1960s and through the 1970s (Kaiser, in preparation; Freeman 1976). More recently the expansion of science doctorates has led to a decline in the appeal of those degrees to prospective students (Teitelbaum 2008). This certainly should not be taken as implying that we should unduly restrict the supply of engineers. The tight control over the number of medical degrees offered in the United States has kept that field highly desirable to qualified young people, but at the cost (to society) of physician shortages. Neither, though, do we want to artificially inflate the numbers and thus distort the market and devalue the attractiveness of the profession.

The lessons learned from past decades of demand and supply in the science and engineering labor market are that disequilibria have significant consequences and that market-driven adjustments seem to occur reasonably well, albeit with a short lag given the years of preparation needed before workforce entry (Freeman 1976; Teitelbaum 2008).

Rather than focusing on quantity, more attention should be paid to training engineers who will thrive in this third generation of globalized knowledge work. Our interviews suggest that it is certain new types of engineers that are proving to be the most desired. An engineering manager at a major U.S. MNE told us, for example, how one of his most valuable young engineers was no more than average (though certainly well-trained) by traditional criteria (university attended, grades, courses taken, recommendations, etc.). This young person, however, had a strong desire to experience other cultures and was very open-minded and was thus hired over other applicants with much superior technical qualifications. He proved highly effective when sent to help coordinate product development activities with facilities in China and elsewhere. One can understand the potential appeal of American engineering graduates who have had part of their education or their co-op experiences in emerging economies.

Brains: From Absorption to Circulation

The ability of the United States to attract and incorporate into its society people from around the world has been a major factor in its technological, economic, and societal success. We have been able to draw on the skills, intelligence, and inventiveness of machinists, nurses, doctors, university faculty, engineers, and scientists from every country. The ability to offer these people the chance to become Americans, to become a genuine part of our social fabric, has set us apart from other economically advanced countries.

Until recently, however, the impact on economic or technological competitiveness was not the major driver of U.S. immigration policy, and guest worker visa programs were not central to supplying the technology workforce. U.S. immigration policies generally have been most explicitly concerned with controlling the total number of immigrants coming to the United States and restricting the numbers coming from most parts of the world. At various points in our history, policy makers notoriously feared that the United States would be overwhelmed by the influx of people different from those already in the country—with "different" being defined in terms of religion, ethnicity, nationality, ideology, or race. Sometimes a strong concern has been that the newcomers would draw unduly on government finances or take jobs from native-born Americans. Understandably but unfortunately, the legacy of these past immigration debates is clouding an analysis of the current high-skill immigration policy analysis.

To be sure, there were periods when immigration was encouraged (or at least allowed) as an offer of humanitarian refuge to those escaping strife in other countries. After World War II, German rocket scientists were brought to the United States—adding significantly to U.S. aerospace capabilities, keeping the Soviet Union from acquiring those capabilities, and reducing the ability of Germany to again become a threat to world peace. More recently, after the repression at Beijing's Tiananmen Square, green card status was granted automatically to Chinese in the United States. A benefit of this humanitarian policy was that it added to the stock of scientists and engineers in the United States As one immigration lawyer noted, "This is a gold mine for the U.S. We are getting the best and the brightest of the most populous nation in the world" (Hart and Chow 1993:1).[1]

Given the attractiveness of U.S. universities, opportunities for challenging jobs in technology, and high income levels, the United States also became the destination for thousands of talented people from around the world, who often stayed after graduation and became part of the U.S. workforce (see Figure 3). Although enriching the U.S.

FIGURE 3
Foreign-Born Scientists and Engineers in the United States S&E Occupations, by
Degree Level and Field: 1993 and 2003.

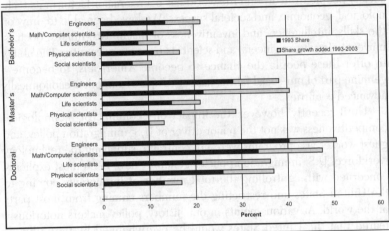

Note: For 1993, data include all people residing in the United States at the time of the survey with a degree in science and engineering, regardless of where that degree was earned.
Source: National Science Foundation, Science and Engineering indicators, 1998 and 2010.

workforce, this immigration raised concerns that these were the people their home countries needed to reach higher technological levels. The gains to the United States were clear from this pattern of immigration, but the impacts on the countries sending the immigrants were mixed at best.

With the advent of third-generation globalization, things have changed. Earlier the United States had such powers of attraction that talented immigrants found ways to come despite policy and procedural barriers that made it difficult to gain entry. Recently, the U.S. advantage in this regard has begun to diminish. High-profile universities in India and elsewhere have garnered attention for their quality. Some science and technology programs in India and China, thanks in part to alliances with foreign MNEs and foreign universities, may soon equal or exceed some of the better U.S. universities. Moreover, U.S. universities are globalizing, and many now offer courses and programs offshore, often with some U.S.-based faculty. Indeed, some emerging economies are beginning to court U.S. universities, much as they earlier courted MNEs. Just as India changed policies to encourage investments by foreign MNEs in the 1990s, it is now proposing changes that would allow foreign universities to establish colleges in the country (Chang 2010). Although entire U.S. university campuses are unlikely to be established offshore in any great numbers, a range of joint programs with Indian and Chinese institutions and high-demand degrees through offshore and online programs are likely to expand. While the top-ranked U.S. universities may not be the most aggressive in moving offshore, it is important to remember that it is universities outside the top tier that provide most of the S&T workforce in the United States and elsewhere. When students graduate, whether from U.S. or their home country universities, they find opportunities in MNEs offering them jobs in the emerging economies on par with those available in the Triad. They are also finding exciting entrepreneurial possibilities in their home countries or other emerging economies. As one young student at a leading Indian university said to us, explaining why he wouldn't think of going to the United States after graduation, "India is the new wild, wild west. . . . Here [India] is where all the opportunity is now."

As these trends progress, immigration policies that would target the acquisition and retention of foreign human capital are being proposed as competitiveness strategies. To some degree, these policies are based on a zero-sum perspective. They would not only build up U.S. human capital in science, technology, and entrepreneurship but would deprive other countries of some of their most valuable human capital. In the past, "brain drain" was seen as being driven by those seeking opportunity in the United States or escaping hostile conditions in their own country. It was justified on humanitarian grounds or as the inevitable outcome of global mobility. It also was seen as ultimately providing some benefit to the sending country, as the new immigrants sent money home. U.S. immigration policy was not proposed so nakedly as an effort to corner the world's human capital to gain competitive advantage. Now this new approach to immigration policy is being embraced by those across the political spectrum, from free-market capitalists to liberal commentators. Ironically, the proposed policies are often intended to monopolize human capital, but unlike policies to control oil and other natural resources, they come at a time when there is an expansion of available highly skilled and educated human capital. On one hand, the problem seems to be defined as the United States needing to gain control over scarce human resources; on the other hand, the problem seems to be defined as the large increase in certain countries of scarce human resources. Beyond such inconsistencies, the skill development policies that are currently proposed are strategically wrong and morally questionable, and they are based on a particular and historically specific notion of globalization and human capital flows that no longer pertains.

We believe that many of the proposed policies do not sufficiently recognize the conditions characterizing the emerging global environment for technology development in this "third-generation" globalization. For example, while some S&T and entrepreneurial people from emerging economies return to their countries of origin, many maintain their linkages to the United States and often develop globally linked businesses (Lynn and Salzman 2008; Lynn and Salzman, forthcoming). We interviewed a number of entrepreneurs and engineering managers who divided their time between the United States and India or China. For example, after a good deal of difficulty we were able to arrange an interview with an engineering manager in Shanghai, only to discover that he spent about half of his time in Cleveland, Ohio. We did not need to go to China to interview him. He lived in both countries. Like a number of managers, he worked primarily in China but had his family in the United States. An entrepreneur from Taiwan had received his education in the United States and then returned to his family's business in Taiwan. Under his leadership the family established plants employing several thousand mainland Chinese in Zhuhai, Guangzhou. At the time of our interview he was completing the takeover of a U.S. firm. His plan was to have the U.S. site design products for the U.S. market and the Chinese site manufacture the product while keeping the corporate headquarters in Taipei. He said he spent about 85% of his time away from his home in Taiwan.

It is thus that both firms and a new cadre of managers have multiple affinities and do not view the world as partitioned into competing teams in the same way as did their predecessors and as do many current policy makers. Instead, they may view linkages as especially attractive because they are a means of furthering the development of emerging economies while they expand their company's profits and market reach. They view such developments as providing benefit to the United States, but they have no particular interest in, or see any need for, U.S. dominance of the global system if it comes through disadvantaging other nations. While they may favor relaxed immigration policy, this is viewed as supporting global human capital circulation, not promoting unidirectional flows to and accumulation by the United States.

More generally, it is important to recognize that global flows of S&T human resources reflect not just individual choices but firm structures, firm hiring policies, and firm location decisions. As we have noted, global business strategies have led MNEs to be less tied to national identities than in the past. To some extent the same is true of people. In a world of inexpensive and extensive travel, people relocating to distant places no longer need to sever ties with their countries and localities of origin. This is also a part of third-generation globalization.

In previous eras it may have been possible and desirable to try to monopolize science and technology human resources. But in this era of third-generation globalization of knowledge work, businesses and people within a country are far less allied in a common interest against business firms and people in other countries than they were in previous stages of globalization. This new configuration of global connectivity does not intensify competition (as implied by the flat-playing-field metaphor), but rather transforms it. As national boundaries no longer delineate a firm's political or economic interest, as people circulate and develop multiple affinities, a global commons begins to emerge. "Competition" on a fragile commons that all depend on requires different strategies from competition aimed at seeking disproportionate use of common goods. In fact, the loss incurred by others on the commons may ultimately be a loss to all (e.g., cf. Ostrom 1990). It is thus the search for collaborative advantage that can most advance the interests of a nation's citizens on the global commons (Lynn and Salzman 2006).

It is essential that the United States ensure that its visa policies are *not* antiquated relics of past eras of globalization and obsolete world views. The policies should not antagonize the rest of the world by seeking to steal others' human resources. They should recognize the new realities of MNE globalization and labor force flows. Above all, they should find ways to take advantage of the opportunities presented by brain circulation, especially since the United States is particularly well positioned to benefit while developing an inclusive collaborative globalization.

Conclusions

Our analysis suggests three fundamental areas in which U.S. policy makers need to reconceptualize their understanding of S&T labor markets: 1) how and why firms are organizing their S&T work globally; 2) how strategies of monopolizing stocks of S&T human capital within the United States, often by raiding other countries, are unlikely to work and may backfire; and 3) how "competitiveness" can best be achieved through developing a global commons rather than by efforts to resurrect historic technonationalist policies.

Most scientists and engineers, with the exception of those working for the military and some government laboratories, are employed in firms that are globalized or affected by globalized firms. These firms distribute their S&T work across national boundaries largely to gain access to a foreign market or source of technology, not because of serious shortages of S&T workers in the United States The science and technology workforce is international and mobile with multiple affinities and geographical preferences. Indeed, the geography of S&T employment opportunities is constantly changing, resulting in an ever-increasing global circulation of S&T workers. U.S. universities are also increasingly globalizing in the location of their campuses and courses, their alliances with foreign institutions, and in the composition of their faculty and students. The development of knowledge and invention now occurs in a largely porous, open international system in which science and ideas flow freely.

For all these reasons, U.S. national boundaries can no longer be used to significantly contain knowledge that is developed here or to sequester the world's best and brightest talent. Human resources and knowledge that are incubated in the United States, once transferred to a global firm (through employment, acquisition, or invention) will flow around the globe as the firms decide what is best for their own strategic interests. U.S. MNEs make the decision of whether to move technology development activities to China or India based on their perceptions of profit and risks, not on whether the move would enhance or undermine the technological strength of the United States. Similarly, U.S. universities, even though most of their research is funded by U.S. taxpayers, are globalizing as part of their own growth and survival strategies. They have to if they are to maintain their operations in the face of ever-declining public support, and as a means of recruiting advanced graduate students as U.S. students increasingly find graduate-level sciences and engineering less attractive than other postgraduate career opportunities (Lowell, Salzman, Bernstein, and Henderson 2009) and as international students are increasingly drawn to universities outside the United States.

In brief, scientific and technical skills have become globally available and do not provide the distinctive advantage they did when they were monopolized by the Triad. In what Chris Hill (2007) has termed the "Post-Scientific Society," science skills and capacity are becoming globally available and are a unique characteristic only when embedded or realized in an innovation. Breakthrough innovation is increasingly the result not of a push from science but of a complex of knowledge and skills that encompass a wide range of fields such as design, marketing, entertainment, and general creativity. In Hill's words, increasingly breakthrough innovation occurs when science and engineering move from the laboratory to the "studio, the think tank, the atelier, and cyberspace." In the era of third-generation globalization, technology developed or captured by a U.S. firm may quickly flow to another country. But the goal should not be to prevent that flow; rather, it should be to establish the means by which the United States can capture the enhancements that come from it and, importantly, gain access to indigenous innovations in other countries (Lynn and Salzman 2007, 2008). Firms have already figured out how to profit from cooperatively developed platforms and open source innovation. We should seek lessons and models from their experience in crafting national competitiveness strategies.

Policy discussions concerning education and skills formation become counterproductive when couched in zero sum, "us versus them" terms. This is true both in emerging economies determined to catch up and regain what they regard as their rightful place in the world and in the current leading economies fearful of losing their place in the world. It is understandable that large countries such as India and China that led the world in technological achievement over much of human history and then were humiliated by the newly ascendant West are attracted by the notion of regaining their dominant positions (Lynn 2009). It is also understandable that people in the Triad countries are concerned about losing what they now have, and fear a threat to their values if other cultures come to dominate the global economy. In both the emerging economies and the Triad, appeals to nationalism may also seem an attractive way to garner resources for good causes, such as education and investment in science and technology.

The result is a form of technonationalism that feeds on itself as countries try to gain advantages over each other. If one views the world as being engaged in zero-sum competition, it seems unpatriotic not to mobilize resources to enter the competitive fray. If other countries are seen as picking up the pace in the race, can "we" afford to be left behind? The risk is that such technonationalistic competitions can damage the commons, and turn destructive for all involved. The United States should take the lead by example to lessen the chance that that will happen. The answer is not to copy the policies of countries such as China and India, countries with very different human resource needs. Rather, it is to train people who can engage internationally in a constructive manner.

To summarize some other points made earlier in this chapter, new skill development strategies for the United States should focus on participation rather than partition. In third-generation globalization, trying to graduate more scientists and engineers than countries that have three or four times the U.S. population and have much faster growing economies is no more than a fool's errand. Worse yet, it can tempt us to disregard the needs of our labor market. The U.S. needs to identify the skills that allow its firms to work in the global commons. It needs to find ways to impart those skills through its educational systems. And it is in this type of education, rather than scoring well on math tests, that the United States can develop its true global advantage.

Profiting from the new era of globalization will require an ability to craft strategies that make use of global technology supply chains without giving up essential core competencies, to operate in different political and cultural environments, and to draw on S&T human resources from around the world in an effective and ethical manner. It also means developing public policies that provide a "return" to the United States rather than policies that enhance globalization patterns facilitating outward flows of capital, innovation, human resources and providing low levels of economic and social benefits to the United States.

Skill development policy should focus on a workforce portfolio of skills across the spectrum rather than narrowly defined skill and education areas or segments of the workforce. Even in technical areas, leading firms we interviewed rarely mention technical skills but focus almost exclusively on breadth and nontechnical skills (Lynn and Salzman 2004, 2009). IBM, for example, frequently mentions the company's greatest demand being people with a "T" skills profile—deep technical expertise in an area embedded in a broader or overarching knowledge of technical and nontechnical fields and skills. It also involves reconceptualizing the academic disciplines to address new interdisciplinary approaches and new skill sets, as is being done in some professional science master's degrees. Similarly, the national workforce skill portfolio is one of strong skills and education across the spectrum, from retail clerk to skilled laborer to technician and accountant to scientist and engineer. It is an approach that seeks to develop skills along the normal distribution of our population in an economy and workforce that, similarly, is composed of a normal, or near normal skill distribution of jobs and activities[2].

Workforce and social policy should not be led by the tails of the distribution, such as the "college for all" policies some advocate. These policies are based on a misperception about future workforce skill and occupational profiles. They also overlook the greater potential rewards of focusing on reducing the 40% noncompletion rate of those who currently enter college rather than seeking ways increase the inflow. While it is attractive to lay claim to developing important innovations, it can be more beneficial to quickly and effectively adopt, implement, and diffuse the best innovations that are available in a global system, whether they be new miracle cures or electronics. Microsoft learned early on that the training of technicians was as essential as the hiring of innovators. Without a large workforce of, for example, competent network administrators able to keep networks running, there would be a very small market for Microsoft's latest technology offerings (Lerman, Salzman, and Riegg 2001). Productivity gains in the economy stem from the effective implementation of innovations, not from creating brilliant innovations that sit on the shelf or that are poorly used.

In sum, we see the potential emergence of a new global commons in technology development, and the United States has the opportunity to take leadership in this commons. The United States has the advantage of experience in developing and engaging in an open system. Taking a position of leadership will require a change in mindset, of going beyond technonationalism. It will entail focusing on the development of the kind of indigenous human capital that can help us participate in this new global commons. It will mean fostering brain circulation rather than attempting to monopolize S&T human capital or undermine domestic labor markets. With the participation of other nations it will provide increased access to the global stock of innovators and innovations. It will require a structural strategy of establishing the organizations and institutions that support a global commons—global research labs, global universities, and other global institutions or platforms for S&T development. To be sure, for the commons to function in a way that is beneficial to the United States as well as to other participants, institutions will have to be developed to address the problems of supply, credible commitments, and mutual monitoring to inhibit free riding (Ostrom 1990). This is done through full and open engagement rather than just occasional forays beyond a nation-state palisade.

Acknowledgments

The research was supported through grants from the National Science Foundation (Human and Social Dynamics Program, #SES-0527584; Social Dimensions of Engineering, Science and Technology #0431755), the Alfred P. Sloan Foundation (with Lindsay Lowell), and the Ewing Marion Kauffman Foundation to study technology entrepreneurship and globalization. We are grateful for research assistance provided by Purba Ruda, superb editorial assistance by Robb C. Sewell-Wolff and Jeff Stoller, and comments by David Finegold.

Endnotes

[1] A newspaper article at the time reported that "immigration specialists, business and academic leaders have hailed the Chinese Student Protection Act as a humanitarian act and an economic boon for the United States" and "this is a gold mine for the U.S. We are getting the best and the brightest of the most populous nation in the world," while also noting that at the same time the U.S. Supreme Court ruled Haitians could be forcibly returned to their country (Hart and Chow 1993:1).

[2] Although skill levels in all occupations may be trending upward, the composition of jobs may be favoring higher-skilled jobs, and there may be some lengthening of the tails, it is still generally more of a normal distribution of skill and education levels than it is a highly skewed or bifurcated distribution, as some analysts and policy groups would suggest.

References

Bartlett, Christopher A., and Sumantra Ghoshal. 1989. *Managing Across Borders: The Transnational Solution* (1st ed.). Boston: Harvard Business School Press.
Bartlett, Christopher A., and Sumantra Ghoshal. 1998. *Managing Across Borders: The Transnational Solution* (2nd ed.). Boston: Harvard Business School Press.
Baumol, William J., and Ralph E. Gomory. 1998. *A Country's Maximal Gains from Trade and Conflicting National Interests.* Working Papers 98–22. New York: C.V. Starr Center for Applied Economics, New York University.
Bruton, Henry J. 1998. "A Reconsideration of Import Substitution." *Journal of Economic Literature*, Vol. 36 (June) pp. 903–36.
Bureau of Labor Statistics, U.S. Department of Labor. 2008. *Occupational Employment Statistics.* <http://www.bls.gov.oes>. [March 2, 2010].
Chang, Arlene. 2010. "Indian Cabinet Approves Foreign University Proposal." *Wall Street Journal*, March 15. <http://online.wsj.com/article/SB10001 4240527487039098045751233931167113392.html>. [March 16, 2010].
Coase, Ronald. 1937. "The Nature of the Firm." *Economica*, Vol. 4, no. 16, pp. 386–405.
Correa, Carlos M. 1995. "Innovation and Technology Transfer in Latin America: A Review of Recent Trends and Policies." *International Journal of Technology Management*, Vol. 10, no. 7/8, pp. 815–46.
Council on Competitiveness. 2004. *Innovate America*. Washington, DC: Council on Competitiveness.
Farrell, Diana, and Andrew Grant. 2005. "China's Looming Talent Shortage." *McKinsey Quarterly 2005*, No. 4, p. 72.
Flecker, Jorg, and Pamela Meil. Forthcoming. "Organisational Restructuring and Emerging Service Value Chains: Implications for Work and Employment." *Work, Employment, and Society.*
Frank, Andre Gunder. 1967. *Capitalism and Underdevelopment in Latin America.* New York: Monthly Review Press.
Freeman, Richard B. 1976. "Cobweb Model of the Supply and Starting Salary of New Engineers." *Industrial and Labor Relations Review*, Vol. 29, no. 2, pp. 236–48.
Gomory, Ralph E., and William J. Baumol. 2000. *Global Trade and Conflicting National Interests*. Boston: Massachusetts Institute of Technology.
Hamilton, Stephen F. 1994. "The School-to-Career Transition in Germany and the United States." *Teachers College Record*, Vol. 96, no. 2, p. 329.
Hart, Jordana, and Cheong Chow. 1993. "Joy, Envy at Green Cards for Chinese." *Boston Globe*, June 27, p. 1.
Hill, Christopher. 2007. "The Post-Scientific Society." *Issues in Science and Technology*, Fall. <http://www.issues.org/24.1/c_hill.html>. [March 17, 2010].
Hymer, Stephen H. 1960. "The International Operations of National Firms: A Study of Direct Investment." Ph.D. dissertation, published as a book in 1976 by MIT Press.
Kaiser, David. In preparation. *American Physics and the Cold War Bubble.* Chicago: University of Chicago Press.
Kogut, Bruce, and Udo Zander. 1993. "Knowledge of the Firm and the Evolutionary Theory of the Multinational Corporation." *Journal of International Business Studies*, Vol. 24, no. 4, pp. 635–45.
Lederman, Doug. 2009. "College for All." *Inside Higher Education*. <http://www.insidehighered.com/news/2009/02/25/obama>. [March 26, 2010].
Lerman, Robert. 2008. "Are Skills the Problem? Reforming the Education and Training System in the United States." *A Future of Good Jobs*. Kalamazoo, MI: Upjohn Institute.

Lerman, Robert, Harold Salzman, and Stephanie Riegg. 2001. "Community Colleges: Trainers or Retrainers of IT Workers." *Community College Journal of Research and Practice*, Vol. 71, no. 6, pp. 41–4.

Lowell, B. Lindsay, and Harold Salzman. 2007. *Into the Eye of the Storm: Assessing the Evidence on Science and Engineering Education, Quality, and Workforce Demand*. Paper presented at the annual meeting of the Association for Public Policy Analysis and Management, Madison, WI, November 3.

Lowell, B. Lindsay, Harold Salzman, Hamutal Bernstein, and Everett Henderson. 2009. *Steady As She Goes? Three Generations of Students through the Science and Engineering Pipeline*. Paper presented at the annual meeting of the Association for Public Policy Analysis and Management, Washington, DC, November 7.

Lynn, Leonard. 2009. "Technology Development in Asia." In Harukiyo Hasegawa and Carlos Noronha, eds., *Asian Business and Management: Theory, Practice and Perspectives*. New York: Palgrave MacMillan, pp. 55–76.

Lynn, Leonard, and Harold Salzman. 2004. "Third Generation Globalization: The New International Distribution of Knowledge Work." *International Journal of Knowledge, Culture and Change Management*, Vol. 4. pp. 1511–21.

Lynn, Leonard, and Harold Salzman. 2006. "Collaborative Advantage." *Issues in Science and Technology*, Winter, pp. 74–82.

Lynn, Leonard, and Harold Salzman. 2007. "'Innovation Shift' to the Emerging Economies: Cases from IT and Heavy Industries." *Sloan Industry Studies* (Occasional Paper WP-2007-22).

Lynn, Leonard, and Harold Salzman. 2008. *Multinationals, Techno-entrepreneurs, and the Globalization of Technology Value Chains*. Paper presented at the annual meeting of the Industry Studies Association, Boston, May 2.

Lynn, Leonard, and Harold Salzman. 2009. "The 'New' Globalization of Engineering: How the Offshoring of Advanced Engineering Affects Competitiveness and Development." *Economics, Management, and Financial Markets*, Vol. 4, no. 1, pp. 11–46.

Lynn, Leonard, and Harold Salzman, eds. Forthcoming. *Technology Entrepreneurs in the Emerging Economies: The New Shape of Global Innovation*. Northampton, MA: Elgar Publishing.

National Academy of Sciences. 2007. *Rising Above the Gathering Storm: Energizing and Employing America for a Brighter Economic Future*. Washington, DC: National Academies Press.

National Association of Manufacturers. 2005. *The Looming Workforce Crisis*. Washington, DC: National Association of Manufacturers.

National Center on Education and the Economy. 2007. *Tough Choices or Tough Times: The Report of the New Commission on the Skills of the American Workforce*. Washington, DC: National Center on Education and the Economy.

National Commission on Excellence in Education. 1983. *A Nation at Risk: The Imperative for Educational Reform, A Report to the Nation and the Secretary of Education United States Department of Education*. Washington, DC: National Commission on Excellence in Education.

National Science Board. 2010a. *Science and Engineering Indicators 2010*. Arlington, VA: National Science Foundation.

National Science Board. 2010b. *Globalization of Science and Engineering Research: A Companion to Science and Engineering Indicators 2010*. Washington, DC: National Science Foundation.

Organisation for Economic Co-operation and Development. 2003. *Problem Solving for Tomorrow's World: First Measures of Cross-Curricular Competencies from PISA 2003*. Paris: Organisation for Economic Co-operation and Development.

Organisation for Economic Co-operation and Development. 2004. *Learning for Tomorrow's World: First Results from PISA 2003*. Paris: Organisation for Economic Co-operation and Development.

Organisation for Economic Co-operation and Development. 2006. *PISA 2006: Science Competencies for Tomorrow's World Report*. Paris: Organisation for Economic Co-operation and Development.

Ostrom, Elinor. 1990. *Governing the Commons: The Evolution of Institutions for Collective Action*. New York: Cambridge University Press.

Ravitch, Diane. 2010. *The Death and Life of the Great American School System: How Testing and Choice Are Undermining Education*. New York: Basic Books.

Reddy, N. Mohan, and Liming Zhao. 1991. "Technology Transfer from Developed Countries to Less Developed Countries: Some Emerging Issues." *ASCI Journal of Management*, Vol. 21, no. 2/3, pp. 142–50.

Rothstein, Richard. 1998. *The Way We Were? The Myths and Realities of America's Student Achievement*. New York: Century Foundation Press.

Rothstein, Richard, Rebecca Jacobsen, and Tamara Wilder. 2006. *"Proficiency for All"—An Oxymoron*. Paper prepared for the symposium "Examining America's Commitment to Closing Achievement Gaps: NCLB and Its Alternatives," Columbia University, New York, November 13–14.

Salzman, Harold. 2000. *The Information Technology Industries and Workforces: Work Organization and Human Resource Issues*. Report for the National Academy of Sciences Committee on Workforce Needs in Information Technology.

Salzman, Harold. 2007. *Globalization of R&D and Innovation: Implications for U.S. STEM Workforce and Policy, Testimony before the U.S. House Subcommittee on Technology and Innovation*. Statement submitted to the Subcommittee on Technology and Innovation of the Committee on Science and Technology, U.S. House of Representatives.

Salzman, Harold, and Lindsay Lowell. 2008. "Making the Grade." *Nature*, Vol. 453, pp. 28–30.

Salzman, Harold, and Radha Roy Biswas. 2000. *The Indian IT Industry and Workforce*. Report for the National Academy of Sciences Committee on Workforce Needs in Information Technology.

Statistics Finland. 2010. *Labour Force Survey 2010, February*. <http://www.stat.fi/til/tyti/2010/02/tyti_2010_02_2010-03-23_tau_015_en.html>. [April 9, 2010].

Teitelbaum, Michael. 2008. "Structural Disequilibria in Biomedical Research." *Science*, Vol. 321, no. 1, pp. 644–5.

Tyson, Laura. 1992. *Who's Bashing Whom? Trade Conflict in High-Technology Industries*. Washington, DC: Institute of International Economics.

United Nations Development Program. 2009. *Human Development Report 2009: Overcoming Barriers, Human Mobility and Development*. <http://hdr.undp.org/en/reports/global/hdr2009/>. [April 9, 2010].

U.S. Department of Education. Institute of Education Statistics. 2008. *Table 8. Percentage of Persons Age 25 and Over and 25 to 29, by Race/Ethnicity, Years of School Completed, and Sex: Selected Years, 1910 through 2008*. <http://nces.ed.gov/programs/digest/d08/tables/dt08_008.asp>. [April 9, 2010].

Vernon, Raymond. 1966. "International Investments and International Trade in the Product Cycle." *Quarterly Journal of Economics*, Vol. 80, no. 2, pp. 190–207.

Vernon, Raymond. 1971. *Sovereignty at Bay*. New York: Basic Books.

Wadhwa, Vivek. 2009. "The Global Innovation Migration." *Business Week*, March 9. <http://www.businessweek.com/technology/content/nov2009/tc2009119_331698. htm>. [April 12, 2010].

Walker, Joe. 2010. "Engineering Grads Earn the Most." *Wall Street Journal*, March 12. <http://online.wsj.com/article/SB10001424052748703625304575116170339369354.html>. [March 12, 2010].

Wells, L. 1968. "A Product Life Cycle for International Trade." *Journal of Marketing*, Vol. 32, no. 3, pp. 1–6.

CHAPTER 4

Raising Skill Demand: Generating Good Jobs

GEORGE S. BENSON
University of Texas at Arlington

EDWARD E. LAWLER III
University of Southern California

Calls for businesses and policy makers to promote high-involvement management practices are not new. *Work in America* (O'Toole et al. 1973) advocated involvement as a means to increase productivity along with the employee skills and wages in the 1970s. So did *America's Choice: High Skills or Low Wages!* (National Center on Education and the Economy 1990) in the 1990s. More recently *The New American Workplace* (Appelbaum and Batt 1994) repeated the call and reviewed the large amount of research evidence that shows the benefits of employee involvement practices, including teams, employee development, gain sharing plans, and participative leadership.

There have been profound changes in the global economy and corporate landscape over the last 40 years, but "high-road" management approaches that emphasize highly skilled and involved employees continue for several reasons. Employees have always been and continue to be motivated to perform at a high level when they are in a high-involvement work setting. Second, society's need for companies to provide good jobs and remain competitive continues to be strong. Finally, the continuing trends toward globalization and the growth of knowledge work in the U.S. economy require higher productivity from workers in order for them to compete with low-wage workers around the world.

High-involvement management has helped to both increase productivity and provide good jobs as it has been adopted by a large number of companies over the last 40 years. In November 1970 a *Time* magazine cover story lamented the plight of blue-collar workers and detailed their diminished status, lost sense of control, and declining real wages ("Business: The Blue Collar Worker's Lowdown Blues" 1970). It suggested that the issues might be addressed through participative management and job enrichment but that "the ideas are so new that only a handful of companies have tried them" (p. 69). By the 1990s some form of high-involvement practices were in place in two thirds of Fortune 1000 companies (Lawler, Mohrman, and Ledford 1998). Today there are many notable success stories of the power of employee involvement in industries ranging from steel production (Nucor) and automobiles (Honda) to airlines (Southwest) and retail chains (Men's Warehouse, Whole Foods). There is research evidence that employee-involvement management practices are related to productivity and job satisfaction as well as quality, customer satisfaction, and firm financial performance (Combs, Liu, Hall, and Ketchen 2006). Over the last 40 years involvement programs have significantly improved the quality of work in large and small companies across most sectors of the U.S. economy and in many countries around the world.

At the same time it is also clear that "high-road" management strategies have not realized their full potential. A large proportion of organizations still do not utilize most high-involvement management practices. Many reasons have been cited for the unfulfilled promise of involvement practices, but chief among these appears to be ongoing concerns over competitiveness in the United States and the fact that many companies have held down wages and other investments in employees to control their costs. Instead of increasing productivity by changing their management practices, many companies have chosen to focus instead on technology or outsourced work if it can be done cheaper elsewhere in the United States or overseas. Instead of involvement, some companies have sought competitiveness through reduced head counts and work intensification, leading to employee stress and the potential for injury. Interest in high-involvement management practices among both academics and managers has declined after a significant push to study and promote them in the early 1990s.

What Are "High Road" Employment Strategies?

Companies that pursue so-called high-road employment strategies invest in production and service employees and ask them to provide more than repetitive physical and/or mental labor in return. They adopt high-involvement management practices that emphasize high levels of employee decision-making authority. They use an integrated set of human resource and work design practices that are designed to give all employees the skills, information, power, and incentives to make decisions in the workplace (Lawler 1986, 1992, 1996). This approach has evolved from very early work in the 1940s showing the benefits of self-direction or self-control in an era when manufacturing was organized by the principles of Fordism and scientific management (Nobles and Stanley 2009). The move toward involvement-oriented job designs began in earnest in the 1950s and 1960s as a movement for "industrial democracy" and "participative management" (McGregor 1960; Likert 1961). Since then, high-involvement management has taken many forms but generally includes elements such as self-managing teams, cross-training, gain sharing, and participative decision making.

While high-involvement management is a proven means to improve productivity and quality, these practices have always been intended to have the parallel goal of increasing the quality of work life through employee experience. While there are different theories of employee involvement, they generally call for employees to have decision-making power, incentives to take responsibility for their performance, information to make decisions, ongoing skill development, and a long-term employment relationship that preserves the value of these investments in human capital.

Companies using "high-road" employment strategies and high-involvement work practices are found across all sectors of economy but are more prevalent in some industries and business models. There has been considerable debate over the years within the related literature on strategic human resources and high-performance work practices as to whether these are best practices that universally lead to increase organizational performance or are dependent on context, including business strategy (Delery and Doty 1996; Boxall and Macky 2009; Kaufman 2010). There is some evidence they are more common in manufacturing firms and less likely to be found in firms that compete based on price (Youndt, Snell, Dean, and Lepak 1996; Datta, Guthrie, and Wright 2005; Blasi and Kruse 2006; Cooke 2007). Low-cost operators are more common in sectors with heavy price competition (e.g., commodities production, fast food, and retail), which are also the least likely to use high-involvement work systems.

History of Adoption

Although they have been around for at least 50 years, the practices associated with employee involvement were not widely known and adopted in the United States and Europe until the late 1970s. In the 1990s several large, multi-industry studies showed a significant growth in participative work practices. The studies differed in their samples and techniques, but the results showed that employee involvement practices, including teams, suggestion plans, and incentive compensation plans, were in use at a third to half of U.S. firms (Osterman 1994; Gittleman,

Horrigan, and Joyce 1998). Employee involvement practices were relatively common in the early 1990s and continued to grow slowly though the middle of the decade. In 1993 the Bureau of Labor Statistics Survey of Employer-Provided Training found that 32% of establishments used team-based work for at least a portion of their employees (Gittleman, Horrigan, and Joyce 1998). Total quality management (TQM) programs were in place in 46%, and 16% used quality circles. A quarter of the establishments had job rotation. Similar results were found in other surveys, including the National Establishment Surveys (NES), which showed small across-the-board increases in involvement practices (Cappelli and Neumark 2001) from 1994 to 1997. The percentage of establishments with self-managed teams increased modestly, from 31.8% to 34% (Blasi and Kruse 2006).

One picture of the changes that took place in 1990s comes from five Center for Effective Organizations surveys of the Fortune 1000 conducted from 1987 to 2005. While this was not a firm-by-firm longitudinal look due to changes in the composition of the Fortune 1000, the surveys indicate a large increase in the number of companies using involvement practices as well as the percentage of employees affected over the 1990s. For example, the number of companies using self-managed teams for at least a fifth of employees increased from 8% in 1987 to 32% in 1996. The use of individual pay for performance for at least 20% of employees increased from 38% to 57% (Lawler, Mohrman, and Ledford 1998). However, the findings from the later surveys indicated that the adoption of employee-involvement practices slowed in the late 1990s (Lawler, Mohrman, and Benson 2001). The percentage of large firms using many practices, including quality circles, gain sharing, profit sharing, pay for skills, and cross-training, remained relatively stable or declined slightly by the time of the last survey in 2002. Figure 1 shows data from surveys of the Fortune 1000 conducted by the Center for Effective Organizations during the 1990s.

Trends in adoption of high-involvement practices since the 1990s are harder to gauge, as there have been no new nationally representative surveys or follow-ups conducted in the last ten years in the United States. It is clear that the attention given to high-involvement work practices has decreased. A search of LexisNexis shows the number of articles appearing in major U.S. newspapers that mention "employee involvement" grew consistently starting in the 1980s, from 7 in 1980 to a high of 123 in 1993, but then began a steady decline, with only 53 articles mentioning it in 2009 (see Figure 2).

FIGURE 1
Percentage of Fortune 1000 Firms with at Least 20% of Employees Covered by
Three Involvement Practices.

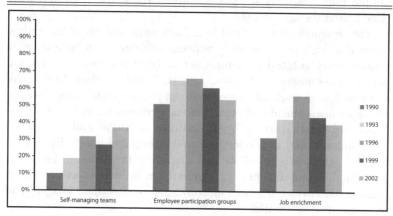

FIGURE 2
Number of Mentions in Major U.S. Newspapers for "Employee Involvement," 1980–2009.

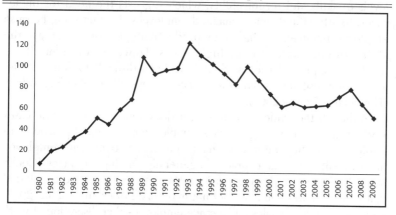

Benefits and Unfulfilled Potential of High-Road Strategies

Ironically, the drop in interest in and adoption of high-involvement strategies comes at a time when evidence of the benefits of these practices has never been stronger. A growing body of research over the last 20 years, while not unanimous, very clearly shows that high-involvement management practices are correlated with a variety of organizational performance measures, including return on assets, sales, entrepreneurial growth, customer satisfaction, and productivity. These business-unit, establishment-level, and single-industry studies are too numerous to mention and have been thoroughly reviewed elsewhere (e.g., Appelbaum, Bailey, Berg, and Kallenberg 2000). Several large-sample multi-industry studies, including Huselid's well-cited work (1995), show the same results.

This research, summarized in a 2005 meta-analysis of 92 studies, found that high-performance practices, including participation, were significantly related to a number of financial and operational performance measures (Combs, Liu, Hall, and Ketchen 2006). This accumulation of work has demonstrated a positive relationship between employee involvement and organizational performance in Fortune 1000 firms and small start-up organizations, in union and non-union environments, and in service, manufacturing, and nonprofits. Taken together, these studies show that employee involvement increases individual, team, and unit productivity in industries as diverse as professional services, steel manufacturing, apparel, medical imaging, and semiconductor fabrication.

Advocates of employee involvement also note that these practices should lead to higher wages. Employee involvement requires higher levels of skills and responsibility, which suggests the need for higher wages to attract and retain qualified employees. Furthermore, because employee involvement increases productivity, it should increase the ability of companies to pay high wages. However, the benefits of involvement practices for workers have been difficult to demonstrate, and several researchers have questioned the overall benefits for workers (Handel and Levine 2004).

Although the evidence is mixed, it does appear that in some cases workers have seen wage gains when employee involvement practices are implemented. Several studies have shown that firms with employee involvement and related practices generally pay higher wages (Cooke 1994; Freeman and Lazear 1995). Other researchers have concluded that wages rise in some cases but not in others. For example, Batt (2002) found in samples of sales and service employees that discretion at work was positively related to wages, while the use of individual practices such as problem-solving teams was not. Hunter and Lafkas (2003) found positive effects for the use of quality circles but not discretion in general in a study of call center employees. Black, Lynch, and Krivelyova (2004) found that wages rise when firms implement involvement practices but only when unions are present.

While there is a set of studies that conclude that wages do not rise with the adoption of high-involvement management practices, more recent research suggests this may be due to the fact that the wage benefits of employee involvement are not spread evenly across different types of employees (Osterman 1994, 2000; Handel and Gittleman 2004). Osterman (2006) concluded that core blue-collar employees enjoy higher wages in high-performance work systems while managerial and clerical employees do not. He argues that this may account for the findings in some studies and that higher wages for front-line employees in high-involvement workplaces may be offset by the likely reduction in the need for higher-paid managerial employees.

The impact of employee involvement on wages is also uneven across sectors. Specifically, wage increases are more pronounced in traditional low-wage manufacturing than in other sectors. For example, Appelbaum, Bailey, Berg, and Kallenberg (2000) found significantly higher wages associated with high-involvement practices in steel and apparel manufacturing industries, but not in medical imaging. Employee involvement reduces demand for unskilled labor (Caroli and Van Reenen 2001) and increases the investment in employee development (Black and Lynch 1997; Frazis, Gittleman, and Joyce 2000; Lawler, Mohrman, and Benson 2001). Firms that adopt employee involvement are also likely to invest in technology, particularly information technology, which requires additional education and training to operate (Black and Lynch 1997; Bresnahan, Brynjolfsson, and Hitt 2002).

There have been many studies showing the benefits of high involvement on employee attitudes and perceived job quality. Freeman and Rogers (1999) found that 79% of participants in employee involvement programs reported having "personally benefited" from increased influence over how they perform their jobs. Hodson and Roscigno (2004) coded organizational practices and work–life experience from 204 English-language ethnographies published in books and sociology journals and concluded that employee involvement showed positive relationships with employee well-being. Other studies have found that employee involvement practices promote positive attitudes toward the organization, which in turn leads to extra effort (Cappelli and Rogovsky 1998), prosocial behavior (O'Reilly and Chatman 1986), safety (Probst and Brubaker 2001), and employee retention (Koys 2001).

Research suggests that high involvement contributes to a workplace climate associated with greater employee commitment and discretionary effort (Takeuchi, Chen, and Lepak 2009). For example, Vandenberg, Richardson, and Eastman (1999) found that employee involvement led to positive employee attitudes, which in turn led to improved individual and organizational performance in an insurance company. Employee involvement was directly related to the commitment and satisfaction of workers, which in turn were associated with higher individual performance rankings for the employees and greater customer satisfaction in their work units. Similarly, Morrison (1995) and Koys (2001) found that employee attitudes, organizational citizenship behavior, and turnover likely mediate the effects of employee involvement and other human resource practices on customer satisfaction and organizational effectiveness.

In general this work clearly demonstrates that employees working in high-involvement organizations are more satisfied with their jobs, more committed to their organizations, more likely to trust management, and more likely to find meaning in their jobs (Freeman, Kleiner, and Ostroff 2000). These positive attitudes toward employee involvement may be dependent on trust in management and perceptions of a positive climate, but this research does show strong benefits for both firms and employees when organizations adopt high-involvement work practices.

National Impact of Involvement

While the evidence is strong that high involvement has positive impact on firms, there is a striking difference between this work and the results of aggregate national research on job perceptions and wages across the United States. Research on employee reactions to high-involvement practices consistently finds positive effects on employee attitudes and wages. However, aggregate trends across the U.S. economy show conflicting evidence on whether the adoption of high-involvement management has led to wage increases or overall improvements in perceived job quality and job satisfaction among workers.

A negative picture of workplace change emerges when one looks at the situation of workers over the last several decades. The stagnation of real wages for hourly and entry-level workers has been well documented. While aggregate productivity of all U.S. workers has increased significantly, the wages of middle-class workers have not seen a commensurate increase. For example, from 2000 to 2007 productivity in the United States increased by 11% while the median hourly wage remained the same. By all measures, income inequality is increasing in the United States. In 1979 the top 10% of wage earners took in around 20 times the income of the bottom 90%. In 2006 the top earners took in 77 times the bottom 90% (Mishel, Bernstein, and Shierholz 2009).

In terms of job quality, there has been considerable debate over whether actual and perceived job quality improved over the years in which involvement practices gained popularity (Handel 2005). While the experience of work has improved for many workers with the adoption of high-involvement management, this trend has been accompanied by increases in work intensification, reduced job security through downsizing and outsourcing, and temporary employment. Some researchers have suggested that, when faced with the harsh realities of economic crises and global competition, companies have cut costs by reducing head counts and pressuring employees to produce more (Goddard 2004).

There is no evidence that workers reported an overall increase in perceptions that their jobs were interesting or autonomous over the last 20 years (Kallenberg and Vaisey 2005). Using the *General Social Survey,* Handel (2005) found that aggregate perceived job quality changed little during the 1990s. Around 85% of workers reported being satisfied or very satisfied with their jobs in both 1989 and 1998. These numbers are unchanged today (Smith 2007). Because some companies began to widely adopt high-involvement practices during this same period, this suggests that these numbers may mask a growing gap among workers. The occupations that report the lowest job satisfaction today are also those whose jobs are the least likely to be affected by employee involvement efforts: low-skill manual jobs (e.g., laborers, roofers, and packers) and low-skill service occupations (e.g., food servers, cashiers, and retail salespersons).

Some research has gone so far as to tie workplace transformation to increases in workloads, work hours, stress, and workplace injuries over the 1990s. Practices including just-in-time (JIT) inventory systems, TQM, performance-based pay, and team-working have been labeled "management by stress." For example, Fairris and Brenner (2001) and Brenner, Fairris, and Ruser (2004) investigated the relationship between "flexible" work practices and workplace safety and note that cumulative-trauma injuries, such as carpal tunnel syndrome, increased significantly during the same periods that new work practices became popular in the United States. They conclude that there is evidence that practices including quality circles and JIT are related to repetitive motion injuries. Others have argued that self-managed teams encourage workers to monitor each other and that this can be an even more coercive and stressful form of control than traditional supervision (Barker 1993). Finally, there is some evidence that employee involvement leads to greater stress and insecurity for supervisors (Batt 2004, Mahony 2007).

These negative national findings stand in contrast with the far larger number of studies showing positive effects of employee involvement on job satisfaction and employee commitment. While there are certainly examples where employee involvement practices are associated with negative worker outcomes in terms of stress and workload, these appear to represent unusual or extreme versions of involvement practices. In a telephone survey of Canadians, Goddard (2001) found that teamwork and similar work practices had positive effects on belongingness, empowerment, satisfaction, and esteem. However, he also found that these benefits were diminished at high levels of implementation, suggesting that there are limited or potentially negative impacts of extreme levels of teamwork and participation.

In general, the benefits of high-involvement management practices have been unevenly distributed across American workers. There is a group of workers in the United States who have seen significant improvements in the quality of their work lives—the discretion they have on the job, the training they receive, and the relationships they enjoy with management. Moreover, these workers are earning more than their counterparts in similar organizations. On the other hand, a number of workers have been marginalized into temporary jobs or menial low-wage full-time jobs as part of their companies' efforts to reduce labor costs.

Factors Limiting the Continued Adoption of High-Road Strategies

Trends in the adoption of high involvement depend in part on the larger economic trends in the United States. Most of the companies that switched to high-involvement practices in the 1960s and 1970s were in traditional manufacturing. These are much less common today as the national economy and employment have shifted significantly toward knowledge and service work. The percentage of the U.S. GDP coming from manufacturing has declined over the last 30 years, and the proportion of American workers employed in manufacturing has dropped from 21% in 1980 to 8% in 2009 (Mishel, Bernstein, and Shierholz 2009).

During this same period there has been significant growth in sectors including computer hardware, software, financial services, health care, and others that require higher-skilled employees and lend themselves to involvement-oriented job designs and practices. Many of the large employers in these sectors are companies that have been formed in the last 20 to 30 years. In leading-edge companies such as Microsoft, Intel, Google, and others, employee involvement and engagement through teamwork, pay for skills, and individual incentives are simply a way of doing business rather than a new program or innovation.

However, the growth in "new economy" companies does not necessarily mean that all these new jobs reflect the high-road principles of involvement and high wages. Knowledge work does not automatically imply employee involvement and discretion, and there has been a significant increase in the number of state and federal lawsuits over improper classification of employees as exempt workers. The world's largest video game developer, Electronic Arts, recently settled an overtime lawsuit with its programmers, who complained of long hours and repetitive work, with little input or recognition. This is precisely the type of high-skill and high-wage job that is supposed to be the hallmark of the new economy.

The shift away from low-value manufacturing in the United States suggests fewer low-cost operators in the U.S economy. In general, firms that compete based on innovation, service, quality, and speed are much more likely to adopt involvement programs (Lawler 2008). As companies move from low cost to differentiation strategies based on product quality or service, they are more likely to implement involvement programs (Youndt, Snell, Dean, and Lepak 1996).

On the other hand, there are kinds of work where management practices are limited in being able to translate into competitive advantage. Encouraging employee participation and carrying higher labor costs in the form of wages, training, and incentives only make economic sense if companies can achieve additional productivity and/or higher prices. This is not realistic for some kinds of service work (e.g., fast-food restaurants, price-driven retailing, and harvesting) where the work is low value and companies must aggressively control costs to remain competitive. The retail and hospitality industries employ 21% of all workers in the United States, but 46% of all minimum wage earners work in these sectors (Mishel, Bernstein, and Shierholz 2009). It should be noted, however, that even in low-margin industries there are multiple examples of successful companies using high-road employment strategies, including Costco, Men's Warehouse, and Whole Foods.

Today's trends in human resources (HR) and management are also likely to impact the future adoption of high involvement and suggest that companies will be more selective in their use of high-involvement management practices. There is a growing trend in HR management toward employee differentiation or segmentation as a means to focus on groups of employees deemed the most critical to execute strategy. Not surprisingly, these are the employees whose work makes high-involvement management practices a good fit. As a result, organization-wide efforts at high involvement may be less common and the growth in high-involvement programs slower.

Differentiation began in practice as firms pared workforces and increasingly used temporary employees and contractors to more aggressively buffer against variability in demand and production cycles. It has divided the workforces of many companies into a high-wage group of core employees and a low-wage group who do not share the same benefits or job security. The trend toward differentiation is likely to continue as the popular HR literature advocates that managers differentiate jobs and focus their efforts on those with maximum impact on organizational performance. While multiple theoretical models for differentiating employees and jobs have been proposed, they have in common that at least one of the differentiating factors is the strategic "value" of the jobs or tasks that employees perform. Lepak and Snell (1999) suggest differentiating on the dimensions of value and uniqueness of skills. Huselid, Beatty, and Becker (2006) suggest distinguishing among "A, B, and C" jobs. Boudreau and Ramstad (2007) focus on performance variance and strategic impact of jobs. They all conclude that HR practices should differentiate how people are treated based on the different types of work they do.

Doskocil Manufacturing provides an instructive example of differentiation. It runs a large plant in Arlington, Texas, that produces the Pet-Mate brand kennels and pet carriers. While the plant runs two shifts daily for lines of injection-molded plastic, they employ no full-time operators. Instead they have a long-standing relationship with a local staffing company that provides temporary employees to run the machines and package the products. Since the plant's production runs vary daily, the company can give 12 to 24 hours' advance notice to the agency on the number of people they need for these low-value-added jobs. HR managers focus their recruiting and retention (as well as their involvement efforts) on product designers and production engineers.

Perhaps the most important obstacles to the adoption of high-involvement practices are negative experiences. Clearly not all high-involvement initiatives have been successful. In a study of unionized organizations, Eaton (1994) found that up to 20% of employee involvement programs were ultimately abandoned, for a variety of reasons. Chi, Freeman, and Kleiner (2007) used detailed interviews with 51 manufacturing firms to look at the adoption of employee involvement over ten years. They found, mirroring the increase in employee involvement nationally in the early 1990s, a 65% increase in the number of involvement practices in place from 1986 to 1995, and the number of firms with at least one program in place increased from 77% to 96%. However, they also found that firms were dropping specific programs during this time much more frequently than expected. A primary reason for terminating programs was the lack of short-term financial returns. Programs were terminated if they were perceived not to bring the added productivity needed to justify their expense and the disruptions caused during implementation.

Determinants of Success

Research has identified a number of potential reasons for the failure of high-involvement programs—lack of managerial support (Fenton-O'Creevy 1998), lack of trust in management (Eaton 1994), and lack of job security

(Preuss and Lautsch 2002) for those affected are all frequent causes of problems. Another important reason for failure is the implementation of practices in an isolated or piecemeal fashion. Fifteen years ago Ichniowski, Shaw, and Prenushi (1995) examined steel-finishing lines and found that individual involvement practices such as work teams, flexible job design, pay for skills, and incentive pay had little to no effect on productivity when used in isolation. Recently Combs, Liu, Hall, and Ketchen (2006) confirmed in a meta-analysis of 92 firms that high-performance work "systems" were more strongly correlated with performance than individual practices, including teams and participation. Chi, Freeman, and Kleiner (2007) found that practices implemented in isolation or with few other supporting practices were the most likely to be abandoned. In such cases one can easily imagine the frustration of managers as the cost and disruption of implementing these practices yielded little or no tangible increase in productivity. This potentially leads to the abandonment of these individual practices even though research clearly demonstrates that organizations with robust involvement programs enjoy significantly increased productivity over workplaces with "traditional" work systems.

While the impact of employee involvement on organizational performance, employee attitudes, skills, and wages is for each practice an important consideration, the success of these practices now depends on whether employees benefit in terms of their experience at work. For employees to act on the additional decision-making opportunities and use their skills to the fullest, they need to see the practices as beneficial and truly internalize the principles of involvement. There is a perspective that argues that employee involvement practices are often implemented as a means to subvert unionism and increase workloads rather than to benefit employees (Goddard 2004; Bodah, McHugh, and Kim 2008). The potential for organizations to use employee involvement in a negative way is a clear threat to its continued adoption and success.

There is the possibility of firms' using the expanded responsibility of front-line employees to increase job demands, raise production targets, and decrease head counts without supporting employees, developing their skills, and increasing their wages. If increased performance demands are accompanied by an abrupt layoff with no safety net or by replacement of workers who are not able to adapt to an environment of higher expectations, then employee involvement will ultimately be labeled as the next chapter in the continuing efforts of management to squeeze employees. Indeed, the overall success of employee involvement and the willingness of workers to embrace participative practices appear to be strongly related to how the workers perceive the intention of the practices.

Employee involvement is not suited to every firm, sector, or strategy, and it is becoming increasingly clear where it fits and where it does not (Lawler 2008). In the late 1980s and 1990s employee involvement became increasingly popular, and some firms no doubt implemented the practices simply because everyone else was pushing them. It is now clear that what once looked like an easy universal route to productivity improvement is actually a complex change that requires the right type of work, the right motives, and a sustained commitment.

Future of Involvement Management

The tone of the discussion concerning employee involvement has evolved significantly since the 1970s. While there is debate over the extent to which it should be implemented and discussion of how to maximize the returns from investments in employees, the benefits of the practices and the ability of workers to adapt and thrive in high-involvement workplaces are no longer questioned. The importance of involved and skilled employees has entered the public consciousness and the managerial mindset. Indeed, most new manufacturing plants in the United States are organized around the basic principles of employee involvement. Over the past several decades, organizations' work practices, such as pay for skills, job rotation, teams, total quality management, and open business information, have become routine and are no longer seen as part of an involvement program or change effort.

The newest automobile manufacturing plants in the United States all use job rotation, teams, and discretion for front-line employees. Twenty-five years ago the GM–Toyota joint-venture NUMMI plant in Fremont, California, was hailed as a new model for American manufacturing and a way for GM to learn how to change its work practices and culture. Though the plant has been shuttered, Toyota has not abandoned high-involvement practices. Production of Toyota Tacoma trucks has been shifted from Fremont to a state-of-the-art Toyota facility in San Antonio, Texas, which has been hailed as a critical source of high-wage manufacturing jobs in the community. The degree to which teamwork, discretion, and participation are embedded in the culture and practices of this plant is demonstrated by a help-wanted ad that appeared in a local newspaper describing the key responsibilities for a tool and die maker: "working in a diverse team," "problem-solving," and "adjusting . . . in a fast paced environment" were all listed ahead of machining and fabricating.

Given all that has been learned about high involvement over the last 40 years, the path is clearly marked for organizations that choose high-road strategies. As recently as 1994 the Commission on the Future of

Worker–Management Relations advocated that the government encourage organizations to adopt employee involvement practices. However, the limitations of government influence over private sector management practices in the United States must be recognized. Researchers and policy makers need to continue to promote high involvement and recommit to demonstrating the benefits for both companies and American workers through information gathering and sharing.

We suggest that the best way to encourage the use of employee involvement and high-road employment strategies is to continue to publicize information about their use and impact on organizational performance. This should include additional resources for new large-scale surveys of high-involvement and management practices in general, similar to the 1994 Bureau of Labor Statistics Survey of Employer-Provided Training or the National Establishment Surveys conducted in 1994 and 1997. Follow-ups using similar methodology would demonstrate trends over the last 15 years and hopefully generate new interest in these practices in companies.

Policy makers and business leaders might also consider requiring that more information be made available on the use of such practices in individual companies. Currently there are no standard reporting requirements for investments in employees or management practices in annual reports or the "Management's Discussion and Analysis" (MD&A) sections of annual 10-K filings with the SEC. This makes it very difficult to know which companies are actively using high involvement. Financial analysts and investors today have very little information about management practices to use in decision making. Reporting requirements related to investments in employees and management practices would help the public make better investment decisions and might in turn encourage firms to consider high-involvement management.

Benson, Young, and Lawler (2006) examined the accuracy of earnings forecasts of professional stock analysts for companies with high adoption rates of high-involvement practices over the 1990s. We found that stock analysts systematically underestimated by 7% the annual earnings of companies with above-average adoption of high involvement and overestimated by 9.1% on average the earnings of companies with low use of employee involvement. This suggests that these professional analysts have a difficult time incorporating the positive impact of high-involvement management practices on corporate earnings into their models. Moreover, we found that very little information was available on the degree to which companies use employee involvement in either in the business press or in company annual reports. Only 27% of the Fortune 1000 companies examined appeared in a newspaper article that mentioned involvement, and 60% of the annual reports we examined over the study period contained no mention of HR practices in general or high-involvement practices in particular.

Some investors have already shown interest in high-road employment strategies. Bassi Investments, based in Golden, Colorado, markets an investment fund that selects equities using a proprietary model based primarily on organization investments in human capital. The Yucaipa Companies, a private equity firm founded by Rob Burkle, invests in turnarounds based on a strategy of implementing employee-oriented management practices in underperforming businesses.

The other major public policy levers available to encourage high involvement are the minimum wage and employee education. In real terms the minimum wage has fallen significantly over the last several decades. From 1979 to 2007 the average entry-level hourly wage for a high school–educated male in the United States fell by 18% in real terms (Mishel, Bernstein, and Shierholz 2009). Raising the minimum wage means that organizations face increasing pressure to use people more effectively. If they are required to pay more for hourly jobs, organizations need to see commensurate increases in productivity to remain competitive. One way to achieve this is by becoming high-involvement workplaces.

Improving the education and skills of the U.S. workforce may be the most significant action that government can take to promote high involvement. The poor preparation of the American workforce has been well documented for some time, most recently in *The Ill-Prepared U.S. Workforce*, a research report by the Conference Board in conjunction with The American Society of Training and Development and the Society for Human Resource Management (Casner-Lotto, Rosenblum, and Wright 2009). Better-educated workers reduce the risk for organizations implementing involvement policies and allow employees to demand higher pay through additional productivity. Better-prepared workers might also increase the incentives for firms to provide additional firm- and job-specific training if they do not have to conduct remedial training for employees.

Conclusion

The continued use and further adoption of employee involvement practices is particularly important in developed economies that are dominated by complex knowledge work and educated workforces. Questions remain concerning the use of some employee involvement practices, but given the evidence that many involvement work practices yield a consistent competitive advantage, there is good reason to believe that employee involvement practices will continue to be used. We are likely to see less talk about the "transformation" of workplaces and how employee involvement is a progressive approach to management. Many practices that are associated with employee involvement have simply become standard operating procedures in companies and will continue to be adopted and used as such. Thus, rather than being seen as part of a new approach to management, employee involvement management practices will simply be adopted because they are seen as the right way to manage an effective organization. Indeed, the transformation of work for hourly manufacturing and service workers through high involvement continues to be the best means available to provide working men and women with more rewarding jobs and to increase the competitiveness of U.S. corporations in the global economy.

References

Appelbaum, E., T. Bailey, P. Berg, and A. Kallenberg. 2000. *Manufacturing Advantage: Why High-Performance Work Systems Pay Off.* Ithaca, NY: ILR Press.

Appelbaum, E., and R. Batt. 1994. *The New American Workplace: Transforming Work Systems in the United States.* Ithaca: ILR Press.

Barker, J. 1993. "Tightening the Iron Cage: Concertive Control in Self-Managing Teams." *Administrative Science Quarterly,* Vol. 38, no. 3, pp. 408–37.

Batt, R. 2002. "Managing Customer Services: Human Resource Practices, Quit Rates, and Sales Growth." *Academy of Management Journal,* Vol. 45, no. 3, pp. 587–97.

Batt, R. 2004. "Who Benefits Most from Teams? Comparing Workers, Supervisors, and Managers." *Industrial Relations,* Vol. 43, no. 1, pp. 183–212.

Benson, G., S. Young, and E. Lawler. 2006. "High Involvement Work Practices and Analysts' Forecasts of Corporate Earnings." *Human Resource Management,* Vol. 45, no. 4, pp. 519–37.

Black, S., and L. Lynch. 1997. *How to Compete: The Impact of Workplace Practices and Information Technology on Productivity.* Working Paper No. 6120. Cambridge, MA: National Bureau of Economic Research.

Black, S., L. Lynch, and A. Krivelyova. 2004. "How Workers Fare When Employers Innovate." *Industrial Relations,* Vol. 43, no. 1, pp. 44–66.

Blasi, J., and D. Kruse. 2006. "High-Performance Work Practices at Century's End: Incidence, Diffusion, Industry Group Differences and the Economic Environment." *Industrial Relations,* Vol. 45, no. 4, pp. 547–78.

Bodah, M.M., P.P. McHugh, and S.J. Kim. 2008. "Employee Involvement Programs and Collective Bargaining: The Role of Labor Relations Climate. *Journal of Collective Negotiations,* Vol. 32, no. 3, pp. 245–60.

Boudreau, J., and P. Ramsted. 2007. *Beyond HR: The New Science of Human Capital.* Cambridge, MA: Harvard Business School Press.

Boxall, P., and K. Macky. 2009. "Research and Theory on High-Performance Work Systems: Progressing the High-Involvement Stream." *Human Resource Management Journal,* Vol. 19, no. 1, pp. 3–23.

Brenner, M.D., D. Fairris, and J.W. Ruser. 2004. "'Flexible' Work Practices and Occupational Safety and Health: Exploring the Relationship Between Cumulative Trauma Disorders and Workplace Transformation." *Industrial Relations*, Vol. 43, no. 1, pp. 242–66.

Bresnahan, T., E. Brynjolfsson, and L. Hitt. 2002. "Information Technology, Workplace Organization, and the Demand for Skilled Labor: Firm-Level Evidence. *Quarterly Journal of Economics*, Vol. 117, no. 1, pp. 339–76.

"Business: The Blue Collar Worker's Lowdown Blues." 1970. *Time*, November 9, p. 69.

Cappelli, P., and D. Neumark, D. 2001. "Do 'High-Performance' Work Practices Improve Establishment-Level Outcomes?" *Industrial and Labor Relations Review*, Vol. 54, no. 4, pp. 737–75.

Cappelli, P., and N. Rogovsky. 1998. "Employee Involvement and Organizational Citizenship: Implications for Labor Law Reform and 'Lean Production.'" *Industrial and Labor Relations Review*, Vol. 51, no. 4, 633–53.

Caroli, E., and J. Van Reenen. 2001. "Skill-Based Organizational Change? Evidence from a Panel of British and French Establishments." *Quarterly Journal of Economics*, Vol. 116, no. 4, pp. 1449–92.

Casner-Lotto, J., E. Rosenblum, and M. Wright. 2009. *The Ill-Prepared U.S. Workforce: Exploring the Challenges of Employer-Provided Workforce Readiness Training.* Research report. New York: The Conference Board, Inc. <http://www.cvworkingfamilies.org/system/files/Ill_preparedWorkforce_RR.pdf>. [October 21, 2010].

Chi, W., R. Freeman, and M. Kleiner. 2007. *Adoption and Termination of Employee Involvement Programs.* Working Paper 12878. Cambridge, MA: National Bureau of Economic Research.

Combs, J., A. Liu, Y. Hall, and D. Ketchen. 2006. "How Much Do High-Performance Work Practices Matter? A Meta-Analysis of Their Effects on Organizational Performance." *Personnel Psychology*, Vol. 50, no. 59, pp. 501–28.

Cooke, W. 1994. "Employee Participation Programs, Group-Based Incentives, and Company Performance: A Union–Nonunion Perspective." *Industrial and Labor Relations Review*, Vol. 47, no. 4, pp. 594–609.

Cooke, W. 2007. "Integrating Human Resource and Technological Capabilities: The Influences of Global Business Strategies on Workplace Strategy Choices." *Industrial Relations*, Vol. 46, no. 2, pp. 241–70.

Datta, D., J. Guthrie, and P. Wright. 2005. "Human Resource Management and Labor Productivity: Does Industry Matter?" *Academy of Management Journal*, Vol. 48, no. 1, pp. 135–45.

Delery, J. and H. Doty. 1996. "Modes of Theorizing in Strategic Human Resource Management: Tests of Universalistic, Contingency, and Configurations Performance Predictions." *Academy of Management Journal*, Vol. 39, no. 4, pp. 802–35.

Eaton, A. 1994. "The Survival of Employee Participation Programs in Unionized Settings." *Industrial and Labor Relations Review*, Vol. 47, no. 3, pp. 371–89.

Fairris, D., and M. Brenner. 2001. "Workplace Transformation and the Rise in Cumulative Trauma Disorders: Is There a Connection?" *Journal of Labor Research*, Vol. 22, no. 1, pp. 15–28.

Fenton-O'Creevy, M. 1998. "Employee Involvement and the Middle Manager: Evidence from a Survey of Organizations." *Journal of Organizational Behavior*, Vol. 19, no. 1, pp. 67–84.

Frazis, H., M. Gittleman, and M. Joyce. 2000. "Correlates of Training: An Analysis of Both Employer and Employee Characteristics." *Industrial and Labor Relations Review*, Vol. 53, no. 3, pp. 443–62.

Freeman, R., M. Kleiner, and C. Ostroff. 2000. *The Anatomy of Employee Involvement and Its Effects on Firms and Workers*. Working Paper No. 8050. Cambridge, MA: National Bureau of Economic Research.

Freeman, R., and E. Lazear. 1995. *An Economic Analysis of Works Councils*. Working Paper No. 4918. Cambridge, MA: National Bureau of Economic Research.

Freeman, R., and J. Rogers. 1999. *What Workers Want*. Ithaca, NY: Cornell University Press.

Gittleman, M., M. Horrigan, and M. Joyce. 1998. "'Flexible' Workplace Practices: Evidence from a Nationally Representative Survey." *Industrial and Labor Relations Review*, Vol. 52, no. 1, pp. 99–115.

Goddard, J. 2001. "High Performance and the Transformation of Work? The Implications of Alternative Work Practices for the Experience of Outcomes at Work." *Industrial and Labor Relations Review*, Vol. 54, no. 4, pp. 776–805.

Goddard, J. 2004. "A Critical Assessment of the High-Performance Paradigm." *British Journal of Industrial Relations*, Vol. 42, no. 2, pp. 349–78.

Handel, M. 2005. "Trends in Perceived Job Quality, 1989–1998." *Work and Occupations*, Vol. 32, no. 1, pp. 66–94.

Handel, M.J., and M. Gittleman, 2004. "Is There a Wage Payoff to Innovative Work Practices?" *Industrial Relations*, Vol. 42, no. 1, pp. 67–97.

Handel, M. and D. Levine. 2004. "Editor's Introduction: The Effects of New Work Practices on Workers." *Industrial Relations*, Vol. 43, no. 1, pp. 1–43.

Hodson, R., and V. Roscigno. 2004. "Organizational Success and Worker Dignity: Complementary or Contradictory?" *American Journal of Sociology*, Vol. 110, no. 3, pp. 672–708.

Hunter, L., and J. Lafkas. 2003. "Opening the Box: Information Technology, Work Practices and Wages." *Industrial and Labor Relations Review*, Vol. 56, no. 2, pp. 224–43.

Huselid, M. 1995. "The Impact of Human Resource Management Practices on Turnover, Productivity, and Corporate Performance." *Academy of Management Journal*, Vol. 38, no. 3, pp. 635–72.

Huselid, M., R. Beatty, and B. Becker. 2006. "'A Players' or 'A Positions'?" *Harvard Business Review*, Vol. 84, no. 3, 143–4.

Ichniowski, C., K. Shaw, and G. Prenushi. 1995. *The Impact of Human Resource Practices on Productivity*. Working Paper No. 5333. Cambridge, MA: National Bureau of Economic Research.

Kallenberg, A., and S. Vaisey. 2005. "Pathways to a Good Job: Perceived Work Quality Among the Machinists in North America." *British Journal of Industrial Relations*, Vol. 43, no. 3, pp. 431–54.

Kaufman, B. 2010. "A Theory of the Firm's Demand for HRM Practices." *International Journal of Human Resource Management*, Vol. 21, no. 5, pp. 615–36.

Koys, D. 2001. "The Effects of Employee Satisfaction, Organizational Citizenship Behavior, and Turnover on Organizational Effectiveness: A Unit-Level Longitudinal Study." *Personnel Psychology*, Vol. 54, no. 1, pp. 101–14.

Lawler, E. 1986. *High-Involvement Management: Participative Strategies for Improving Organizational Performance*. San Francisco: Jossey-Bass.

Lawler, E. 1992. *The Ultimate Advantage: Creating the High Involvement Organization*. San Francisco: Jossey-Bass.

Lawler, E. 1996. *From the Ground Up: Six Principles for Creating the New Logic Organization*. San Francisco: Jossey-Bass.

Lawler, E. 2008. *Talent: Making People Your Competitive Advantage*. San Francisco: Jossey-Bass.

Lawler, E., S. Mohrman, and G. Benson. 2001. *Organizing for High Performance: The CEO Report on Employee Involvement, TQM, Reengineering, and Knowledge Management in Fortune 1000 Companies*. San Francisco: Jossey-Bass.

Lawler, E., S. Mohrman, and G. Ledford. 1998. *Strategies for High Performance Organizations: Employee Involvement, TQM, and Reengineering Programs in Fortune 1000 Corporations*. San Francisco: Jossey-Bass.

Lepak, D., and S. Snell. 1999. "The Strategic Management of Human Capital: Determinants and Implications of Different Relationships." *Academy of Management Review*, Vol. 24, no. 1, pp. 1–18.

Likert, R. 1961. *New Patterns of Management*. New York: McGraw-Hill.

Mahony, D. 2007. "How Participatory Work Practices Affect Front-Line Supervisors." *Journal of Labor Research*, Vol. 28, no. 1, pp. 147–68.

McGregor, D. 1960. *The Human Side of the Enterprise*. New York: McGraw-Hill.

Mishel, L., J. Bernstein, and H. Shierholz. 2009. *The State of Working America 2008/2009*. Ithaca, NY: Cornell University Press.

Morrison, E. 1995. "Organizational Citizenship Behavior as a Critical Link Between HRM and Service Quality." *Human Resource Management*, Vol. 35, no. 4, pp. 493–512.

National Center on Education and the Economy. 1990. *America's Choice: High Skills or Low Wages! The Report of the Commission on the Skills of the American Workforce*. Washington, DC: National Center on Education and the Economy.

Nobles, B., and P. Stanley. 2009. "Freedom-Based Management." *MLAB Labnotes*, no. 12, pp. 19–23.

O'Reilly, C., and J. Chatman. 1986. "Organizational Commitment and Psychological Attachment: The Effects of Compliance, Identification, and Internalization on Prosocial Behavior." *Journal of Applied Psychology*, Vol. 71, no. 3, pp. 492–9.

Osterman, P. 1994. "How Common Is Workplace Transformation and Who Adopts It?" *Industrial and Labor Relations Review*, Vol. 47, no. 2, pp. 173–89.

Osterman, P. 2000. "Work Restructuring in an Era of Restructuring: Trends in Diffusion and Effect on Employee Welfare." *Industrial and Labor Relations Review*, Vol. 53, no. 2, pp. 179–96.

Osterman, P. 2006. "The Wage Effects of High Performance Work Organization in Manufacturing." *Industrial and Labor Relations Review*, Vol. 59, no. 2, pp. 187–204.

O'Toole, J., E. Hansot, W. Herman, N. Herrick, E. Liebow, B. Lusignan, H. Richman, H. Sheppard, B. Stephansky, and J. Wright. 1973. *Work in America: Report of a Special Task Force to the U.S. Department of Health, Education, and Welfare*. Cambridge, MA: MIT Press.

Preuss, G., and B. Lautsch. 2002. "The Effect of Formal versus Informal Job Security on Employee Involvement Programs." *Industrial Relations*, Vol. 57, no. 3, pp. 517–39.

Probst, T., and T. Brubaker. 2001. "The Effects of Job Insecurity on Employee Safety Outcomes: Cross-sectional and Longitudinal Explorations." *Journal of Occupational Health Psychology*, Vol. 6, no. 2, 139–59.

Smith. T. 2007. *Job Satisfaction in the United States.* Chicago: National Opinion Research Center, University of Chicago.

Takeuchi, R., G. Chen, and D. Lepak. 2009. "Through the Looking Glass of a Social System: Cross-level Effects of High Performance Work Systems on Employee Attitudes." *Personnel Psychology*, Vol. 62, no. 1, pp. 1–29.

Vandenberg, R., H. Richardson, and L. Eastman. 1999. "The Impact of High Involvement Work Practices on Organizational Effectiveness: A Second-Order Latent Variable Approach." *Group and Organization Management*, Vol. 24, no. 3, pp. 300–39.

Youndt, M., S. Snell, J. Dean, and D. Lepak. 1996. "Human Resource Management, Manufacturing Strategy, and Firm Performance." *Academy of Management Journal*, Vol. 39, no. 4, pp. 836–66.

CHAPTER 5

Technology-Assisted Learning for Adult Basic Education, Skills, and English as a Second Language

MARY MCCAIN
TechVision21

> This past century's concept of "literacy" grew out of our intense belief in text, a focus enhanced by the power of one particular technology—the typewriter.
>
> John Seeley Brown, "Growing Up Digital" (2000:12)

The 2003 National Assessment of Adult Literacy (NAAL) found that 43% of the adult population in the United States scored at the lowest levels for prose literacy and that 55% scored at the lowest levels for quantitative literacy—levels that correspond to the ability to perform, at best, the most basic everyday activities (National Assessment of Adult Literacy 2003).[1] Of equal concern, these data have remained unchanged or grown worse since the 1993 NAAL survey. Among the estimated 150 million adults in the labor force, more than 18 million lack high school diplomas, and more than 51 million have high school diplomas but no postsecondary education (National Commission on Adult Literacy 2008). Unsurprisingly, lower levels of education correlate with lower literacy levels.

Compounding this already dismal picture are the projections for job growth and for the skills that will be required for new jobs. According to estimates by the Bureau of Labor Statistics and other data, occupations that require postsecondary education and training are projected to grow much faster than those with lower education requirements. The fastest growth will be among occupations that require an associate's degree or a postsecondary vocational award (Council of Economic Advisors 2009; Lacey and Wright 2009).

Despite this increasing gap between labor force qualification and skill demand, fewer than 10% of the more than 80 million adults who need additional education to improve literacy, obtain high school diplomas, or pursue postsecondary education and training are served by the public and private sector systems in place to serve them.[2] Further, these systems for adult basic education and English as a Second Language (ESL) are typically delivered by untrained instructors, using curriculum, material, and methods frequently unsuited to the adults' needs.

In recent years, educators and policy makers have turned their focus to community colleges as the most feasible existing option to address the growing importance of degree and/or certification attainment in enabling individuals—and the nation—to compete for and win 21st-century jobs and economic success. Community colleges, however, already struggle with limitations in physical and instructional capacity, funding, and other issues as they face the prospect of millions of new, and often unprepared, students. In turn, such students frequently face significant barriers to attaining high school and/or postsecondary degrees, including lack of financial resources, insufficient education course prerequisites and/or required levels of knowledge, available time because of family and/or job responsibilities, transportation, and other issues.

In response to these challenges, the public and private sectors have fallen back on traditional remedies, such as increased funding for college plant, equipment, and instructors; expanding eligibility for financial aid; increasing the postsecondary offerings of remedial courses; and providing evening and weekend classes. Employers are urged to make more investments in basic education, GED attainment, and skills for their employees. Nonetheless, the capacity and capability of community colleges to assume responsibility for adult literacy, ESL, education, and skill development is unrealistic, if only because of already inadequate funding. Perhaps more important, the continued format of classroom-based, instructor-led, defined curriculum and course sequence with assessment based on assigned content and seat time no longer suits the education and job requirements of adults with a variety of learning needs and limited time and resources.

Technology alone cannot solve these issues, but it offers the option to transform access to learning in ways that benefit adults in need and the systems that struggle to serve them. The rapidly increasing availability, sophistication in delivery, value of content, ease of use, and multiple options for work and life that technology offers helps to expand the ability of existing education systems to serve more individuals and enables underserved adults to learn in ways that suit their immediate and longer-term needs. There are other, equally compelling, reasons beyond degree completion for adults to use technology for learning, including the necessity of being able to use computers and the Internet—"ICT literacy"—to get and keep jobs and to participate in the community and access its services.

A growing body of evidence supports the effectiveness of using technology in adult basic education, ESL, and skill development. There also is considerable evidence that adults—even those with low levels of literacy, limited English language ability, and minimal or no exposure to computers—are willing and eager to use technology for multiple purposes. Nonetheless, hesitation remains in initiating real change. If the United States is to take advantage of technology's options and potential, it must provide resources to the existing systems to enable wider and more effective uses of technology for education and must begin to put into place a new system that enables learning outside of institutional structures, integrates adult education and workforce development, and prepares adults for working, living, and continually learning in a technology-driven economy and society.

Changing the Context

The challenges to changing existing systems for learning are philosophical as well as practical, and they often have less to do with commonly cited issues—funding, access, computer skills, support systems—than with strongly held views about what constitutes "education" and "learning" and how these are best achieved. Using technology in learning is as much about information, communication, and the learning environment as it is about technology. Traditional education is built on the premise that access to information is limited—to particular locations, choices about content development and access made by others, and options and credentials that are based on defined sequences of curriculum, courses, time, and instructors. "Teaching" is considered to be the source of "learning." While this structure for education has served the nation well, in a technology-driven economy and society of almost limitless information and access to people and places, it can inhibit learning instead of promote it. Until the classroom ceases to be viewed as the focal point of learning, no great change can occur.

The practical challenges to change include an absence of the infrastructure that helped to ensure quality and credibility of the previous generations of education: assessment of the institutions that provided education and of the student's knowledge acquisition, verification and credentialing of the assessment, and credibility and acceptance of the credential as a proxy for demonstration of knowledge. The oversight and funding of education are designed to ensure adherence to these practices. With the change in access, these safeguards are a barrier to change, yet dismantling them is neither straightforward nor without risk.

In an effort to avoid these challenges, officials and educators have crafted a strategy that attaches technology to the adult basic education and ESL systems that exist, essentially using computers and access to the Internet to deliver the traditional curriculum using traditional methods rather than beginning to transform learning. This "distance education" typically refers to the delivery of instruction to students who are separated from the instructor through some type of technology that is used to support regular and substantive interaction between the students and instructor, synchronously or asynchronously. When combined with classroom attendance, distance education is described as "blended" learning. It is designed to replicate the traditional educational experience, with the advantage of flexibility for the individual who cannot attend a class in a particular location at set times.

Distance delivery of adult basic education and ESL has been proven to be a successful option for adults studying for GED, advancing ESL levels, and improving literacy, numeracy, and work-related skills. Comparative studies in the United States, Canada, Australia, and the United Kingdom have found that adults taking the GED or studying to improve reading and/or English ability have slightly higher results than those with either classroom-only or distance-only study (Askov, Johnston, Petty, and Young 2003; Brennan 2003; Porter and Sturm 2006; Reder and Strawn 2006; Stiles and Porter 2007). The caveat to these encouraging outcomes is that the adults in the majority of these studies are those enrolled in formal programs. We know far less about the habits and successes of the remaining 90% of the adult population in need.

One of the few studies that provides information about adults both in and out of formal programs is the Longitudinal Study of Adult Learning (LSAL) that followed a cohort of 900 adults in Portland, Oregon, from 1998 to 2008. Among the significant findings of this study was the routine practice of "self-study" among a majority of these adults, including those who enrolled periodically in formal courses. Further, those who self-studied alone outperformed those who participated in classes alone: Of adults who were enrolled in a basic skills program for the GED but did not self-study, about 17% were successful, compared with 24% of those who engaged in self-study but did not participate in a program (Reder and Strawn 2006).

The LSAL included questions about access to and use of technology in the annual surveys and interviews with the study cohort, and these responses demonstrated both expanding access, increasing perceptions of effectiveness and value among the participants, and the mediating capability of technology between an individual's need for and/or interest in learning and options for assistance, whether a community service organization or an online tutor. Differences among learners' preferred modes of learning, their life circumstances, and the accessibility of learning resources such as classes shaped their choices about how to pursue literacy development (Reder 2003).

Access

Access to computers and the Internet in classrooms is limited and, when available, too often lacks the software, speed, and/or bandwidth necessary to make effective use of available technology-assisted content. Public spaces with IT access, such as libraries, are overwhelmed with the numbers of people who seek to use computers, often needing assistance from limited staff. However, while adults without high school diplomas who are unemployed or have low-wage jobs or who don't speak English continue to be less connected to computers and the Internet than other segments of the population, the growth in connectivity for this group is expanding rapidly (Horrigan 2009a).

There are three challenges to expanding the use of technology in learning for adults with lower levels of literacy, English, and basic skills: lack of physical access to computers and the Internet; lack of the basic level of ICT skills necessary to use the technology to advantage; and lack of sufficient quantity and range of and necessary conditions for learning.

Access to computers and the Internet continues to expand significantly among all demographic groups in the population, although the numbers continue to remain lowest among individuals with low levels of education, employment, and income as well as among blacks and Hispanics—groups that typically include those adults who need basic education and ESL study. Lack of home access is compounded by the absence of computers in most adult education classrooms and overwhelming demand in publicly available options such as libraries and community centers. The availability of mobile devices, which tend to be cheaper than computers and to provide more options for communicating with others, offers the promise of rapid adoption of some type of technology-accessible device (U.S. Census Bureau 2007; Horrigan 2009b).

A survey by the Pew Internet and American Life Project (2009) found that 77% of all adults have a computer in the home, a figure that rises to 95% for adults who are married with child or children. However, 84% of all adults have a cell phone (Kennedy et al. 2008), and a 2009 survey (Marist Institute 2009) found that 82% of those with incomes less than $50,000 a year had a cell phone.

A companion survey by Pew on Internet use the same month (Pew Internet and American Life 2009) found that, of the 79% of all adults who used the Internet at least occasionally, 60% had incomes below

$30,000 a year, 50% had less than a high school education, and 67% were black and 84% Hispanic. The highest percentage of activity was e-mail use (90%), but 88% used a search engine to find information.

As the sophistication of technology and content has grown, broadband connection to the Internet has become more necessary. Despite the higher costs and absence of broadband availability in some geographic areas, 63% of Americans have broadband at home. Further, the growth rates in broadband connection are significant from year to year, even among those with low levels of income and education. In households with annual incomes under $20,000, adoption increased from 25% in 2008 to 35% in 2009; with annual incomes between $20,000 and $30,000, adoption increased from 42% to 53%. Among high school graduates, the rate of adoption grew from 40% to 52% and among rural Americans, from 38% to 46% (Horrigan 2009a).

Physical access must be complemented with the ICT skills necessary to use computers/devices and the Internet, including not only the ability to manage the functions of computers and the Internet but also the abilities to search, evaluate, share, store, and connect information and processes. The traditional view has been that such skills must be taught in classes, such as those frequently offered in community technology centers, but recent research indicates that adults tend to prefer to learn ICT skills with the help of friends, family, and colleagues. A 2006 survey in the United Kingdom found that while 44% of respondents were using ICTs at home and 32% at the workplace, only 21% had ever participated in formal training to use computers. Despite the efforts to provide widespread public access, the survey found few adults, only 11% of the sample, using public computers. The researchers conclude that the government campaign and investment has overlooked the realities of adults' patterns of access, use, and need for further and online learning (Silver-Pacuilla and Reder 2008). Early usage data from http://www.usalearns.org, a recently developed online portal sponsored by the U.S. Department of Education to serve adult learners in ESL at a distance, suggests that students with lower levels of education in their home countries (sixth grade or lower), at beginning ESL levels, and with only modest computer skills were able to effectively use the site.

Further, there are many CD-ROM and online sources that provide either tutorials or interactive instruction in using computers and accessing the Internet that use voice, text, and images to enable individuals at any level of literacy to follow the steps. Increasingly, "user-friendly" hardware devices, such as those having a touch screen instead of a keyboard, that originally were developed for people with disabilities have begun to penetrate the adult education market.

An analysis of literacy scores between technology users and nonusers who answered the 2003 NAAL survey questions about technology use and access found that across demographic categories on Prose, Document, Quantitative, and Health literacy, scores revealed a pattern of higher scores among technology users than nonusers. One example: Among those who did not complete high school, more than 50% of technology nonusers have below basic document literacy scores, compared with 38% of technology users (Silver-Pacuilla and Reder 2008).

Technology and Work

As information and communications technologies have become more pervasive in every workplace, more and more workers have had to learn about computers, software, and communication and collaboration tools and technology as well as the practices associated with their use—whether or not these skills are intrinsic to a worker's actual job. By 2014, more than 77% of all jobs in the United States will require at least a basic level of ICT skills, according to Bureau of Labor Statistics projections (Saunders 2005).

Adult learners appear to be strongly motivated to attain ICT skills because of the importance of these skills in work (Bynner, Reder, Parsons, and Strawn 2008; Silver-Pacuilla and Reder 2008). An analysis of multiple surveys and research during the last ten years in several countries concluded that adults find the use of technologies in learning to be motivating, both because of the relationship of ICT skills to employment and because they enable greater flexibility for the teacher and the learner (Silver-Pacuilla and Reder 2008). Mobile technologies (tablets, personal digital assistants, mobile phones) in particular encouraged student interest and participation (Mellar et al. 2007).

The centrality of work readiness to adults' learning lives can provide strong leverage in encouraging acquisition of basic literacy and language skills. A 2008 comparison of longitudinal data from studies in Portland, Oregon, and London looked at ICT and literacy within the context of the rising importance of the use of and access to computers as part of contemporary employability. The central conclusion of this study was that "employment and ICT use support the development of literacy proficiency. Hence, enhancement of literacy proficiency is aided substantially by time spent in employment and exposure to ICT" (Bynner, Reder, Parsons, and Strawn 2008:5).

In 2003 the New Jersey Department of Labor piloted an innovative workforce development program in which poor, single, working mothers received a computer, Internet access, and courses online in their homes. There was a very high retention rate, with 92% of the 128 participants completing the program. Participants in the program experienced an average annual wage increase of 14%, and several enrolled in other educational programs, such as community college. All of the women stated that they would not have been able to complete a training program if it were not available at home. Through online learning, women also increased their facility with computers and the Internet (Gatta 2003).

Technology makes possible an entirely new environment and learning experience that can add to or go beyond the traditional classroom experience of instructor-led text-based formats. In using computers and the Internet, individuals can expand their communities to include other learners or members of a "community of practice." This experience can lead to new practices introduced by the new users and by developing technologies. In a paper that analyzed computer-usage data from the LSAL and other studies, Clare Strawn (2008) puts forth the concept of "computer-mediated literacy practices," defined by the relationships among literacy proficiency, fluency with technology, and contexts of practices. She goes on to note that "a computer application does not stand independent from the social context of its use" (p. 1) and that "popular culture and informal learning through computer use may offer avenues for development of new kinds of literacy not available in formal programs" (p. 4).

Supporting the Learner, Not the System

Credible credentials must be based on accepted and acknowledged standards for content, assessment, and outcomes together with assurance that the individual who is credentialed is the individual with the knowledge. Online provision of course curriculum, sample assessments for particular lessons or modules, opportunity for periodic communication with an instructor or regular access to an online tutor, and other methods will allow adult learners to track the formal education in order to be fully prepared for the formal assessment.

Adults who need basic education, ESL, work-readiness training, and other knowledge to attain or complete a degree or find employment must seek and maintain some connection to the adult education system. Technology offers a means for making such connection possible, whether an adult participates in all, some, or no formal programs.

Yet new structures and processes also must be developed for the transformation of learning that technology enables. With technology, the institutions, the determination of how and in what format content is available, and the design for assessment are no longer sufficient. Individuals can access knowledge, skill, information—learning—not only using multiple media at any time or place but also in different formats and structures and quantities. Beyond these concerns, there are questions about developing different methods of assessment and certification of learning for individuals and about quality and credentialing for learning providers.

English-language ability may be necessary for an immediate purpose, such as a job or promotion, financial requirements, or family responsibilities. A short-term, targeted language option is not sufficient for the long term but can serve an immediate need. Access to web-based vocabulary and translation can offer a missing word or phrase "just in time." This and similar examples already are in place, but they represent little more than transplanting the traditional and familiar process of education to an online environment.

Successful programs that lead to employment and further education for low-skilled adults, whether or not technology is involved, frequently have designed the experience to suit the needs of the learner rather than the requirements of the system. As governments, educators, employers, and technology developers consider how to take advantage of technology without losing the value of supporting systems, it will be necessary to determine what the new environments can be.

Results from the LSAL project suggest that new program designs are needed to facilitate and support the learning of adults engaged in self-study and to link self-study activities with program services. Learners engaged in self-study may benefit from assistance with identifying learning goals, skill assessment, selection of study materials (whether print-based, online, or multimedia), mentoring or tutoring, and progress assessment (Reder 2008). What good technologies and good uses of technology offer is the potential to enable and support that can be customized to the learner, whether he or she is in an instructor-led classroom or learning independently at a distance (McCain 2002, 2009).

The current system for adult basic education, ESL, and basic skills is isolated from the traditional pipeline of pre-K through postsecondary education and isolates adult learners. As individuals become more mobile and freer to choose where, how, and when they can access education and training, they will become aware of and have access to options beyond the traditional narrow offerings of "adult basic education."

The Role for Government

The necessary period of transition and integration between the systems in place and those that can support a technology-enabled environment requires changes that are substantively, culturally, financially, and politically overwhelming. In business, the information and communications technology industries paved the way for the use of technology for learning and work in business, developing and introducing purpose-designed communications and technology tools and infrastructure suited to the needs of economy and efficiency in a global economy. Business and other sectors of the economy and population provide a market for developers, manufacturers, and providers of technology.

Most programs for adult literacy and English learners have been funded by government and nonprofit organizations; for-profit companies rarely develop technology-based learning for these adults because the market is diffuse, small (in terms of organizations that buy products), and lacking financial resources to justify for-profit sales. As technology becomes more widely available and more individuals are familiar with its use and as programs and learning applications expand, current divisions among education levels—K–12, postsecondary, adult education, and training—may begin to blur, providing the necessary market for products aimed at low-literacy and ESL adult learners. Until this occurs, however, government must in the face of market failure take the lead in establishing the mechanisms to fund and promote development, evaluation, marketing, dissemination, and a framework for learning assessment and credentials.

There are already innovative and effective models on which to build such an effort, including those that provide a structured approach that can supplement traditional instruction or be used independently; those that immediately offer the learner access to content and learning, regardless of knowledge and ability; those that provide sophisticated interaction for particular learning "modules"; and many others. (See brief descriptions of selected models in the appendix to this chapter.)

To take advantage of the opportunity for using technology in learning for all individuals, an essential first step is redesigning the adult education and workforce-skills system to provide a framework and support to learners outside of formal programs. Such a system would include provisions, such as online assessment, to certify knowledge and competence achieved via distance learning. These online certifications would carry the same eligibility for course and/or program credit—whether in postsecondary institutions or job training programs—that classroom-based certification enjoys.

The Obama administration's 2009 "American Graduation Initiative" proposed a comprehensive plan and funding to produce 5 million additional community college graduates by 2020. Unlike many proposals, the initiative called for a significant role for technology, not only for delivery but also for courses developed specifically for an online audience—courses that will be free and freely accessible and that community colleges will be encouraged to align with their course requirements for degree programs. If funded, this initiative would make a significant difference in establishing a connection between independent learning and credit for credentials.

There are many organizations, state and local governments, and other entities that are involved in technology and learning for adult literacy, ranging from the implementation of statewide systems to a local organization's offer for access to computers and the Internet. But there is little awareness or acceptance of these beyond local borders, nor are there any serious moves to use technology to serve areas beyond the governmental, geographic boundaries of states and communities. Nor have there been successful efforts to link the adult basic education/ESL system to workforce and economic development, despite the ultimate goal of employment for most adult learners. Assembling this information and these policies and practices can provide a solid base on which to develop specific strategies and actions.

A much-needed mechanism to provide information about available programs, content, locations, and other options is a web portal. The available options that technology offers for adult learning are expanding rapidly but with little to no visibility among the adults and communities who need them. Development and management of a national web portal that aggregates information about technology-assisted learning for adults with low levels of literacy and/or English language fluency and limited ability to use computers and the Internet would make a significant difference in awareness and use. Even websites that purport to serve these adults rarely provide links to other sources and are not designed for ease of access for these adults.

There are many and varied technology-assisted and -oriented programs, content, tools, and other information accessible via the Internet—whether they are designed for supplements to formal education programs or for independent online learning. These are designed for and available to adults with basic skills or language needs, instructors or advisors with professional development needs, officials and administrators with management and measurement needs, employers with specific occupation or professional needs, and many more. Information of all kinds for adults with low levels of literacy and/or English language fluency and limited ability to use computers and the Internet is not easily found or accessible.

Technology is changing the acceptance that education as it exists today is what "must be" to a belief that learning is what "can be." Abandoning the current systems is not a practical or even desirable option, nor is continuing to focus primarily on "fixing" these systems. Failure to determine and develop the systems appropriate and necessary to support individuals and organizations in using technology for learning will constrain the nation's ability to compete with a world-class workforce and will put national and individual prosperity at risk. Incremental change can be more difficult and often less interesting than revolutionary change, yet this is the challenge that confronts us. And it is one that the nation must and can address.

Endnotes

[1] Basic literacy capabilities include finding, in a pamphlet for prospective jurors, an explanation of how people were selected for the jury pool; using a television guide to find out what programs are on at a specific time; and comparing the ticket prices for two events (http://nces.ed.gov/NAAL/index.asp?file=KeyFindings/Demographics/Overall.asp&PageId=16).

[2] In FY2004, the federal allocation for grants to states was $564,079,550, which represented approximately 26% of the total amount expended at the state and local levels to support adult education and literacy. The program enrolled just under 2,600,000 learners. (U.S. Department of Education 2007).

Appendix: Selected Program Models

Interactive Learning Using Multiple Media. Sed de Saber (Thirst for Knowledge) (http://www.seddesaber.com) is an electronic English language program for Hispanic adults who have limited English proficiency. It is a portable, interactive, self-paced program that uses storytelling, voice recording, games, and review exercises to build and improve English language skills. *Sed de Saber* combines ESL curriculum with the Leapfrog Quantum Pad Plus Microphone, which allows the learner to record, play back, and compare his or her voice to the word or phrase being learned, increasing confidence in pronunciation skills.

Web Portal and Online Learning Environment for Adult Learners in Basic Education. The Learner Web (http://www.learnerweb.org) is a free web- and telephone-accessed application that provides customized, guided instructional support to adults seeking to improve their basic skills, prepare for the GED, or pursue other learning goals, such as citizenship, family literacy, or college prep. A learner's goals and skill needs are matched to supporting resources available online or offline in the local community.

Web Applications. USA Learns (http://www.usalearns.org) is a free ESL instructional program developed primarily for immigrant adults with limited English language skills who cannot attend traditional classroom programs. The site offers practice activities in listening, reading, writing, and speaking skills as well as life skills necessary for success at work and in the community. All instructional materials are online; there are no videos, workbooks, or other materials for printing. USA Learns is designed primarily for individual distance learning outside of the traditional classroom. Learners do not need advanced computer skills to use USA Learns, and there are no proxy contact hours assigned to it. However, as there is a unit mastery quiz for every unit in the two courses, a mastery model should fit (Fleischman 2008).

BuildingSkills4Work (http://buildingskills4work.org) aims to equip out-of-school adults and youth with the workforce skills that will prepare them to qualify for and be successful in higher-paying entry-level jobs. This free online program is designed to engage adult learners with and without the intervention of a teacher or tutor. It teaches entry-level workplace skills, including both academic and interpersonal skills, and targets the needs of individuals at the low to middle end of the NAAL Basic Literacy skill range (Level 2), people whose reading and quantitative skills are often not sufficient to successfully complete a GED program or apprenticeship, to matriculate in community college or university degree programs, or to qualify for jobs that pay self-sufficiency wages.

References

Askov, E., J. Johnston, L.I. Petty, and S.J. Young. 2003. *Expanding Access to Adult Literacy with Online Distance Education.* Cambridge, MA: National Center for the Study of Adult Literacy, Harvard Graduate School of Education.

Brennan, Roslin. 2003. *One Size Doesn't Fit All: Pedagogy in the Online Environment. Volume 1.* Kensington Park SA, Australia: National Vocational and Educational Training System, Australian Flexible Learning Framework.

Brown, John Seely. 2000. "Growing Up Digital." *Change,* March–April, pp. 10–20. <http://johnseelybrown.com/Growing_up_digital.pdf>. [June 13, 2009].

Bynner, John, Steve Reder, Samantha Parsons, and Clare Strawn. 2008. *Research Summary: The Digital Divide: Computer Use, Basic Skills and Employment: A Comparative Study in Portland, OR, USA and London, England.* <http://www.nrdc.org.uk/publications_details.asp?ID=149#>. [May 10, 2009].

Council of Economic Advisors, Executive Office of the President. 2009. *Preparing the Workers of Today for the Jobs of Tomorrow.* <http://www.whitehouse.gov/administration/eop/cea/Jobs-of-the-Future>. [May 10, 2009].

Fleischman, John. 2008. "New Designs in Online and Distance Learning: USA Learns." National Institute for Literacy Discussion List Special Topics. November. <http://lincs.ed.gov/pipermail/englishlanguage/2008/003049.html>. [October 17, 2010].

Gatta, Mary L. 2003. *Findings from the Field: Early Findings of the New Jersey Online Learning Project for Single Working-Poor Mothers.* <http://www.itwd.rutgers.edu/PDF/FindingsfromField.pdf>. [December 10, 2008].

Horrigan, John. 2009a. *Home Broadband Adoption, June 2009.* Washington, DC: Pew Internet and American Life Project. <http://www.pewinternet.org/Reports/2009/10-Home-Broadband-Adoption-2009.aspx>. [August 12, 2009].

Horrigan, John. 2009b. *Wireless Internet Use, July 2009.* Washington, DC: Pew Internet and American Life Project. <http://www.pewinternet.org/~/media//Files/Reports/2009/Wireless-Internet-Use.pdf>. [August 12, 2009].

Kennedy, John, Tracy L.M. Hoops, Aaron Smith, Amy Tracy Wells, and Barry Wellman. 2008. *Networked Families,* October 19. Pew Internet and American Life Project. <http://www.pewinternet.org/Reports/2008/Networked Families.aspx>. [May 10, 2009].

Lacey, T. Alan, and Benjamin Wright. 2009. "Occupational Employment Projections to 2018. Employment Outlook 2008–2018." *Monthly Labor Review,* November. <http://www.bls.gov/opub/mlr/2009/11/art5full.pdf>. [January 12, 2010].

The Longitudinal Study of Adult Learning (LSAL): 1998–2008. Portland, OR: National Center for the Study of Adult Learning and Literacy, Portland State University. <http://www.lsal.pdx.edu>. [May 11, 2009].

The Marist Institute for Public Opinion Poll. 2009, March. <http://www.marketing charts.com/interactive/employment-age-top-factors-in-cell-phone-pda-use-9678>. [August 12, 2009].

McCain, Mary. 2002. *Leapfrogging the Status Quo: E-Learning and the Challenge of Adult Literacy.* Boston: Jobs for the Future. <http://jff.org/publications/education/leapfrogging-over-status-quo-e-learning-/216>. [March 22, 2009].

McCain, Mary. 2009. *The Power of Technology to Transform Adult Learning: Expanding Access to Adult Education and Workforce Skills Through Distance Learning.* New York: Council for the Advancement of Adult Literacy. <http://caalusa.org/POWER_OF_TECH.pdf>. [October 1, 2010].

Mellar, Harvey, Maria Kambouri, Kit Logan, Sally Betts, Barbara Nance, and Viv Moriarty. 2007. *Effective Teaching and Learning: Using ICT.* London: National Research and Development Centre for Adult Literacy. <http://www.nrdc.org.uk/publications_details.asp?ID=87#>. [June 4, 2009].

National Assessment of Adult Literacy. 2003. U.S. Department of Education, Institute of Education Sciences, Center for Education Statistics. <http://nces.ed.gov/naal>. [January 10, 2010].

National Commission on Adult Literacy. 2008. *Reach Higher, America: Overcoming Crisis in the U.S. Workforce.* New York: Council for the Advancement of Adult Literacy. <http://caalusa.org/report.html>. [July 15, 2008].

Pew Internet and American Life Project. 2009, April. *Demographics of Internet Users.* <http://www.pewinternet.org/Static-Pages/Trend-Data/Whos-Online.aspx>. [April 12, 2009].

Porter, Paul, and Matthew Sturm. 2006. *Crossing the Great Divides: Distance Learning and Flexible Delivery in Adult Basic Education.* Toronto, ON: Human Resources and Social Development Canada, AlphaPlus Centre. <http://www.distance.alphaplus.ca/pdfs/CrossingTheGreatDividesFullRpt.pdf>. [April 20, 2010].

Reder, Stephen. 2003. "Giving Literacy Away, Again: New Concepts of Promising Practice." In Lisa Soricone, ed., *Summaries of Papers Presented at Twentieth Annual Rutgers Invitational Symposium on Education (RISE),* October 22–23. Co-sponsored by National Center for the Study of Adult Learning and Literacy (NCSALL), Institute for the Study of Adult Literacy, and the Rutgers Graduate School of Education, pp. 21–2. <http://www.ncsall.net/fileadmin/resources/research/rise_summaries.pdf>. [August 21, 2009].

Reder, Stephen. 2008, November. "New Designs in Online and Distance Learning," National Institute for Literacy Discussion List, Special Topics. <http://lincs.ed.gov/pipermail/englishlanguage/2008/003049.html>. [October 17, 2010].

Reder, Stephen, and Clare Strawn. 2006. "Self-Study: Broadening the Concepts of Participation and Program Support." *Focus on Basics*, Vol. 8, Issue C (November), pp. 6–10. <http://www.ncsall.net/index.php?id=1152>. [October 17, 2010].

Saunders, Norman C. 2005. *A Summary of BLS Projections to 2014*. <http://www.bls.gov/opub/mlr/2005/11/art1full.pdf>. [December 1, 2005].

Silver-Pacuilla, Heidi, and Stephen Reder. 2008. *Investigating the Language and Literacy Skills Required for Independent Online Learning*. Washington, DC: National Institute for Literacy. <http://www.lsal.pdx.edu/docs/pdf/language_literacy.pdf>. [October 17, 2010].

Stiles, Richard, and Dennis Porter. 2007. *The California Adult Education 2005–2007 Innovation and Alternative Instructional Delivery Program: A Review*. Carson, CA: California State University, Dominguez Hills. <http://www.cdlponline.org/pdf/InnovationProgramsReport2005-2007.pdf>. [February 28, 2009].

Strawn, Clare. 2008. *The Relationship Between Literacy Proficiency and the Digital Divide Among Adults With Low Education Attainment*. Portland, OR: National Center for the Study of Adult Learning and Literacy, Portland State University. <http://www.lsal.pdx.edu/Documents/PDF/littech.pdf>. [May 12, 2009].

U.S. Census Bureau. 2007. *Computer and Internet Use in the United States: October 2007*. Table 4: "Reported Computer and Internet Access for Individuals 15 Years and Older, by Selected Characteristics: 2005. Table 5. Reported Internet Access and Activity, For Individuals 15 Years and Older Who Use the Internet, by Selected Characteristics: 2005." <http://www.census.gov/population/www/socdemo/computer/2007.html>. [April 12, 2009].

U.S. Department of Education. 2007. *Adult Education Report to Congress: 2004–2005*. <http://www2.ed.gov/about/offices/list/ovae/pi/AdultEd/congressionalreport04-05.pdf>. [April 29, 2009].

CHAPTER 6

Connecting the Dots: Creating a Postsecondary Education System for the 21st-Century Workforce

SUSAN J. SCHURMAN
Rutgers University

LOUIS SOARES
Center for American Progress

For much of this century and, indeed, right up to the present, American enterprise has been organized on the principle that most of us do not need to know much to do the work that has to be done. This system may have worked brilliantly for us until recently, but it will do so no longer.

> Ray Marshall and Mark Tucker, *Thinking for a Living* (1992:xii)

One clear measure of how much the economy has changed in the past two decades can be seen by reviewing the last LERA research volume that examines new developments in worker training (Ferman, Hoyman, Cutcher-Gershenfeld, and Savoi 1991). That volume contains few references to the nation's higher education system. Two decades later it is impossible to imagine a national system of workforce development without including colleges and universities. In 1976, Richard Freeman argued that an oversupply of college graduates, stemming from expanded access to higher education in the 1960s, had caused income returns from a college degree to decline so precipitously that additional social or private investments in colleges would yield only marginal benefit for the foreseeable future. Shortly thereafter, the economic returns to a bachelor's degree began a steady, uninterrupted rise that by 2006 yielded nearly a $50,000 advantage in median annual income compared to a high school diploma alone (Haskins, Holzer, and Lerman 2009). This trend is not limited to bachelor's degree completion; recent research shows an average income return of 4% to 6% for each 30 college credits (two semesters) earned, and a 29% earnings increase for those with associate's degrees compared to those with only a high school diploma (Furchgott-Roth, Jacobson, and Mokher 2009). Most experts predict that this trend is likely to continue. According to the Bureau of Labor Statistics, the U.S. economy will produce 15.6 million net new jobs between 2006 and 2015, nearly half of which will require some type of postsecondary education credential. A recent national poll by the Pew Economic Mobility Project indicates that the general public has taken these data to heart: 80% of respondents said that having a good education is very important to economic mobility, and 55% said that getting a college degree "almost perfectly describes their definition of the American Dream" (Haskins, Holzer, and Lerman 2009:4).

It is not surprising, then, that enrollment in U.S. colleges and universities has reached an all-time high, with over 65% of recent high school graduates and nearly 60% of the total birth cohort reporting some collegiate participation by their mid-twenties (Turner 2007). Unfortunately, neither colleges and universities themselves nor public higher education policies have yet adjusted to this enormous change in demand. After three decades of rising enrollments, the overall bachelor's degree completion rate for those who enter college is not only lower today than in the 1970s (Bound, Lovenheim, and Turner 2009; Haskins, Holzer, and Lerman 2009), but it also reveals a growing pattern of inequality. At the most selective public institutions (and most private institutions) completion rates have *increased* by 10% (Bound, Lovenheim, and Turner 2009). But at the nation's public two-year and less selective four-year colleges, where the largest increases in enrollment have occurred, completion rates have declined (Carey 2005; Bound, Lovenheim, and Turner 2009; Haskins, Holzer, and Lerman 2009;).[1] Community colleges in particular, because of their greater elasticity in responding to increased demand, have received the largest share of increasing enrollments from the least prepared students; completion rates for this group—always low—declined further, from 5.6% to 5% (Bound, Lovenheim, and Turner 2009). During this same period, expenditures per student *increased* at private and selective public institutions but *decreased* at nonselective public four-year and two-year institutions, resulting in decreasing student–faculty ratios at private and selective public institutions and increasing ratios at less selective four-year and two-year institutions (Bound, Lovenheim, and Turner 2009). In their analysis of why college completion rates have declined, Bound, Lovenheim, and Turner (2009) found that declining student academic preparedness explains 88% of the decline in completion rates at community colleges, while increasing ratios of students to faculty account for 81% of the decline at less selective public four-year institutions.

The net effect of these changes is that, at the very moment a national consensus calls for a significant increase in college degree completion as a centerpiece of the nation's workforce development strategy, the trend at colleges and universities—with the exception of the nation's most selective and/or most expensive institutions—is in the opposite direction. Meanwhile, completion rates in other countries are increasing. While the United States still has the highest proportion of bachelor's degrees in the 55- to 64-year-old age group, it has fallen to 6th place in the 25- to 34-year-old group among the 30 richest countries (Organisation for Economic Co-operation and Development 2007). When associate's degrees are included, the United States has fallen to 12th place in degree completion among 25- to 34-year-olds (Organisation for Economic Co-operation and Development 2007).

In response, President Obama has proposed an ambitious agenda aimed at restoring U.S. leadership in postsecondary educational attainment. He has called for the United States to have the world's highest proportion of college graduates by 2020, to add 5 million people with community college credentials in the form of occupational credentials or associate's degrees, and to ensure that all adults have at least one year of postsecondary education.[2] This agenda poses a major question: How will the nation's postsecondary education system, already strained beyond capacity, meet this challenge?[3]

The purpose of this chapter is to describe a "pathway" by which the nation's existing postsecondary education and training system can be modified to help achieve these goals. In particular, our focus is on enabling the approximately 75 million incumbent workers who lack a recognized postsecondary education credential to resume their education (Soares and Mazzeo 2008). Soares (2009:13) terms these individuals "working learners . . . individuals between the ages of 18 and 64 who are already in the workforce and who currently lack a postsecondary credential." Working learners are of particular interest because data suggest that it will be impossible to meet the president's goals without helping them obtain a postsecondary credential. One recent study estimates that the United States will need to enroll as many as 10 million such working learners to retake the global lead in the proportion of adults with a postsecondary credential (Jones and Ewell 2009). Another study suggests that the focus for many of these prospective students should be at the two-year-college level (Holzer and Lerman 2007).

Despite wide variation on virtually all demographic characteristics, working learners share one important distinction: All are needed wage earners for themselves or their families. To obtain a postsecondary credential, these individuals must be able to maintain their employment and family responsibilities while they are pursuing further education. Many of these working learners share another important attribute: They have some college credits but no credential. They are among the large number of high school graduates who entered college but left without completing a degree. A growing body of evidence indicates that to be successful, working learners require flexible education programs, courses of study that yield educational credentials that employers value, career guidance, and easy-to-use financial assistance (see, for example, Soares 2009 for review).

Serving these working learners requires a significant rethinking of the very idea of a "college education." The traditional view of college—four to six years of full-time study in the cloistered environment of a college campus before entering the "real world" of work—is simply not relevant to working learners. This traditional view needs to be replaced by a "lifelong learning" view (e.g., Fischer 2000; Field 2006; Smith 2010) in which education and training resources of different kinds are accessible to individuals throughout their lives, enabling them to build successful careers, update their competencies in response to economic shifts, and increase their understanding, as citizens in a democracy, of the complex issues affecting their lives.

We argue that the current structure of U.S. higher education lacks the flexibility to permit movement between work and learning on the scale required to meet the challenge. In contrast, job training programs provided by employers and unions or through the public workforce development program contain the needed flexibility but seldom yield recognized credentials. We outline here a conceptual framework for rethinking the role of postsecondary education in workforce development and give examples and policy recommendations to facilitate such a transformation.

Our framework is constructed around the fact that, in the knowledge economy, workers' knowledge no longer represents merely a set of competencies required to produce goods or services as was true in the mass-production economy. Rather, knowledge itself has become a commodity—"raw material that can be claimed through legal devices, owned and marketed as a product or service" (Slaughter and Rhoades 2004:17). The magnitude of this change has yet to be widely understood by policy makers at any level. It has triggered the most dramatic change in the nature of work and the competencies demanded by labor markets since the advent of mass production. To sustain a broad national prosperity, our workforce development system must adapt to the knowledge economy. This cannot be accomplished without transforming postsecondary education to integrate the rigor of our traditional higher education system with the labor market flexibility of our workforce development and employer-based job training systems (Soares 2009).

We refer to our framework as "connecting the dots" to underscore the fact that there is no need to reinvent the wheel. Most of the elements needed for the postsecondary education system we outline exist but operate on policies that are still aligned with the mass-production economy rather than the knowledge/information economy. This lack of alignment and connectivity causes Smith (2010:21) to argue that postsecondary education is "not a system at all . . . [but] actually resembles a large and diverse cottage industry"—a plethora of education providers including colleges and universities, community colleges, community-based organizations, employers, and labor unions, each of which implements and measures learning processes in unique ways and confers course credit and credentials based on different criteria. Connecting the dots refers to integrating this array of providers in three ways:

1. Reducing the sharp divide between the traditional liberal arts and vocational/professional curricula and integrating the competencies of both in new ways

2. Building new connections among various types of postsecondary education providers so that learners can progress smoothly from one to another

3. Enabling working learners to "earn while you learn" by making educational opportunities available in formats and with funding structures that permit people to continue working while acquiring new knowledge and skills

These three types of integration, we propose, will enhance economic competitiveness and improve individual opportunity, providing Americans with the ability to creatively apply knowledge to real-world situations and to bring knowledge gained in the real world to the classroom. Such integration also ensures that education is delivered in a way that meets working learners' need for flexible learning options that accrue credit and credentials across many providers. Facilitating these types of integration requires significant policy changes at institutional, state, and federal levels. The challenge is to adopt new policy levers that will encourage broader diffusion of innovations that increase access to postsecondary education for working learners while maintaining and increasing the breadth, rigor, and standards of excellence associated with college-level learning.

Workers' Knowledge Requirements in the Knowledge/Information Economy: A Framework

Human resource scholars identify four different types of knowledge that the workforce of any enterprise must possess: general, occupation-specific, firm-specific, and industry-specific (e.g., Lepak and Snell 2003). This focus on workforce knowledge has given rise to an "architectural view" (Lepak and Snell 2003; Morris, Snell, and Lepak, 2005) in which the knowledge-based firm is viewed as a "portfolio of human capital" that constitutes a significant source of sustained competitive advantage (Lepak and Snell 2003). Figure 1 depicts a typology of these different types of knowledge. "Knowledge" in this framework includes both *declarative* knowledge (e.g., facts, concepts, theories, events) and *procedural* knowledge (integrating physical and cognitive skills for action; Anderson 1976).

FIGURE 1
The "Architecture" of Knowledge in Organizations.

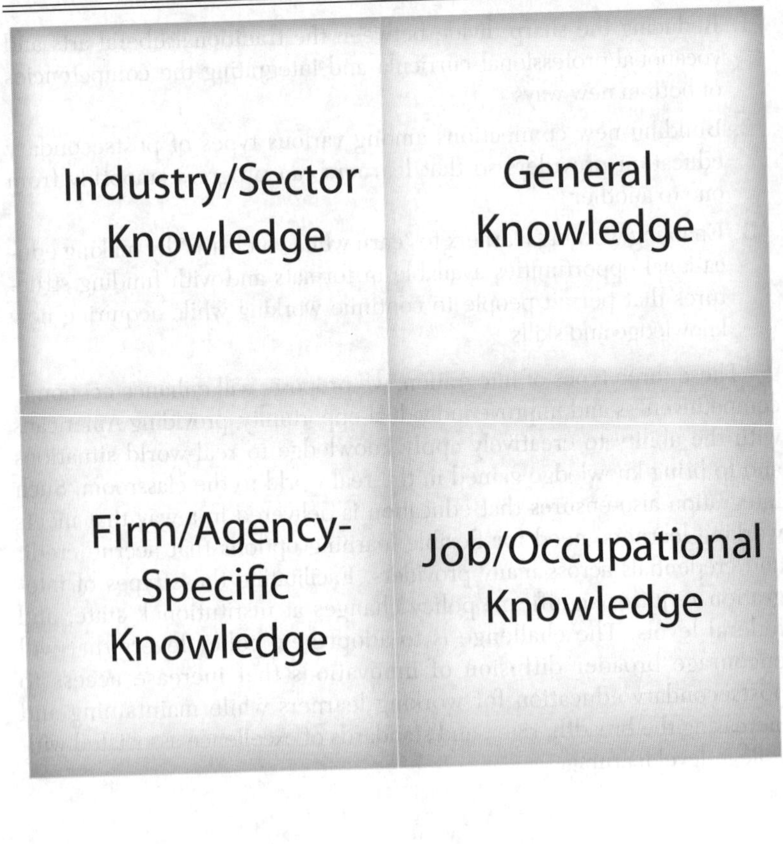

In the typology shown in Figure 1, each type of work-related knowledge is assumed to include both declarative and procedural knowledge that varies depending on the specific nature of the occupation or industry. Products or services and the structure of work in different industries and occupations generate different demands for knowledge in the workforce.

- *General knowledge,* acquired primarily through formal schooling, refers to such academic competencies as analytic skills, quantitative reasoning, written and oral communications, critical thinking, and problem-solving skills as well as mastery of specific subjects or disciplines.
- *Occupation-specific knowledge* pertains to specific jobs or occupations and may be acquired through formal education, training, on-the-job experience, or a combination of these, depending on the occupation.
- *Firm- or agency-specific knowledge* may result from some combination of formal schooling, training, and on-the-job experience and is, by definition, unique to the firm.
- *Industry-specific knowledge* can also be acquired through either experience or formal schooling, but in an increasing number of industries significant levels of both experience and education are required.

The mass-production paradigm of organization that dominated the American economy in the 20th century required a workforce knowledge profile very different from the profile required by the knowledge- and information-based organizations that form the primary engines of the 21st-century economy. Meanwhile, the existing postsecondary education system is still geared to the needs of the old economy.

The Mass-Production Education and Training System

Figure 2 depicts the education and workforce development system that evolved to meet the needs of the mass-production economy. Three features are most relevant to the present discussion. First is the separation of "academic" from "vocational" knowledge; second is the specialization of education providers to serve these different education markets; third is the autonomy of the provider institutions, with poorly developed connectivity between and among them. These features stem in large measure from Fredrick Taylor's (1911) *Principles of Scientific Management.*

Taylor sought to improve the efficiency of production by finding the "one best way" to perform a task. His methods led to assigning the newly created industrial engineering department the task of decomposing workers' traditional occupational knowledge into discrete tasks, separating the conception of tasks (thinking) from their execution (doing), and giving management control over each step of the production process.

FIGURE 2
Structure of 20th-Century Postsecondary Education.

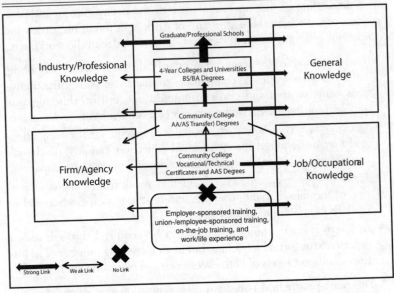

Taylor's methodology greatly facilitated the massive substitution of machines for human labor that made mass production possible and also enabled the mass employment of low-skilled workers to operate the machines. Front-line workers' jobs in Taylor's system are highly circumscribed, requiring little knowledge beyond the occupation level, where "occupation" often involved only one basic task that could be mastered with little training or experience. Higher-skilled workers, such as tool and die makers, electricians, and machine repairers, require more occupational and general knowledge and hence more training. Depending on the size of their firm, front-line workers may know a fair amount about the firm or even the industry, but this knowledge would not be integral to task performance.

Supervisors in the mass-production paradigm get promoted from the ranks of the front-line workforce, and their knowledge profile is very similar to those they supervise. They are required to have job/occupational knowledge and may also acquire additional knowledge about the firm, but, like front-line workers, they may know relatively little about their industry and do not require a high level of general knowledge.

As the mass-production economy evolved, higher-level managers were less likely to rise through the ranks and more likely to be professional managers trained at academic institutions. Executives were required to have higher levels of general knowledge as well as specialized firm and industry knowledge. At the same time, such managers often had less knowledge of the specific jobs at the front line of the firm. Perhaps most importantly, this system required increasing numbers of specialists—professional and technical workers like engineers and applied scientists with specialized technical and occupational knowledge acquired through formal schooling.

The principles of job design initially developed for manufacturing and food processing enterprises spread throughout the economy to other enterprises and industries, including, and most especially, the education sector (Tyack 1974; Marshall and Tucker 1992). Taylor's "principles" proved applicable to virtually any task—cognitive or physical—that can be decoded and described using "rules-based logic." Rules-based logic applies whenever it is possible to specify an action for every contingency; such "condition–action–outcome" (CAO) rules permit the specification of step-by-step procedures for workers to follow in executing tasks (Levy and Murnane 2004), thus achieving standardization—the foundation of mass production.

For nearly a century the mass-production workforce development system created broadly shared prosperity in the United States. However, as Marshall and Tucker (1992) point out, the system was a double-edged sword: It made front-line workers in the United States part of "the largest, richest middle class the world has ever seen" but at a very high long-term cost. Taylor's premise of separating "thinking" from "doing" ultimately yielded the world's highest and most expensive ratio of managers, support staff, and technical specialists to front-line workers. The result was a system "far more vulnerable than anyone imagined. There was one thread that ran through almost all its weaknesses—its elitist character. We had built a system of 'coolie labor' surrounded by a managerial, technical and support elite" (Marshall and Tucker 1992:10). Figure 2 sketches the structure of the postsecondary education and job training system that supported this system and emphasizes the key features that require alteration.

Separation of Academic and Vocational Knowledge. Paradoxically, the "elitist" character of the U.S. mass-production system spawned an "anti-elitist" education reform movement based on the notion that the traditional American intellectual ideal for schooling was aristocratic and had no place in a democracy. During the first half of the 20th century, the American secondary education system introduced increasing structural differentiation accompanied by increasing curricular differentiation between "academic" and "vocational" studies. According to Cremin

(1988:232; see also Tyack 1974), the progressive school-reform movement argued that the "attractiveness, or 'holding power,' of the schools would be increased only as studies were seen by pupils and their families as more useful[, i.e.,] . . . more vocational." The logic of this argument led to providing different curricula for different students depending on their occupational destinations. The result was a division of schooling into vocational—supplying large numbers of front-line workers who had "mastered the three R's, had some vocational skills and were well disciplined" (Marshall and Tucker 1992:20)—and academic, preparing students destined to be managers and specialists for advanced instruction at colleges and universities. Despite all claims to the contrary, this "tracking system survives to this day" (Marshall and Plotkin, Chapter 12, this volume).

Specialization of Education Providers. The separation of academic and vocational curricula initially developed in the K–12 system became the foundation of the nation's postsecondary education and training system as well. As Figure 2 shows, the mass-production education paradigm spawned a wide variety of education and/or training institutions specialized to serve either vocational or academic markets. In 2006, there were 4,829 two- and four-year colleges, of which about 35% are public, another 35% are private not-for-profit, and the remainder are private for-profit. Of the 14.9 million undergraduate students attending these institutions, 11.7 million attend public institutions, 2.4 million attend private not-for-profit institutions, and 0.8 million attend private for-profit institutions. Public two-year and four-year institutions are funded by, in addition to tuition and fees, state legislatures. Despite shrinking state appropriations and concomitant increases in tuition and fees, four-year public institutions continue to post tuition levels about 25% below the level charged by private institutions, and tuition at two-year public institutions remains a tenth of the private level.

By far the fastest-growing segment of degree- or certificate-granting postsecondary education is the private for-profit institutions, which now enroll close to 10% of all college students. (For a theory and detailed analyses of penetration of market logic into higher education, see Slaughter and Leslie 1997 and Slaughter and Rhodes 2004). These institutions range from small, specialized, career-oriented institutions to large universities that confer credentials ranging from occupational certificates to doctoral degrees (e.g., DeVry and the University of Phoenix). Their rapid growth in the last decade can be attributed to the adoption of a new model that is specifically geared to working learners and consistent with many of the proposals that we outline below. The model is student-centric, linking course delivery and pedagogy specifically to the needs of students, and also labor market–centric, based on developing close ties with employers for the purposes of curriculum development and career placement. These institutions also tend to be early adopters of innovations, such as web-based instruction, as well as standardized curricula. However, the for-profit institutions have also generated growing criticism about program quality, enrollment practices, and financial models (Government Accountability Office 2009; Eisman 2010).

Consistent with the academic/vocational divide we have described, the public workforce development system is almost entirely separate from the formal higher education system and is geared to provide short-term training, mostly for hard-to-employ and dislocated workers to obtain jobs that require little skill. Its services, funded each year under the Workforce Investment Act (WIA) of 1998, are an amalgam of 16 different categories of programs housed in four different government agencies. These funds are managed at the state level by 650 local Workforce Investment Boards (WIBs) made up of business, labor, community, and education leaders. WIB staff contract for training services with a diverse set of certified education institutions, including community colleges (mostly noncredit programs), high school vocational centers, community-based organizations, and private training firms. At about $4 billion a year, funding for these WIA training services is only about a third of that invested in college programs such as the Pell Grant and has decreased 40% since 1985. Of the total, only 40% is invested directly in training and serves about 416,000 individuals per year. Most importantly, with a few exceptions, WIA-sponsored training does not offer recognizable occupational credentials or academic credit that provides meaningful benchmarks of achievement with value in the job market or that links to a college-degree pathway. (For a more complete description and critique of the public workforce development system, see, e.g., Soares 2009 and Marshall and Plotkin, Chapter 12, this volume).

An Autonomous and Disconnected "System." The diverse group of colleges and universities in the postsecondary education system is regulated and governed in a highly decentralized fashion. Compared with many other nations, higher education policy and funding in the United States is concentrated in the states rather than in the federal government. Some scholars argue that the relatively limited federal role helps explain why other countries have surpassed the United States in college degree completion. Since the 1980s, virtually all developed and many developing nations have adopted policies redirecting public resources in efforts to more tightly link postsecondary education to economic competitiveness; most of the nations that have made rapid gains (e.g., Australia and the United Kingdom) have strong national education ministries (Slaughter and Leslie 1997; Slaughter and Rhoades 2004). In the United States each individual state sets up its own public higher education system and provides regulation and oversight for the public, private nonprofit, and for-profit higher education sectors. States establish and implement rules governing the creation of private nonprofit and for-profit universities and specify the minimum requirements that all institutions operating in the state must meet in order to grant academic degrees. There is considerable variation in the specific details of state regulations, policies, and outcomes among the 50 states (see Jones and Ewell 2009 for an overview). Quality control of provider offerings is maintained largely through a voluntary accreditation system composed of privately run accrediting agencies that review the qualifications of member institutions. Though it is possible to forego accreditation, the Higher Education Act stipulates that an institution must be accredited by one of 61 nationally recognized accrediting agencies designated by the U.S. Department of Education to be eligible for Title IV federal financial aid programs. Within this framework of federal, state, and accrediting body requirements, education institutions have a high degree of local control over core policies such as admission standards, curricula, degree requirements, and the award of institutional financial aid.

Similarly, the workforce development system, as funded through WIA, is equally decentralized, with the 650 local workforce boards mentioned above certifying vendors in their service area and having limited communication with other boards. This service and governance model makes it exceedingly difficult to achieve the funding flexibility needed to serve increasing important regional labor markets (Marshall and Plotkin, Chapter 12, this volume).

As Figure 2 illustrates, within this vast network of educational providers, job or occupational knowledge for most "front-line" workers is primarily acquired through direct work experience supplemented by on-the-job training exclusively. At higher skill levels, training is provided through the private postsecondary education and training system or through vocational certificates and degrees at the public community colleges. As the figure also shows, there is little opportunity to translate this work-based training into a recognized and portable credential. Very little of the training provided by private education offers recognized certificates or credentials. Workers with only this type of knowledge are largely unable to apply their occupational knowledge to a pathway leading to formal credentials. A notable exception is the registered apprenticeship system, which provides an important model (see, e.g., Lerman 2007, 2009).

By the second half of the 20th century, the two-year community college system emerged to provide both general education and vocational training needs beyond high school but short of the baccalaureate degree. As can be seen in Figure 2, the community college is the linchpin in the nation's postsecondary system. It is the only institution whose mission is explicitly directed toward serving all four areas of work-based knowledge. Little wonder that many have argued that the community college mission is too broad, and as a result these institutions struggle to perform their many functions well (Pusser and Levin 2009) with a funding formula that in some states is less than elementary schools per full-time-equivalent student (e.g., Murphy 2004).

A particular tension exists between the community college's *transfer* role, offering lower-division liberal arts courses to students who will move on to four-year schools to complete bachelor's degrees, and its *vocational* function, where it offers a variety of occupational certificates as well as associate of applied science (AAS) degrees. AAS degree curricula contain a core of technical credits in an occupational specialty (e.g., heating and air conditioning technician, electrician) as well as a number of general education courses geared to the occupation (e.g., applied math, business English), and the degree is considered a terminal degree. In many (but not all) cases, general education courses are not considered equivalent to those offered in the AA/AS curricula, and hence fewer than half of the credits awarded on an AAS degree transcript are considered "transferable" to baccalaureate degree institutions. However, earning an AA or AS degree at a community college is also no guarantee that all degree credits will be accepted in transfer at four-year institutions. In the absence of statewide transfer policies or negotiated articulation agreements, each degree-granting institution decides what credits it will accept from other institutions (see, e.g., Jones and Ewell 2009), which can result in a significant loss of credits.

At the higher end of the postsecondary system, the baccalaureate degree system is geared primarily to providing general knowledge. Although, as Figure 2 shows, it does have some links to firm or industry knowledge for some degree areas, these are relatively weak and provide little in the way of specific work-based knowledge except in those programs that combine internships or cooperative work experience with the curriculum. As Figure 2 also shows, by far the best-developed link in the system is between baccalaureate and graduate institutions where there are well-developed pathways to advance from bachelor's degree to graduate study. The link between graduate professional education and industry and firm knowledge is also quite robust, especially in some technical fields, such as pharmacy and engineering.

Overall, as Figure 2 shows, with the exception of bachelor's degree to graduate study, there are seldom well-developed pathways among these different types of education institutions and providers. Until very recently, most employer-sponsored training programs—even those that offer recognized certificates or credentials such as registered apprenticeships—have not been considered part of the formal postsecondary education system. Despite the fact that there is a well-developed methodology for assessing the college-credit equivalence for life and work experience and job training ranging from military training to registered apprenticeships to employer-sponsored training, many academic institutions refuse to accept this form of learning as part of an official transcript. Exacerbating this lack of alignment, training funded through the workforce development system has yet to develop the consistent measures of quality and credentialing that would allow for integration with postsecondary educational programming (Soares 2009).

Even within the formal higher education system, transferring credentials from two-year to four-year schools or between four-year schools has been subject to institutional policies that cause transfer students to lose many credits earned at other schools. A 2005 study by the Government Accountability Office found that 60% of students—2.5 million a year—transfer at least once before completing an undergraduate degree. On average, transferring requires the student to attend at least one additional semester and can add an additional year or more of study. The total "transfer tax" paid for this lack of portability of credits has been estimated to include $7 billion in additional costs to students for credits not applied to degree transcripts, $14 billion in state subsidies for instruction delivered but not counted, $5 billion in financial aid to cover credits taken and not counted, and $6 billion in delayed or reduced tax revenues because students take longer to complete their degrees (Smith 2010). In total, the transfer tax adds more than $30 billion in redundant costs to students, institutions, and governments for the 50% of students who actually complete degrees within eight years of starting. This figure does not include the costs associated with the 50% who do not finish. The Gates Foundation claims that fully half of all annual postsecondary education expenditures, including financial aid, go to people who never receive a certificate or a degree (Wallis 2008; also cited in Smith 2010).

Even if these calculations turn out to overestimate the cost, there is little doubt that modifying the postsecondary education and training system in ways that reduce the inefficiencies and inequities attached to transferring credits is crucial to making college possible for working learners. However, while improving the efficiency and effectiveness of the transfer system has the potential to dramatically improve working learners' access to postsecondary education and improve completion rates at a much lower total societal cost per credit hour, it will not automatically lead to the kinds of knowledge these workers need to succeed in the knowledge/information economy. Increasing the number of people with *both* college-level credentials *and* long-term sustainable employment with middle-class incomes requires preparing them with the kinds of knowledge and competencies that the knowledge economy demands.

Creating a 21st-Century Postsecondary Education for Knowledge-Based Work

The emerging knowledge economy creates both a major challenge and opportunity for postsecondary education. Knowledge-based work reduces the disparity between some academic and vocational competencies but introduces new ones. For example, the analytic, critical thinking, and problem-solving skills traditionally attributed to a liberal arts education are important to knowledge-based firms along with other foundational skills of the academic curriculum, including quantitative reasoning, writing, information literacy, and demonstrated mastery of a major subject. However, knowledge work also places a high premium on collaboration and the ability to apply such skills when working in teams on real problems—skills not taught in many undergraduate liberal arts majors. Figure 3 depicts modifications that would "connect the dots" in order to alter the postsecondary education system in ways that meet the workforce knowledge requirements of a knowledge-/information-based economy and the needs for working learners. The figure shows stronger integration both horizontally, between the various types of work-based knowledge, and vertically, between and among the education and training institutions. These changes reflect the significant difference between knowledge as a *means* to enable the mass production of goods and services and to produce highly specialized goods and services and knowledge as the *end* of the production process (Slaughter and Leslie 1997, Slaughter and Rhoades 2004). Knowledge work requires reversing Taylor's principles. Instead of viewing workers' knowledge and capacities for innovation and learning as an impediment to standardization, knowledge-based firms need to "harness" these capacities as the basis for competitive advantage (see, e.g., Jackson, Hitt, and DeNisi 2003; Smith 2010). The result is a very different workforce knowledge profile and a demand for increases in all four types of work-based knowledge among all types of employees.

Managing knowledge work for competitive advantage also requires major change in organizational structures and processes to enable workers to contribute their specialized knowledge and capacity for creating and innovating. This leads to a major reduction in the number of layers of managerial employees, "flattening" the organization hierarchy or shifting

FIGURE 3
Toward a 21st-Century Structure of Postsecondary Education.

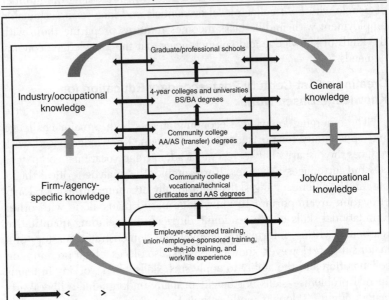

from a hierarchical structure to a more lateral or horizontal structure (for more in-depth discussions of these changes, see Piore and Sable 1984; Marshall and Tucker 1992; and Benson and Lawler, Chapter 4, this volume). Not all types of knowledge will be rewarded, however.

One feature of the mass-production paradigm persists and has become more prevalent in the knowledge economy: the substitution of machines or less-skilled (hence lower-paid) workers for higher-skilled labor. Levy and Murnane (2004) describe the effect of computers on "routine" (i.e., rule-based) tasks: "Computers excel at the rapid application of rules. A task that can be fully described by rules is a strong candidate for computer substitution" (p. 30). Rule-based tasks are not confined to the "low-skilled" end of the labor market. In fact, many so-called low-skilled occupations are among the least amenable to computer substitution. For example, Gatta, Boushey, and Appelbaum (2009) describe the complex face-to-face skills of interactive service occupations typically termed low-skilled that make them less susceptible to computerization or off-shoring. On the other hand, at the higher end of the labor market, Levy and Murnane (2004) describe how computers eliminated the jobs of "open-pit" bond traders and significantly reduced the salaries of their replacements, who now conduct their business from their offices. These authors argue that the knowledge economy will increasingly relegate routine (rule-based) tasks, at both the high and low ends of the labor market, to computers while investing in people to perform tasks that require "expert thinking" and "complex communication."

Expert thinking involves pattern recognition (often called intuition), which Levy and Murnane (2004) describe as information processing based on nonroutine CAO rules that are too complex to specify. A better definition might be this: inductive information processing based on CAO rules that must be inferred using complex perceptual processes in complex, cluttered information contexts (see Holland, Holyoak, Nisbett, and Thagard 1986). Expert thinking requires mastery of both declarative and procedural knowledge in a specialized area. Computers, thus far, lack the capabilities for such advanced inferential thinking and for physical tasks like changing bandages on nursing home patients, serving dinner at fine dining establishments, and performing heart transplants. Humans, on the other hand, have highly evolved inferential and physical capabilities that can be enhanced with education and experience and augmented by computers' capacity to perform routine tasks.

Complex communication refers to the ability to engage in expert thinking in the variety of new contexts contained in the knowledge-based workplace, such as multidisciplinary teams (both face-to-face and virtual), new forms of social media (like Facebook), and telecommuting. For example, Gittell (2009) describes the enhanced quality and efficiency outcomes obtained in health care organizations where patient care is organized to emphasize "relational coordination" so that the various specialized occupations work in teams to contribute their expertise. Gittell's research also highlights the fact that current educational programs in the various professional specialties—especially medicine—do not prepare practitioners to engage in such collaborative processes.

In summary, the emergence of the 21st-century knowledge and service economy has both elevated the education level needed for economic competitiveness to a postsecondary level and changed the mix of skills needed by workers to add value in the workplace.

"Connecting the dots" requires changes in postsecondary policy and practice at the federal, state, and institutional levels. Using several examples, we will highlight the policy issues and propose solutions. Our focus is primarily state and institutional levels, since many of the challenges outlined earlier are governed by these policies (Jones and Ewell 2009). Marshall and Plotkin (Chapter 12, this volume) propose federal policy changes that support those we present below.

Integrate Liberal Arts and Vocational/Professional Curricula

A growing number of colleges and universities now provide work-based learning opportunities, such as service learning, internships, and research and teaching assistantships, all of which add valuable applied experience to liberal arts curricula. For the most part, however, such experiences do not reflect broader integration of occupational/professional knowledge with traditional liberal education or vice versa. Here we want to highlight some new initiatives that seek to achieve a higher level of integration between the knowledge demands of work and the academic curriculum. We begin at the bottom of Figure 3 with the concept of linking work-based training to a college-degree pathway.

Connect Workforce Development and Job Training Programs to Degree Paths. As we have described, workforce development programs at their best deliver outcomes-based training, build partnerships, and provide support to help working learners navigate changes in the labor market. There is a well-established methodology for assessing the credit course equivalent of noncredit courses and experiential learning. The process can lead to the inclusion of more general learning outcomes in job training and work-based learning outcomes in college programs (see, e.g., Jones and Ewell 2009). Two examples illustrate the potential impact of expanding this process. The Washington State Community and Technical Colleges "Integrated Basic Education and Skills Training" (IBEST) program seeks to move low-income, nonnative English speakers quickly through a combination of English as a Second Language, intensive adult basic education, and skills training linked to occupation credentials (Washington State Board for Community and Technical Colleges 2005). Innovative models such as IBEST are an essential first step, helping working learners obtain a recognized credential. The next step is to connect such credentials to degree pathways. The New Jersey Pathways Leading Apprentices to a College Education program (NJ PLACE; http://www.njplace.com) is a the result of a statewide collaboration among all the major stakeholders to workforce development: New Jersey's 19 community colleges, employer associations, organized labor, the State Employment and Training Commission, and a number of registered apprenticeship programs. The goal of the program is to integrate apprenticeship courses offered by noncollegiate providers with general education offered by the community colleges to yield an AAS degree in technical studies that will be transferable to baccalaureate institutions. The experience of NJ PLACE reveals one of the major obstacles to creating a degree pathway for noncredit job training: the most widely accepted source of assessing the credit equivalence of noncredit courses—The American

Council on Education's College Credit Recommendation Service—is cost prohibitive for many providers. In New Jersey discussions are under way about the need to establish a state-based assessment service.

Define and Assess Learning Outcomes at Community Colleges. As noted earlier, community colleges are the key institutions for serving working learners. Through their vocational and technical programs, community colleges have always had close partnerships with employers in their service areas and have the capacity to adapt quickly to changes in the local labor market. Many community colleges have already created articulation agreements to award credits for employer or joint union–employer training programs as part of an AAS degree. The challenge for community colleges is to better integrate their general education (transfer) and technical missions. The following example illustrates both the possibilities and the challenges inherent in achieving such integration.

The Learning College project, initiated by the League for Innovation in the Community College in 2000 with 12 "vanguard" institutions, now involves a group of 72 institutions around the country committed to creating innovative instructional forms focused on learning outcomes and interdisciplinary learning. In particular, these colleges have created faculty, staff, and student communities aimed at transforming both general and occupational education by transforming instruction from "learner-centered"—which most community colleges have always been—to "learning-centered," with a focus on the *outcomes* of the educational process. The most significant of the many challenges that these colleges faced is also the most essential for "connecting the dots": defining, assessing, and documenting student outcomes. Evaluating the Learning College project, McClenney (2002, emphasis added) observes that, despite considerable experience with outcomes-based learning, most colleges had difficulty applying the process to all college courses, programs, and degrees—in particular, *"general education courses and critical across-the-curriculum skills (e.g,. writing, critical thinking, problem-solving, and the like) remain a considerable challenge."* McClenney found that few of the colleges were satisfied with their methods for assessing the acquisition of skills and knowledge identified in the outcomes statements, and none had created satisfactory models to document and transcript the learning outcomes. Developing a common approach to the definition, delivery, and assessment of required learning outcomes at the course, program, and degree levels is essential both for integrating occupational and general education and for reducing the inefficiencies and inequities in the transfer of credits discussed earlier.

Create a "Practical Liberal Education" at Baccalaureate Institutions. One promising example of integration at bachelor's-degree-granting institutions is the Liberal Education and America's Promise initiative (LEAP), where over 150 members of the Association of American Colleges and Universities are striving to integrate the elements of a liberal education across all collegiate disciplines, including career and professional disciplines (Association of American Colleges and Universities 2007). As one of its primary goals, LEAP seeks to "challenge the widespread belief that students must choose either a practical or a liberal education by building widespread support for educational changes that already are producing a new synthesis of practical and liberal education" (from the LEAP website). LEAP member colleges identify essential learning outcomes in four categories: knowledge of human cultures and the physical and natural world; intellectual and practical skills; personal and social responsibility; and integrative learning. LEAP colleges work with both employers and public schools to help college and college-bound students "understand, prepare for and achieve a challenging, public-spirited and practical liberal education" (Association of American Colleges and Universities 2007; from the LEAP website).

As is clear from the examples described, experimentation with integrating liberal and occupational/professional education is occurring along the continuum of postsecondary education providers. State and federal policy initiatives could increase both the pace and scale of these changes by grants supporting the following types of initiatives:

1. Support for faculty and staff to develop a common approach to the definition, delivery, and assessment of required learning outcomes at the course, program, and degree levels as well as to develop commonly accepted measures of the college equivalency of work-based learning.

2. Grants to create partnerships that align integrated curricula across postsecondary education providers. Colleges, universities, training providers, employers, and unions must be able to articulate areas of knowledge, skills, and attitudes that are being developed across their programs so that students and instructors can define an educational pathway. The federal Departments of Education and Labor could invest in these types of partnerships through regional skills initiatives that encourage standards and curriculum development in high-demand occupations.

Build New Connections Between Various Types of Postsecondary Education Providers

As noted through this chapter, working learners are mobile learners. For these learners, connecting the dots means facilitating the ability to earn college degrees by transferring credits among education providers. As outlined in the previous section, this cannot be accomplished on any large scale without a better alignment of standards among institutions. Since the majority of transfers occur within states, we concur with Jones and Ewell (2009) that the most effective policy interventions would encourage states to target their policy and resource leverage toward helping working learners obtain recognized and portable postsecondary credentials. Space limitations prohibit a comprehensive discussion, but the following recommendations are illustrative (for more detailed recommendations, see Jones and Ewell 2009 and Soares 2009).

Align Transfer Policies for Lower-Division General Education Courses Among All Colleges and Universities Receiving State Operating or Capital Assistance. Some states already have such policies in place while others, such as California, do not (Jones and Ewell 2009). New Jersey's statewide transfer policy applies to AA/AS degrees, but the legislation does not cover students who complete the general education credits equivalent to the AA degree at four-year schools that do not offer the associate's degree. After aligning outcomes and standards for lower-division courses, the two- and four-year schools will also need to align assessment mechanisms so that transfer students will be prepared to perform as well as students who enter four-year institutions directly. Properly implemented, such policies should lead to improved completion rates with fewer lost credits without negatively affecting four-year schools' ability to control the content and standards of their major baccalaureate programs of study.

Create a State-Based "Assessment Center." To capture the credits and/or learning that would help working learners earn formal credentials, there must be a system that coordinates the assessment of credits and provides information and guidance to all students and potential students, regardless of their current status. The optimal location of such a center would be statewide. Specific functions of such an assessment center might include these:

1. Assessing individuals' prior learning (PLA). Research indicates that students who can apply PLA credit in the most flexible way possible—for general education credits, major requirements, waiving course prerequisites, and obtaining advanced standing—have much higher graduation rates than students who lack this flexibility (Klein-Collins 2010). PLAs should be treated as transfer credits rather than as "recommendations," for which many colleges require students to pay tuition in order to receive the credit. To encourage institutions to offer more PLA credit and to expand the ways that such credits can be applied, states will need to establish a coordinated effort to ensure that common standards apply.

2. Assessing credit equivalence of noncredit courses. Assessing non-credit courses for credit equivalence is far more strategic and cost-effective than assessing individuals' prior learning. States should follow Ohio's lead (Jones and Ewell 2009) and establish clear guidelines for converting noncredit learning to credit that counts toward associate's or bachelor's degrees. State-based entities like the National Program on Noncollegiate Sponsored Instruction, based at the State University of New York, have the ability to assess training programs offered by noncollegiate postsecondary providers. States should also work together to ensure that these credits can be portable across state lines.

3. Providing guidance to students. Working learners need guidance as to the pathways they may have toward a credential or a degree. Currently such guidance is primarily available from advisors at the college or university where students are enrolled or where they are considering enrolling. These advisors may not have complete information or may be focused on competitive recruitment and therefore not be willing to provide full information. A state-based center can inform students about articulation agreements that easily enable students to transfer one set of college credits to another institution, and this center should also provide guidance on other options such as degree-completion institutions, competency-based institutions, and credit transfer services (see Soares 2010).

4. Expanding articulation agreements. To better serve student needs while ensuring institutional diversity, the United States needs a much more universal system of articulation agreements. Currently, the existence of articulation between institutions depends on the individual college or university, occasionally facilitated by a systemwide agreement. A more universal articulation system that is intentional rather than haphazard is essential to improving degree-completion rates among working learners. States should encourage the development of agreements systemwide between noncollegiate providers and two- and four-year public institutions as well as between four-year public institutions; these agreements should also extend, wherever possible, to private institutions.

Earn While You Learn

As we stated at the outset of this chapter, a very large group of U.S. workers needs—and wants—to combine work, family responsibilities, and lifelong learning. This poses a challenge to the design of the postsecondary education system at all levels. Those who do not start college right after high school and attend full-time while depending on their parents for income and support are considered "nontraditional" students by colleges and universities and do not fit into the traditional structure of college learning. Workers who have lost their jobs are considered "dislocated workers" in need of quick intervention by workforce training programs to get them new jobs. In combination, these two groups comprise around half of all college students. Serving these working learners requires a postsecondary education system that allows them to earn a living while continuing their education.

Community colleges are the ideal place to foster an "earn while you learn" system because data show that many working learners will either begin their journey in community college, gain a postsecondary credential there, or pass through on their way to more education (Berker and Horn 2003). For the most part, community colleges are still designed primarily to serve the needs of traditional students. In addition to many of the changes already discussed, earning while learning can be facilitated by such innovative practices as tightly defined course sequences, compressed class formats, consistent class schedules, competency-based educational advancement, coordinated support services between classes and work, and whole program registration (with students registering once rather than every semester).

Research indicates that these innovations at the institutional level make it more likely that a working learner will be successful at getting a degree or credential (Bosworth 2007). They modify community college practices in ways that support the learning style and work and life responsibilities of people who are needed wage earners in their families. Ivy Tech Community College of Indiana is pioneering these earn-while-you-learn innovations through its College for Working Adults (CWA), which enables working learners to obtain an associate's degree in under 24 months while working full-time (Ivy Tech Community College 2010).

Federal policy makers can support these types of innovations with targeted investments through competitive grant processes. For example, President Obama's 2011 budget includes a $321 million Workforce Innovation Fund that redirects current budget dollars from the Departments of Education and Labor into a co-managed, competitive grant program to support and test new ways to deliver workforce training programs that yield postsecondary credentials through earn-while-you-learn models. The Center for American Progress (Soares 2010) recommends that 50% of this fund be directed toward community college partnerships with business, unions, and nonprofit organizations that use apprenticeship and career pathways programs linked to regional economic growth initiatives to help working learners complete associate degrees. Such an investment could be significantly expanded by adding lifelong learning accounts to Section 529 of the Internal Revenue Code and allowing contributions from individuals, employers, and the state. In addition, federal financial aid policies are currently geared to completing the bachelor's degree in four years, which pushes working learners toward full-time study and consequent failure because they do not have sufficient time to complete the coursework. Fewer and fewer students— even among the traditional age group—complete in four years, and the standard for completion by which institutions and individuals are measured should be increased from six to eight years.

Conclusion

President Obama has proposed an ambitious agenda aimed at restoring U.S. leadership in postsecondary educational attainment. This will require changes to postsecondary education practice and policies that will make it possible for working learners to persist and succeed in postsecondary education. The great strength of higher education in the United States is that individuals and families view it as an investment. Unlike many countries in the world, it is "normal" for Americans to go back to school multiple times to retrain or pursue additional credentials. Connecting the dots between academic and occupational curricula within postsecondary institutions and making better connections among the various institutions will make it possible for many more people to do so. Making these changes is essential to a national workforce development strategy that will ensure that the knowledge economy not only produces the kind of broadly shared prosperity as the mass-production economy but also restores to American workers the opportunity to develop their capacity for learning, creativity, and innovation.

Endnotes

[1] Bound, Lovenheim, and Turner (2009) define completion rates as the proportion of students who attend college within two years of high school graduation and obtain a BA within eight years of high school graduation. Student ability is measured by senior-year scores on the National Assessment of Educational Progress.

[2] Remarks by the president on the American Graduation Initiative at Macomb Community College, July 14, 2009. <http://www.whitehouse.gov/the_press_office/Remarks-by-the-President-on-the-American-Graduation-Initiative-in-Warren-MI>. [March 15, 2010].

[3] Not everyone agrees that the focus on increasing credentials is the right policy (e.g., Mishel and Rothstein 2007). These critics argue that there are more skilled workers than demand for their skills and that the solution lies in labor policy, not education policy. However, employment data from February 2010 (Bureau of Labor Statistics 2010) showed that despite the overall loss of seven million jobs, there was strong job growth in three sectors: educational services, health care, and social

assistance. All but one of the growing occupations had average incomes above the national average ($42,270), and most of the higher-income jobs required at least some college. These data suggest that adjusting to the knowledge/information economy will require changes in both labor and education policy.

References

Anderson, J.R. 1976. *Language, Memory and Thought*. Hillsdale, NJ: Erlbaum.

Association of American Colleges and Universities. 2007. *Liberal Education and America's Promise (LEAP)*. <http://www.aacu.org/leap/goals.cfm>. [May 15, 2010].

Berker, Ali, and Laura Horn. 2003. *Work First, Study Second: Adult Undergraduates Who Combine Employment and Postsecondary Enrollment*. Washington, DC: National Center for Education Statistics. <http://nces.ed.gov/pubsearch/pubsinfo.asp?pubid=2003167>. [April 20, 2010].

Bosworth, Brian. 2007. *Lifelong Learning: New Strategies for the Education of Working Adults*. Washington, DC: Center for American Progress.

Bound, John, Michael Lovenheim, and Sarah Turner. 2009. *Why Have College Completion Rates Declined? An Analysis of Changing Student Preparation and Collegiate Resources*. Working Paper 15566. Cambridge, MA: National Bureau of Economic Research. <http://www.nber.org/papers/w15566>. [January 15, 2010].

Bureau of Labor Statistics. 2010. *Current Employment Statistics—February 2010*. <http://www.bls.gov/ces>. [April 5, 2010].

Carey, Kevin. 2005. *One Step from the Finish Line: Higher College Graduation Rates Are Within Our Grasp*. Washington, DC: Education Trust. <http://www.edtrust.org/sites/edtrust.org/files/publications/files/one_step_from.pdf>. [October 15, 2009].

Cremin, L. 1988. *American Education: The Metropolitan Experience 1876–1980*. New York: Harper and Row.

Eisman, S. 2010. *Subprime Goes to College*. Speech to Ira Sohn Conference. <http://www.insidehighered.com/news/2010/05/27/qt#228602>. [May 27, 2010].

Ferman, L., M. Hoyman, J. Cutcher-Gershenfeld, and E. Savoi, eds. 1991. *New Developments in Worker Training: A Legacy for the 1990s*. Madison, WI: Industrial Relations Research Association.

Field, John. 2006. *Lifelong Learning and the New Educational Order*. Staffordshire, UK: Trentham Books.

Fischer, G. 2000. "Lifelong Learning: More Than Training." *Journal of Interactive Learning Research*, Vol. 11, no. 3/4, pp. 265–94.

Freeman, R.B. 1978. *The Overeducated American*. New York: Academic Press.

Furchgott-Roth, D., L. Jacobson, and C. Mokher. 2009. *Strengthening Community Colleges' Influence on Economic Mobility*. <http://www.economicmobility.org/reports_and_research/other/other?id=0010>. [January 5, 2010].

Gatta, M., H. Boushey, and E. Appelbaum. 2009. "High Touch and Here to Stay: Future Skills Demands in US Low Wage Service Occupations." *Sociology*, Vol. 43, no. 5, pp. 968–89.

Gittel, J.H. 2009. *High Performance Health Care: Using the Power of Relationships to Achieve Quality, Efficiency and Resilience*. New York: McGraw-Hill.

Government Accountability Office. 2005. *Transfer Students: Postsecondary Institutions Could Promote More Consistent Consideration of Coursework by Not Basing Determinations on Accreditation*. <http://www.gao.gov/new.items/d0622.pdf>. [March 15, 2010].

Government Accountability Office. 2009. *Proprietary Schools: Stronger Department of Education Oversight Needed to Help Ensure Only Eligible Students Receive Financial Aid.* <http://www.gao.gov/new.items/d09600.pdf>. [May 1, 2010].

Haskins, R., H. Holzer, and R. Lerman. 2009. *Promoting Economic Mobility by Increasing Postsecondary Education.* <http://www.economicmobility.org/assets/pdfs/PEW_EMP_POSTSECONDARY_ED.pdf>. [January 3, 2010].

Holzer, H., and R. Lerman. 2007. *America's Forgotten Middle Skills Jobs: Education and Training Requirements in the Next Decade and Beyond.* Washington, DC: Workforce Alliance.

Holland, J., K. Holyoak, R. Nisbett, and P. Thagard. 1986. *Induction: Process of Inference, Learning, and Discovery.* Cambridge, MA: MIT Press.

Ivy Tech Community College. 2010. <http://www.ivytech.edu/cwa>. [April 25, 2010].

Jackson, S., M. Hitt, and A. DeNisi, eds., 2003. *Managing Knowledge for Sustained Competitive Advantage: Designing Strategies for Effective Human Resource Management.* San Francisco: Jossey-Bass.

Jones, D., and P. Ewell. 2009. *Using College Access and Completion Funds to Improve Postsecondary Attainment in California.* Boulder, CO: National Center on Higher Education Management Systems. <http://www.nchems.org/pubs/docs/Utilizing%20College%20Completion%20Program%20Funds.pdf>. [March 16, 2010].

Klein-Collins, R. 2010. *Fueling the Race to Postsecondary Success: A 48-Institution Study of Prior Learning Assessment and Adult Student Outcomes.* Chicago: Council for Adult and Experiential Learning.

Lepak, D., and S. Snell. 2003. "Managing the Human Resource Architecture for Knowledge-Based Competition." In S. Jackson, M. Hitt, and A. DeNisi, eds., *Managing Knowledge for Sustained Competitive Advantage: Designing Strategies for Effective Human Resource Management.* San Francisco: Jossey-Bass, pp. 127–54.

Lerman, R. 2007. "Career-focused Education and Training for Youth." In H. Holzer and D. Nightingale, eds., *Reshaping the American Workforce in a Changing Economy.* Washington, DC: Urban Institute Press, pp. 41–90.

Lerman, R. 2009. *Training Tomorrow's Workforce: Community College and Apprenticeship as Collaborative Routes to Rewarding Careers.* Washington, DC: Center for American Progress.

Levy, F., and R. Murnane. 2004. *The New Division of Labor: How Computers Are Creating the Next Job Market.* Princeton, NJ: Princeton University Press.

Marshall, R., and M. Tucker. 1992. *Thinking for a Living: Education and the Wealth of Nations.* New York: Basic Books.

McClenney, A. 2002. *Learning from the Learning Colleges: Lessons from the Journey.* Phoenix: League for Innovation in the Community College. <http://www.league.org/league/projects/lcp/lessons_learned.htm>. [April 15, 2010].

Mishel, L., and R. Rothstein. 2007. *Response to Marc Tucker.* Washington, DC: Economic Policy Institute. <http://www.epi.org/publications/entry/responsetotucker>. [January 5, 2010].

Morris, S., S.A. Snell, and D. Lepak. 2005. *An Architectural Approach to Managing Knowledge Stocks and Flows: Implications for Reinventing the HR Function.* CAHRS Working paper #05-15. Ithaca, NY: Cornell University School of Labor and Industrial Relations, Center for Advanced Human Resource Studies. <http://digitalcommons.ilr.cornell.edu/cahrswp/283>. [May 4, 2010].

Murphy, Patrick. 2004. *Financing California's Community Colleges*. San Francisco: Public Policy Institute of California. <http://www.ppic.org/content/pubs/report/R_104PMR.pdf>. [May 27, 2010].

Organisation for Economic Co-operation and Development. 2007. *Education at a Glance 2007*. <http://www.oecd.org/dataoecd/4/55/39313286.pdf>. [January 4, 2010].

Piore, M.J., and C.F. Sabel. 1984. *The Second Industrial Divide: Possibilities for Prosperity*. New York: Basic Books.

Pusser, B., and J. Levin. 2009. *Re-imagining Community College for the 21st Century: A Student-Centered Approach to Higher Education*. Washington, DC: Center for American Progress. <http://www.americanprogress.org/issues/2009/12/reimagining_community_colleges.html>. [April 20, 2010].

Slaughter, S., and L. Leslie. 1997. *Academic Capitalism: Politics, Policies, and the Entrepreneurial University*. Baltimore, MD: Johns Hopkins University Press.

Slaughter, S., and G. Rhoades. 2004. *Academic Capitalism and the New Economy: Markets, State and Higher Education*. Baltimore, MD: Johns Hopkins University Press.

Smith, P. 2010. *Harnessing America's Wasted Talent: A New Ecology of Learning*. San Francisco: Jossey-Bass.

Soares, L. 2009. *Working Learners*. Washington, DC: Center for American Progress.

Soares, L. 2010. *Community College 2.0*. Washington, DC: Center for American Progress.

Soares, L., and C. Mazzeo. 2008. *College-Ready Students, Student-Ready Colleges: An Agenda for Improving Degree Completion in Postsecondary Education*. Washington, DC: Center for American Progress.

Taylor, F.W. 1911. *Principles of Scientific Management*. New York and London: Harper.

Turner, S. 2007. "Higher Education Policies Generating the 21st Century Workforce." In H. Holzer and D. Nightingale, eds. *Reshaping the American Workforce in a Changing Economy*. Washington, DC: Urban Institute Press, pp. 91–116.

Tyack, D. 1974. *The One Best System: A History of American Urban Education*. Cambridge, MA: Harvard University Press.

Wallis, C. 2008. "Bill and Melinda Gates Go Back to School." *Fortune*, November 26. <http://money.cnn.com/2008/11/25/magazines/fortune/GatesFoundation_Wallis.fortune/index.htm>. [May 15, 2010].

Washington State Board for Community and Technical Colleges. 2005. *Integrated Basic Education and Skills Training (IBEST): Program Guidelines and Planning Process*. Olympia, WA: Washington State Board for Community and Technical Colleges. <http://www.highereducation.org/reports/Policy_Practice/IBEST.pdf>. [May 15, 2010].

CHAPTER 7

Employer-Led Training: Extensive and Intensive Approaches

ROBERT I. LERMAN
American University

Skills are central to achieving robust economic growth and to reducing economic inequality. When assessing these relationships, researchers usually focus on a narrow range of skill indicators that are easily measured, such as years of schooling completed and test scores. Some of these indicators have been closely linked to economic growth and to the distribution of earnings. In one study, for example, Hanushek and Woessmann (2009) find that variations in math and science test scores across countries have a substantial association with variations in economic growth, but years of schooling have no significant association, once test scores are taken into account. Researchers analyzing inequality generally emphasize the increasingly positive association between years of schooling and earnings, often highlighting the rising earnings gap between college graduates and high school graduates (for example, Goldin and Katz 2008).

Despite the extensive literature linking worker skills to economic growth, few studies measure skills in a comprehensive manner or examine how skills generate the added productivity and economic rewards associated with human capital. Rarely do studies describe exactly how added years of schooling and/or test scores translate into more productive workers who are able to increase value. To perform valuable tasks in the workplace, workers have to become knowledgeable and proficient with the tools and technologies of their occupations and be able to work with other people in their organizations. Several competencies are required to do so. General academic competencies are necessary but often insufficient. Workers typically require occupational skills as well as communication, problem-solving, and teamwork skills. Often they need skills specific to the firm to achieve high productivity.

Schooling, job training, and work experience help workers attain these skills. Vastly more resources are spent in the education sector than

153

on job training. In the United States, expenditures on all levels of education reached nearly $1.1 trillion in 2009 (National Center for Education Statistics 2009; see Table 27), while annual public spending on job training is less than $10 billion (Mikelson and Nightingale 2004).

Government spending on job training in the United States is relatively low in comparison to other countries in the Organisation for Economic Co-operation and Development (OECD). As of 2000, government dollars for training as a percentage of GDP was only 0.04% in the United States, compared with 0.28% in France, 0.34% in Germany, and 0.30% in the Netherlands (O'Leary, Straits, and Wandner 2004). Of course, spending by private (and public) employers on job training may narrow these differentials. Japan, a country with a strong emphasis on training, spends only 0.03% of GDP when one includes only government training dollars. Another comparative study of participation in employer-led training indicates that the United States had participation rates in training above those in Switzerland, the Netherlands, and Canada (Leuven and Oosterbeek 1999). On the other hand, intensity was lowest in the United States.

Employer-led training, both formal and informal, helps workers achieve a variety of skills. High-level worker training such as formal apprenticeships helps firms as well, partly by allowing them to delegate authority to a well-trained workforce. Between the late 1940s and the late 1990s, job training programs among U.S. employers proliferated, rising from less than 20% to more than 70% of organizations (Yang 2006). Although a body of research has documented high returns to workers and employers from employer-led training (Bartel 1995, 2000; Bishop 1997; Parent 2000; Organisation for Economic Co-operation and Development 2004), the data on employer-led training are limited, and the findings have attracted little interest from policy makers.

The nation spends about $400 billion on postsecondary education, some of which goes toward career-oriented coursework. At the same time, the size of employer-led training investments is highly uncertain because of the paucity of reliable data based on well-structured samples. According to a 1990 study by the Congressional Office of Technology Assessment, "human resource practices in most American firms place a low value on training" (U.S. Congress 1990:13). The study suggests that large firms that might be expected to offer training choose instead to use extensive screening and above-average wages to attract skilled workers. Small firms are said to use training provided by the equipment vendor to help workers adjust to new technologies.

Still, evidence from a variety of available data sources shows that considerable employer-led training takes place in the United States, though often in very short spurts. According to survey data published by the American Society for Training and Development (2009) based on voluntary participation of larger firms, the scale of employer-led training was about $130 billion per year and about 2.4% of payroll for the years 2007 to 2009. Unfortunately, the federal government no longer collects data from employers on their training activities. The last nationally representative *employer* survey providing data on the incidence and intensity of formal employer-led training took place in 1997, over 13 years ago (Lerman, McKernan, and Riegg 2004).

An extensive body of research documents the high economic returns to workers resulting from employer-led training (Bishop 1997). Training benefits not only workers and firms, but other external parties as well. Bishop highlights several external benefits, including gains for subsequent employers and for the public in avoidance of disasters as well as network externalities (as more are training in a common means of communication). Moreover, the government generally gains by paying little for the training while reaping tax benefits from the increased earnings of workers.

Given the high returns to workers and firms as well as the external benefits, it is puzzling that policy makers do not place a high priority on determining the size and effects of employer-led training.[1] Spending on employer-led training is much higher than outlays on government training programs, yet far more research and policy attention has been directed toward government programs. One reason may be that governments in the United States have little influence on training efforts by private firms. Another may be that the public role in preparing workers for skilled careers is assumed to fall under the authority of the school system and postsecondary education institutions. A third reason is that employer-led training is difficult to measure.

Despite the absence of nationally representative data drawn from employers, this chapter reviews recent trends and patterns of employer-led training on the basis of data drawn from nationally representative surveys of workers. I begin with a brief look at why employers might train their workers, especially with skills that can be productive elsewhere, then go on to consider prior research on the incidence of employer-led training. The next sections examine new evidence concerning the types of workers who participate in and do not participate in formal training, the intensity and duration of training, and whether employer-led training has been increasing or decreasing. I pay close attention to one distinctive form of employer-led training—apprenticeship training. Although apprenticeships cover a very small share of all workers, they involve intensive, long-term, and economically rewarding employer-led training; I present evidence of the effectiveness of apprenticeship training from the employer and worker perspectives. In the final section I discuss policy implications and recommendations for enhancing the role of employer-led training in expanding the skills and earnings of American workers.

Why Should Employers Fund Training?

Nearly all discussions of training begin with the work on human capital put forward by Mincer (1958) and Becker (1964). In considering the incentives for workers and firms to pay for training, Becker distinguishes between general training (defined as training that enhances skills that are valuable outside the firm) and specific training (training that adds to the worker's productivity within but not outside the firm). According to Becker's theory, firms have no incentive to finance general training. Since the added productivity makes the worker more valuable both inside and outside the firm, firms financing the training will be unable to recoup their investment by paying the newly trained worker a wage less than his or her newly enhanced level of productivity. If firms tried to pay the worker less, as a way of recouping some part of their investment, competitors would hire the worker or bid up the trained worker's wage to the new productivity level.

This theoretical argument notwithstanding, researchers have found a large body of evidence that employers offer and pay for general training. One possibility is that employers pay more for training but less for workers, as workers receiving training accept a lower-than-normal wage in return for the compensating benefit of training. However, most of the empirical evidence rejects this implication—trainees show little wage sacrifice when obtaining general training. Acemoglu and Pischke (1999) show that imperfect information and other market imperfections can allow employers to pay trained workers less than the gain in their productivity without losing them to other firms. One reason is that the employers providing the training are in a better position to judge the worker's productivity than are outside employers. An employer knows only a modest amount about workers when they enter the firm. One way of learning more is to observe how they learn, especially on the job. Another possibility is that general skills complement specific skills. As a result, increasing general skills raises workers' ability to use their specific skills.

Still another rationale comes from Cappelli (2004), who argues that imperfect information might be a reason to offer tuition benefits. It is difficult to sort workers whose qualifications are similar on paper. But when tuition benefits are offered, the applicants with more interest in learning relative to other applicants with the same paper qualifications are more likely to apply and use the general training. These workers may have more motivation and an unmeasured skills advantage. Cappelli (2004) finds evidence to support the notion that workers who take up tuition benefits are more effective than other workers with the same observed characteristics.

Other studies highlight the impacts of organizational attributes and strategies on worker training. For example, the incentive to train should be higher for those organizations that have to delegate decision making, that are large and have high monitoring costs, and that promote from within instead of hiring from the labor market for high-level positions. Knoke and Kalleberg (1994) find that organizations that are large, promote from within, and have formalized job structures provide more worker training. Osterman (1995) shows that organizations make trade-offs between training existing workers and hiring workers with previously developed skills and that organizations train more when they use flat hierarchies, worker involvement, and teamwork and devolve decision making to the line level. Surprisingly, his estimates reveal no increase in training related to job ladders.

How Much Employer-Led Training Takes Place in the United States?

Companies engage in training for a variety of purposes. Nearly all employers provide new workers with an orientation and training about safety, company procedures, compensation policies, and other procedures. Another common form of employer-led training takes place when organizations implement new technologies or change their organizational structure. A recent story highlights the six-week training program that the United Parcel Service (UPS) provides to its drivers (Levitz 2010). Many companies go well beyond these measures and offer in-depth training that can substantially improve career outcomes. This includes registered apprenticeships, other long-term occupational training that involves certification, special courses at work sites, and tuition support for degree or nondegree programs. With the aging of the population and the retirement of a large number of experienced, skilled workers, the demand for effective training is likely to increase substantially over the next decades. On the other hand, major employers that used to rely on internal labor markets and complementary training are said to have less interest in the long-term relationships with workers that would justify heavy investments in training.

National Data Sources on Employer-Led Training

Several nationally representative data sets are available to document employer-led training in the 1990s, including two employer-based surveys (Lerman, McKernan, and Riegg 2004). The 1997 National Employer Survey (NES), administered by the U.S. Bureau of the Census, involved telephone interviews with 3,000 establishments representing more than 5,400 private establishments with 20 or more employees. The 1995 Survey of Employer-Provided Training (SEPT) collected information about formal and informal training from about 1,000 private establishments with 50 or more employees. The SEPT is distinctive in that it includes interviews with about 1,000 employees at these establishments. SEPT also collected information about a broad measure of informal training. Neither of these employer surveys has been repeated since 1997.

Other nationally representative data on employer-led training come from household surveys. These include the National Household Education Survey (NHES), the Survey of Income and Program Participation (SIPP), and the National Assessment of Adult Literacy (NAAL). The adult education components of the NHES surveys involve interviews with about 20,000 adults who are 16 and over and not enrolled in elementary or secondary school. Although NHES focuses on education and training courses, it covers employer-provided instruction as well as employer-supported training. NHES data are available for 1995, 1999, and 2005. The SIPP, a longitudinal national survey of about 36,000 households per panel, collects data mostly on employment, incomes, assets, and program participation. In addition, the SIPP includes topical modules on a variety of topics, including information on work-related training that helps persons search for or be trained in a new job and/or helps workers improve their skills in their current jobs. The main NAAL surveys nearly 18,000 adults 16 and over to determine the prose, document, and quantitative literacy of American adults. It also includes information on an array of personal characteristics, including educational background, labor force participation, and job training and skills.

Various other data sets have been used to examine training for subgroups of individuals. These include the National Longitudinal Survey of Youth (NLSY, especially the 1979 panel), the 1982 Employment Opportunity Pilot Project survey (EOPP), and the 1993 National Assessment of Vocational Education (NAVE).[2] In addition to reviewing reported training estimates from other studies, this chapter offers a set of new tabulations based on three years of SIPP data (the 1996, 2001, and 2004 panels), two years of NHES data (1999 and 2005 surveys), and the 2003 NAAL. These data sets offer a profile of workers who may or may not receive employer-led training.

The surveys vary in terms of coverage. Some do not include informal training, while others provide little data on employer support to workers for credit courses that may or may not be related to their current jobs. Rarely do the surveys offer information on the role of training in adapting to new technologies or firm reorganization operations, though these are major rationales for company-provided training.

One of the most intensive forms of employer-led training is apprenticeship training. While national data sets rarely have sufficient cases to investigate this form of training, over 25,000 employers or union–employer programs offer apprenticeship training to at least 480,000 workers in the registered apprenticeship system and probably a similar number in unregistered programs (Lerman, Eyster, and Chambers 2009). Although nearly 1 million apprentices constitute a small share of the workforce of about 140 million and each year's completers represent less than 10% of an age cohort, this training is quite intensive and of long duration. I draw here on a survey of apprenticeship sponsors to shed light on this type of training.

Indicators of the Employer-Led Training Based on Selected Studies

Employers generally offer some training, especially for new employees. About 93% of establishments with 50 or more workers provided formal training in 1994 (Lerman, McKernan, and Riegg 2004). Although the rate is lower for smaller establishments, 72% of those with 20 or more workers offer formal training. An even higher share (97%) provide some form of informal training. Much of the training is orientation and safety training that takes place when workers start their jobs. One survey indicated that over 90% of recently hired workers receive at least some on-the-job training (Barron, Berger, and Black 1999). Employers reported in 1992 that their most recent hire averaged 19 hours of formal training, 59 hours of informal training by managers, 34 hours of informal training by co-workers, and 41 hours of informal training by watching others (Bishop 1997). Although training for new hires may have declined since 1992, these results highlight the importance of informal training.

Between the 1980s and mid-1990s, surveys of employer-led training show gradual increases in the incidence of employer-led training. For example, the percentage of workers reporting receiving training in the SIPP rose from about 6% in 1984 to about 20% in 1996. Using a common definition for training, the incidence of training in the NHES increased from 19% to 27%. Training incidence as measured by the

NHES was consistently higher than that in the SIPP. However, the highest figure comes from the SEPT, where 70% of workers in establishments with 50 or more workers reported receiving training. Although the incidence of training appeared substantially higher in the SEPT than in other data sets, the SEPT recorded mean hours of training per worker that were much lower than in the NHES, though about the same as in the SIPP (Lerman, McKernan, and Riegg 2004).

For all data sets, the incidence of training was lowest for the least educated workers and highest for workers with a BA degree or more. But in the case of the NHES, workers with some college but no BA degree averaged 56 hours of training in the prior six months, compared to only 34 hours for college graduates.

The most common form of employer-provided training involves occupational safety training. Employer surveys (NES and SEPT) report about 70% of workers obtaining this form of training, much of which is specific to the firm. At the same time, only a small share of firms provide basic skills training. Lynch and Black (1998) find that about 75% of employers provide specific training but only 25% offer remedial skills training.

While some have argued that U.S. firms place a low value on training, the incidence of training is not particularly low among American workers. Using data from the 1994–95 International Adult Literacy Survey (IALS), Kletzer and Koch (2004) report that the incidence of career- or job-related training among 25- to 54-year-old workers is 49% in the United States, 38% in Canada, 20% in Germany, and 58% in the United Kingdom. In terms of career- or job-related training with some indication of employer support, the United States ranks second out of 11 OECD countries. Only the United Kingdom showed a higher proportion.

These figures take no account of the variations in employer training for the under-25 workforce. Certainly, Germany's dual system of workplace and school-based training for youth is far more extensive and lengthy than any comparable training in the United States. Although few U.S. firms offer anything comparable to the intensity and duration of German apprenticeship programs, a strikingly high share of employers do offer tuition assistance for postsecondary courses. Employers interviewed in the 1997 NES were asked if they reimburse the cost of tuition for an approved course. Over 80% reported doing so for managers, supervisors, and administrators; in 69% of firms, tuition subsidies were available for front-line workers. Although only a minority of workers use tuition subsidies in a given year, 53% of adults enrolled in postsecondary degree programs received employer support from a tuition subsidy or paid leave (Lerman, McKernan, and Riegg 2004).

The ASTD surveys capture the extent of training in large firms (American Society for Training and Development 2009). As of 2008, the 301 firms providing data on their training expenditures averaged over 15,000 workers per firm, and their payrolls accounted for just below 10% of the private sector wage and salary outlays. Although these data are not even necessarily representative of large firms, since the results come from a voluntary sample, their training patterns are still of interest. Spending on training for these firms consistently exceeds 2% of payroll; as a share of profits, spending has ranged from 12.5% in 2003 to 6.9% in 2006. Learning hours per employee have increased a good deal from the 25.5 figure in 2003 to over 36 in 2008. While workers on average use about 36 hours for training, the amount of hours of training opportunities available is about ten times higher. These options include hours available for employees through such mechanisms as live classes, workshops, seminars, online courses, and video and print materials. Spending on tuition reimbursement has remained fairly steady, at about 12% of all training expenditures.

Recent Patterns of Employer-Led Training Among Adult Workers

To update the information on employer-led training for all adult workers, I tabulated data drawn from the 1996, 2001, and 2004 SIPP panels, the 2003 NAAL, and the 1999 and 2004–05 NHES. The recent data yield information on formal training but do not capture the extensive informal training documented in other studies (Bishop 1997). The surveys differ somewhat between surveys, though it is not clear why these differences should account for differences in the trends. The SIPP questions ask respondents two questions, one dealing with whether they have received training to look for a new job and the other whether they have received training to improve skills in the job they already have. The wording changed slightly between 2001 and 2004 in the SIPP. In addition, the SIPP asks a general question about training experiences in the last ten years.

The main NHES questions ask about any work-related course, apprenticeship program, or vocational degree/diploma program taken in the prior 12 months. Unlike the SIPP, the NHES survey instrument reminds workers by mentioning "work or career-related courses, seminars, training, or workshops whether or not you had a job when you took them." By far the most frequent participation was work-related courses, which involved 40% of all full-time workers in the 2004–05 survey. Employers provided financial support for nearly all of these courses, including tuition and materials (86% of cases), worker salaries during the training (81%), and programs offered at workplaces.

The NAAL survey questions are these: "During the past year, did you participate in any training or education, including courses, workshops, formal on-the-job training or apprenticeships to: A. Help you do your job better? B. Help you get a promotion? C. [Asked only of those not employed the past year] Help you get a job?" One might think that the NAAL questions would yield less training frequencies among workers than the SIPP, since the SIPP asks workers about training for a new job. However, the NAAL also might jog the memory of workers by mentioning the list of possible training outlets. The SIPP data include much larger samples than the NHES and the NAAL. However, the SIPP questions on training do not include examples, as do the other surveys. In any event, the NAAL responses are substantially higher than even the NHES figures.

As shown in Table 1, both the levels and trends in the incidence of training (within a one-year period) vary by data set. The differences are striking. According to the SIPP, the share of 25- to 64-year-old workers receiving employer-led training in the prior 12 months fell sharply, from

TABLE 1

Incidence of Training (in Percentages) in the Prior 12 Months of Employed 25- to 64-Year-Olds, by Survey, Year, Sex, and Education.

	Survey of Income and Program Participation			National Assessment of Adult Literacy	National Household Education Survey	
	1996	2001	2004	2003	1999	2005
Total	32.8	27.9	21.8	56.9	31.0	42.4
Male	30.4	25.3	19.7	53.6	29.4	31.8
Female	35.7	31.0	24.2	60.6	32.8	46.0
Males by education group						
Less than high school	10.1	6.9	4.8	20.0	7.2	5.8
High school graduate	20.7	15.4	11.3	40.8	20.6	18.7
Some college	34.8	27.1	22.9	60.2	29.5	36.1
Bachelor's degree	41.8	35.5	26.5	70.6	42.7	50.3
Females by education group						
Less than high school	11.2	9.3	5.7	28.2	7.3	8.4
High school graduate	26.0	19.9	14.7	47.7	22.3	31.5
Some college	35.7	26.2	24.5	64.2	34.3	49.6
Bachelor's degree	46.8	42.3	31.5	76.6	47.3	65.1

Source: Tabulations by author from the Education and Training History Modules of the 1996, 2001, and 2004 panels of the Survey of Income and Program Participation, from the National Assessment of Adult Literacy, and from the National Household Education Survey.

33% in 1996 to 28% in 2001 to 22% by 2004. On the other hand, data from the NHES show upward trends in the share of workers receiving training, from 31% in 1999 to 42% in 2005. The NHES figure for 1999 falls between the 1996 and 2001 SIPP percentages. However, the 2004 SIPP indicates a sharp decrease in training, while the 2005 NHES shows a substantial increase. Further complicating the picture is an overall figure of 56.9% observed in the 2003 NAAL.

The reasons for these patterns are unclear. Although the survey instruments and the sample sizes vary, all three data sets are nationally representative of the workforce. Given the differences in estimates, it is difficult to provide a definitive figure for the share of workers engaged in any formal training over the prior year. The SIPP figures are low and decreasing. The NHES estimates show increases, and the NAAL indicates that well over half of all workers take part in some employment-related training, financed mainly by employers.

Types of Trainee and Training

While the magnitude of training differs across surveys, the patterns of training are qualitatively similar. In all the surveys, women workers receive training at slightly higher rates than men (Table 1). The largest differential is in the 2005 NHES, where the gap is about 14 percentage points, with the incidence of training at 46% for women and 32% for men. The 1999 NHES showed a female–male gap of only about 3 percentage points (32.8 vs. 29.4), which is in the same range as the other surveys.

Educational differences show up largely as expected. All the data sets show much lower rates of participation in job training among the lowest educated groups. According to the recent SIPP and NHES surveys, less than 10% of high school dropouts participated in any training. By contrast, in the NAAL, 28% of those with less than a high school degree reported participating in some training. Training is markedly higher for high school graduates, especially in the NHES and NAAL and among women. Note that in 2004, 32% of female high-school-graduate workers participated in training, as compared to 19% of similarly educated men. Workers with some college, both male and female, see significantly higher levels of training in all the data sets. Rates of training are much higher for college graduates than for other groups. However, the gap between the NAAL and the SIPP is largest in this category, with the NAAL showing about 71% of male workers with a college education participating in some training, a figure over 40 percentage points higher than is reported in the SIPP. In addition, the proportion of college graduates receiving training in the last 12 months dropped dramatically between 1996 and 2004, according to the SIPP.

Companies might prefer to upgrade those with weaker skills or to give preference to trainees with a solid set of prose and math literacy skills. In the NAAL, data are available on literacy levels linked to data on training, but the literacy tests are applied after individuals experience the training. Thus, while higher test scores among trainees than non-trainees probably means that employers are more likely to train more skilled workers, it might mean that training increases test scores. The NAAL does indeed reveal about 11% higher literacy levels for workers receiving training than for other workers at the same level of formal education. Among individuals who did not complete high school, those who received training have mean skill levels that were 13% higher than those not receiving training. At higher levels of education, differences in literacy levels between trainees and others were only about 6% to 8%.

The occupational patterns are similar across data sets, with managers and professionals receiving training at a substantially higher rate than among other broad occupations. Sales workers and those in office and administrative support are the groups next most likely to receive training. Workers in construction, installation, and production are least likely to have received any training in the prior year. The gaps across surveys are quite large in all occupational categories but are largest by far among managers and professionals. While only 20% of managers and professionals report receiving training in the 2004 SIPP, the incidence of training for these two occupational categories reached 43% in the 2005 NHES and 58% in the NAAL.

Training levels vary surprisingly little by age through age 55. In the 2004 NHES, for example, 38% of 45- to 54-year-olds participated in work-related courses or apprenticeship, just above the 35% participation rate of 25- to 34-year-olds. However, the percentage falls to 27% among 55- to 64-year-olds. The other surveys indicate a mild reduction in training participation as workers age.

The SIPP divides training into several categories, ranging from basic skills to preparing for a job outside the organization. The first distinction lies in timing: whether the training took place within the last 12 months or the last 10 years. A second distinction is whether the training is to help prepare for a new job or to improve skills for one's current job. A third deals with ways of improving on one's current job. As Table 2 reveals, a significant share of workers have not received any training for the last 10 years, especially as of 2004. Low training levels are especially common among high school dropouts. Most of the training within the last 12 months is for upgrading skills. Within this broad category, the highest share is for training to teach new specific work skills, such as how to use equipment, machinery, or technical processes (not shown in

TABLE 2
Incidence of Training (in Percentages) Based on Responses
in the 2004 Surveys of Income and Program Participation.

Worker characteristics and year of survey	No training	Training in last 10 years but not last 12 months	Training in the last 12 months		
			Training for a new job	Improve skills on current job	Both types of training
2004, total	60.8	17.4	2.1	18.8	1.0
Male	62.6	17.5	1.7	17.4	0.8
Female	58.7	17.2	2.5	20.4	1.2
Highest schooling					
Less than high school	88.0	6.5	1.5	3.6	0.3
High school graduate	72.2	14.6	1.8	10.8	0.6
Some college credit	57.1	19.3	2.6	19.9	1.2
1 year of college	61.0	18.9	2.3	16.9	0.9
Associate's degree	51.4	19.8	2.4	25.2	1.3
Bachelor's degree	49.8	21.1	2.3	25.7	1.2
Advanced degree	48.4	18.2	1.3	30.5	1.6
1996, total	48.6	18.4	2.6	28.4	2.1
Male	50.7	18.8	2.2	26.4	1.9
Female	46.2	18.0	2.9	30.7	2.3
Highest schooling					
Less than high school	59.3	17.5	2.7	19.1	1.5
High school graduate	43.6	21.4	3.0	29.2	2.8
Some college credit	39.0	21.3	2.6	34.3	2.9
1 year of college	40.4	17.9	3.1	36.2	2.4
Associate's degree	34.6	21.4	2.3	38.9	2.9
Bachelor's degree	35.7	20.0	2.4	39.3	2.6
Advanced degree	32.8	18.4	1.6	45.1	2.1

Source: Tabulations by author from the Survey of Income and Program Participation, Education and Training Modules, 1996 and 2004 panels.

the table). About 54% of trainees obtained this type of training. Another 35% reported receiving other training to upgrade their skills and knowledge. These are the types of training reported in the SIPP by the more than 25 million adult workers who participated in some form of training.

In the 2004 NHES, of the 57 million adults in formal work-related courses or training, nearly all were trying to maintain or improve skills (95%) or to learn new skills and methods (83%). Over 40% took up training to get or keep a state, industry, or company certificate or license. Only 19% took the training to get a raise and only 10% to get a job with a different employer. Well over half (63%) of adults in this work-related training participated because they were required to do so by their employer. This figure for employer-required training is similar to the 57% level reported in the NAAL.

The workers most likely to take these courses were in professional and managerial occupations; over 56% of these workers reported taking formal work-related courses, and 70% took part in some formal adult education. Participation in work-related courses was much lower for sales, service, and clerical workers but still engaged about a third of workers; nearly a fourth of trade and labor workers participated in training of one form or another.

Sector differences in training vary with the data set. In the 2004 SIPP, workers in public sector or nonprofit private sector jobs were much more likely to report participating in job training. Local government workers—a group that includes teachers—had a 38% rate of participation in training, 20 percentage points higher than workers in for-profit firms. The nonprofit private sector workers were almost as likely as government workers to obtain training. In contrast, the NAAL data indicate that private employees were more likely to take part in training than government employees (53% to 42%).

Employer Financing of Postsecondary Education Programs

Employers frequently offer tuition assistance to their workers for postsecondary education courses. Evidence from a range of employer surveys taken in the 1990s reveals that over 80% of employers offer tuition assistance, at least for approved courses (Cappelli 2004). A 2002 survey by the firm Eduventures of human resource professionals in over 500 firms finds that over 70% offer tuition reimbursement benefits (Flaherty 2007). Many provide tuition help even for courses that are not directly tied to the worker's job. Recent data on the share of students and workers who receive this form of assistance are available from the SIPP interviews conducted during June–September 2005 and from the 2005 NHES. The estimates of students with employer subsidies range from about 2.1 million (SIPP) to nearly 3 million (NHES).

Although these numbers are large in absolute terms, they represent only about 2% of the workforce. On the other hand, employer subsidies extend to a significant share of degree seekers. Among students pursuing a master's degree, between 25% (SIPP) and 31% (NHES) received employer subsidies. The SIPP reports that employers subsidized over 13% of those pursuing a certificate or license program or taking college courses without a degree objective. A lower percentage of BA seekers—from 5% to 7%—take advantage of employer subsidies. However, the absolute numbers subsidized toward a BA range from about 500,000 to 800,000 students.

For half the students receiving employer support for postsecondary education, employers provided the assistance without any requirements linked to the job.[3] About one in four assisted students took the courses as an employer requirement for maintaining skills on their current job. For over 20% of cases, the employer-assisted courses were a requirement for gaining higher pay. The data clearly show employers were willing to spend money to enhance general skills. But how did they recoup these investments? One possibility is that workers had to remain with the employer in return for the subsidy. In about a third of cases in which the courses were not required, employers did impose a requirement that workers remain for a period after the training. Yet the requirement to stay with the employer after training was not more frequent when the courses looked general than when the courses were linked to improving skills on a current job or to improving one's salary.

One requirement common to tuition reimbursement programs is that participants earn at least a "C" or have to repay the firm for the tuition costs (Flaherty 2007). To qualify for beneficial tax treatment so that the tuition reimbursements are not taxable income, firms must have a written plan, meet nondiscrimination clauses, and not offer other compensation for those who do not take up tuition reimbursement. In addition, the courses must be job-related.

Some employers view tuition reimbursements as helping to reduce turnover. But theoretically, the provision of general training of the type learned in courses should increase the worker's market value and potentially increase turnover. A case study of the impact of tuition reimbursement in a nonprofit organization found convincing evidence that workers' use of tuition reimbursement led to sharply lower turnover, as much as a 50% reduction over five years (Flaherty 2007). The analysis took account of the possibility that workers taking up the tuition benefit would have naturally stayed longer with the organization. Although the detailed results covered only one firm, the in-depth analysis shows that some organizations are right to view tuition reimbursement as at least partly offset by cost saving through lower turnover. Also, as noted above, Cappelli (2004) finds tuition benefits may act as a screening device to attract workers with higher-than-average skills.

Duration of Training and Employer Involvement

Most workers receiving job-related training undertook at least a full day of instruction. In the 2004 NHES, only a third of trainees had 10 instructional hours or less. Over 40% had at least 26 hours and 22% had more than 50 hours of classroom instruction. According to the SIPP, the time spent in training among trainees is considerably less than reported in the NHES. Like the NHES, two thirds had training durations of more than one day, but no more than 10% of trainees (or about 2% of workers) reported more than a week of training.

Nearly all workers in formal work-related courses or training (in the 2004 NHES) received some employer support. The most common form (at 86%) was financial support from employers in the form of tuition, books, and/or materials. In addition, 80% of trainees were allowed to take the training during regular work hours and were paid for the time spent in training. In over half of the training cases (57%), employers provided the programs at the workplace. In the NAAL, employers fund 91% of the training they require of their employees. In addition, employers also pay for 62% of job-related training not required by the employer. The training for less educated workers is more likely to be required by employers than the training for the highly educated. For workers with less than a high school degree, over 80% of employer-funded training is required by the employer. For college grads, only 58% is required.

Intensive Employer-Led Training

Although tens of millions of workers obtain some employer-led training every year, the scale of long-term, intensive training is modest. The best example of intensive training is occupational training that leads to certification, often through formal apprenticeships. Apprenticeships are programs through which individuals achieve the skills of a fully skilled worker in an occupation primarily through supervised, work-based learning along with related academic instruction. Employers, joint union–employer agreements, government agencies, and the military all sponsor apprenticeship programs. Apprentices are employees at the firms and organizations where they are training; productive work is combined with learning experiences that lead to demonstrated proficiency in a significant array of tasks. The programs usually last three to four years and require students to complete coursework that includes math, verbal, and occupation-specific content. The coursework is generally equivalent to at least one year of community college.

The U.S. apprenticeship system is decentralized, although many programs are governed by state and federal regulations under the registered apprenticeship system. Programs that are part of the registered apprenticeship system operate under the supervision of the U.S. Labor Department's Office of Apprenticeship (OA) and state apprenticeship agencies. The responsibilities of the OA include issuing certificates of completion to apprentices, protecting the safety and welfare of apprentices, providing guidance and technical assistance to program sponsors, monitoring program equal opportunity plans to prevent discrimination against women and minorities, and expanding the use of apprenticeship by employers.

As of 2008, about 28,000 registered apprenticeship sponsors operated training for about 465,000 apprentices, implying an average of about 18 apprentices per sponsor (Lerman, Eyster, and Chambers 2009). The number of registered apprentices is comparable to the combined number of individuals receiving training through three federally sponsored Department of Labor programs: the Workforce Investment Act's Adult and Dislocated Worker programs, a formula-funded federal program that provides local workforce boards with funds for training and other services; the Job Corps, which is an intensive residential training program for the most at-risk youth; and the Trade Adjustment Act, which provides training dollars in addition to unemployment cash benefits to workers displaced because of trade (Mikelson and Nightingale 2004).

Registered apprentices are highly concentrated in construction, energy, manufacturing, transportation and communication, and public administration occupations. However, transportation and communication occupations jumped nearly fivefold between 2003 and 2007, the fastest growth in percentage terms of any occupation. Despite increases in recent years, registered apprentices still make up only about 0.3% of the workforce; the number of registered apprentices exiting their training each year is about 4% of a typical cohort's annual entrants to the workforce.[4]

In addition to the registered apprentices, a large but unknown number of workers receive intensive and long-term occupational training sponsored by employers who do not register their apprenticeship programs with the U.S. Department of Labor. One of the few data sources that ask about all U.S. apprenticeships (including the unregistered) is the NHES. The specific question asked in the NHES is, "During the past 12 months, were you in a formal apprenticeship program leading to journeyman status in a skilled trade or craft?" Although the absolute number of individuals who reported having been in an apprenticeship is small, the weighted figure is 1.8 million workers. If this figure is accurate, apprenticeships that are not registered would be about three times the number of registered apprenticeships. Unfortunately, it is difficult to know how accurate this estimate is, since the total NHES sample is only about 9,000 individuals.

Apprenticeships involve a considerable upfront investment on the part of employers. Although no cost study in the United States has uncovered the incremental costs of training apprentices, the amounts based on other cost estimates are probably on the order of at least

$10,000 per apprentice. Assuming a conservative estimate of the costs at $5,000 per year per apprentice, employer investment in this intensive type of training would reach over $5 billion.

Benefits of Intensive Apprenticeship Training to Workers and Employers

Evidence is accumulating that demonstrates the value of intensive, occupational-based training, especially in the context of apprenticeships. The gains for the workers are showing up in research comparing alternative modes of training. In a careful study that compared matched groups of workers entering job centers in Washington state, Hollenbeck (2008) found that the returns to apprenticeship training far exceed the returns to other types of training, including community college programs. For apprentices, the present value of their post-program increases in earnings, net of any earnings foregone during the training period itself, amounted to over $50,000 for the first 2.5 years after exiting their program. In contrast, estimates using the same approach for workers entering community college occupational programs indicated gains of only about $8,000 or less in the short term. Although community college occupational programs yield much higher long-run returns ($104,000 to $130,000 for workers through age 65), the projection for the present value of long-term gains to apprenticeship training is about $266,000. The public costs of community college were about $5,000 more than the public costs of apprenticeship. Of course, as in the case of any postsecondary education and training, the net gains are likely to vary, depending on the occupation and geographic area. Moreover, more research is certainly necessary to determine the variability in earnings gains across occupations and other dimensions of apprenticeship training.

From the perspective of employer sponsors, apprenticeship training is a sound approach to skill development. One body of evidence comes from a 2007 survey of sponsors of registered apprenticeship programs conducted for the U.S. Department of Labor's Employment and Training Administration (ETA; Lerman, Eyster, and Chambers 2009). The survey obtained data from 947 sponsors concerning the sponsor's program characteristics, benefits of registered apprenticeship, drawbacks or costs of registered apprenticeship, views on the apprenticeship system, interactions with the larger workforce investment system, and related instruction. The results showed strikingly positive attitudes by sponsors. Nearly all reported they would recommend the program to others, with 86% stating they would "strongly" recommend it and 11% indicating they would recommend it with reservations, due primarily to problems with accessing related instruction.

The benefit cited by over 80% of sponsors was the apprenticeship program's role in meeting the demand for skilled workers. Another major benefit was that the apprenticeship programs show reliably which workers have the skills needed. Other benefits, cited by 68% of sponsors as very important, were raising productivity, strengthening worker morale and pride, and improving worker safety. A majority of sponsors also reported benefits in worker recruitment and retention and in meeting licensing requirements.

One common concern about encouraging intensive, employer-led training is that firms will be unable to recoup the costs of training because others firms will drive up the wages of the newly skilled workers. The process by which competitor firms bid away trained workers after their apprenticeship is commonly called "poaching"; it is viewed as a major disincentive to employer involvement in any training that raises the productivity of workers outside the firm. Some apprenticeship sponsors viewed poaching as a significant problem, but surprisingly, 46% of sponsors did not perceive it as a problem at all. Moreover, even among sponsors who perceived poaching as a problem, about 85% would still strongly recommend apprenticeship to others.

Sponsors generally did not find costs to be a significant problem. Sixty-three percent of sponsors said related instruction costs were not a problem, although 30% viewed costs as a minor problem and 6% as a major problem. Similarly, only 7% of respondents saw the cost of experienced workers' time to instruct apprentices as a significant problem, while 34% indicated it was a minor problem.

Occupational Certification

Apprenticeships document to employers that employees have mastered the occupational skills employers demand. In the survey of apprenticeship sponsors (employers and union–employer programs), 95% report that apprenticeships reliably show which workers have the skills to do the job (Lerman, Eyster, and Chambers 2009). Completing an apprenticeship generally is sufficient to meet state licensing and certification standards in the field. Other employer-led training can also lead to a license or certification. Obtaining a license or certification may raise wages in one of three ways: Licenses limit entry into a profession, restricting the supply and driving up wages; employers and other buyers are willing to pay more for licensed and/or certified workers because the licenses give buyers the assurance that the worker has mastered the profession's relevant skills; and passing the licensure test requires workers to learn skills that upgrade their performance in their profession.

Although the literature on returns to occupational certification and licensure is modest, one study based on a national poll indicates about 29% of workers were licensed and 35% were either licensed or certified by a government entity (Kleiner and Krueger 2009). In addition, the authors find that the wage gains to licensure are significant, about a 14% increase. The wage impacts on certification were much smaller and not statistically significant in some specifications.

The NAAL data reveal high percentages of workers with some form of certification. About 14% of workers reported information technology (IT) skill certification that was "sponsored by a hardware or software manufacturer or an industry or professional association." Nearly three out of four had to pass a test to earn the IT certification. Over one in three workers had a job-related skill certification that was "recognized by a licensing board or an industry or professional association." About 90% of these certifications required passing a test. The share with either form or both forms of certification reached 42%, somewhat higher than but not enormously different from the 35% figure reported by Kleiner and Krueger (2009). Having a vocational degree or some college raised the chances of having a certification by 36%, an increase similar to the increased probability of college graduates.

Workers reporting skill certifications in the NAAL generally earned much more than other workers, after controlling for educational attainment. The only exception was among college graduates, for whom an IT certification was associated with modestly higher wages but for whom non-IT certifications showed no association with weekly earnings. On the other hand, those with a high school degree or less earned considerably higher wages if they had either type of certification. Consider those with only a high school equivalency or GED. Those with a non-IT skills certificate were much less likely to earn under $500 per week than those without a non-IT skills certificate (26% versus 51%) and much more likely to earn over $1,150 per month (27% versus 17%). The gains were generally even higher for those with IT certificates relative to those without IT certificates at the same level of educational attainment. For both types of certification, the earnings advantage showed up in all education groups; the lower the level of education, the higher was the gain.

Taken together, the two sets of results about certifications reinforce the findings concerning apprenticeship training that achieving a recognized credential raises earnings. Because some certifications are not as in-depth as apprenticeship training, one would not expect the same jump in earnings. Still, the evidence strongly suggests that earnings gains result from recognized occupational skills, whether obtained in an employer-led training program or through some other mechanism.

Accounting Practices and Employer-Led Training

Managers often cite the skills and commitment of their employees as their companies' most precious assets. But at the same time, they also admit that they can only manage what they can measure. Currently, productive investments in building the skills of a company's workforce count as current costs to firms, though they are in fact intangible investments. When companies invest in capital goods and plants, only a modest portion of the purchase counts as current-year costs in determining profits. The remaining value is counted as an asset on the company's balance sheet. In contrast, all of the spending on skill development is a cost in the current year, despite the reality that the company will gain benefits from these expenses over a period of years.[5]

According to Corrado, Hulten, and Sichel (2006), the magnitude of the overall intangible investment component of firm spending on training and organizational change was about $365 billion in the period 1998 to 2000. However, for the training component alone, they use Bureau of Labor Statistics figures to suggest that the annual training component of employer investments is about $116 billion, counting direct firm expenditures on trainers, tuition, and outside training contracts as well as firm spending on wages during the time workers are undergoing formal and informal training.

For tax purposes, expensing training costs in the year they are borne saves money relative to treating training costs as an investment. However, this accounting treatment distorts the profitability of training investments relative to investments in capital equipment that firms depreciate over time. If investments in training were treated more closely in line with economic reality for measuring profits and assets (but not for tax purposes), the contributions of training investments might be measured more precisely and the benefits would become more apparent. Firms might then undertake considerably more training and increase skills of their workforce. Employer training appears to yield high returns to workers as well as to firms. Thus, any measure that increases the incentive for companies to increase spending on training could raise the useful skills of the U.S. workforce substantially. If businesses increased their training outlays by 1% of wages and salaries, the added investments in human capital would amount to nearly $80 billion per year, or about double the entire education-related expenditures by all community colleges in the United States. Of course, the impact of accounting changes might be much smaller, but it is plausible to expect added training outlays in the billions of dollars.

One problem is how to measure the benefit to firms of added worker capabilities and the duration of the benefits. Another worry is that companies will overstate their training outlays relative to other labor costs. Such actions could cause an inappropriate reduction in current costs. Of course, similar judgments are required for allocating the costs of physical capital as well, especially the length of the depreciation period. A major distinction between physical and human capital is that firms have no property rights in the added human capital, as they have with added physical capital. Workers may leave if the added human capital is not rewarded with wage increases. Thus, training investments should count as assets to the company only to the extent that the company can benefit from the increased human capital. Certainly, the very fact that companies now finance lots of training indicates their ability to capture some of the gains. Hankanson, Johanson, and Mellander (2003) provide a more detailed treatment of these issues.

Valuation problems are real, but approximations are better than ignoring the reality that training constitutes an investment that should not be treated like other services used up in the current year. After all, the idea of counting the cost to the firm of providing financial options to employees was initially greeted with skepticism about the theory and the feasibility of calculating an appropriate dollar amount. In fact, some measures of the costs of options depend on assumptions about longevity with the firm. Moreover, some firms already amortize some training expenses when workers are learning how to operate new equipment.

It will take time to develop a consensus in the United States that accounting for the firm's human capital assets makes sense and to agree on a practical method for doing so. But the increase in the importance of human capital to the firm (and not just to the worker) should stimulate action.

Conclusions and Implications for Policy and Research

High levels of worker productivity and wages generally require high levels of skills. Employer-led training plays a significant role in developing and upgrading the skills of American workers. Involving employers in training can lead to high returns, to skill development that is relevant to the workplace, and to high levels of worker engagement. Yet research on employer-led training remains modest, especially in light of the more than $70 billion to $100 billion that employers spend every year. There is far more research available on public sector job training programs that spend under $5 billion per year. In a sense, employer-led training is a hidden part of the nation's human capital development system. Given its potential benefits and large scale, policy makers should place a high priority on learning more about the employer-led system.

Using current data on the incidence and trends of employer-led training, we are not sure about the scale or the trends in employer-led training. Data from one major national survey show a decline between the late 1990s and 2004–05 in the share of workers who took part in job-related training in the prior year, while another survey indicates increases in the same period. Moreover, the proportion of workers reporting training varies from about 20% in the SIPP to a range of 42% to 57% in the other surveys. None of the recent national surveys offer detailed information on the widespread amount of informal training in the United States.

Another important gap in descriptive information is the extent to which employers collaborate with each other. The workforce field is increasingly looking into sectoral approaches, whereby all firms in similar industries and in the same local or regional job market come together to define skills and training needs. Although a third party often provides the training, employers also participate in the training process (Conway, Blair, Conway, and Dworak-Muñoz 2007). Evidence from Britain suggests that interfirm collaborations bear fruit (Gospel and Foreman 2006), but there is little hard data on this issue in the U.S. context.

Other open questions deal with the returns to employer-led training. What are the gains for workers and firms from employer-led training? Although a few studies show high rates of return to apprenticeship training (Hollenbeck 2008), few *recent* studies have analyzed the impacts of employer-led training on workers and employers. Another important consideration is how the returns of employer-led training in the workplace compare with learning skills in a school-based context. Only Hollenbeck's studies of training in Washington state provide this comparative analysis, with results showing apprenticeship training—which has the highest employer involvement and workplace learning—yielding substantially higher returns than community college training.[6] More research on this topic is important; if this finding has general validity, the United States could increase substantially the cost effectiveness of training dollars by shifting dollars toward encouraging apprenticeship and other employer-led training. Already, the Organisation for Economic Co-operation and Development (2009) has concluded that the United States should expand apprenticeship training substantially, especially for young workers.

To many, the provision of employer-led training falls short of optimal levels because of positive externalities (Bishop 1997; Greenhalgh 1999). Certainly, available evidence indicates that in-depth employer-led training, such as apprenticeship training, improves outcomes for workers and yields benefits for employers. For these reasons, policy makers may want to encourage the expansion of employer-led training. But what are the best tools for expanding training?

One tool would be to expand apprenticeship training through a combination of increased marketing, technical assistance, and subsidies to employers. Currently, the federal budget for the Office of Apprenticeship (OA)—the agency charged with regulating and managing registered apprenticeship programs in the United States—is only about $22 million per year. This sum is tiny in comparison with federal dollars spent on training in other programs for a far smaller number of workers. For example, funding for the Job Corps is over $1 billion for 60,000 workers, while over 480,000 workers participate in registered apprenticeship programs. Tripling the current budget for OA would cost $40 million per year, but the increase could more than pay for itself if employers increased their apprenticeships by even a very modest amount. Combining the added marketing with tax credits for expanding apprenticeships would no doubt increase a very productive form of employer-led training. A recent effort in South Carolina (Apprenticeship Carolina) demonstrates the potential of an approach combining marketing and tax credits. With a budget of $1 million per year and tax credits of $1,000 per apprenticeship, Apprenticeship Carolina managed to develop at least one new apprenticeship program per week over a year-and a-half period. Moreover, once employers build apprenticeship training into their training and recruitment strategies, they are likely to continue to finance serious and productive worker training.

Another appropriate tool to expand apprenticeship would be for state and federal governments to share in the costs of the academic-instruction component of apprenticeship training. Already some states do so by providing discounts for community college courses. The effort should be expanded. Apprenticeships are growing in many European countries and play a major role in developing skills for a wide range of careers (Steedman 2005). For example, the Leitch Review of Skills (Leitch Commission 2006) in the United Kingdom recommended expanding the number of apprenticeships to 500,000. In the U.S. context, meeting this target would require about a fourfold increase in apprenticeships, to about 2.3 million.

Another promising tool is to expand sectoral programs, which involve the collaboration of firms in the same industry with training providers and community-based organizations. Employers work with local intermediary organizations to specify their skill requirements and to provide openings for those gaining skills. These programs have achieved some success in ensuring that the training is linked to careers and real jobs.

Upgrading the capacity of employers to deliver training toward specific skill levels is another potential tool for expanding training. A recent parliamentary report in the United Kingdom calls for government and nongovernment groups to strengthen the capacity of the training function of employers, with the goal of helping workers attain a formal accreditation for the skills they have learned and demonstrated in a work context (House of Commons Innovation, Universities, Science and Skills Committee 2009). Certifying the capacity of training organizations, along with technical assistance to small firms, encourages more productive employer-led training.

One element of this approach could be to increase the utilization and effectiveness of employer tuition assistance programs. Often, current assistance is a stand-alone offer viewed as an employee benefit but not closely linked to employers' skill objectives. Because of the large share of workers who can access tuition reimbursement from employers, improving the productivity and wage gains of these investments could generate a sharp increase in employer-led training. At this point, research and demonstrations are appropriate to answer questions about the low take-up rates, the match between the uses of tuition assistance and the productivity improvements of workers and firms, and the cost effectiveness of the strategies. International experience suggests that linking tuition assistance and other training initiatives to the attainment of recognized standards and qualifications would make existing training dollars more productive and would encourage more workers to participate in training and more firms to offer training. The House of Commons report cited earlier (House of Commons Innovation, Universities, Science and Skills Committee 2009) offers one example of a training initiative aimed at upgrading workers to a particular standard.

Altering accounting procedures to recognize the asset value of human capital is another low-cost intervention to encourage employer training. The change would recognize in income statements and balance sheets that training investments generate assets that yield future benefits. Although the modification in practice would not be easy to construct, the result would be to make accounts better reflect current operations and company assets. Managers focusing on short-term or long-term profits would have more incentive to invest in training. Since employer-sponsored training yields a high return, additional employer-sponsored training is likely to increase productivity by improving worker skills and qualifications.

Overall, employer-led training contributes substantially to the earnings, skills, and productivity of millions of American workers. It is time for policy makers to recognize its importance by strengthening policies that promote employer-led training and by sponsoring additional research and data collection about the scope, impacts, and strategies for improving outcomes for workers and employers.

Acknowledgment

I thank Joanna Stork for excellent research assistance.

Endnotes

[1] For a noteworthy exception, see the report on worker training produced by the U.S. Congress, Office of Technology Assessment in 1990.

[2] See Barron, Berger, and Black (1999) for a description of these sources.

[3] The data from this paragraph come from the SIPP.

[4] According to the website of the U.S. Bureau of Labor Statistics, the U.S. labor force stood at 153.6 million at the end of 2007. Dividing the 468,000 apprentices by the 153.6 million in the labor force equals 0.3%. A cohort of 22-year-olds entering the labor force is about 3.4 million. Since apprenticeships usually last about 3.5 years, the number of apprentices per single year of age is 134,000. Dividing 134,000 by 3.4 million equals 3.9%.

[5] Thanks to Laurie Bassi for alerting me to this point.

[6] A study in France also demonstrates that gains to apprenticeship training exceed the returns to school-based vocational education, especially for men (Mendes and Sofer 2002).

References

Acemoglu, Daron, and Jörn-Steffen Pischke. 1999. "Beyond Becker: Training in Imperfect Labour Markets." *The Economic Journal*, Vol. 109, no. 453, Features (Feb.), pp. F112–42.

American Society for Training and Development. 2009. *2009 State of the Industry Report: ASTD's Annual Review of Trends in Workforce Learning and Performance.* Alexandria, VA: American Society for Training and Development.

Barron, John, Mark Berger, and Dan Black. 1999. "Replacing General with Specific Training: Why Restricting Alternatives Makes Sense." In Soloman Polachek and John Rust, eds., *Research in Labor Economics, Vol. 18.* Stamford, CT: JAI Press, pp. 281–302.

Bartel, Ann. 1995. "Training, Wage Growth, and Job Performance: Evidence from a Company Database." *Journal of Labor Economics*, Vol. 13, no. 3, pp. 401–25.

Bartel, Ann. 2000. "Measuring the Return on Employer Investments in Training: Evidence from the Literature." *Industrial Relations*, Vol. 39, no. 3, pp. 502–24.

Becker, Gary. 1964. *Human Capital: A Theoretical and Empirical Analysis, with Special Reference to Education.* Chicago, IL: University of Chicago Press.

Bishop, John. 1997. "What We Know About Employer-Provided Training: A Review of the Literature." In Soloman Polachek, ed., *Research in Labor Economics, Vol. 16.* Greenwich, CT, and London: JAI Press, pp. 19–87.

Cappelli, Peter. 2004. "Why Do Employers Pay for College?" *Journal of Econometrics*, Vol. 121, nos. 1–2, pp. 213–41.

Conway, Maureen, Amy Blair, Steven Conway, and Linda Dworak-Muñoz. 2007. *Sectoral Strategies for Low-Income Workers: Lessons from the Field*. Washington, DC: Aspen Institute.

Corrado, Carol, Charles Hulten, and Daniel Sichel. 2006. *Intangible Capital and Economic Growth*. Finance and Economics Discussion Series. Washington, DC: Federal Reserve Board.

Flaherty, Coleen. 2007. *The Effect of Tuition Reimbursement on Turnover: A Case Study Analysis*. NBER Working Paper 12975. Cambridge, MA: National Bureau of Economic Research.

Goldin, Claudia, and Lawrence Katz. 2008. *The Race Between Education and Technology*. Cambridge, MA: Belknap Press of Harvard University Press.

Gospel, Howard, and Jim Foreman. 2006. "Inter-firm Training Coordination in Britain." *British Journal of Industrial Relations*. Vol. 44, no. 2, pp. 191–214.

Greenhalgh, Christine. 1999. "Adult Vocational Training and Government Policy in Britain and France." *Oxford Papers on Economic Policy*, Vol. 15, pp. 97–113.

Hankanson, Christina, Saku Johanson, and Erik Mellander. 2003. *Employer-Sponsored Training, Stabilisation, and Growth: Policy Perspectives*. Working Paper 9-2003. Uppsala, Sweden: Institute for Labour Market Policy Evaluation.

Hanushek, Eric, and Ludger Woessmann. 2009. *Do Better Schools Lead to More Growth? Cognitive Skills, Economic Outcomes, and Causation*. NBER Working Paper 14633. Cambridge, MA: National Bureau of Economic Research.

Hollenbeck, Kevin. 2008. *State Use of Workforce System Net Impact Estimates and Rates of Return*. Paper presented at the Association for Public Policy and Management. Los Angeles, CA, November 6–8.

House of Commons Innovation, Universities, Science and Skills Committee. 2009. "Re-skilling for Recovery: After Leitch, Implementing Skills and Training Policies." London: House of Commons.

Kleiner, Morris, and Alan Krueger. 2009. *Analyzing the Influence of Occupational Licensing on the Labor Market*. NBER Working Paper 14979. Cambridge, MA: National Bureau of Economic Research.

Kletzer, Lori, and William Koch. 2004. "International Experience with Job Training: Lessons for the United States." In Christopher O'Leary, Robert Straits, and Stephen Wandner, eds., *Job Training Policy in the United States*. Kalamazoo, MI: Upjohn Institute, pp. 245–88.

Knoke, David, and Arne Kalleberg. 1994. "Job Training in U.S. Organizations." *American Sociological Review*, Vol. 59 (August), pp. 537–46.

Leitch Commission. 2006. *Leitch Review of Skills: Prosperity for All in the Global Economy—World Class Skills*. London: Her Majesty's Treasury. <http://webarchive.nationalarchives.gov.uk/+/http://www.hm-treasury.gov.uk/media/6/4/leitch_finalreport051206.pdf>. [July 6, 2010].

Lerman, Robert, Signe-Mary McKernan, and Stephanie Riegg. 2004. "The Scope of Employer-Provided Training in the United States." In Christopher O'Leary, Robert Straits, and Stephen Wandner, eds., *Job Training Policy in the United States*. Kalamazoo, MI: Upjohn Institute, pp. 211–44.

Lerman, Robert, Lauren Eyster, and Kate Chambers. 2009. *The Benefits and Challenges of Registered Apprenticeships: The Sponsors' Perspective*. Washington, DC: Urban Institute. <http://www.urban.org/UploadedPDF/411907_registered_apprenticeship.pdf>. [July 6, 2010].

Leuven, Edwin, and Hessel Oosterbeek. 1999. "The Demand and Supply of Work-Related Training: Evidence from Four Countries." In Solomon W. Polachek, ed., *Research in Labor Economics*, Vol. 18. Stamford, CT: JAI Press, pp. 303–30.

Levitz, Carol. 2010. "UPS Thinks Out of the Box on Driver Training." *Wall Street Journal*, April 6, p. B-1.

Lynch, Lisa, and Sandra Black. 1998. "Beyond the Incidence of Employer-Provided Training." *Industrial and Labor Relations Review*, Vol. 52, no. 1 (October), pp. 64–81.

Mendes, Sylvie, and Catherine Sofer. 2002. "Apprenticeship vs. Vocational School: A Comparison of Performances." In Catherine Sofer, ed., *Human Capital Over the Life Cycle: A European Perspective*. Northampton, MA: Edward Elgar Publishing, pp. 118–36.

Mikelson, Kelly, and Demetra Nightingale. 2004. *Estimating Public and Private Expenditures on Occupational Training in the United States*. Report to the U.S. Department of Labor, Employment and Training Administration.

Mincer, Jacob. 1958. "Investment in Human Capital and Personal Income Distribution." *Journal of Political Economy*, Vol. 66, no. 4 (August), pp. 281–302.

National Center for Education Statistics. 2009. *Digest of Educational Statistics*. Washington, DC: U.S. Department of Education. <http://nces.ed.gov/programs/digest/d09/tables/dt09_027.asp>. [July 6, 2010].

O'Leary, Christopher, Robert Straits, and Stephen Wandner. 2004. "U.S. Job Training: Types, Participants, and History." In Christopher O'Leary, Robert Straits, and Stephen Wandner, eds., *Job Training Policy in the United States*. Kalamazoo, MI: Upjohn Institute, pp. 1–22.

Organisation for Economic Co-operation and Development. 2004. "Improving Skills for More and Better Jobs: Does Training Make a Difference?" *Employment Outlook: 2004*, Chapter 4, pp. 183–224. Paris: Organisation for Economic Co-operation and Development.

Organisation for Economic Co-operation and Development. 2009. *Jobs for Youth: United States*. Paris: Organisation for Economic Co-operation and Development.

Osterman, Paul. 1995. "Skill, Training, and Work Organization in American Establishments." *Industrial Relations*, Vol. 34, no. 2, pp. 125–46.

Parent, Daniel. 2000. "Wages and Mobility: The Impact of Employer-Provided Training." *Journal of Labor Economics*, Vol. 17, no. 2, pp. 298–316.

Steedman, Hilary. 2005. *Apprenticeship in Europe: "Fading" or Flourishing?* Centre for Economic Performance Discussion Paper no. 710. London: London School of Economics.

U.S. Congress, Office of Technology Assessment. 1990. *Worker Training: Competing in the New International Economy*. OTA-ITE-457. Washington, DC: U.S. Government Printing Office.

Yang, Song. 2006. "Organizational Sectors and the Institutionalization of Job-Training Programs: Evidence from a Longitudinal National Organizations Study." *Sociological Perspectives*, Vol. 49, no. 3, pp. 325–42.

CHAPTER 8

Creating a Sector Skill Strategy: Developing High-Skill Ecosystems

DAVID FINEGOLD
JOHN MCCARTHY
Rutgers University

Along with health care, the most pressing domestic issue facing the Obama Administration is how to create and retain good jobs following the deepest recession since the Great Depression. One key piece of this effort will be ensuring that the American workforce has the right skills needed to fill these jobs through the redesign of the public U.S. workforce development system and related education reforms. The reauthorization of the Workforce Investment Act (WIA) faces similar challenges to health care reform, albeit with far more modest resources. It starts from an existing public system that was never designed to meet the challenges of a 21st-century global economy. Instead, it has evolved over time—from CETA to JTPA to WIA—into a large government bureaucracy that is only tangentially related to the competitive drivers and skill needs of the private sector. Likewise, despite the influx of $4 billion in stimulus dollars to fund additional workforce training in response to the deep financial crisis of 2008–09, the system appears inadequate to serve the needs of the largest number of individuals facing unemployment since the Great Depression.

Gordon Lafer (2002) offers a comprehensive critique of the U.S. public workforce development system, arguing that it starts from two false premises: that the market and private sector employers will, except during cyclical downturns, provide a sufficient quantity of good jobs for the American workforce, and therefore that any persistent unemployment must be due to inadequate skills supply or a "skills mismatch," as individuals who are displaced from declining sectors need to be retrained for areas of job growth. He provides evidence that, even before the deep recession of 2007–09, the problem lies instead on the demand side of the labor market, where the number of jobs required to lift all working Americans out of poverty in the boom period of the 1990s (nearly 26 million) exceeded the available supply of job openings offering a living wage (2.1 million) by nearly 13:1: "There simply are not enough decent paying jobs for the number of people who need them—no matter how well trained they are—suggest[ing] that training programs cannot hope to address more than a small fraction of the poverty problem" (Lafer 2002:4–5). Lafer shows that while public sector training programs have generally failed to produce meaningful increases in individual earnings or career success, they have been a successful political strategy, attracting bipartisan support. Investments in training, and the accompanying assumption that individual skill deficiencies are to blame for unemployment and wage stagnation, are more politically viable than addressing the underlying causes of the insufficient supply of good jobs and growing income inequality.

The policies that Lafer proposes—raising the minimum wage, better enforcing existing labor laws, strengthening unions' right to organize so they can protect worker rights and increase their bargaining power—are, however, for the most part directed at improving the quality of jobs on offer. Even if these policies were adopted and succeeded, they would not address the core problem of stimulating the growth of new jobs, since by raising marginal labor costs they will likely reduce or at best retain existing levels of employment. The main exception to this is Lafer's call for a return to CETA's origins, with a greater role for public sector job creation programs. Particularly during a severe economic downturn, there is clearly an important role for the government to play in creating living-wage jobs. But neither direct public employment nor stimulus spending on infrastructure projects and other public goods is likely to offer a sustainable, long-term solution to the problem of creating enough good jobs to restore the United States to full employment and reversing the generation-long stagnation or decline in the average living standards of the average American worker.

Is there a skill policy alternative—a "third way" between reliance on free markets and the government itself—to create good jobs? We will argue that the most viable, though still difficult and unproven, option is for the government and private sector to partner, along with education providers, investors, and nonprofits, to foster the development of sustainable skill systems. This extends the earlier concept of high-skill ecosystems (HSEs; Finegold 1999), regional clusters of enterprises and skill providers in one or more common sectors that are key drivers of innovation and accompanying job growth. HSEs are growing in importance as the United States shifts from a manufacturing to a more protocol-based economy, where the creation of new knowledge that is embedded in products or services is the key to creating wealth and employment. Sustainable skill systems encompass HSEs but also recognize the benefits that sectorally focused partnerships can have in helping lower- and intermediate-skill workers prepare for high-demand jobs in particular industries in a regional economy. Placing sustainable skills systems at the core of a new U.S. skills strategy could address at least three major, related deficiencies in the current public workforce development system that must be remedied if the U.S. workforce is to compete more effectively in the global economy:

- Lack of sectoral and regional capabilities
- Failure to serve the majority of the workforce
- Poor connections with economic development and job creation

We begin by exploring why regional clusters have grown rather than diminished in importance as globalization and the ease with which work can be moved around the world are increasing. We then look at the roles government policy can play in fostering the development of sector-specific skills and HSEs, analyzing leading international examples of sectoral skill policy—from Germany, Singapore, and Australia—as well as from innovative U.S. states: Wisconsin, New York, and Connecticut. The key success factors from these cases are then applied to an assessment of the largest U.S. federal government effort to date to foster HSEs, the U.S. Department of Labor's $325-million Workforce Innovation in Regional Economic Development (WIRED) initiative, which funded 39 clusters between 2006 and 2010. We focus in particular on one of these efforts, Bio-1, that has sought to foster the growth of a bioscience-based HSE along the Route 1 corridor in central New Jersey that connects Princeton and Rutgers and including the University of Medicine and Dentistry of New Jersey (UMDNJ). We conclude by distilling the lessons from WIRED and Bio-1 for redesigning the U.S. skill system.

The Importance of Clusters in Today's Global Economy

Deregulation, globalization, and technological change have combined to make increasingly obsolete the bureaucratic model of vertical integration that was the dominant corporate form for the last century. It is giving way to vertical *dis*integration, where firms keep fewer core competencies in-house, contracting out the remaining functions to specialized partners or peripheral agents. Piore and Sabel (1984) described the shift away from mass production as a "second industrial divide." They argued that, where mass production is characterized by rigidities that prevent innovation and adaptation, vertical disintegration allows for both flexibility and specialization as each partnering organization becomes adept in some service or facet of production. Such "flexible specialization" provides nimbleness in response to, or anticipation of, environmental uncertainties, including technological changes, changing consumer tastes, and concomitant fluctuations in labor demand (Piore and Sabel 1984; Best 1990).

The proliferation of global value chains indicates the magnitude of this organizational transformation; indeed, Kelly (1998) has argued that contemporary economies exist in dynamic webs of global networks, as opposed to locations in their traditional sense. This has been fostered by advances in communication technology that have made over a billion additional workers available in global labor markets and prompted leading multinationals to invest heavily in India, China, and other locations where lower-cost talent and suppliers are available. Given the global scope of modern business, does it make sense for policy makers to focus on workforce and economic development policies that aim to create clusters of related enterprises and sector-specific skills?

Research finds significant and enduring benefits to the geographic clustering of related industries and institutions. One benefit relates to the strength of relationships made possible through proximity (Porter 2000). Applegate (2006) has emphasized that "stronger, deeper differentiated nodes in a network are required in environments characterized by increased complexity, uncertainty and turbulence" (p. 359). These forces help to explain why, as Scott (1998) has pointed out, we may tend to find clustering "wherever we find industries that face unstable markets whose contestability is focused mainly on product quality and innovativeness rather than cost" (p. 61). Physical proximity facilitates trust, norms, and shared understandings between local buyers and suppliers, but it may also give rise to a broader range of partnerships between business and K–12 schools, universities, and government. These forms of social capital are difficult to imitate along globally dispersed networks (Porter 2000).

Knowledge spillovers represent another potential benefit of HSEs. Griliches (1992) has explained that spillovers occur as organizations and people are "working on similar things and hence benefiting from each other's research" (p. 112). In clusters, tacit information disseminates by way of professional relationships, job mobility, and other informal exchanges among scientists and the regional workforce (Saxenian 1994; Almeida and Kogut 1999). For example, Gittelman (2006) found that patents were more likely to be co-authored by the scientists of firms and universities that were proximate to one another. Zucker, Darby, and Brewer's (1998) study of 183 biotechnology regions found that the ascent of biotechnology firms corresponded to the dispersion of a small cohort of star scientists who played "a crucial role in the process of spillover and geographic agglomeration over and above that which have been predicted by university reputation and scientists supported by federal grants alone" (p. 298). To use von Hippel's (1994) language, therefore, the "sticky," tacit knowledge that disseminates may strengthen a region's competitive position as it becomes spatially embedded and therefore inaccessible to those operating outside of the region's corridors.

A related advantage may come from catalyzed investment, from supply-side businesses as well as the migration of talented, job-seeking workers into the area. Cooke (2002) has noted that being part of a successful cluster lowers entry barriers for start-up companies: Gaps in service and unmet needs are more readily perceived. Specialized suppliers are established and locally available. Human capital is plentiful and well-trained. The availability of jobs across common industries may attract additional workers to the region (Storper and Scott 1992; Saperstein and Rouach 2002). This in turn can attract investment from firms seeking to tap into world-class talent, like the decision by Novartis to move its global R&D headquarters from Switzerland to Cambridge, Massachusetts, to be at the heart of a thriving biotech cluster. In this way, once established, clusters can become self-sustaining. As these outsiders are likely to be adept in some cluster-specific capacity, the region may grow increasingly specialized and thus of greater value to local businesses. For example, labor market specialization may reduce the costs borne by local employers on training and recruitment.

Can Government Create Clusters?

Despite the growth in cluster initiatives, the appropriateness of government intervention in regional economic development has been hotly contested. Sabel (1993:141), for example, stated that most "economic development programs . . . are either well-intentioned failures or publicity-minded frauds." Stam's (2009) recent review of the literature concluded that top-down efforts at cluster building are almost always unsuccessful. Indeed, the world's most successful high-tech industrial clusters—e.g., Silicon Valley, Cambridge, Massachusetts—have been more the result of world-class university and industrial serendipity than intentional government policy making. The growth of La Jolla's strong biotech cluster surrounding the University of California in San Diego provides a useful illustration of unplanned cluster evolution, as the founders of over 80 key companies in La Jolla emerged from a single failed merger between Hybritech and Eli Lilly (Casper 2007). This example notwithstanding, the appeal of generating relatively high-skilled, "sticky" jobs has prompted many recent government-led efforts trying to consciously stimulate cluster development.

Cluster development strategies have taken many forms. Some efforts have sought merely to improve the general business environment through tax policy, business-friendly regulation, or R&D incentives. Others have tackled infrastructural issues by funding technology parks and/or better modes of public transportation, or by addressing market imperfections, including imperfect information, by publicizing "economic trends as well as information and data on markets, customers, competitors, and technological trends specific to clusters" (Enright 2002:118). Some governments have even supplied risk capital, providing seed funding for emerging technologies and firms committed to creating good jobs in the regions (e.g., Bresnahan, Gambardella, and Saxenian 2001). Complementing these specific policy initiatives, some governments have sought ways to enhance collaboration among actors in a region (Lagendijk and Charles 1999; McEvily and Zaheer 2004). In Scotland, Wales, and England, for example, "cluster initiatives have emerged both as a part of the desire to improve the benefits from foreign investment by supporting supply chains and other forms of interfirm relationships, and to support networking among local firms" (Lagendijk and Charles 1999:127).

Developing human capital targeted to the common needs of firms in a sector has been another important component of regional economic development. Finegold (1999) has argued that, like real ecosystems, successful HSEs require four key elements: catalysts (research generating new intellectual property and innovation to spur economic momentum); supportive environments (social, institutional, or regulatory frameworks) to maintain vitality and support new firm creation; connectivity (social capital) between key regional stakeholders; and, finally, sustained nourishment (skills, human and financial capital) to facilitate innovation and improve the quality and relevance of the local labor market. Overseas, to a far greater extent than in the United States, regional economic development efforts have been complemented by sectorally focused public workforce training programs designed to improve employment opportunities for workers and strengthen the human capital available to local employers. While efforts to create clusters from scratch often fall well short of the intended goal (Sabel 1993; Stam 2009), international experience suggests that such sector-focused skill-building policies can be beneficial for all levels of workers, as well as for local businesses.

Cluster Skill Experiments: International Examples

We explore here three models of sectoral skill development: Singapore (high-tech), Germany (intermediate skills), and Australia (entry-level and up).

Singapore: From MNCs to a Biotech HSE

Singapore is perhaps the leading global example of sustained government effort to develop an HSE. It has a very successful track record over the last 40 years of using the education and training (ET) system as a key means to drive economic development. Starting with virtually no industrial base but having the assets of a very high literacy rate, a central-Asia location, a stable government, good infrastructure, and an English-speaking population, the state used generous investment incentives and other policies to attract multinational corporations (MNCs) to locate manufacturing, distribution, and regional headquarters in Singapore. It then used a reimbursable training levy to encourage firms to provide ongoing training to help the workforce move into increasingly high-value-added jobs (Magaziner and Patinkin 1989). Companies like Apple Computer discovered that Singapore's well-educated workforce was not only very productive, but also contributed numerous suggestions for incremental innovations, helping to make their plants in Singapore among the most effective in their global operations (Magaziner and Patinkin 1989).

Concerned that Singapore would eventually lose its competitive edge in information technology and manufacturing to lower-cost and much larger emerging powers of China, India, and other Asian nations, Singapore's leaders sought to foster the leap from incremental to radical innovation through the development of the most R&D-intensive of all sectors: the biomedical industry. While most other governments think in electoral cycles, Singapore's approach is distinguished by its long-term orientation. This feature is particularly vital in the bioscience sector, where a new drug typically takes more than a decade to make it from the research lab to the market. Through its powerful Economic Development Board (EDB), which created one of the first sovereign wealth funds, Singapore became an early investor in many of the first generation of successful U.S. biotech companies. These investments not only produced strong financial returns but also provided the government with key insights into the primary success factors required for this emerging sector.

The government recognized that succeeding in the biosciences would require a radical shift in Singapore's labor supply. While strong at producing a high and uniform level of basic skills, Singapore's ET system has historically been weak at generating research breakthroughs, creative risk-takers, and entrepreneurs. Creating new biotech firms requires a tolerance for failure and a free exchange of ideas among those with different viewpoints, characteristics that are not yet well incorporated into Singapore's ET system or culture. The government developed short-, medium-, and long-term approaches to build the necessary capabilities. In the short term, it offered generous financial incentives to attract Nobel Prize–winning scientists to set up research labs in Singapore and experienced scientists and managers from foreign bioscience firms to help lead new start-up companies. These provided immediate credibility to Singapore's nascent research efforts and attracted other top young scientists to work and train in Singapore. The medium-term strategy involves sending Singapore's top students to leading foreign research universities for graduate science and technology education. The government pays for their education provided that they return to Singapore when they complete their studies. In the long term, the government hopes that reforms of Singapore's education system, designed to encourage more freedom and creativity, and the expansion of its own universities and research institutes, bolstered by alliances established with top universities such as Johns Hopkins and MIT, can grow their own bioscience brainpower to generate the intellectual property for future local start-ups.

Along with human capital, the EDB has focused on putting in place the other key elements needed for an HSE. It has provided over $2 billion in financial capital for life-science firms, split between investments in venture capital funds that provide funding for new biotech ventures and financial incentives to attract MNCs to locate manufacturing, clinical development, and, most of all, centers of biomedical research in Singapore (Economic Development Board 1999; Saywell 2001). And to foster connections among the different players and provide the specialized infrastructure this industry requires, they invested US$500 million to build the Biopolis and nearby Tuas Biomedical park for bioscience manufacturing. This ambitious "city within a city" is near the National University of Singapore and the national hospital and contains five biomedical research institutes, along with a large vivarium to house the mice essential for preclinical studies. Thus far, the Biopolis strategy has had more success in growing academic research and attracting leading MNCs—GSK, Novartis, Chiron—to Singapore than it has in fostering the creation of new bioscience enterprises, but the government's long-term orientation and strong track record suggest that they will persist until they evolve a model that fits the Singapore context. (For more details on Singapore, see Finegold, Wong, and Cheah 2004.)

Germany: Sector Skills and Innovation

Germany has been less focused than Singapore on developing specific clusters; it has instead maintained national institutions that have closely connected workforce and economic development, and helped create the conditions in which HSEs can develop. This begins with an apprenticeship system through which the majority of the workforce obtains a strong educational foundation combined with a set of occupational skills. The close fit between training and local employer needs is ensured through tripartite governance and updating of national skills standards, a major on-the-job training component, and administration of the system through the local chambers of commerce and industry. This strong base of intermediate skills, combined with government-supported applied research institutes (Fraunhofer, Max Planck), has been a key enabler of continuing product and process innovation that has sustained Germany's place as a leading global manufacturer. The skill system has been complemented by institutions—works councils, patient capital, cooperative industrial relations—that have encouraged German manufacturers to pursue high-road strategies (e.g., Streeck 1989).

While Germany's coordinated-market-economy approach has been well documented (Hall and Soskice 2001), three features of how the system has evolved in response to recent global economic pressures are worth considering as part of the development of sectoral skill strategies. First, German apprenticeships have been modernized to include opportunities for individuals to progress into higher education, thereby retaining a majority of young people in the dual system and expanding coverage to the growing service sector (see Schurman and Soares, as well as Lerman, Chapters 6 and 7 in this volume). Second, Germany has been able to successfully transfer its traditional approach to become a leader in new high-technology, green sectors—such as solar energy and environmental technology—by combining strong demand-side incentives for investment with a highly skilled workforce. And finally, German public policy helped firms within clusters preserve their core capabilities during the deep global recession—by providing financial incentives to retain workers on reduced hours—rather than resorting to large layoffs that have resulted in sharp increases in unemployment in the United States.[1]

Australia: Promoting Skill Ecosystems

In response to concerns about low-skill demands for a high percentage of its workforce and growing competition from Asia, Australia has gone farther than any country in adopting HSEs as an explicit framework to guide its workforce development strategy (Windsor and Alcorso 2008). This began by expanding the HSE's original focus from solely high-technology clusters to embrace any sectoral skill system in a region "shaped by interlocking networks of firms, markets and institutions" (Buchanan et al. 2001). While substantially broadening the definition of HSEs, the approach retained "the core insight": the need to address the range of contextual factors that shape approaches to skill formation and usage within a particular ecosystem (Payne 2007), including these:

- Business settings (e.g., the type of product market, competitive strategies, business organizations/relations, financial system)
- Institutions and policy frameworks (vocational education and training [VET] and non-VET)
- Modes of engaging labor (e.g., labor hire)
- Structure of jobs (job design and work organization)
- Level and type of skills formation (e.g., apprenticeships, informal on-the-job training)

To this list we would add the factors that shape not just the formation and use of skills, but also the generation of new innovations that will both create new jobs and new skill needs.

With this broad approach to HSEs, the Australian national government and two state governments (New South Wales and Queensland) embarked on an ambitious set of pilot initiatives to test the relevance of the HSE concept in a variety of sectors, ranging from horse racing to health care (Windsor and Alcorso 2008). These 44 pilot initiatives, begun in 2003, all integrated skill provision with regional and economic development, addressing four main issues: "1) skill and labour shortages; 2) the role of VET as an innovation partner; 3) quality improvement across supply chains and networks; and 4) reshaping work and labour market measures aimed at supporting industry efforts to develop, utilise and retain a highly skilled workforce" (Payne 2007:3). The pilot experiments encountered many challenges—most notably, the ability to shift from a traditional supply-side focus to also address skill demand issues, as well as finding project managers capable of bridging the worlds of ET, industry, and other stakeholders—but they made sufficient progress that the promotion of HSEs has become a central tenet of the Australian government's future strategy. This shifts the focus from skill development to workforce development, recognizing the need to promote the demand for higher-level skills along with the effective use of those skills in the workplace. This will require (Skills Australia 2010):

- Enabling new industry connections—identification of an industry cluster or regional program through which to support multifaceted solutions to address skill demand issues and business performance and to lift capability across a range of workplaces
- Addressing skill use directly in enterprises. For instance, where public funds are involved for training, support could be linked to other interventions taken by enterprises to tackle job design, work organization, or organizational performance and to engage workers
- Developing the capacity of enterprises—examination of opportunities to build the internal capacity of enterprises as learning organizations by developing leadership and management capacity

United States Examples

The U.S. has failed to develop well-recognized sector skill standards and a strong sectoral dimension to public workforce training initiatives found in these other nations. Recent local and regional experiments, however, suggest that sector skill strategies not only can be successful in stimulating the development of innovation and new job creation, but can also do a better job of improving the career prospects of disadvantaged workers than the traditional offerings from the U.S. public workforce development system. Some leading examples are highlighted below.

Regional Workforce Funding Collaboratives

As part of the National Sector Strategy Partnership (NSSP), a number of leading private foundations have come together with the public workforce development system, employers, and education and training providers to support the development of regional collaborations focused on the skill needs of particular sectors (Mills 2010). A prominent early example of their efforts is the Bay Area Workforce Funding Collaborative initiative in the biotech and health care sectors. Founded in 2004, this public–private partnership's first round of $3.4 million in grants funded the development of new targeted programs and training for over 700 unskilled and displaced workers to assume career-ladder jobs in these sectors, paying $27,000 to $60,000. SkillWorks in Boston has taken a similar approach, placing over half of the 500 displaced workers it has trained in new jobs and upgrading the skills of over 1,000 incumbent workers to assist with career advancement (Mills 2010).

Public/Private Ventures (Maguire, Freely, Clymer, and Conway 2009) used an experimental design to compare three leading sector skill programs:

- The Wisconsin Regional Training Partnership, a labor–management cooperation that brought together stakeholders from manufacturing, construction, and health care to provide 40- to 160-hour technical and general skills training in areas tailored to local industry demand

- Jewish Vocational Services in Boston, which provided 21- to 25-week training courses, including a 4- to 6-week internship, in medical and basic office skills

- *Per Scholas* in The Bronx, New York, a nonprofit social venture that refurbished computers and provided 500 hours of computer technician training

Public/Private Ventures recruited 1,285 low-wage workers who were eligible for public training assistance, having earned under $10,000 and worked seven months prior to the trial. They were randomly assigned to one of the three programs or a control group that could receive free employment services and training, and were followed for 24 months. A third of the control group received training; 8% of those in the treatment groups did not. The results were quite dramatic: Those who took part in the sectoral training earned 29% more on average in the year after the training than those in the control group, and they were more likely to receive benefits. The effect was due to a combination of participants being more likely to find steady jobs, working more hours, and earning a higher hourly wage.

New York City

In 2002, when Michael Bloomberg took office as mayor, he replaced New York City's Department of Employment with a new Department of Business Services (DBS) that would focus on tying workforce development and other programs more closely to employer needs. This combined funding from WIA, the Economic Development Administration, private foundations, and other sources to create the largest Workforce Investment Board (WIB) in the United States, which oversees seven One-Stops spread across the city. Three years ago, inspired by the research on the effectiveness of sector approaches, the DBS launched two small pilot efforts in health care and biotechnology. In 2008, this was expanded into a $5-million competition soliciting proposals from public and private providers to create three sectoral One-Stops: The first one, for transportation, was established in Queens in June 2008, followed by health care and manufacturing in fall 2009. Chris Neale, who oversees the program, explained the selection and rationale (Finegold 2010):

> We didn't specify sectors, although we eliminated IT and Finance because we wanted to focus on industries that would work for the low-income population we were targeting. A big part of what makes sector strategy successful is having an organization running it that has strong employer connections and is able to bring the full range of stakeholders. We chose providers that demonstrated these capabilities. There were other sectors we would like to have, but need a great organization to make it work.

The transportation center already appears to be generating success, helping 1,800 individuals in its first 18 months of operation either to find a job in the sector or to retrain for higher-level work within their existing employer. The new health care and manufacturing centers are focusing on helping individuals move up the occupational ladder, developing longer-term training and placement programs for high-demand areas such as emergency medical technicians, paramedics, diesel mechanics, and CNC machinists. All have employer advisory bodies that guide the development of training to meet job needs. As they continue to evolve, one of the key issues will be how well they coordinate with the area One-Stops to provide a seamless service for employers and individuals in particular sectors.

Chicago

In an effort to make WIA programs more relevant to local businesses, the City of Chicago in 2005 launched Manufacturing Works (MW) and Service Works (SW), two sector-based service centers designed to serve as brokers among regional employers, workforce and economic development programs, employees, and job seekers in manufacturing, hospitality, and customer service (Schrock 2009). These initiatives were intended to integrate a range of discrete state- and federally funded services, targeting business as their primary customer. Their brokerage role allows them to provide recruitment services, human resource support, and worker training, among other features. Together MW and SW have served 315 local employers and placed 878 workers. Their placed manufacturing workers have averaged a starting wage of $12.49 per hour, while service sector workers have averaged $10.89 (Schrock 2009).

Connecticut

Workplace Inc., located in southwest Connecticut, is one of the most entrepreneurial workforce development organizations in the United States. It has evolved a multipronged business model that combines serving as one of the state's four regional WIBs with a non-profit 501(c)3 that allows it to leverage public and private funds to meet the skill and economic development needs of individuals and employers in the region (Finegold 2009a, 2009b). Workplace Inc. created the Center for Capacity Development, which serves as a consulting, grant-writing, and outsourcing service (human resources, information technology, finance) for over 150 small and medium-sized enterprises and nonprofit and public sector organizations, working with them to bring in nearly $15 million in external resources to the region. Workplace Inc. has identified four key sectors as vital for maintaining Connecticut's position as one of the states with the country's highest living standards: finance, health care, green jobs, and advanced manufacturing. Through TechLine, for example, it has built a supply-chain partnership that starts with ASML U.S. Inc., a provider of advanced microlithography manufacturing systems, and works with six of its suppliers in the region to enhance their workforce and organizational capabilities.

A National Cluster Strategy: WIRED

As these examples suggest, there is a small but growing number of promising sector skill initiatives under way in some of the U.S.'s largest clusters. With a few notable exceptions, however, these have continued to concentrate on displaced and lower-skilled workers who have been the traditional clients for the U.S. public workforce development system, rather than developing high-skill ecosystems that might stimulate the development of high-skill jobs in the United States. In a major departure from past policy, the Bush administration launched the Workforce Innovation and Regional Economic Development (WIRED) initiative in November 2005. The program was driven by a belief "that national competitiveness and regional prosperity are possible if communities learn how to link their varied knowledge resources with their business and innovation assets, and ensure that their workforces have the new skills and knowledge required to work effectively in new and emerging industries" (Almandsmith et al. 2008:i).

The government sought to stimulate HSE development by inviting competitive bids from regions across the United States (see Figure 1). Applicants were to focus on the sectors of greatest importance to their economies and to define regions that corresponded to true local labor markets, unlike the existing WIB structure that often corresponded to local or county governments. Rather than treat this as another new government program, grantees were supposed to leverage WIRED funds with other public and private sector resources to build a coherent workforce and economic development system. The U.S. Department of

FIGURE 1
Thirty-Nine WIRED Regions.

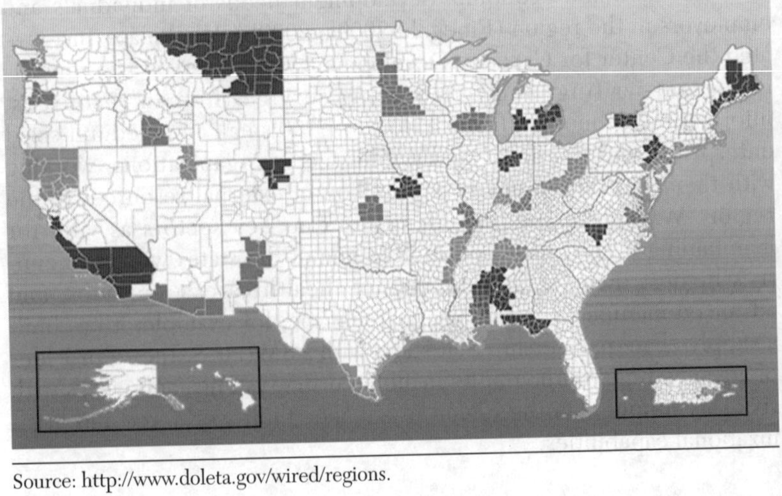

Source: http://www.doleta.gov/wired/regions.

Labor awarded $325 million in three rounds that began in 2006 ($15 million over three years to the first 13 winners and $5 million over three years to the second- and third-generation grantees), with the last round of grants expiring in June 2010.

The WIRED initiative, despite its seemingly bipartisan objectives, was controversial from the outset. It was one of the few significant new initiatives announced by the Labor Department during the Bush administration's eight-year tenure, and it was perceived by many existing players as a way to work around and undermine the workforce development system in place rather than as a potential basis for transforming it. The funds, which came from H1-B visa program fees, were redirected from existing programs to train displaced workers without congressional approval. Despite these concerns, the lure of a new initiative to a system that had faced steadily declining resources was very attractive, creating a highly competitive application process. Below we focus on one WIRED region that explicitly sought to use WIRED funds to build an HSE.

Bio-1 Case Study[2]

For most of the 20th century, the bioscience industry, in particular large pharmaceutical companies, was a core sector of the New Jersey economy. Over the last decade, however, this industry has undergone major restructuring, as research and development costs have risen dramatically while the rate of new product approvals has fallen, driving average costs per new approved molecule to over $1 billion (Burrill 2007). This has forced large pharmaceutical companies to rethink their vertically integrated business models and to begin reaching out more to biotech companies and other partners to fuel innovation in their pipeline. At the same time, they have sought to maintain profits through consolidation, using mergers and acquisition to cut costs and combine product pipelines. New Jersey, which had already seen its share of U.S. bioscience employment fall from 20% to 13% (Heldrich Center 2007), has been hit particularly hard by this merger trend, losing three corporate headquarters in 2009 alone as a result of the mergers between Pfizer-Wyeth, Merck-Schering Plough, and Roche-Genentech.

To try to reverse this trend, in 2007 central New Jersey applied for and was awarded one of the third-generation WIRED grants. Titled Bio-1, this effort has targeted the bioscience-based cluster that runs along the Route 1 corridor that connects Princeton with Rutgers and the University of Medicine and Dentistry of New Jersey (UMDNJ). At the core of Bio-1's strategy was the labor market analysis that suggested the region had more individuals who had brought products successfully through the FDA and to market than anywhere on the planet. Drawing on the analogy of the growth in the San Diego cluster that came from the talent emerging from the Hybritech-Lilly merger, Bio-1 has sought to turn the hardship created for the thousands of experienced bioscience professionals displaced by the mergers and industry restrictions into an opportunity by matching this talent with bioscience firms from around the world and across the United States that are interested in investing in New Jersey. Rather than training and developing workers itself, Bio-1 operates by bringing various state, local, and federal entities, educational institutions, venture capitalists, business and industry leaders, and other stakeholders together around issues of sectoral skills and workforce and economic development. Through the course of its funding, it has also served as a network facilitator among key regional stakeholders, including universities, businesses, and venture capitalists.

Bio-1 Accomplishments

Bio-1 had two main types of achievement during its first two years of operations, from the time the grant kicked off in November 2007 through the end of 2009. The first, more concrete successes were those achieved by 30 projects that were funded with the majority of the $5 million available, with the remainder going to staff and overhead expenses. The less tangible but potentially more important long-term achievements were the new relationships that were built through these activities between and among New Jersey's education providers, employers, and other stakeholders in the bioscience industry, which will be illustrated using network analysis.

A key criterion for the projects that were funded was the potential to have a lasting impact beyond the life of the grant. Bio-1 had the luxury of focusing most of its expenditure on this form of long-term capacity and system building, rather than direct training of individuals, since it was able to leverage an additional $300,000 a year in state custom training grants for bioscience employers, which appeared adequate to meet industry demand. Among the highlights of what the Bio-1 participants have produced are these:

- *Bioscience careers website, brochure, and jobs portal.* The website http://www.bio-one.org is a one-stop destination for bioscience career information, featuring descriptions of and labor market information for all of the main jobs in the New Jersey bioscience industry, video profiles of diverse individuals in these jobs, and a custom online jobs board built around the national biotechnology competency framework that helps match individuals and employers for internship and employment opportunities. These are supported by a popular career brochure distributed across the state and by curriculum and training for biology teachers and careers counselors to integrate the material into their practice.

- *Global partnerships to foster new firm and job creation.* New Jersey is already home to the U.S. headquarters of many international bioscience companies, attracted by the proximity to potential large pharmaceutical partners, strong air and transport infrastructure, a very diverse, highly educated population, and proximity to both New York financial markets and the FDA. Bio-1 sought to attract new foreign investment in New Jersey by funding development of a "mini-MBA" in global bio-entrepreneurship, an innovative combination of workforce and economic development. The first of two sessions of this one-week intensive program brought together a dozen companies from 10 countries around the world, matched carefully with 18 talented bioscience professionals in New Jersey who together had over 350 years of experience bringing drugs from the lab to the market. They worked together in teams with academic and industry experts to refine business plans for new companies to be created in New Jersey that they then presented to top bioscience investors. Within a week after the first session, a New Zealand bioinformatics company had begun hiring talent for its U.S. operations in Newark, and a Chinese biotech start-up had decided to shift its U.S. headquarters from Maryland to New Jersey as a result of the program.

- *Master's of Business and Science (MBS) degree.* Bio-1 provided an initial seed grant of $400,000 to enable Rutgers to create a new professional science master's (PSM) degree framework and an associated Certificate in Management of Science and Technology for individuals who already possess an advanced technical degree. The MBS integrates a science or engineering specialty—such as biotechnology, drug development, and advanced food technology—with a set of business courses geared toward science-based industries. It was designed in close partnership with New Jersey employers to meet their need for integrators who can bridge between PhDs and MBAs to help develop new technologies. It is part of a growing national trend, with more than 100 PSM programs now in existence, although New Jersey had just one small program before the MBS. Rutgers was able to leverage the Bio-1 funding to bring in an additional $2 million in support to launch the degree framework, which spans 14 schools across all three Rutgers campuses. The new degree was officially approved in December 2009 and had 22 different specializations up and running by fall 2010 (http://www.psm.rutgers.edu). The goal is not just to make Rutgers a national leader in this new form of graduate education, but also to help stimulate the growth of new biobusinesses in the region, since each student's capstone project will be to join a team that develops business plans for new innovations emerging from Rutgers' labs or its partner institutions.

- *Articulation agreements between community colleges and four-year universities.* These agreements should facilitate smooth transfer of credits and hence improve the speed of degree completion for students from the region's four community colleges to New Jersey public universities with the strongest bioscience programs.

- *Creating a system for the alternative route to teacher training.* New Jersey already had a number of programs designed to address the shortage of well-qualified science and math teachers in the public schools by enabling individuals with relevant degrees and work experience to train to become teachers. Bio-1 provided support to expand some of the top programs, created a brochure and marketing program, devoted a section of its website to make it easy for interested individuals to identify available programs, and created a virtual support network to help these new teachers make the transition to the classroom. The program was seen as a potential dual win for Bio-1, increasing the supply of science, technology, engineering, and mathematics (STEM) teachers and providing new career opportunities for individuals displaced from the pharmaceutical industry.

- *Retraining of displaced workers.* In addition to the alternative-route programs for teacher training, Bio-1 supported the creation of a number of innovative workforce development programs not covered by the state's custom training program. These include a Biotech Boot Camp for workers affected by the closure of Fort Monmouth to help them retrain for regulatory and compliance jobs in the bioscience sector and a mini-MBA in global biopharma innovation that will teach 15 experienced displaced workers interested in starting their own biobusinesses or joining new enterprises, along with 15 individuals from countries around the world who are seeking to enter the U.S. market by establishing operations in New Jersey, the key elements needed to create a bioscience business plan.

- *Bioscience Fellows Program.* The deep recession has created a very weak job market for new graduates. Bio-1 addressed this issue in 2009 by emulating a successful program from its partner WIRED region, the Delaware Valley Innovation Network, to provide a $3,000 grant to employers to encourage them to take on new graduates on six-month fellowship. The goal is to create 101 placements, and some of the fellows have already moved into full-time jobs.

Social network analysis was conducted to measure what impact Bio-1 has had on relationships among stakeholders in the region. Figure 2 illustrates the pre- and post-WIRED Bio-1 Initiative interorganizational communication patterns as given by 38 participants, each in some way affiliated with the initiative.[3] The shapes represent different institutional sectors. Participating organizations from the sample reported a 70.54% growth in ties in the post-initiative network relative to the pre-initiative network. Additional statistics for these data, as well as a more detailed

FIGURE 2
Growth in Network Ties Among Bio-1 Stakeholders.

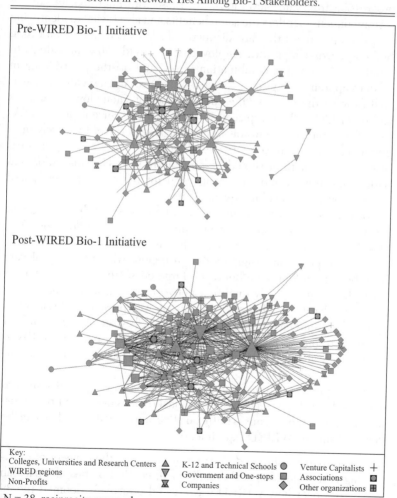

Pre-WIRED Bio-1 Initiative

Post-WIRED Bio-1 Initiative

Key:
Colleges, Universities and Research Centers	▲	K-12 and Technical Schools	◯	Venture Capitalists	+
WIRED regions	▽	Government and One-stops	◼	Associations	⬓
Non-Profits	✕	Companies	◆	Other organizations	⊞

N = 38, reciprocity assumed

explanation of the context and sampling procedures, are available in McCarthy, Rubinstein, and Finegold (2010).

Conclusions and Ways Forward

Both international experience and experiments now under way across America suggest that there would be significant benefits to creating a strong sectoral focus for workers at all levels in a transformed U.S. workforce development system. For lower-skilled workers, a sectoral approach offers better connections with employers and the potential to build career ladders that would allow for ongoing skill development and progression from entry-level jobs. For those with intermediate skills, a sectoral dimension offers the same benefits and also is vital to identifying those competencies that are distinctive to key occupations, and then building partnerships with employers that would allow individuals to build these through a combination of on- and off-the-job training in modern apprenticeships or technician programs. And a sector strategy is vital to meet the needs of the large number of unemployed graduates and other high-skilled displaced workers that the current public workforce development system was never designed to serve. By closely integrating economic and workforce development to develop HSEs in areas of regional strength, it should be possible to stimulate innovation and with it address the most pressing need for the coming decade and beyond: the creation of high-quality jobs.

Best of all, in the current environment of severely constrained resources, a sector strategy can be pursued at relatively low cost. The experience from Bio-1 and other WIRED areas, as well as other successful sector experiments, suggests that in regions where the key players have begun working together, each targeted sector can be sustained through a single, highly qualified network broker, an administrative assistant, a local travel budget, and a strong web presence. Through this approach, a state might be able to cover eight key sectors for $2 million per year, resources that could be generated by consolidating WIBs to more closely align with regional labor markets as part of the reauthorization of the WIA.

In the process of transforming the workforce development system to combine both strong sectoral and regional dimensions, it will be important to apply the lessons—both positive and negative—that can be derived from the WIRED experiment:

- *Avoid partisanship and short-termism.* While the concept of creating HSEs should appeal broadly to all political parties, the partisan battles over how WIRED was created effectively doomed the 39 pilots as soon as there was a change in presidential administration. Future efforts should seek to build a bipartisan consensus and a small core of sustainable funding for HSEs that can demonstrate their effectiveness.

- *Integrate workforce and economic development.* Although this was a core part of the original WIRED vision, subsequent rule changes prohibited grantees from spending WIRED funds on economic development, effectively removing the "ED" from the WIRED remit. A future system needs close integration at both national and regional levels between the Departments of Commerce and Labor and the Economic Development Administration.

- *Focus on the system.* One of the most valuable lasting contributions of Bio-1 and the efforts of many WIRED regions was shifting public workforce development programs from operating in relative isolation to being a more integrated part of a sector-based regional development system. This included building connections among different levels of education and training providers (from K–12 schools through to research universities and training organization) and between them and employers, investors, and other key stakeholders.

- *Minimize bureaucracy.* It is important to ensure that the public's money is well spent, so engaging employers actively in the workforce development system requires a streamlined process that minimizes paperwork and allows rapid and flexible local responses to changing labor market conditions.

Through this type of integrated approach, the role of the government in workforce development might gradually shift from *provider of last resort* for workers on the margins of the labor market to *climate setter* and *network facilitator*, where government establishes the regulatory and other conditions needed to stimulate HSEs and proactively fosters interorganizational relationships.

Endnotes

[1] It is important to note, however, that the strong employment protections and generous benefits in Germany have produced a much higher level of structural unemployment than in the United States.

[2] Author David Finegold was the principal investigator on the Bio-1 grant.

[3] This research tried to incorporate responses from a broad range of organizations (e.g., private sector, government, universities) as well as from organizations with varying levels of involvement. For example, some of the surveyed organizations were extensively involved in task teams that were coordinated by WIRED Bio-1 administrators, while others were not. A forthcoming article by McCarthy, Rubinstein, and Finegold elaborates the context and analytic sample for this study.

References

Almandsmith, Sherry, Mary Walshok, Kay Magill, Linda Toms Barker, Pamela Surko, Mary Vencill, Tommy Smith, Hannah Betesh, and June Chocheles. 2008. *Early Implementation of Generation I of the Workforce Innovation in Regional Economic Development (WIRED) Initiative.* Interim capital evaluation report prepared by Berkeley Policy Associates. Washington, DC: U.S. Department of Labor, ETA/OGCM.

Almeida, P., and B. Kogut. 1999. "Localization of Knowledge and the Mobility of Engineers in Regional Networks." *Management Science,* Vol. 45, no. 7, pp. 905–17.

Applegate, Lynda 2006. "Building Inter-firm Collaborative Community: Uniting Theory and Practice." In C. Heckscher and P. Adler, eds., *The Firm as a Collaborative Community.* Oxford, England: Oxford University Press, pp. 355–416.

Best, Michael H. 1990. *The New Competition: Institutions of Industrial Restructuring.* Cambridge, England: Polity Press.

Bresnahan, T., A. Gambardella, and A. Saxenian. 2001. " 'Old Economy' Inputs for 'New Economy' Outcomes: Cluster Formation in the New Silicon Valleys." *Industrial and Corporate Change,* Vol. 10, no. 4, pp. 835–60.

Buchanan, J., K. Schofield, C. Briggs, G. Considine, P. Hager, G. Hawke, J. Kitay, J. Meagher, A. Mounier, and S. Ryan. 2001. *Beyond Flexibility: Skills and Work in the Future,* Sydney: New South Wales Board of Vocational Education and Training.

Burrill, Steven. 2007. *Biotech Industry Report 2007.* San Francisco: Burrill & Co.

Casper, Steven. 2007. "How Do Technology Clusters Emerge and Become Sustainable? Social Network Formation and Inter-Firm Mobility within the San Diego Biotechnology Cluster." *Research Policy,* Vol. 36, no. 4, pp. 438–55.

Cooke, Philip. 2002. "Biotechnology Clusters as Regional, Sectoral Innovation Systems." *International Regional Science Review,* Vol. 25, no. 1, pp. 8–37.

Economic Development Board. 1999. *Annual Report: Life Sciences.* <http://www.sedb.com/edbcorp/an_1999_13.jsp>. [July 6, 2010].

Enright, M. 2002. "Regional Clusters: What We Know and What We Should Know." In J. Brocker, D. Dohse, and R. Soltwedel, eds., *Innovation Clusters and Interregional Competition.* Berlin: Springer Publishers, pp. 99–129.

Finegold, D. 1999. "Creating Self-Sustaining High-Skill Ecosystems." *Oxford Review of Economic Policy,* Vol. 15, no. 1, pp. 1–22.

Finegold, David L. 2009a. "National Skills Strategy Needed." *Washington Times,* April 8. <http:www.washingtontimes.com/news/2009/apr/08/national-skills-strategy-needed/>. [July 27, 2010].

Finegold, D. 2009b. Personal interview with Joseph Carbone, director of Workplace Inc Southwestern Connecticut Workforce Investment Board, April 22.

Finegold, D. 2010. Personal interview with Chris Neale, director of Sector Skill Initiatives, NYC Department of Business Services, January 26.

Finegold, David, Poh-Kam Wong, and Tsui-Chern Cheah. 2004. "Adapting a Foreign Direct Investment Strategy to the Knowledge Economy: The Case of Singapore's Emerging Biotechnology Cluster." *European Planning Studies,* Vol. 12, no. 7, pp. 921–41.

Gittelman, Michelle. 2006. *Does Geography Matter for Science-Based Firms? Epistemic Communities and the Geography of Research and Patenting in Biotechnology.* Unpublished paper, Stern School of Business, New York University.

Griliches, Zev. 1992. "The Search for R&D Spillovers." *Scandinavian Journal of Economics,* Vol. 94 (Supplement), pp. 29–47.

Hall, P., and D. Soskice, eds. 2001. *Varieties of Capitalism,* Oxford, England: Oxford University Press.

Heldrich Center. 2007. *The Workforce Needs of New Jersey's Pharmaceutical and Medical Technology Industry.* New Brunswick, NJ: Rutgers University, John J. Heldrich Center for Workforce Development.

Kelly, K. 1998. *New Rules for the New Economy: Ten Ways the Network Economy Is Changing Everything.* London: Fourth Estate.

Lafer, Gordon. 2002. *The Job Training Charade.* Ithaca, NY: Cornell University Press.

Lagendijk, A., and D. Charles. 1999. "Clustering as a New Growth Strategy for Regional Economies? A Discussion of New Forms of Regional Industrial Policy in the UK." In *Cluster-Analysis and Cluster-Based Policy: New Perspectives and Rationale in Innovation Policy-Making.* Paris: Organisation for Economic Cooperation and Development, pp. 127–55.

Magaziner, I., and M. Patinkin. 1989. *The Silent War.* New York: Random House.

Maguire, S., J. Freely, C. Clymer, and M. Conway. 2009. *Job Training That Works: Findings from the Sectoral Employment Impact Study,* P/PV in Brief, issue 7, May. Philadelphia: Public/Private Ventures.

McCarthy, J., S. Rubinstein, and D. Finegold. 2010. *Catalyzed Networks: Government as a Network Facilitator in Regional Economies.* Unpublished paper, Rutgers University.

McEvily, B., and A. Zaheer. 2004. "Architects of Trust: The Role of Network Facilitators in Geographical Clusters." In R. Kramer and K. Cook, eds., *Trust and Distrust in Organizations: Dilemmas and Approaches.* New York: Russell Sage Foundation, pp. 189–213.

Mills, J. 2010. *Overview of Regional Workforce Funding Collaboratives.* Oakland, CA: National Network of Sector Partners.

Payne, Jonathan. 2007. *Skill Ecosystems: A New Approach to Vocational Education and Training Policy.* SKOPE Issue Paper no. 14. Oxford, England: ESRC Centre on Skills, Knowledge and Organisational Performance.

Piore, Michael J., and Charles F. Sabel. 1984. *The Second Industrial Divide: Possibilities for Prosperity.* New York: Basic Books.

Porter, Michael E. 2000. "Location, Competition, and Economic Development: Local Clusters in a Global Economy." *Economic Development Quarterly,* Vol. 14, no. 1, pp. 15–34.

Sabel, Charles F. 1993. "Studied Trust: Building New Forms of Cooperation in a Volatile Economy." *Human Relations,* Vol. 46, no. 9, pp. 1133–70.

Saperstein, J., and D. Rouach. 2002. *Creating Regional Wealth in the Innovation Economy: Models, Perspectives, and Best Practices.* Upper Saddle River, NJ: Financial Times, Prentice Hall.

Saxenian, Anna Lee. 1994. *Regional Advantage: Culture and Competition in Silicon Valley and Route 128.* Cambridge, MA: Harvard University Press.

Saywell, Trish. 2001. "Medicine for the Economy." *Far Eastern Economic Review,* November 15.

Schrock, G. 2009. "Re-working Workforce Development: Chicago's Sector-Based Workforce Centers." *Report to the Chicago Workforce Investment Board and the Joyce Foundation,* pp. 1–28.

Scott, Alan J. 1998. *Regions and the World Economy: The Coming Shape of Global Production, Competition, and Political Order.* Oxford, England; New York: Oxford University Press.

Skills Australia. 2010. *Australian Workforce Futures: A National Workforce Development Strategy.* Barton, ACT: Commonwealth of Australia. <http://www.skills australia.gov.au/PDFs_RTFs/WWF_strategy.pdf>. [October 20, 2010].

Stam, E. 2009. "Cluster Creation." *Regional Studies,* Vol. 43, no. 2, pp. 319–23.

Storper, M., and A.J. Scott. 1992. *Pathways to Industrialization and Regional Development*. London, New York: Routledge.

Streeck, W. 1989. "Skill and the Limits of Neo-Liberalism: The Enterprise of the Future as a Place of Learning." *Work, Employment and Society*, Vol. 3, no. 1, pp. 89–104.

Von Hippel, Eric. 1994. " 'Sticky Information' and the Locus of Problem Solving: Implications for Innovation." *Management Science*, Vol. 40, no. 4, pp. 429–39.

Windsor, K., and C. Alcorso. 2008. *Skills in Context: A Guide to the Skill Ecosystem Approach to Workforce Development*. Sydney: NSW Department of Education and Training and Commonwealth Department of Education, Employment and Workplace Relations.

Zucker, Lynn G., Michael Darby, and Michael Brewer. 1998. "Intellectual Human Capital and the Birth of U.S. Biotechnology Enterprises." *The American Economic Review*, Vol. 88, no. 1, pp. 290–306.

CHAPTER 9

Joint Union–Management Workforce Development Model

DANIEL MARSCHALL
ELLEN SCULLY-RUSS
The George Washington University

In their early synthesis of the features shared by joint training programs, Ferman, Hoyman, and Cutcher-Gershenfeld (1990:160) argued that such programs, as they emerged from the industrial restructuring of the 1980s, represented a distinctive innovation in worker training and career development with the potential to become "a stable and significant domain" in labor–management relations. The authors described joint training programs as an emerging set of institutional arrangements that included large-scale, negotiated, and jointly administered trust funds providing technical training, personal development, and access to education for union members. Though there were many examples of joint union–management training activity prior to the appearance of the industrial joint training program model, earlier programs were narrowly focused on single-issue training or time-bounded training efforts. In contrast, the new model spanned many areas of training activity, covered divergent populations of workers and managers, and incorporated service delivery strategies guided by a philosophy of worker involvement and jointly determined decision making. Among other research implications, the authors identified the classification of joint training activities as a challenge for understanding the structural tendencies within these young organizations.

Notably, the authors speculated that the emergence of these innovative joint training programs marked a historic change in traditional collective bargaining practices and past attitudes of both union and management toward the centrality of education and training activities. Gomberg (1967), writing during a time when union density was near its postwar high and the mechanisms of collective bargaining were finely tuned, argued that special labor–management committees, including those covering human relations issues, were transitory formations that reflected (inherently unstable) experiments in class collaboration and focused on supplementary issues (such as worker displacement). Such efforts would survive, he said, only if they remained subsidiary to the collective bargaining process. Contemporary industrial relations experts disagree. Based on the experience of employee involvement programs, Cutcher-Gershenfeld, Kochan, and Verma (1991) concluded that jointly sponsored participative initiatives that involved unions as full partners and were directly connected to collective bargaining contracts were likely to be sustained over time because they bore the capacity to broaden out to encompass many issues, helping to institutionalize the program into the overall operations of the organization. Joint programs were not isolated phenomena, these authors argued, but signaled a fundamental restructuring of labor–management relations. As both management and labor came to understand the need for continuous workplace learning for employees and adjusted the services in joint programs according to competitive pressures, scholars predicted that such programs could become "permanent social institutions" (Ferman, Hoyman, and Cutcher-Gershenfeld 1990:161).

Our research into the current status of joint training and continuous workplace learning programs bolsters the argument of latter-day scholars. We examine the extent to which these programs have been institutionalized as well as the potential role of the joint union–management training model in helping to craft the comprehensive workforce development system called for in this volume.

In the two decades since the first edition of this volume was published, new joint training programs have emerged, while diminishing resources have forced several existing programs to modify their offerings and others to shut their doors altogether. Still other programs have expanded their service offerings beyond the provision of formal education and training in the workplace and now include a wide array of services that intervene at the point of production to improve quality and firm performance, increase the level of worker skill and expertise, and help U.S.-based firms meet the demands of global competition. In addition, many joint union–management training programs now engage in regional and sector partnerships, taking on new functions as workforce development intermediaries in the external labor market to extend their services beyond individual firms and to new population groups in the wider community. Importantly, the joint training program model has spread its reach across the domestic economy, expanding from its manufacturing roots in the Midwest to service sector firms spread across the nation.

Our review suggests that joint training programs have proven to be resilient institutions with the capacity to respond to the great need for ongoing education among active and laid-off workers. In this chapter we argue that the involvement of joint union–management partnerships in internal and external labor markets not only strengthens the joint training program model but also adds value to the broader workforce development system, helping improve the system's effectiveness in those industries and regions where joint programs exist. Furthermore, we argue that joint training programs not only represent a shift in the strategic importance of jointness within the U.S. labor movement, but that these efforts were the primary mechanisms by which this shift occurred.

We begin the chapter with a discussion of two seminal works on joint training programs that together codified the joint training model, including its organizational structure and worker-centered pedagogy (Sarmiento and Kay 1990). We continue with a review of the literature about joint training published between 1990 and 2009. The aim of this review is to identify the features of the model that have been institutionalized and to discuss the innovations that have occurred. In order to highlight the structural features of joint programs that contribute to their sustainability, we present a five-part classification of key features.

This review is followed by a discussion of the Institute for Career Development (ICD), a joint education and training partnership between the United Steel Workers union and multiple employers in the steel and rubber industries. Though the program has at times faced threats to its sustainability, it has also experienced tremendous growth in its scope and reach over 20 years. This growth contrasts with other programs in the manufacturing industry that have contracted or in some cases been dismantled all together. Our purpose is to explore the features, mechanisms, and processes that have made the ICD a resilient and sustainable institution of worker education. We conclude with a discussion of the policies that may help strengthen and expand the role of joint training programs in the 21st-century workforce development system.

The Legacy of the 1980s: The Joint Training Program Model

The joint training model first emerged in 1982 when, faced with massive industrial restructuring, the United Automobile, Aerospace and Agricultural Implement Workers of America (UAW) and the Ford Motor Company negotiated the UAW–Ford Education, Training and Development Program to retrain thousands of displaced auto workers in new careers (Ferman, Hoyman, and Cutcher-Gershenfeld 1990). The parties realized before long that industrial restructuring required active workers to develop deeper technical skills and broader capacity for critical thinking and problem solving. The UAW–Ford program was broadened to offer education and training to incumbent workers. The UAW quickly distributed the model throughout the auto sector, first by negotiating new programs with the other two U.S. automakers, General Motors and Chrysler, and then with the larger auto supply firms. Soon the Communications Workers of America (CWA) and the International Brotherhood of Electrical Workers (IBEW) took up the model and negotiated a joint training fund in the 1986 contract with AT&T, forming the Alliance for Employee Growth and Development.

By the early 1990s, the model had become widely distributed among large, unionized firms. In their early years, joint programs represented a significant new investment in the education and training of a segment of the American workforce, front-line industrial workers, who had been largely ignored by the training sponsored by employers and the public system. The new programs were massive, well-funded operations that offered services to thousands of workers across the country. In addition, training delivery was largely decentralized, designed and administered by local committees and functioning through contracts with local education providers. The limited history and the complex nature of these programs meant little could be known about their operations and their outcomes. Indeed, the authors acknowledged that there was limited scholarship available to draw on in their discussion of the model.

To compensate for the lack of systematic research on joint programs, the authors drew on data from a survey of 102 labor–management pairs and the anecdotal accounts of program leaders and practitioners in large, national programs (Ferman, Hoyman, Cutcher-Gershenfeld, and Savoie 1991) to outline the basic program model and explain how joint programs were an innovation to workforce development and training (see Table 1). In its simplest form the model consisted of three basic elements: a negotiated training trust fund, a joint governance structure including a single union and a single employer, and a mission to upgrade the skills and meet the personal development needs of union members. Their description of the model elaborates on these basic features.

> The picture that emerges is a training activity characterized by codetermination in decision making, with high degrees of local control, that is providing services to active and displaced workers via a mix of internal worker-trainers and external service providers, all of which may be supported with internal funds and public dollars (pp. 164–65).

In the same year the AFL-CIO Human Resources Development Institute (HRDI) published *Worker-Centered Learning: A Union Guide to Workplace Literacy* (Sarmiento and Kay 1990). Rather than focus on the institutional arrangements, funding mechanisms, and institutional relationships, these authors offered a prescription for a worker-centered

TABLE 1
Distinctive Features of Joint Training Programs.

- Are rooted in and defined by collective bargaining that specifies mission, governance, and coverage and provides a financial formula.
- Target broad populations, including displaced and active workers.
- Emphasize career development, employment security, and broad training and education that would increase workforce flexibility.
- Developed under an implicit agreement that joint training programs would not replace existing union and company training obligations such as apprenticeship training and specific job- or production-related training.
- Include codetermination in decision making.
- Present participant-driven content, with training based on workers' expressed needs and aspirations.
- Exhibit high degree of local control over training, with local joint committees determining needs, organizing training, and developing service delivery systems and relationships.
- Make extensive use of local community networks for counseling, assessment, and training.
- Evaluate based on outcomes for workers.

Source: Ferman, Hoyman, and Cutcher-Gershenfeld 1990.

pedagogy to guide the development of joint training programs and their relationships with workers. By combining trade union values for workplace democracy and equity with established principles of adult learning, worker-centered learning places the learners' needs and interests at the center of the educational process. Workers are engaged in every step of the process, from design to delivery to evaluation. In addition, basic education and job-related training are broadly contextualized so that the participants are encouraged to explore the social, economic, and political structures that shape their work and skill requirements. The authors articulated several worker-centered learning principles (depicted in Table 2), which they suggested union leaders and program operators use to guide the development, delivery, and evaluation of education and training provided by joint training programs.

Since 1990 the literature on the industrial joint union–management training programs has largely followed these two tracks. Authors often anchor their discussion of joint training programs on the basic structural and pedagogical principles set forth in these seminal works, providing very little systematic analysis or critical inquiry to confirm, extend, or invalidate them. Ironically, though Ferman, Hoyman, and Cutcher-Gershenfeld (1990) called for rigorous research to refine the joint program principles and cultivate the model, no one, not even the authors themselves, took up the systematic study they proposed. While much has been published about joint training programs in the last 20 years, it is largely anecdotal, drawing on the accounts of program leaders and practitioners as well as publicly available documents, program materials,

TABLE 2
Worker-Centered Learning Principles.

- Education that builds on what workers already know, taking the workers' strengths, not their deficiencies, as the starting point in the educational program.
- Education for the whole person, not just the learning needs related to the workplace.
- Codetermination in development and planning of program.
- Participatory, bottom-up decision making to ensure that programs are responsive to needs of workers and learning goals.
- Equal access to programs, with barriers to entry such as current skills and responsibilities mitigated by a complement of support services.
- Worker involvement in the design of skill assessments, which in turn are used to support individual learning goals and provide feedback on individual progress, not as tools to screen workers for placement in jobs.
- Confidentiality of classroom records.
- Integration of basic skills education into a larger education program.

Source: Sarmiento and Kay 1990.

and journalistic accounts to describe individual programs. Thus much of this work appears to be motivated by advocacy rather than the goal of evaluation guided by social scientific methods.

This approach to the research on joint training programs lies in stark contrast to the rigorous and substantial line of research that exists on joint programs focused on single issues like health and safety (Schurman and Israel 1996; Schurman, Hugentobler, and Robins 1990) as well as extensive research that exists on broad, strategic, and firm- or industrial-level labor–management partnerships (MIT 2001; Luria, Vidal, Wial, and Rogers 2006; Kochan, Eaton, McKersie, and Adler 2009). Indeed, many authors acknowledge the lack of rigor in the literature on joint training programs and offer several explanations. Some claim joint programs lack the resources to invest in data collection and program evaluation (Tao, Richard, Tarr, and Wheeler 1992), so they also lack the systems and knowledge to track program quality and performance (Bloom and Campbell 2002). Harris (2000) attributes his lack of investment in data collection and analysis to the politicized nature of the union–management partnership. Union and management leaders, fearful that poor evaluations might cause their partners to withdraw support from the program, limit the availability and access to the hard data researchers need to conduct rigorous analyses. The end result is that there are few agreed-upon metrics to evaluate the effectiveness of joint programs (Bloom and Campbell 2002). A systematic research agenda is hampered by the lack of a validated set of descriptive variables that can be used to compare one program to another (Ferman, Hoyman, and Cutcher-Gershenfeld 1990).

In a review of the literature on joint training programs from 1990 to 2009 we observed that, except for a few evaluations of specific courses and initiatives sponsored by joint training programs, the literature has largely been written by practitioners for practitioners. It is heavily focused on a set of principles and practices that closely resembles those first articulated in the 1990s, which the authors claim contribute to the effectiveness of joint training programs. These claims are backed up by anecdotal evidence gleaned mainly from the authors' experience or through interviews with program leaders.

The endurance of an anecdotal set of principles in the literature on joint programs is evidence to us of a shared body of knowledge cultivated by a community of practitioners who govern and operate joint training programs. Communities of practice are often thought of as a shared history of learning that over time builds a domain of knowledge and a set of tools and practices that enable the practical application of the knowledge (Wenger 1998). Central to the cultivation of this shared knowledge is a group of people who, sharing a common concern or passion about a topic, interact on an ongoing basis to deepen their knowledge and expertise. We argue that the literature on joint training may represent the articulation of a community of practice. It also may be one of the mechanisms by which the community of joint program practitioners and its knowledge domain has been constituted and is distributed.

The Practice of Joint Training (1990–2009)

Five features of joint training programs emerged in the review of the literature on such programs published between 1990 and 2009. Though built on the basic principles first outlined in 1990 (Ferman, Hoyman, and Cutcher-Gershenfeld 1990; Sarmiento and Kay 1990) these features have been extended, distributed, and institutionalized in the structure and operations of joint training programs by a community of practitioners who share common values for promoting economic and educational equity. These institutionalized features include reliance on a pedagogy of worker-centered learning, a wide array of services and programs, delivery of services to multiple population groups, development of multiple labor market capacities and functions, and a partnership organizational structure in which labor and management share in the governance and balance multiple interests in workplace training.

Worker-Centered Pedagogy

Worker-centered learning is a functional, contextualized learning experience in which workers engage and come to know more about real workplace issues and performance problems as they develop new

FIGURE 1
Example of Worker-Centered Learning.

Nursing homes care for patients with complex needs who require the services of diverse professional groups. Yet the nurse aides, the front-line caregivers, are often marginalized, and this impacts the quality of patient care. The training, which involved 130 members of multidisciplinary work teams, focused on helping the team develop communication and team skills while increasing the knowledge base and empowering the front-line staff to take on a broader role in care.

In the beginning of the program, participants decided on critical questions to focus their leaning and teamwork during the five-week training program. The training consisted of three days of didactic instruction in palliative care and team-building skills and two days of mentored practice. Teams also worked between sessions to explore their questions and to experiment with solutions to structural problems.

King (2009) found participants were more aware of their impact on patient care and increased their understanding of patient needs. They also reported a clearer understanding of the role of other team members. Front-line workers reported gaining more confidence and more self-esteem. Indeed many participants requested further training in gerontology and patient care. Some enrolled in vocational training programs leading to new credentials. Managers also reported observable improvement in the teams' ability to resolve conflicts and to solve problems.

Source: King 2009.

knowledge and skills. General education and skills training are contextualized in the functional aims of workers who voluntarily enroll in training to improve job performance, advance in their careers, or develop and grow as a person. Educators and participants often construct the curriculum together by drawing upon workplace, union, or political-economic issues to contextualize the learning program. Figure 1, an example of a worker-centered program for nursing home workers sponsored by the SEIU 1199 Education and Upgrading Fund, shows how the pedagogy is part of a broader process of individual empowerment and economic development. It is a systematic approach to workplace learning that builds new learning structures and relationships into the daily experience of workers, which supports the application of new skill and knowledge on the job.

Harris (2000) explains worker-centered pedagogy as a strategic union response to two contradictions in the practice and theory of workplace learning. First, though employers wanted more skilled workers, they faced strong economic pressure against making the investments needed to increase the level of learning and engagement among a large number of line employees. Second, he pointed out that though the literature called for a new worker who is responsible for his or her learning and careers and is more engaged in the workplace, the voice of the worker was often missing from academic discussions and research on perceived workforce skill gaps and learning needs. Worker-centered pedagogy addresses these discontinuities.

Worker-centered pedagogy places learners at the center of the educational program, engaging them directly in the entire learning process.

According to Schied (1994), this is accomplished through the active role of the union in the education program.

> Worker-centered learning recognizes that workers, through their unions, play a central role in developing their own educational programs. A worker-centered approach makes the worker, in context of his/her union, the cornerstone of the educational program. . . . The learner and union educational staff are actively involved in the development of the curriculum (p. 9).

Kemble (2002) argues that union involvement adds value to workplace education and training in two ways. First, unions negotiate training funds that serve to address a major gap in human capital investments in U.S. industries because they extend training to the front-line, active workforce, a population often overlooked by employer training and public workforce development programs. Second, the involvement of the union in program design tends to mitigate the power differential that exists between workers and managers in the training needs assessment process. Workers who work though their unions are often more candid when talking about performance problems, and this candor results in more accurate training needs assessment and better, more relevant program design.

Though joint programs have an institutionalized pedagogy that places the worker at the center of the learning process, programs will contextualize the training in the workplace, so education and training must also take production-centered issues and goals into account. The dual focus of joint training programs ensures that all stakeholder interests are considered, and in the design and delivery of training that inevitability leads to conflict inside programs that must be resolved.

Bloom and Campbell (2002), in a study of nine courses offered by three joint training programs, found that joint programs developed and institutionalized organizational codes and structures that help the partners manage conflicting needs and interests. The way in which programs are structured to manage this creative tension can be observed in the mission statement that delineates the goals of the program. Some programs emphasize individual development, signaling an emphasis on individual learning and development. It is assumed that greater awareness of and response to individual learning needs and interests can be aggregated to bring workforce needs and outcomes into focus (Bloom and Campbell 2002). Programs that emphasize individual development invest in a comprehensive system of educational and career counseling that helps individuals assess their skills and learning styles, set goals, and select training programs that can help them meet their short- and long-term goals. Program practitioners and leaders aggregate and tap this information to gain a broader perspective on skill gaps and needs in the workplace. There is an assumed value chain in this approach—as individual skill and knowledge levels increase, workers gain more employment security and firm performance is improved (Marschall, forthcoming).

Some challenge the notion that programs can achieve broader results in the workplace by merely aggregating individual learning. This is why some programs have adopted more systematic focus on the employers' strategic goals and skill needs to ensure training is linked back into the workplace. For example, joint training programs have customized their training to meet the needs of specific business units or occupational groups within the company. Many joint programs work extensively with hiring managers and shop stewards to ensure that training is designed to meet the needs of hard-to-fill positions and that trainees are hired when they complete the program.

Some practitioners argue that these customized efforts run counter to the basic principles of worker-centered learning because they focus on the needs of a select group of workers and not the community as a whole. Critics of this approach claim it risks resulting in narrow job- or employer-specific training that cannot provide workers with portable credentials and skills required for employment security in the current labor market. Thus the dual focus of joint programs presents challenges and causes tension inside joint programs that must be managed. However, Bloom and Campbell (2002) observe that these challenges and tension lead to dialogue and creative problem solving and "helps to ensure that the training plans and delivery are genuinely relevant to the learning needs of both workers and their employers" (p. 22).

Expansion of Training Offerings and Services

Surveys of joint program leaders (Bloom and Campbell 2002) as well as reviews (Roberts and Wozniak 1994; Harris 2000; Kemble 2002; Marschall, forthcoming) and case studies (Tao, Richard, Tarr, and Wheeler 1992; Hensley 1996; Fischer 2003; Takahashi and Melendez 2004) of joint programs reveal that they provide a variety of career and educational counseling, basic and occupational skills training, education leading to personal development and widely recognized credentials, and job placement services. Indeed, these studies include reviews of programs in a wide range of industries (telecommunications, entertainment and food service, industrial manufacturing, health care, construction, building, and maritime trades). The consistency of this finding leads us to conclude that another institutionalized feature of joint training programs is the provision of a wide array of services to program participants.

For example, out of the 14 joint training programs studied by the AFL-CIO Working for America Institute, 12 had at least three of the following services: tuition reimbursement, instruction in English as a Second Language, basic skills and entry-level training, technical and occupational training, and skills upgrade training for particular jobs (Working for America Institute 2001). Hensley (1996) analyzed 700 labor–management workplace training agreements and found that joint training programs expanded the focus of traditional negotiated training benefits beyond generally required job skills and new technology implementation, including career counseling, general education, upgrade training, and personal development.

Program offerings expand over time. The early joint programs, as well as many new programs in the early stages of their development, are first initiated to respond to a specific event or problem that calls for a training solution. For example, though the UAW–Ford Education, Development and Training Program was negotiated to serve the retraining and job placement needs of laid-off auto workers, the program was quickly expanded to include active workers when the parties realized a number of factors: increasing skill demands in the workplace; the need to upgrade the basic skills of active workers so that they would be prepared to participate in vocational retraining should they be laid off; the effectiveness of the joint training model over the unilateral employer training model in workforce training; and the willingness of union workers to participate in and complete a course of study offered by the joint training program. The variety of the services offered naturally expanded along with the growth of the training population and the variety of needs they and their sponsors presented to the program. (The program in the steel and rubber industries, described below, provides another example of this evolution.)

A similar developmental cycle was observed by Korshak (2000) in a joint training partnership negotiated by the Hotel Employees and Restaurant Employees (HERE) with union hotels in San Francisco in the late 1900s. The program began with a focus on soft skills training and workplace interventions aimed at improving communications and relationships among workers and between workers and their supervisors. In the Holiday Inn, a joint training study team surveyed the bargaining unit and found that management-provided training programs were not relevant to workers' needs. Workers wanted English language education and training in communications and problem-solving skills, and they expressed a strong preference for on-the-job training over classroom training.

The program developed training in the workers' expressed needs and incorporated training in critical thinking and technical skills. The program was piloted in a highly contentious work group that was charged with developing a plan for managing the renovations of the hotel's restaurant. The employees did not trust that management would rehire them after the renovations. To allay their concerns, the team formulated a multifaceted plan to help the employees support themselves during the closing period and to prepare them for jobs in the new restaurant by training them in new customer service skills, food safety, and alcohol awareness. In addition, workers were crossed-trained in banquet skills, which provided them with new salary streams as well as a career pathway out of the restaurant. The team also agreed to new job classifications, redefined jobs, and new hours of operations. The project helped transform the once narrow, dead-end restaurant jobs into a new work structure that created career ladders to more challenging and better-paying jobs in the industry. The program had such payoffs for all parties that the partners agreed to expand it into other areas. Over time the program helped workers and supervisors establish a new culture of learning, leading them to question the way hotel jobs and careers were organized and motivating them to work with the joint program to reconfigure work and provide new training that improved the career opportunities for workers and business performance for the employer (Korshak 2000).

In these and other cases, joint programs build up a constellation of services, developed one on top of another, until gradually a robust set of direct services emerge to respond to the needs of multiple stakeholders. This gradual and pragmatic developmental process fosters change in stakeholders' understanding of the joint program—they move from seeing it as "a program" designed to help the parties respond to an event (industrial or workplace restructuring) to seeing it as a resilient institution with robust capacity to support continuous learning among the front-line workforce and to intervene in and improve the performance of the firm and the functioning of the internal labor market.

Expansion of Services to Multiple Population Groups

The discussion of the developmental trajectory of joint programs points to another salient feature of the model. Joint programs have institutionalized a practice of delivering services to multiple and distinct population groups, including incumbent workers, dislocated workers, and persons in need of education and training in basic skills, including English language training. Though many programs, such as those involving the UAW and the CWA, started with a mission to serve displaced workers, they soon expanded to other population groups. In addition, as other partnerships took up and replicated the joint training model, they adapted it to their particular condition and needs.

In some cases this has meant that the program model expanded to include the provision of services to groups not covered by the collective bargaining agreement. For example, the CWA–IBEW–AT&T Alliance for Employee Growth and Development created Alliance Plus, a not-for-profit 501(c)(3) to extend training to AT&T managers and business units that sought their assistance on narrow job-related training not allowable under the training programs' guidelines. At first this innovation was viewed as an administrative mechanism that allowed the program to respond to an expressed need of a major stakeholder. But when the company began to downsize in mid-1990, this seemingly administrative mechanism became a central strategy in efforts to ensure the future viability of Alliance Plus. Like other programs, Alliance Plus is funded on a per-capita basis, so a reduction in the number of employees had a significant, long-term effect on the program's budget. Not only did the program experience significant decrease in its revenues, but the per-unit cost of training also increased because the program had lost a critical mass of participants in many locations. The training program used Alliance Plus to reach out to other CWA bargaining units to offer and provide short- and long-term training to other groups of union workers.

On the other hand, the Garment Industry Development Corporation (GIDC), a joint labor–management sector partnership in New York City, was originally launched to address the education and training needs of the entire industry, including owners, managers, union leaders and representatives, buyers, suppliers, contractors, and retailers as well as bargaining unit members. Conway (1999) claims that sector partnerships like GIDC give new meaning to joint programs' dual mission because they actively intervene at the site of production to improve both the supply and demand sides of the labor market. GIDC and other sector partnerships provide a bundle of services, including the provision of ongoing education and training for all stakeholder groups (e.g., employers and supervisors) to develop new cognitive capacity and attitudes on every level of the industry that can help the industry as a whole convert to new, more competitive organizational structures and processes (Conway 1999).

New York City is home to one of the most concentrated and diverse union training centers in the United States. There are union and joint training programs in almost every sector of the city, including construction, health care, education and public sector, building maintenance, transportation, entertainment, manufacturing, hospitality, and food preparation (Fischer 2003). In 1985 the Consortium for Worker Education (CWE) was formed as a nonprofit conduit for the distribution of New York State workplace literacy funds to union programs in New York City (Fischer 2003). The consortium has grown to become one of the more extensive examples of the expansion of joint programs to new population groups. Today, with a budget of over $100 million, it is the largest worker education and training organization in the city.

CWE developed by bringing the extensive union training industry together under one umbrella to share and improve programs. CWE also drew on the wide array of programs and services, the industry knowledge, and the employer relationships that resided inside of joint programs to leverage public and private foundation dollars and extend the programs to new population groups. Though the CWE's role in the public workforce development system is controversial in the job training industry in New York City, it is widely recognized that many of the consortium's programs result in better performance outcomes for individual participants because they often result in placement for low-income, underemployed, and unemployed community members in union jobs that offer continuous education and career opportunities (Fischer 2003).

By expanding the resources of joint training programs in New York City beyond the boundaries to individual partnerships and opening them up to other population groups, the CWE has helped align the joint training programs more closely with each other while simultaneously leveraging the critical mass of joint programs to improve the functioning of the external labor market. CWE has emerged as the center of a system of joint training programs in New York City that has helped reduce redundancies among programs while allowing the public system to leverage and benefit from the worker-centered, dual-focused approach to worker education to improve services to a broader, more diverse population. The question remains as to whether and how these gains will help mobilize a new generation of workers, especially those from within professional ranks, to support and join labor unions (Kemble 2002; Scully-Russ 2006).

Multifunctional Intermediaries

CWE is also an example of a fourth feature of joint programs: Some programs systematically intervene in external labor markets—often organized in a regional area and/or as a cluster of companies in a discrete industry—to provide services that address skill gaps and improve the functioning of the workforce and economic development system. Though this feature is thought to be a recent innovation in joint programs, it really is more than 30 years old.

The District 1199C Training and Upgrading Fund in Philadelphia was established through collective bargaining in 1974 to provide education benefits to union members and members of the community interested in careers in health care. The program has grown since then into a multifunctional workforce intermediary that provides a myriad of workforce development functions (such as setting skill standards, developing a common curriculum, and educating and training workers), educational programs leading to certificates and pathways to higher education, and job development and placement for displaced, underemployed, and low-wage workers in the Philadelphia region. The program combines these efforts with economic development functions such as layoff aversion, modernization services to upgrade the performance of health care providers, and other activities that help union employers create good jobs for workers and the community.

Over the last 30 years, the 1199C Training and Upgrading Fund has brought together key stakeholders in a local community and labor market to "fashion" a workforce and economic development infrastructure to provide career pathways for low-wage workers and to grow and articulate their demands for skilled labor in health care. Indeed, the program meets Giloth's (2004) description of a workforce intermediary.

> They are fundamentally brokers, integrators, and learners who entrepreneurially enact workforce development rather than simply "meeting the market" or conforming to a publicly mandated set of roles and responsibilities. . . . They represent such a broad range of institutions and approaches . . . [but embody] distinctive strategy elements as well as organizational characteristics . . . [such as] dual customer, brokering partners, and integrating resources for the purpose of meeting employer and worker needs (pp. 7–8).

A new program that was developed by the Training and Upgrading Fund for front-line behavioral health care workers illustrates how a joint training program can play an important multifunctional role to fill a critical gap in the labor market. The new initiative was aimed at improving the quality of jobs as well as the quality of care in the community. In this example, the fund combined its deep and structural partnership with employers (see joint governance below), with a worker-centered pedagogy and its historic relationships with postsecondary education to upgrade the role of the front-line behavioral health care worker, improve the quality of care to patients, and provide workers with new skills that put them on a pathway to higher education and a good, sustainable career (R. Wilson 2009).

The effort began in 2004 when the fund, along with two of the leading employers of mental health workers in the city of Philadelphia and several area education institutions, joined forces with Jobs to Careers, a national initiative to develop the skills and career pathways for front-line behavioral health care workers. Though the fund had long provided entry-level training for such workers, the new education program was linked to a comprehensive strategy to upgrade the industry's workforce practices. The program worked with the partners to develop new competencies that both met the current minimum requirements for carrying out behavioral health work and also injected new ones to move the work to higher levels of performance and responsibility (R. Wilson 2009). The program worked with employers and the union to use the new competencies to upgrade jobs and improve quality of care.

Meanwhile, the program also worked with its long-time educational partners in the region to develop a new competency-based curriculum and credentialing regime that integrated classroom instruction with on-the-job learning and assessments. This educational strategy had two significant results that helped to meet the dual mission of joint programs. First, it helped to ensure that competencies and new knowledge were embedded into the daily routines of front-line workers—improving the quality of care and firm performance. It also ensured that workers learned while they earned, putting individuals on a pathway to a college degree they once thought was unattainable. This was accomplished because the new curriculum included three instructional modules, each roughly equivalent to six academic credits. The fund crafted a comprehensive education program that combined its original entry-level behavioral health care technician certificate program with 42 hours of college preparation courses and the three new competency-based modules. Workers continued to work while participating in training that led to an award of 21 college credits, putting them halfway along the path toward an associate's degree.

According to the fund's director, Cheryl Feldman (Scully-Russ 2009), their deep, structural relationships with contributing employers provide the program with great insight into the industry's skill needs as well as the insider knowledge required to make programs work for the industry. Employers are integrated into every level of the program. At the board level, employers help decide how funds will be spent, hospital administrators oversee the development and delivery of programs at the worksite, and supervisors help students transfer new learning to the workplace.

In addition, the program invests much time and energy in developing its worker-centered pedagogy to ensure programs respond to workers' interests, needs, and learning styles. Through many years of experience and experimentation, the program has established a niche in the training and development of health care professionals in the region. The program acts as a bridge between education and the workplace that helps bring teachers together with students to integrate work-based skills into instruction as well as to embed learning into the workplace.

The 1199C Training and Upgrading Fund is but one example of how joint training programs that engage in the broader workforce development system both achieve their own mission and help improve the functioning of the labor market. This case also shows that when joint programs move into the broader arena, they may become a vital part of the institutional framework of the regional workforce development system.

Joint Governance

The final feature that has been institutionalized is the establishment of labor–management partnership organizations in which both union officials and management personnel share in governance. When the joint training model first emerged in the early 1980s, the concept and practice of jointness was a subject of intense controversy. Traditionally, union leaders tended to emphasize their adversarial relationship with employers. AFSCME president Jerry Wurf summarized this 1970s-era stance in reference to quality of work life programs:

> I must stress the adversary nature of labor relations. . . . I'm skeptical of any employer, in government or private industry, who states that he's motivated entirely or in part by the quality of his employees' work life. . . . Unionists are justifiably skeptical of quality of work life programs that management attempts to impose unilaterally or to hustle workers into accepting. Very often these programs are nothing more than speed-up or union-busting masquerading in the disguise of trendy social science (Wurf 1982:133).

Though this position began to moderate as U.S. employers encountered the pressures of foreign competition and unionized employees in some industries reached out to their union counterparts, the debate inside the labor movement over jointness as a principle and strategic approach remained unresolved for many years. Some argued that jointness and the "team concept" co-opted union militancy at a time when it was needed most: a period of transformative change in the economy when the workings of capitalism had become more transparent (Moody 1988). Many took a more pragmatic perspective, arguing that though joint activities may be necessary, they should remain marginal adjuncts to the primary labor–management relationship, adversarial collective bargaining. Still, there were strong advocates for jointism who argued that joint activities provided unions and workers with new forms of control and empowerment in work, potentially leading in the long term to the co-management of enterprises (Bluestone and Bluestone 1992) and a more cooperative, associational model of unionism (Heckscher 1988).

The debates led to the formation of the AFL-CIO Committee on the Evolution of Work to provide a forum for the labor movement to deliberate the implications of the changing economic landscape and to forge a consensus among senior labor leaders on a strategic union response. The committee's 1983 initial report, *The Future of Work*, recommended progressive action to reduce the surplus of labor, including devoting greater attention to human resource development "through better education, training, retraining, upgrading, and upward mobility opportunities for all workers, both employed and unemployed" (AFL-CIO 1983:18). A later report recognized that some employers had reached out to unions to create partnerships to modify the organization of work and called upon unions to "take the initiative in stimulating, sustaining and institutionalizing a new system of work organization based upon full and equal labor–management partnerships" (AFL-CIO 1994:2).

Several unions made significant investments of union funds in the development of new resources and tools to help local union leaders take on new roles in joint activities. The CWA, for example, developed a workbook on joint labor–management processes to guide local leaders in using joint programs to solve concrete problems and improve working conditions; international staff were then trained in organizational development skills to provide technical assistance to locals (Sheahan 1993). CWA president Morty Bahr became a national champion for the cause of worker education and training, arguing that "many of us believe we can build our unions by offering education and training services to workers" (Monks and Bahr 2003:5). The International Association of Machinists (IAM) established a partnership training program for union leaders based on rigorous guidelines for union involvement in high-performance work organization systems "where labor and management are interdependent and equally dominant in the revitalization of our industrial base" (Kourpias 1994). The UAW established the Paid Educational Leave (PEL) program to train local and rank-and-file leaders in joint skills and educate them about the global trends affecting their industry. The Service Employees International Union (SEIU) established the Lifelong Education and Development (LEAD) program to help affiliates negotiate and establish career ladder programs in the service sector and to engage with management through quality of work life programs to improve service delivery.

The late 1980s and early 1990s appeared as a crossroads in the evolution of jointness in U.S. labor relations. Ferman, Hoyman, and Crutcher-Gershenfeld (1990) observed that

> in many workplaces there have emerged a broad array of joint committees. . . . Some of these committees are adjuncts to the collective bargaining process, while others are not. There are even

joint committees of top leaders who are responsible for coordinating the activities of many other joint committees. . . . These joint
activities represent an entire domain of contract administration
that can sometimes surpass grievances and arbitration in terms of
the time and even the importance of the activity for union leaders,
which has led some scholars to argue . . . that joint activities can
have a robust, two-way relationship with collective bargaining
instead of just serving as a secondary adjunct (p. 159).

Thus the evolution and institutionalization of jointism in the U.S.
labor movement has occurred on both the policy and operational levels.
The institutionalization of joint programs inside of the labor movement
can be observed in the legacy of many of the early joint training programs that continue today. For example, though AT&T has been racked
by the harsh economic conditions in the telecommunications industry,
Alliance Plus has adjusted and continues to provide services to active
and displaced workers. In addition, other new labor–management partners continue to take up the joint training programs model. In 2005 the
Coalition of Kaiser Permanente Unions, AFL-CIO, negotiated a nationwide workforce development initiative, inclusive of two new Taft–Hartley
trusts, to support the joint development of new systems and programs to
respond to the workforce impacts of the industrial restructuring occurring in the health care industry (Mills 2001).

New forms of jointness have been institutionalized inside the labor
movement, in part because joint training programs have been effective
in helping unions respond to the real challenges facing workers in a
globalized economy. Scholars speculate that union leaders have accepted
the instability in the economy and have taken responsibility to help
union members transition, in part because they hope that workers will
remain loyal to the labor movement (Harris 2000). Generally, main-
stream union leaders have settled on the notion that jointism and
selected partnership activities with management are a legitimate strategy
to help unionized employers maintain the viability of their firms in the
face of global competition and continued industry restructuring—in
those instances in which employers accept the legitimacy of union representation, share corporate information, enable workers and union
officials to participate in decision making, establish labor–management
structures with equal representation, and meet other standards outlined
by the AFL-CIO (1994).

The Institute for Career Development: A Resilient Partnership

The establishment of a resilient, multi-employer partnership on skill
development in the steel industry was contingent on the three factors

identified by Eaton, Rubinstein, and McKersie (2004) as contributing to cooperative labor–management relations, including joint recognition of industry crisis, the presence of dedicated union and management leadership, and the negotiation of strong collective bargaining language. Indeed, the Institute for Career Development developed and expanded over time as the partners formalized their skills partnership, expanded their service offerings and population groups, and gradually broadened the institute's activities from interventions into individual bargaining units, to the industry, and more recently, to the broader workforce development system. This minicase illustrates how the five joint training programs' features evolved over time as well as how they work together to foster a dynamic and resilient institution of worker education and training.

Following the massive destruction of foreign manufacturing capacity during World War II, U.S.-based integrated steel companies emerged as global leaders in steel production. In subsequent decades, as Asian and European firms used advanced technologies and flexible work organization techniques to rebuild their domestic industries, American companies reduced their research and development spending and chose to diversify by purchasing firms in other industries rather than increase their capital investment in steel and deploy new technology (Dertouzos 1998). During the 1970s, industry experts projected that there would be steel shortages for the next decade, leading steel producers to believe that "they could keep running their old mills indefinitely and still make money" (Kaufman 2001). That belief evaporated when restrictive monetary policies and a recessionary economy in the 1980s led to a surge in steel imports and the recognition, by management and union representatives alike, that falling demand, excess production facilities, and foreign competition from more efficient producers would result in plant closings in the context of severe industry restructuring.

The top leadership of the steelworkers union had a history of fostering productive labor–management cooperation, stretching back to the formation of joint committees during World War II and an explicit political commitment to industrial democracy (Rubinstein 2003). Faced with inevitable concessions, United Steelworkers president Lynn Williams adopted a strategic approach to collective bargaining to help offset what he termed the power differential in the industry and contribute to overall company viability. As he described this framework:

> We insisted in the difficult times, during concessionary bargaining, that workers had to have a voice in the industry. Concessions, if they were going to be made, should be looked at as an investment. Workers investing should be treated like shareholders. So

we did stock deals in place of money and we fought for union representatives on company boards and fought for a real voice in the industry and total information (Marschall 2008).

In 1986, following two years of meetings of joint problem-solving teams, the union and National Steel signed a contract that crafted a "cooperative partnership" in which the company agreed to a no-layoff pledge while the union accepted a reduction in job classifications. Importantly, the agreement stipulated that employees who would otherwise be dismissed would be placed in an employment security pool and then assigned to other tasks in National Steel plants. This provision, along with job classification changes, placed a premium on in-plant training and continuing skill development for hourly employees. As one manager said, "Where we had pipefitters and welders, we now have mechanics. Part and parcel of this is an extensive training program that was developed with the union" (Rutigliano 1988:37). Similar terms were enacted at LSE, a joint partnership of LTV Corp. and a Japanese company, where unionized workers achieved the power to make day-to-day operating decisions, determine work schedules, and develop training and job progression schedules. Pursuing a bargaining strategy that elevated employment security for union members, the union elicited management willingness to share authority and information, provide proper compensation for workers when they learned new skills, and share in the increased profits of the enterprise. Skill training played a critical role in this strategy, Williams (1995) said:

> For domestic industry to survive and compete in today's world, workers must be trained in new and old skills. Cross-training of people assigned to a specific area must encompass the duties of more than one classification, and new skills must be learned because of changing technology (p. 142).

Though the steelworkers union made progress on increasing the skill training available to members, their actions could not forestall continued plant closings and mass layoffs. Employment in the steel industry dropped from an average of 422,000 hourly employees between 1966 and 1970 to only 101,000 in 1992 (Locker Associates 1993). The union responded by establishing a headquarters-level task force and bargaining with companies to obtain 90-day prior notice of plant closings, company contributions of cash and office space for services to the unemployed, and joint governance of program operations. Union and company leaders opened more than 50 worker assistance centers during the 1980s, each providing a comprehensive range of services to former employees, family members, and residents in surrounding communities. To cultivate a sense of "worker ownership" over the programs, assistance centers typically were located in convenient plant buildings or familiar union halls. Many services were delivered by peer counselors—fellow union members trained to recruit their colleagues, conduct skill assessments, and arrange suitable vocational training. All members would receive equitable treatment and high-quality services, the union emphasized, with services being available for a year or more after facilities had closed. Working with the national AFL-CIO and experts in dislocated worker services, union and company representatives raised funds from federal government programs and spread their comprehensive, participatory worker assistance model to chemical workers, copper miners, and aluminum workers nationwide (United Steelworkers of America 1986). Notably, union and management at J&L Steel negotiated a small fund for worker transition to be financed by cents-per-hour contributions from the wages of existing workers (similar to such measures in the auto industry).

These two strands—increased joint emphasis on skill training and assistance centers for dislocated workers—came together in 1989 when the union negotiated a contract financing a new organization, the Institute for Career Development (ICD). As Williams recounts the train of events, the union had bargained provisions against contracting out with several companies, but encountered resistance for USX (the former US Steel that had expanded into other industries.) The conflict resulted in a six-month lockout by USX, removing their steel from the market and boosting the sales of competitors. When the next round of bargaining arrived, the union found that other companies had substantial resources and were open to discussing greater investments in skill training. The union had already been working with Ben Fischer of Carnegie Mellon University to examine the joint training partnerships in the auto and communications industries. Williams became convinced of the need for a steel

> industry program when he traveled to local union halls and discovered that it was common around the major plants that people were taking early pensions who didn't really want to. And the reason was that they were intimidated by the new technology they saw coming in and they saw their jobs disappearing and newer, more technical jobs coming along. They didn't have [the skills] and often their math was not up to the demands. . . . Then, in the downsizing, we had all these skilled people but they didn't have any marketable skills. So we decided to come up with some ideas to address this somehow (Marschall 2008).

Their collectively bargained approach was to have 10 cents per hour worked by steelworkers in participating companies set aside in a fund that would support a small central staff, which would set standards for training activities, and a network of local joint committees (LJCs) located near plant sites, where they would be responsive to the needs of incumbent workers and dislocated union members. Operating principles were established, notably that minimal funds would be expended on brick-and-mortar building projects and that training would focus on basic skills instruction in an informal, supportive atmosphere. Over two decades, the ICD has become a respected continuous learning institution, involving the union and 14 steel and rubber companies, whose services are delivered by as many as 72 jointly governed LJCs. Classes sponsored by ICD enrolled nearly 15,000 workers in 2006 and offered more than 2,000 customized courses (United Steelworkers 2008). Their learning philosophy, practices, and structures reflect the key features that we have identified in durable joint training programs.

First, ICD-sponsored courses integrate a worker-centered conception of learning signaled in the organization's mission statement, which emphasizes that "workers must play a significant role in the design and development of their training and education" in order to reach their full potential, both as employees and human beings (Institute for Career Development 2008b:9). To implement what they characterize as a "bottom-up" planning process, each LJC receives training to survey local union members and identify areas of study that would be popular with steelworkers, to respond to promotional opportunities in their facilities, or to help them transition to alternative jobs (for those permanently displaced.) Because ICD leaders found that many steelworkers had negative experiences in the traditional educational system, classes are oriented toward topics with practical applications that will help participants become accustomed to the learning process and enjoy interacting with their peers to accomplish tangible tasks. The ICD views learning as an active process in which persons relate new concepts to their existing understandings and exchange knowledge with their peers, all in the context of real-life actualities (such as fixing broken motors in home appliances) and situated learning contexts. Courses are designed so that the community and social environment facilitate the learning experience, combining the use of instructional technology and group collaboration to reinforce their competency goals (Institute for Career Development 2007). An extensive survey found a high level of satisfaction with ICD courses, with 68% of participants (n = 529) rating the benefits as valuable (Smith Education Associates 2008).

The ICD also provides a comprehensive array of services that address the personal learning goals of unionists and the acquisition of transferable skills necessary for alternative careers. After identifying the interests and goals of workers, center staff are advised to "start small" and offer a few well-defined programs, often involved with computer literacy training and working to repair familiar mechanical equipment. Basic skill enhancement is available in all centers, including preparation for obtaining a GED, effective reading and writing, and refresher training in math skills. To enhance workers' personal development, courses are offered in life skills, preparing for college classes, and financial planning. After career counseling by LJC staff, participants have access to tuition assistance for enrollment in accredited educational institutions (Institute for Career Development 2008b). In 2007, ICD centers held more than 1,547 courses in 28 categories, the most popular being "Computer Basics" and pretechnical courses such as "Auto Body and Repair" and "Heating, Ventilation and Air" conditioning technology (Institute for Career Development 2008a).

As indicated by the roots of the ICD in dislocated worker programs, the organization serves multiple population groups. The recession of 2007 to 2009 contributed to a host of mass layoffs and facility closings, according to reports by LJC coordinators, leading to more laid-off members seeking to make productive use of their time off by enrolling in community college classes, taking customized computer courses, and preparing for craft maintenance jobs (Institute for Career Development 2009a). Those workers whose hours had been reduced but were still on the job had access to skill training to enhance their ability to perform assigned work tasks and use new technology. Program centers continue to be open to services for union family members, enhancing the supportive learning atmosphere, and to community organizations, maintaining the link with outside resources.

With its network of local training centers embedded in a range of communities, the ICD built on its knowledge of industrial manufacturing skill training and its interest in renewable energy and energy efficiency occupations to adopt a workforce intermediary role in selected areas. The ICD responded to the availability of federal grants to propose a "Career Pathways in Green Industries" program that is conducting skill training for incumbent and dislocated steelworkers, veterans, and unemployed adults. Each of the four program sites involves a regional labor market that encompasses urban areas, suburbs, and rural counties. Through its partnership with community colleges and economic development organizations, the ICD is becoming a part of the institutional structure of these regional labor markets, helping them prepare for the emergence of a clean energy economy (Apollo 2008). The training services delivered in each area have been customized to the needs of local employers, notably the expressed desire of steel firms such as Arcelor-Mittal USA to hire and promote "incumbent and new employees with knowledge in green work systems and energy efficiency standards" (Institute for Career Development 2009b). ICD program staff are working with federally funded Workforce Investment Boards to recruit participants and place trainees with employers, the sort of cooperative relationships that will integrate LJC bodies with the ecosystem of education, job training, labor exchange, and community-based organizations that comprise the federally financed elements of the nation's workforce development system.

Finally, the ICD has integrated the principles of jointness throughout its governance structures, reflecting the ideological predilections of United Steelworkers (USW) union leaders. The ICD mission statement emphasizes that union and company leaders are implementing a "shared vision" in which skill training responsive to firm-level economic needs are balanced with the individual enrichment required for workers to "have more stable and rewarding personal and family lives," thus building competencies relevant to workplace, home, and community environments (Institute for Career Development 2008b). The ICD's governing board of directors, which formulates policy and monitors expenditures, is composed of an equal number of representatives from the USW and top company managers. Similarly, a 21-person advisory board draws from human resource professionals, employee relations executives, and USW district-level leaders and staff to counsel and provide assistance to the ICD director. In turn, each LJC, which develops and implements local training projects in concert with employee demonstrated needs, incorporates union and company personnel, including front-line supervisors and experienced workers who are respected by their peers. Attendance at ICD annual national conferences is diverse, encompassing company managers, local USW leaders, training coordinators, site directors, and many "Learning Advocates" who work directly with program participants.

The role of the ICD remains salient in the precarious global economy buffeting steel, rubber, and other manufacturing companies. As layoffs and plant closings occur, the demand for retraining and career development services continues apace. Moreover, services provided by the ICD have the potential to retain jobs in U.S.-based facilities. Of the nine steel companies listed as members of ICD, only two are independent firms with facilities solely in North America. The remaining are part of geographically diverse, multinational firms or joint ventures with Korean, Russian, and European steel makers. Luxembourg-based ArcelorMittal, for example, has steelmaking operations in 20 countries and operates 21 major production complexes, only three of which (employing 12% of its global workforce) are located in the United States (ArcelorMittal 2009). Though skill training programs for employees will not ensure that these domestic facilities remain open, their availability will contribute to the viability, competitiveness, and technological sophistication of those locations, helping unions and management alike make optimal use of their human capital resources.

Implications for Workforce Development Policy

The growth of joint training programs and their integration into the internal operations of firms provides unions with new ability to influence how actors inside the firm adjust to competitiveness and cost and improve the efficiency and effectiveness of the internal labor market (Marschall, forthcoming). Similarly, the movement of joint training programs into institutional arrangements and partnerships external to the firm—such as their involvement in workforce intermediaries or with the public workforce development system—provides unions with new leverage over how multiple stakeholders (employers, public agencies, education institutions) respond to economic change. The interaction between joint training programs and the broader (yet overly fractured) national workforce development system presents opportunities for joint programs to add value to the broader systems because joint programs may help broaden the participation of employers in the public system as well as enable the system to rapidly expand services to the active and laid-off workers who are in great need of continuous learning. Thus we offer four policy recommendations to strengthen and expand the role of unions and joint programs in a 21st-century workforce development system.

Encourage Union and Joint Program Involvement at Every Level of the Public System

Joint programs continue to look beyond the needs of individual workers and firms and engage in collective action to boost regional or sector economies through training. These activities not only improve the joint program model but also help to fill skill gaps, introducing new standards for educational quality that will improve the quality of programs throughout the entire system. Public policies are needed to ensure as well as to expand the involvement of unions and joint programs in public boards that oversee and deliberate investments in training and development of the workforce.

Currently, local union leaders are embedded in the federally financed workforce development system through their mandatory membership on some 600 Workforce Investment Boards (WIBs) established by the Workforce Investment Act of 1998 (WIA). In addition, representatives of unions and joint training programs are involved in policy-making organizations that work with the U.S. Congress to fashion legislation that supports sector strategies incorporating the principles of jointness and proposing target programs to be operated by labor–management organizations. Yet broader involvement of unions and joint program practitioners in the workforce development system is constrained by current workforce policies and the bias of some public officials that leads them to seek out nonunion employers as industry representatives to public workforce development policy and program initiatives. Under the Job Training Partnership Act of 1982, private industry councils were required to include substantial representation from unions and community organizations. The public boards are only required to include two labor representatives under WIA.

Our discussion of worker-centered pedagogy illustrates how union involvement in the development of education and training provides for creative tension that improves the quality of the education and training programs. The worker perspective that unions bring to the workplace learning process will also help balance the broader policy-level discussions and debates about how to expand and improve public investments in the training and development of the U.S. workforce.

Encourage New Investments in Incumbent Worker Education and Training

Initiating a new joint training program is an expensive undertaking that many employers may find difficult to afford in today's economy. New policies are needed to encourage employers to make investments in the training and development of the workforce. For example, a unique opportunity may have been missed in the early release of the economic recovery funds. In addition to providing jobs, an allowable expense could have been education and training to help incumbent workers develop new skills while also providing new jobs to the community. Though long debated in labor, it may now be time to also consider new forms of tax incentives that encourage employer investment in education and training, as proposed by the Center for American Progress (Bosworth 2007).

Support New Partnerships and Revitalize Practitioner Networks

Initiating a new joint training program requires knowledge and expertise that local leaders and employers often lack. In addition, existing practitioners often engage across programs to learn from each other and to partner on developing innovations or solving common problems. In the past, these learning processes were supported by structured networks of joint program practitioners whose mission was to foster new learning among joint programs and to assist in launching new partnerships. For example, the AFL-CIO Working for America Institute as well as the Association of Joint Union–Management Education Programs sponsored research, workshops, annual conferences, and other exchanges that helped to elaborate and distribute the knowledge domain underlying the practice of joint training programs. These networks were well respected inside the community of joint training practitioners and among their partners. However, recent political and economic trends have caused the association to dissolve and have severely limited the ability of the Working for America Institute to foster networking among union leaders interested in workforce development. New policies and resources are needed to support the networking of practitioners and to help them to continue to refine and distribute the knowledge base of joint programs throughout the unionized sector of the economy.

New policies could also help diffuse joint training program practices to other parts of the workforce development system. For example, American unions have long advocated peer counseling, and joint training programs have successfully integrated peer support specialists into comprehensive services for dislocated workers (AFL-CIO 1995). Inspired by the proliferation of "union learning representatives" in the United Kingdom (T. Wilson 2009), the American Federation of Teachers is operating pilot projects in partnership with employers in three locations to help provide training and career development services to members (American Federation of Teachers 2009). The AFL-CIO has proposed that the workforce development system incorporate a learning network of certified "professional workplace learning advisors" who would conduct learning needs analyses for co-workers, recommend pertinent education and skill training programs, and advocate for continuous skill improvement. Advisors would be knowledgeable about the labor exchange services available for public employees in the employment services in One-Stop Career Centers and (if such a program were available) would refer fellow employees to the "career coaches" in the centers, as envisioned by the Center for American Progress (Soares 2009).

Support New Research on the Joint Program Model

Finally, we recommend new policies to support systematic research of the joint program model, with the goal of generating new insight to strengthen and diffuse the model and its effective practices in order to improve the delivery of education and training to the 21st-century workforce. This would require investments in new internal systems of evaluations that would help individual joint programs develop new metrics and tracking systems to help them understand their processes and improve the quality of their programs.

Conclusion

In this chapter we have explored how a set of basic practices and philosophical principles that were first articulated in the early 1990s have been refined, distributed, and institutionalized into the material structures of joint training programs. Together the five joint training program features discussed here have given rise to a robust and flexible model of worker education and training that holds great potential for the 21st-century workforce development system. Though more research may be needed to validate these features and understand how they work together to contribute to effectiveness of worker education and training programs, the lack of rigor does not negate the fact that joint training programs have proven to be sustainable organizations that fill a significant gap in the U.S. workforce development system through providing a wide range of relevant services to diverse populations of front-line workers. These services affect the lives of workers in meaningful ways, and they contribute to performance of firms, and in some cases to the broader regional economy.

The current economic crisis has fostered a level of government investment in the education and training of workers that may be unprecedented. It has also sparked new dialogue about how to make broader, more systematic education opportunities available to all Americans. In addition, it has opened new debate over the responsibility for the funding of workforce education and training as well as the most effective division of labor for the provision of education and training to working adults. For the last 30 years, these issues—including the responsibility for educational funding, the appropriate mix of education and job-related training, the need for particular occupations and jobs as well as the most appropriate credentialing regime, and the most appropriate modes of training delivery—have been the subject of ongoing discussion and innovation inside the community of joint training programs. The experience of meeting the education needs of working adults, and the knowledge of workforce development that underlies the practice of joint training programs, is a valuable resource to all concerned with modernizing the American workforce development system. We argue that the learning and experiences of the community of practitioners who have developed and refined this model must be considered in any discussion of the workforce development system for the 21st century.

References

AFL-CIO. 1983. *The Future of Work.* Washington, DC: AFL-CIO Committee on the Evolution of Work.
AFL-CIO. 1994. *The New American Workplace: A Labor Perspective.* Washington, DC: AFL-CIO Committee on the Evolution of Work.

AFL-CIO. 1995. *Serving Workers in Transition: A Guide to Peer Support*. Washington, DC: AFL-CIO Human Resources Development Institute.

American Federation of Teachers. 2009. "Enhancing Members' Skills and Careers." *American Teacher*, March 2.

Apollo. 2008. *The New Apollo Program: Clean Energy, Good Jobs*. San Francisco: Apollo Alliance.

ArcelorMittal. 2009. *Safe Sustainable Steel: Fact Book 2008*. Luxembourg.

Bloom, M., and A. Campbell. 2002. *Success by Design: What Works in Workforce Development*. Ottawa: The Conference Board of Canada.

Bluestone, B., and I. Bluestone. 1992. *Negotiating the Future: A Labor Perspective on American Business*. New York: Basic Books.

Bosworth, B. 2007. *Lifelong Learning: New Strategies for the Education of Working Adults*. Washington, DC: Center for American Progress.

Conway, Maureen. 1999. *The Garment Industry Development Corporation: A Case Study of a Sectoral Employment Development Approach*. Washington, DC: Aspen Institute.

Cutcher-Gershenfeld, J., T.A. Kochan, and A. Verma. 1991. "Recent Developments in U.S. Employee Involvement Initiatives: Erosion or Diffusion." In D. Lewin and D. Sockell, eds., *Advances in Industrial and Labor Relations*. Greenwich, CT: JAI Press, pp. 1–32.

Dertouzos, M.L. 1998. *Made in America: Regaining the Productive Edge*. Cambridge, MA: MIT Press.

Eaton, S.C., S.A. Rubinstein, and R.B. McKersie. 2004. "Building and Sustaining Labor–Management Partnerships: Recent Experience in the U.S." *Advances in Industrial and Labor Relations*, Vol. 13, pp. 137–56.

Ferman, L.A., M. Hoyman, and J. Cutcher-Gershenfeld. 1990. "Joint Union–Management Training Programs: A Synthesis in the Evolution of Jointism and Training." In L.A. Ferman, M. Hoyman, J. Cutcher-Gershenfeld and E.J. Savoie, eds., *New Developments in Worker Training: A Legacy for the 1990's*. Madison, WI: Industrial Relations Research Association, pp. 157–90.

Ferman, L.A., M. Hoyman, J. Cutcher-Gershenfeld, and E.J. Savoie, eds. 1991. *Joint Training Programs: A Union–Management Approach to Preparing Workers for the Future*. Ithaca, NY: ILR Press.

Fischer, D.J. 2003. *Labor Gains: How Union-Affiliated Training Is Transforming New York's Workforce Landscape*. New York: Center for an Urban Future.

Giloth, R.P., ed. 2004. *Workforce Intermediaries for the 21st Century*. New York: American Assembly, Columbia University.

Gomberg, W. 1967. "Special Study Committees." In J.T. Dunlop and N.W. Chamberlain, eds., *Frontiers of Collective Bargaining*. New York: Harper & Row, pp. 235–51.

Harris, Howard. 2000. *Defining the Future or Reliving the Past? Unions, Employers, and the Challenge of Workplace Learning*. Information Series No. 380. ERIC Clearinghouse on Adult, Career, and Vocational Education, Columbus, OH, p. 70.

Heckscher, C.C. 1988. *The New Unionism: Employee Involvement in the Changing Corporation*. New York: Basic Books.

Hensley, Stephen Michael. 1996. *Labor–Management Training Programs Established and Funded through Collective Bargaining Agreements at Firms Employing 1000 or More Persons*. Blacksburg, VA: Virginia Polytechnic Institute and State University.

Institute for Career Development. 2009a. *District Directors' Reports for USW Districts 1, 2, 4, 7, 8, 9, 10, 11, 12, 13*. Merrillville, IN: Institute for Career Development.

Institute for Career Development. 2009b. *DOL ETA Energy Training Partnership Grant Application.* Merrillville, IN: Institute for Career Development.

Institute for Career Development. 2008a. *Summary of Selected Course Costs in 2007.* Merrillville, IN: Institute for Career Development.

Institute for Career Development. 2008b. *United Steelworkers ICD Participating Companies.* Merrillville, IN: Institute for Career Development.

Institute for Career Development. 2007. *ICD's Vision of Learning: A Position Paper.* Merrillville, IN: Institute for Career Development.

Kaufman, B.E. 2001. "An Interview with Steelworkers' President Lynn Williams." *Journal of Labor Relations,* Vol. 22, no. 1, pp. 145–71.

Kemble, P. 2002. "How Unions Can Help Lift Up America by Its Bootstraps," In P. Kemble, ed. *Workforce Development and the New Unionism.* Washington, DC: New Economy Information Service, pp. 11–22.

King, Kathleen P. 2009. "Workplace Performance-Plus: Empowerment and Voice through Professional Development and Democratic Processes in Health Care Training." *Performance Improvement Quarterly,* Vol. 21, no. 4, pp. 55–74.

Kochan, T.A., A.E. Eaton, R.B. McKersie, and P.S. Adler. 2009. *Healing Together: The Labor–Management Partnership at Kaiser Permanente.* Ithaca, NY: Cornell University Press.

Korshak, Stuart R. 2000. "A Labor–Management Partnership: San Francisco's Hotels and the Employees' Union Try a New Approach." *The Cornell Hotel and Restaurant Administration Quarterly,* Vol. 41, no. 2, pp. 14–29.

Kourpias, G. 1994. *High Performance Work Organization Partnerships.* Upper Marlboro, MD: International Association of Machinists and Aerospace Workers.

Locker Associates. 1993. "Steel Industry Employment Data." *New Directions in Basic Steel: Joint Leadership Level Manual.* Pittsburgh, PA: Locker Associates.

Luria, D., M. Vidal, H. Wial, and J. Rogers. 2006. "*Full-Utilization Learning Lean*" in Component Manufacturing: A New Industrial Model for Mature Regions, and Labor's Stake in Its Success. Sloan Industry Studies Working Paper. Cambridge, MA: Sloan School of Management, Massachusetts Institute of Technology.

Marschall, D. Forthcoming. "The Role of American Unions in the Institutionalization of Workplace Learning: Innovations for New Work Systems and Labor Movement Renewal." In R. Cooney and M. Stuart, eds., *Trade Unions and Workplace Training: Issues and International Perspectives.* London: Routledge.

Marschall, D. 2008. Interview with Lynn Williams, October 3, 2008.

Mills, N. 2001. "New Strategies for Union Survival and Revival." *Journal of Labor Relations,* Vol. 22, no. 3, pp. 599–613.

MIT. 2001. *Collective Bargaining in the Face of Instability: A Resource for Workers and Employers in the U.S. Aerospace Industry.* Cambridge, MA: MIT Labor Aerospace Research Agenda.

Monks, J., and M. Bahr. 2003. *Labor Unions and Workforce Development.* Washington, DC: New Economy Information Service.

Moody, K. 1988. *An Injury to All: The Decline of American Unionism.* London and New York: Verso.

Roberts, Markley, and Robert Wozniak. 1994. *Labor's Key Role in Workplace Training.* Washington DC: AFL-CIO.

Rubinstein, S.A. 2003. "Partnership of Steel? Forging High Involvement Work Systems in the U.S. Steel Industry: A View from the Local Unions." *Advances in Industrial and Labor Relations,* Vol. 12, pp. 115–44.

Rutigliano, A. 1988. "Cooperating to Survive at National Steel." *Management Review* (February), pp. 30–38.

Sarmiento, A., and A. Kay. 1990. *Worker-Centered Learning: A Union Guide to Workplace Literacy.* Washington, DC: AFL-CIO Human Resources Development Institute.

Schied, F.M. 1994. *Worker-Centered Learning: Developing a Basic Skills Curriculum and Materials in a Union Setting.* Harrisburg, PA: Pennsylvania State Department of Education, Bureau of Adult Basic and Literacy Education.

Schurman, S.J., M.E. Hugentobler, and T. Robins. 1990. "How Unions Can Improve the Outcomes of Joint Health and Safety Programs." *Labor Studies Journal,* Vol. 15, no. 4, pp. 16–38.

Schurman, S.J., and Isreal, B. 1996. "Redesigning Work Systems to Reduce Stress: A Participatory Action Research Approach." In G. Keiter, J. Hurrell, and L. Murphy, eds., *Job Stress Interventions: Current Practices and New Directions.* Washington, DC: American Psychological Association, pp. 235–64.

Scully-Russ, E. 2009. Interview with Cheryl Feldman, August 24, 2009.

Scully-Russ, E. 2006. "Learning to Organize: The Challenge and Promise of Democratic Learning in American Unions" In R.v.d. Veen, D. Wildemeersch, J. Youngblood, and V.J. Marsick, eds., *Democratic Practices as Learning Opportunities.* Rotterdam/Taipei: Sense Publications, pp. 151–64.

Sheahan, M. 1993. *Preparing Local Leaders for Their Role in Joint Programs and Restructuring Work: A Strategic Approach.* Taylor, MI: UAW Region 1A IPS Labor–Management Council.

Smith Education Associates. 2008. *2007–08 Career Development Impact Survey: Aggregate Results.* Bridgman, MI: Smith Education Associates.

Soares, L. 2009. *Working Learners: Educating Our Entire Workforce for Success in the 21st Century.* Washington, DC: Center for American Progress.

Takahashi, B., and E. Melendez. 2004. "Union-Sponsored Workforce Development Initiatives." In E. Melendez, ed., *Communities and Workforce Development.* Kalamazoo, MI: Upjohn Institute for Employment Research, pp. 119–50.

Tao, Fumiyo, G.V. Richard, H. Tarr, and J.R. Wheeler. 1992. *Upward Mobility Programs in the Service Sector for Disadvantaged and Dislocated Workers. Volume I: Final Report.* Washington, DC: National Commission for Employment Policy (DOL).

United Steelworkers. 2008. *Resolution: Training, Retraining and Career Development.* Pittsburgh, PA: United Steelworkers.

United Steelworkers of America. 1986. *Responding to Economic Dislocation.* Pittsburgh, PA: International Headquarters Task Force for Dislocated Worker Program Development.

Wenger, E. 1998. *Communities of Practice: Learning, Meaning, and Identity.* Cambridge, UK: Cambridge University Press.

Williams, L. 1995. "Making Everyone a Stakeholder: Strategies for Addressing Conflict Needs." In H. Risher and C. Fay, eds., *The Performance Imperative: Strategies for Enhancing Workforce Effectiveness.* San Francisco: Jossey-Bass.

Wilson, R. 2009. *Jobs to Careers Practice Brief: Promoting Work-Based Learning for Quality Care.* New York: Jobs for the Future.

Wilson, T. 2009. "Union Learning." *National Labor College Seminar on Creating Jobs; Delivering Education and Skills; Expanding Labor's Role.* Silver Spring, MD.

Working for America Institute. 2001. *High Road Partnerships Report.* Washington DC: AFL-CIO.

Wurf, J. 1982. "Labor's View of Quality of Working Life Programs." *Journal of Business Ethics,* Vol. 1, no. 2, pp. 131–7.

CHAPTER 10

Civil Society and the Provision of Services: The Freelancers Union Experience

CHARLES HECKSCHER
Rutgers University

SARA HOROWITZ
ALTHEA ERICKSON
Freelancers Union

The social framework of support for employees in the United States has eroded dramatically in recent decades. On one side, corporations have cut their commitments to employee benefits—reducing training, dropping defined-benefit pension plans, and shifting away from the traditional "lifetime security" model of employment. On the other side, government programs that used to fill in the gap have been squeezed by budgetary and political pressures. As a result, for example, in 2007–08 only 41% of the unemployed nationwide received unemployment benefits (*New York Times* 2009). Unions used to provide another counterweight in the workplace and the political arena, but their loss of membership and influence has left them with little ability to slow these trends.

In part in response to this decline of traditional institutions of social security, there has been a substantial growth of interest, both academic and practical, in institutions that fall outside the traditional categories of companies, unions, and government and that are based instead on voluntary association and communal linkages. Such "civil society organizations," or CSOs, are often seen as a "third way" between the individualism of the market and the bureaucratic mechanisms of the state. The concept of CSOs is still a loose and evolving one, including everything from lobbying to mutual aid to psychological support groups. Though this fluidity makes exact counts difficult, it is generally agreed that the number of organizations has increased significantly since the early 1990s in both the developed world and in many developing nations (Beloe, Elkington, Hester, and Newell 2003; Anheier, Kaldor, and Glasius 2005; Clark 2008).

Freelancers Union is a CSO aimed at representing the needs of independent workers—those without lasting relations with particular employers, including freelancers, consultants, independent contractors, temps, part-timers, contingent employees, and the self-employed. The U.S. Government Accountability Office estimates this group at over 30% of the workforce (U.S. Government Accountability Office 2006)—and that does not even include those working in large firms with increasingly uncertain expectations of long-term employment.

In ten years Freelancers Union has grown to over 140,000 members (and continues to grow rapidly), has achieved financial self-sufficiency, and has developed a portable health insurance program that is often cited as an important alternative to familiar approaches. In the process it has gained a good deal of experience in navigating the set of relations among CSOs, government, and the market. Its efforts in the area of skills and training are still nascent, but the intention is to apply some of the same principles of mutual aid and market aggregation to this arena.

Freelancers Union's efforts in the education and training domain are less developed than in other services, especially the provision of health insurance. In an economy that increasingly demands sophisticated knowledge and technical skill, freelancers face a particular dilemma because they lack access to the major existing means of occupational learning, which is firm-based training programs. Thus this is an important priority for the future. We will focus on the general problems of the emerging role of CSOs in these service areas that have traditionally been driven by markets and hierarchies, and then try to apply these lessons to the early Freelancers Union training programs.

Civil Society

"Third Way" Conceptions

The modern concept of civil society was first articulated by Alexis de Tocqueville (1839),[1] who saw in the American practice of free association an alternative to state-centered European systems. It is in this sense, as an *alternative* model of organization, that the concept of civil society has enjoyed a boom in the last two decades: It has often been presented as a "third way" to the two great organizing principles of modernity, markets and hierarchies (Powell 1990; Giddens 1998; Castells 2000; Adler 2001). As a principle of organization, civil society minimizes both coercive authority and material incentives. It relies instead on motivations of trust and community. It is more collective than markets, which are based on individual exchanges, but less so than hierarchies.

The civil society concept is attractive in large part because it seems to avoid the increasingly visible problems of other ways of organizing. On one side, markets have long been subject to critique from liberals for increasing social inequities and ignoring social obligations to the less successful; this view was given new impetus by the financial crisis starting in 2008. On the other side, hierarchy, especially in the form of government, has been a central target of the conservative movement since the 1980s, and there are growing criticisms of bureaucracy in large firms as well. CSOs, according to their advocates (Skjelsbaek 1971; Wapner 1995; Giddens 1998), can combine the flexibility and entrepreneurship of market incentives with the coordination and focus of bureaucracy. They seem to offer a path between the political–ideological poles, and have in fact attracted interest from both liberal and conservative politicians and political theorists. Even more ambitiously, some scholars (Giddens 1998; Castells 2000) believe CSOs can overcome a persistent problem of modernity: the depersonalization of relations and related alienation of the individual, which characterize both bureaucracies and markets, and which a long line of writers have seen as characteristic of modern society (Durkheim 1933; Reisman, Glazer, and Denney 1950; Smith 2002).

Despite the enthusiasm of scholars and activists, however, CSOs have also manifested major weaknesses. Since the era of major growth is less than two decades old, there has been scant research on their effectiveness and longevity, but partial and anecdotal evidence suggests that they demonstrate neither. "How effective are they?" asks a study of NGOs: "recent research suggests 'not very'" (Beloe, Elkington, Hester, and Newell 2003:21).[2] The associational spirit is regularly undermined by fragmentation, lack of sustained focus, isolation, and poverty of resources. The most successful have generally depended on outside "charity" from governments or foundations; these have proved to be both unreliable and constraining in the long run.

The *theory* of civil society also remains far less developed than the theories of hierarchy and market. Its attractiveness comes in part from the fact that it is unfamiliar and can easily be interpreted, or blurred, to fit divergent views. An enormous range of institutions is often included in discussions of CSOs, ranging from small, coherent local communities at one extreme to large, loose, unbounded associations at the other. Little unites the field except an antipathy to markets and hierarchies; this is not sufficient to build an understanding of the role of CSOs and the conditions for their effectiveness.

Beyond the Third Way: The Complexity of CSOs' Role

From a sociological perspective[3] the problem of the third-way view is that it is one-sided and incomplete: It believes that free associations can stand on their own and *replace* the previous order. The demonstrated weaknesses of CSOs are a result of their frequent tendency to try to "go it alone"—to rely on pure voluntary solidarity and to resist necessary elements of discipline, hierarchy, and economic effectiveness. The strengthening of civil society does not eliminate the need for hierarchies and markets but rather *adds* a set of complex problems around how to integrate them.

Many CSOs have recognized these problems to some degree and have begun a painful process of "maturation" that involves developing more formally organized internal operations that include more differentiation and hierarchy as well as learning to work with external institutions that they have often treated as foreign or hostile. For example, for many years environmentalists and labor representatives refused to have anything to do with coal companies or Walmart, defining them as the enemy. More recently, however, many of these CSOs have engaged in negotiation with corporations, and politicians and have begun hesitantly to accept that they must regularize their relations to firms and economic institutions (Shellenberger and Nordhaus 2004; Sacks 2007). But this is just a first step in a long and necessary process of working through the implications of the rise of CSOs.

The issues can be organized systematically by using Parsons' model of complex social systems as comprised of four key sectors (Parsons 1971). Civil society organizations are the core of the "associational" sector of society; they coordinate activities of mutual interdependencies that require relations of trust. They include all forms of voluntary "coming together," from bowling leagues to interest groups to mutual-aid associations. They are built on webs of diffuse mutual exchange and obligation. Their strength is in their ability to build cooperative relations within defined groups.

In addition to this, however, are three further sectors that fulfill key social requirements:

- Economic institutions are essential for coordinating complex production chains across broad markets. They rely primarily on contracts for specific good and services.
- Political institutions organize people around shared goals, including mutual security, relying primarily on hierarchies of authority.

- Moral/cultural institutions create the unifying orientations and beliefs or "visions" that are common to all members of a society and give confidence that others will "do the right thing," even in situations that are novel or that conflict with narrow self-interest. Modern society has tended to deemphasize shared values in pursuit of individualism. But the crisis of meaning that has produced the current "culture wars" has made clear the continuing need for shared commitments to values. The central institutions in this area historically have been churches, nuclear families, and schools. These are different from voluntary associations because members have obligations to live up to certain values, while members of an association may simply be looking for the benefits of mutual exchange.

Civil society, in this view, has a crucial but incomplete role in social relations and needs to develop effective relations with the other sectors.

Civil society organizations like Freelancers Union are less established than political and economic ones and therefore have an especially

FIGURE 1
The Four Core Social Sectors and Their Central Concerns
(with a Focus on Civil Society).

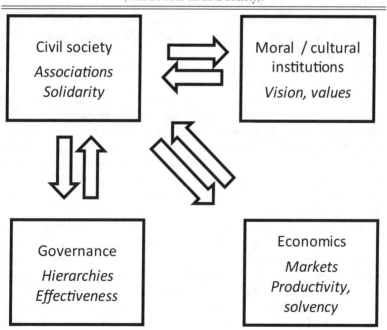

difficult struggle to define their priorities in this balancing act. They need to be able to define their own particular identities and contributions to their members, while at the same time interacting with and mobilizing resources from the three "outside" (and generally more established) social sectors. On one side lies the danger of isolation, maintaining the "purity" of the group identity and solidarity but losing the ability to influence the wider society; on the other lies the danger of assimilation, of losing the group identity and becoming "merely" a political, economic, or cultural body.

The key problem, then, is to understand how CSOs can build on their particular strength, the solidarity of their members, while also finding ways to meet needs for solvency, effectiveness, and value-integrity.

CSOs and the Economy

The most salient balancing act for CSOs is in relation to the economic sphere. CSOs have typically resisted involvement in market economics, often developing moral stances that reject the profit motive. Thus they have rarely sought support from economic institutions or sought cooperative relations with them, preferring to work through government regulation or to create pressure through hostile confrontation. As a result, many have become heavily dependent on charitable foundations, which sharply constrains their freedom of action and their ability to set strategies. Most also operate with very small budgets and pay far lower salaries than the private sector (Beloe, Elkington, Hester, and Newell 2003), hampering their ability to retain high-level employees.

In the past decade there has been a clear move among many types of CSOs to review this stance, to find ways both to draw on the market economy's resources and to exert ongoing influence on major corporations through stabilized relations of alliance and negotiation. In the health care arena, a particularly dramatic example was the sight of the heads of the Service Employees International Union (SEIU) and Walmart standing shoulder to shoulder in 2009 to support reform, despite their bitter disagreements in other domains (Benson 2009).

CSOs have also grown more creative in creating resources through economic activity without abandoning their own identities. AARP has for many years drawn profits from sales of its retirement products to members. Oxfam has developed the fifth-largest retail entity in the United Kingdom (Jennings 2006). Ten Thousand Villages has created networks of local producers in developing countries and connected them to affluent markets. Various fair trade organizations have used profits from sales to maintain their organizations and help producers.

The challenge is to balance the associational and the economic missions without allowing one to crowd out the other. If CSOs become *merely* economic profit-making organizations they lose the distinctive advantage of trust that is built from the mutual solidarity of their members. Large CSOs like AARP are continually faced with the tension between maximizing their size and resources and maintaining the sense of member solidarity. But if they are *merely* solidarity groups, they risk becoming irrelevant to the wider society and having fewer resources for action.

Freelancers Union has since its founding sought economic self-sufficiency. Though foundation grants were important in its early years, it rapidly increased the share of income coming from its health insurance products for members and achieved full self-sufficiency in 2006. It continues to seek a merging of nonprofit sources of revenue with for-profit social enterprises and to avoid excessive dependence on any single source. While combining both associational and economic missions into a single organization creates some tension between the two forces, ultimately it establishes conditions for a stronger whole, where the economic and associational ties reinforce each other.

CSOs and the Polity

A second area of balance is in relation to government. Most CSOs emphasize independence and tend therefore to remain ineffective, unable to sustain coherent strategies (Ghimire 2005). But a set of associations—perhaps the majority worldwide—have become highly intertwined with governments, seeing political influence as the main avenue for getting things done as well as a crucial source of funding. There are serious dangers in this dependence, however. Many experiences, going back to at least the 1960s, have shown that the government connection can rapidly lead to estrangement from the membership (Moynihan 1969; Gittell and Hoffacker 1980).

The strength of CSOs in comparison to government is their ability to focus on needs of particular groups—their members—rather than the electoral math of building majorities. Thus, on this dimension, the effectiveness of CSOs depends on enabling groups to identify their needs and find their own "voices"; assimilation to government programs undermines this effectiveness.

Freelancers Union has been active in the political sphere, lobbying for improvements in the legal framework governing freelance work. Within New York City and State it has become a significant actor, attracting attention from political leaders, mobilizing members, and helping frame the intellectual agenda around freelancers. It has so far avoided the dilemmas that spring from high dependence on government programs. It has also drawn attention on the national level for its advocacy of the interests of independent workers.

CSOs and the Value Sphere

An important dilemma for CSOs is how closely they should identify themselves with broad value claims. Many CSOs been effective by connecting to powerful value-based movements, including ones on the right (evangelical, anti-abortion, and pro-gun groups) as well as on the left (civil rights and environmental groups). But tight links between CSOs and strong value positions may also create problems: A value focus can drive away potential members and also lead to fractures within the membership. Value disagreements leave little room for compromise or working things out amicably. For those reasons, many CSOs have been wary of basing themselves in such broad claims, focusing instead on either relatively narrow, pragmatic interests or on underlying status groupings such as ethnic or regional identity.

Freelancers Union has not adopted a strong value statement or litmus test for membership, but it has begun to sketch out a value-based vision that cuts across current political polarizations: It views freelancing as a potentially positive social institution and suggests that freelancers should be proud of what they do. Thus, rather than fighting for employer guarantees of job security, like many other associations, the organization has fought to make job mobility and independence more rewarding.

Unlike true value-focused organizations, Freelancers Union has not demanded unity around this vision. But it has been seen, by some members at least, as inspirational and a reason to contribute beyond direct self-interest. In a recent survey asking how people felt about Freelancers Union, the 500 respondents used many "vision" words (as analyzed by content analysis software): "community," "movement," "supportive," and "network" were among the key emergent terms, and many people expressed a sense of excitement about the mission.

Freelancing vision cuts across current political polarities. Liberals generally seek to use government to guarantee more stable jobs; conservatives like the flexibility of freelancing but think about it in purely market terms. The notion that freelancers, by joining together in an association, can increase the rewards and security of this kind of work is an unconventional one. Some existing value-defined groups, such as unions and foundations, have found this approach intriguing, but other potential allies, including liberal groups who have a different vision based in a more classic view of corporate responsibility, have at times been hostile.

Perhaps the most significant value-oriented decision was the renaming of the organization in 2007 from "Working Today" to the far less neutral "Freelancers Union." The adoption of the "union" label reflected the values of many of the organization leaders, but it was also found in field-testing to be popular with members—conjuring images of a proud and unified group rather than a mere loose association. But some members, and an unknown number of potential members, are uncomfortable with these connotations. This move, like any value-centered move, tends to narrow the potential range of association but to increase the commitment and activism of members.

Internal Organization and Solidarity of CSOs

A final critical balancing act for CSOs is the *internal* organizational tension among free association, involvement, and disciplined action. Voluntary associations have difficulty sustaining consistent courses of action or getting members to act together; it is too easy for those who disagree to leave. Furthermore, many modern civil society organizations, based in "new social movements," have strong ideologies and almost reflexively resist centralized command (Gamson 1995). As a result, they have difficulty both in developing consistent strategies and in sustaining commitments to others. A community group may succeed, for example, in working out an agreement with a developer, but members who do not agree need not fall into line—they can easily split off and renounce the agreement, or they can stall action by unending debate. This very often renders civil society organizations ineffective as participants in stakeholder agreements: They are too fluid, and their commitments are insufficiently reliable (Newell 2005).

Most CSOs resolve this balance through small, committed staff groups that coordinate diffuse memberships. This has been true of Freelancers Union, which through much of its history conducted most of its work through staff activity. As it has grown larger and more complex, however, especially after about 2008, it has gone through some crucial changes that have helped manage the tensions we have described. The danger is that this can lead to a dependent relation between members and the organization, rather than solidarity, and thus accentuate the tendency of members to pursue their individual interests rather than building the strength of the group.

Internal Differentiation. In 2009, the organization split into several parts that essentially specialize in managing different aspects of the problems described. Most dramatically, it spun off a for-profit health insurance company to provide this crucial member benefit. What makes this relationship highly unusual is that the insurance company is wholly owned by the association; thus, while the company focuses on success in the marketplace, the association is concerned with making sure the company contributes to the overall needs of the solidarity group. This differentiation makes it easier to avoid being pulled too much toward the pole of profit maximization, or conversely to allow the logic of solidarity to undermine economic needs. While the organization is still working through the practical details of this relationship, it is clear that the economic ties members experience through the insurance company create additional opportunities for fostering mutual solidarity.

As part of the reorganization, Freelancers Union also created a Political Action Committee that has begun to focus the political side of the organization's actions, but like the insurance company it is clearly subordinate to "associational" part.

Member Democracy. "Association management" is nearly an oxymoron: The members on whose energy and commitment the system depends cannot be "managed" in any conventional sense. At the same time they tend to view the association from a relatively narrow perspective so that pure democracy is not an option either: Democratic discussions may quickly fall into narrow interest-demands.

The dilemmas were vividly manifested for Freelancers Union during a major shift in insurance provision in 2009. Unlike most providers, Freelancers Union invited members to comment on the changes; though well over 95% were satisfied, the complaints of a small and vocal minority whose rates had gone up were eventually reported in national news media. The organization's response was guided by the fact that it was a CSO rather than a market business: Rather than simply dropping "customers," it sought to engage dissenters in dialogue and to increase mutual understanding throughout the membership. The staff learned a great deal from the exchange, and the bonds of trust with members were probably strengthened by it.

Another relevant dilemma has been the role of members in governance. Until 2009 members did not elect representatives to the board of directors. This is common among associations, because members are often narrowly focused on particular interests and may remain quite disconnected from the broader strategic problems faced by the staff. In 2009, however, the organization developed a process for electing a member representative.[4] It retains considerable safeguards through which the staff and board can reject candidates who are pursuing single issues, but it also develops wider involvement of members, which should help strengthen the bonds of solidarity and trust that are vital to success.

Current efforts focus on web-based communication media, including member-to-member and member-to-organization bulletin boards and chats, sharing of information, and exchange of services. These have been lively and have grown substantially in the past year but still involve a small minority of the membership. The longer-term vision includes ways to involve members more actively in Freelancers Union activities; in this respect the area of education has already shown promise and may play an increasing role. *Freelancers Union as a Hub.* Freelancers Union also hopes to strengthen its internal organization by building capacity as a "hub," linking smaller, more focused organizations and aggregating their power. Thus it has built a web of affiliates such as the Translators and Interpreters Guild and the World Wide Web Artists Consortium with the intention of having them dock onto Freelancers Union health insurance offerings, other products and services, lobbying activities, and communication networks. However, these affiliated groups too have often proved to have little internal solidarity or discipline, and they have generally not proved to be useful partners or intermediaries.

The balances or dilemmas of CSOs—around economics, authority, values, and member relations—can only be resolved through practice and learning. The hopes placed in CSOs in recent decades far outstrip their actual ability to manage these complex relations, so they remain generally marginal and far less influential than traditional "organized" actors such as labor unions and business firms. Those CSOs that have survived beyond an initial burst of enthusiasm have begun to develop more sophisticated conceptions of their relations to markets—the idea of "market intelligence" has begun to take hold—as well as governments, and they have sought to establish credibility as negotiation partners (Beloe, Elkington, Hester, and Newell 2003; Shellenberger and Nordhaus 2004).

The Health Care Experience

Since lack of health insurance was the most urgent problem for its members in the 1990s and 2000s, Freelancers Union focused first on this area. The organization's experience with education and training is still comparatively undeveloped, but the health care experience provides lessons that are beginning to shape plans for the education programs.

Health insurance provides a particularly salient example of the ways CSOs could play a valuable role in providing benefits and services to their members, particularly where the government and the private market fall short. Before the implementation of health care reform, about 15% of Americans, or 45 million people, fell outside of the main organizing mechanisms for health insurance—Medicare, Medicaid, and employer-provided plans.[5] Furthermore, many of those with insurance have inadequate coverage. CSOs could step in to fill that gap and could do a better job of organizing coverage than either government or the market.

The Economic Front

Member-centered CSOs are effective only to the extent that they can retain the trust of their members. This can create dilemmas not faced by "normal" commercial insurance carriers in responding to members whose demands are economically problematic. The experience of Freelancers Insurance Company (FIC) provides first-hand experience about these differences.

Freelancers Union started FIC in January 2009, after years of negotiating group coverage through private insurers, whose interest in the bottom line always seemed to trump Freelancers Union's interest in covering its members. Freelancers Insurance Company is rooted in the growing field of social entrepreneurship, made up of mission-driven organizations that establish for-profit businesses whose primary purpose is to fill a social need.

FIC is a for-profit insurer and must balance its books each month. Yet it is distinct in several ways from a "merely" economic organization. First, it is wholly owned and operated by Freelancers Union, the nonprofit membership organization. There are no shareholders pressuring FIC for higher returns. Thus FIC can make choices different from other insurance companies. Traditional insurers often try to eliminate the sickest, most at-risk from their pool of enrollees. FIC, on the other hand, works to keep people in the group, no matter their health status. So whereas a traditional insurer might cut a plan or benefit that attracts less healthy people, FIC tries to find the right balance of benefits and pricing to keep its members on the plan and works to subsidize their costs in other ways. For example, FIC may decide to take on more actuarial risk to keep prices down and keep people insured.

The long-term relationships and mutual dependence between a CSO and its membership also encourage a CSO to offer better, more comprehensive care. It's in the CSO's best interest to keep its members healthy and to develop a large, sustainable risk pool. Thus it has strong incentives to invest in preventive care to keep members healthy (and hopefully less expensive to insure) over the long term. For example, FIC is developing innovative new nurse practitioner and mental health networks and is using labor and community organizing strategies to "nudge" members into better health practices.

Financing also sets CSOs apart from private providers. Because they are financed by social capital (from foundations, membership fees, or individual donors) as opposed to private equity, CSOs don't have the same profit pressures traditional insurers have. FIC is financed with capital from foundations, which require a 2% rate of return, instead of the 30%

rate private equity investors would likely require. This low-cost capital has a direct impact on premium rates. The federal government should explore new approaches to promoting these models, including offering low-cost capital, setting alternative capitalization requirements, or establishing favorable tax treatment to support health insurers that meet social goals. This approach has a long history in affordable housing (U.S. Treasury 2008) and could be applicable to health insurance as well.

The Political Front

There is of course a strong argument by some that government should take over the provision of health care as a basic and universal right. Freelancers Union has demonstrated some of the benefits of a voluntary associational approach as at least an element of a health care system. Government has in the past largely focused on the needs of those in the primary labor force and has failed rather dramatically to pay attention to independent workers, who have been left to fend in the individual market. Thus a great deal of Freelancers Union's efforts in the first years have been directed at building a picture of the particular needs of independent workers and demonstrating to regulators that they form a viable risk pool with their own distinct needs.

The need for FIC to pay close attention to its members and to retain their loyalty gives it a distinct flavor from government plans. On the other hand, without government-enforced standards, the system would fragment into competing groups that would be both inefficient and vulnerable to manipulation. The ideal is an interaction in which CSOs can act as intermediaries tailoring essential services to particular memberships. This balance is a matter of very practical and detailed experimentation; Freelancers Union has been a pioneer in working it through.

The Value Front

FIC by its nature stakes out an unusual position in a crucial value debate: It implies that neither direct government administration nor free market provision of health care is sufficient. It implies a vision of associational exchanges at the "front lines" of relation to differentiated groups.

There are questions about whether other values should become part of the FIC message. For instance, the company has developed some programs emphasizing long-term health and wellness beyond the industry norms. These are not directly "demanded" by the membership but are more part of the organization's vision. Examples of these programs include a discounted therapist network, communications campaigns to help members save money on health costs, and potential partnerships with nurse practitioners to increase access to affordable primary care.

The FIC has just begun to explore this terrain, since it has achieved independent status. CSOs cannot get too far from members' interests, but they can create a vision of health care that helps to increase commitment and goes beyond concrete member demands.

Internal Relations

One of the ways a CSO can add value is by providing insurance plans that meet the particular needs of its membership. Freelancers (like other groups) have certain specific needs and expectations, and a trusted CSO can become more knowledgeable about this community than a purely economic firm. For instance, Freelancers Union maintains a website open to constant "chatter" from members; this surfaces direct health care issues, like any standard "complaints" forum, but it also provides insight into broader needs and opportunities that may affect the shape of offerings.

The CSO can also leverage the solidarity and community within the group to bring down costs. For example, Freelancers Union organizes a subset of mental health providers from its membership to provide lower-cost services to other members. It can publish the names of high-cost MRI providers and encourage members to go elsewhere to keep prices down for everyone.

The strengths and vulnerabilities of the CSO role have already been clear in the first year of Freelancers Insurance Company. On the positive side, when members had to make an "opt-in" choice to join the new independent company, over 95% made the switch—much higher than the rate expected by industry specialists accustomed to standard commercial processes. The sense of solidarity and loyalty felt by members clearly contributed to this high conversion rate. On the negative side, it was necessary at that time, for economic reasons, to restructure rates so that certain members paid significantly more than before (while others paid less). As indicated earlier, there was a strong protest by some members and a rejection of the economic logic. By communicating openly and actively, the organization was able to come through this dispute with the sense of solidarity and commitment intact.

There is wider evidence that groups of workers can come together and offer benefits that compete effectively in the market, sustain themselves, and provide needed services to their members. Mutual insurance companies (Wikipedia 2010), in which the policy holders are the shareholders, gained significant market share in the United States until Ronald Reagan pushed them to de-mutualize in the 1980s (Chaddad and Cook

2004). The health insurance cooperatives (Van Gelder 2008) of the Emilia Romagna region in Italy are owned and financed by the worker-cooperatives that they have successfully served for the last 80 years. The *mutuelles* in France (Durand-Zaleski 2008) are private, supplementary insurance policies, owned and operated by labor organizations, which complement the public health system. All of these models work, and we should make room for them in our benefits delivery system.

Education and Training: Actual and Potential Efforts

Freelancers Union has not gone nearly as far in the provision of education and training as it has with health insurance, though this is very much in the long-term plan. The educational program currently involves three major components: in-person seminars, online "webinars," and networking meetings. Together these enrolled nearly 1,300 persons in 2009. This represents only the first steps toward what will certainly become a much more central part of the organization's efforts. Many of the issues raised by the experiences of CSOs in general, and Freelancers Union health care efforts in particular, are relevant to aspirations for extending these initiatives.

As with health care, there is an important potential role for CSOs because of the insufficiencies of markets and governments in dealing with the growing complexity of civil society. As the economy has changed in recent decades, significant gaps have become apparent in worker education and training, especially for the growing corpus of free-lancers. Classically, universities provided general education, and companies then added company-specific training for employees who were expected to advance their careers within the organization. As internal labor markets have declined, however (Osterman and Burton 2005; Farber 2007), employers have had less incentive to invest in employee skill development, and corporate training staff have come under pressure (O'Leonard 2009). Employees, widely recognizing that they cannot count on careers within one company, have expressed growing dissatisfaction with company training programs (Conference Board 2010).

Universities, both private and public, have been largely unable to address these changing needs because their entire model is based on general education for precareer students; degree requirements, semester schedules, and many other elements create obstacles to dealing with the needs of working adults seeking help with career advancement. While many universities are currently developing continuing education programs, these are in constant tension with the more "academic" mission. Some online universities, such as Edison College and the University of Phoenix, have tried to address these constituencies through virtual delivery systems, but they have only a narrow single-issue and commercial relationship to their students and are unlikely to gain the level of trust and understanding possible for a member association.

Government has historically played some role in training, but it has been unable to fill the growing demand. In part this is because of the general constraint on social spending of recent decades; more fundamentally, though, government is also not geared to meeting rapidly changing and differentiated needs. Its strength is in the mobilization of resources on a large scale for common goals. For instance, the U.S. Department of Labor sponsors One-Stop Career Centers that link persons to short-term training, certifications, and apprenticeships. However, much of this is geared toward the unemployed and persons working in more traditional industries like agriculture, construction, manufacturing, and mining rather than for independent workers in newer fields like technology. These programs also fail to provide the flexible business and marketing training that workers need to succeed in the new, more mobile workforce.

Other government training services often approach skill building from the perspective of a small business seeking to grow by bringing on more employees rather than from the perspective of an independent worker, who is more concerned with maintaining individual financial stability. This is the case, for instance, with the New York City Business Solutions program.

Overall, programs such as these provide useful skills and fill the gaps left by employer training. However, they don't provide a comprehensive solution to the needs of the new economy. CSOs like Freelancers Union, on the other hand, are focused on the needs of particular membership groups and the coordination of differentiated networks. They have the potential to deliver more targeted and responsive types of training in response to member needs.

Freelancers Union has a closer understanding of the needs of independent workers than most other education and training organizations by virtue of its multifaceted connection to its members. Its members fall outside the traditional employer-centered training mechanisms and have varying levels of educational attainment according to their types of work. Self-employed individuals in the United States, for instance, are more likely to have college and graduate degrees than their wage and salary counterparts. On a national level, 38% of the self-employed have a college or graduate degree, while 32% of standard full-time workers do. In contrast, agency temps have a lower level of educational attainment, with 21% having a college or graduate degree.[6]

No matter what the educational level attained, however, there is a skill set that freelancers and other independent workers need but do not get through traditional, formalized education or on-the-job experience. Independent workers with lower educational attainment like nannies and health aides along with more highly educated ones like technology professionals and therapists all have legal, accounting, and marketing needs that are beyond their areas of expertise. Sole proprietors need to know how to draft contracts, understand copyrights and trademarks, complete complicated tax forms throughout the year, pay additional taxes, and keep a steady stream of clients. To be self-sufficient, independent workers must acquire the skills from a long list of experts (accountants, lawyers, marketing professionals) while actually doing the work that they are paid for. And unlike traditional employees, who have access to on-the-job training, freelancers have to seek out training on their own to keep up on their job-specific knowledge.

How they access these skills varies depending on their occupation or industry. Filmmakers, for instance, may seek out courses offered by the Independent Filmmaker Conference to get more knowledge on "the new hybrid world of distribution and marketing," while writers wanting to switch up their niche market might take an eight-week course on travel writing through mediabistro.com. Someone in a technology-related field might not only take continuing education courses through a traditional educational institution but also attend annual conferences or join a meetup group to exchange ideas.

So far, Freelancers Union has addressed these needs through brief sessions on practical skills required for freelance work, such as accounting, legal basics of contracts, marketing strategies, and new media. In 2009 it held 20 seminars and webinars on these issues, generally in single two-hour sessions of 40 to 60 people. These are taught by independent professionals, often members themselves, with very little administrative overhead.

Networking events would not normally be classed with training, but for many freelancers they are an essential way of gaining information about their field—from market opportunities to new technologies and techniques. The Freelancers Union held three such sessions in 2009 that attracted about 650 people.

These first steps have been positive. An art curator who participated in a recent Freelancers Union online seminar on tax deductions and quarterly statements indicated on an evaluation that "other than a one-on-one session with an accountant I can't imagine a more useful exchange of tax-related information for freelancers," and a writer who participated in a recent seminar on marketing said that it "offered real-world experience and gave you actual tools to use." And these seminars are less than one third the cost an individual would have to pay for one-on-one help from a professional in these areas. At every event over the past year, Freelancers Union has seen many repeat participants, who want to continue to plug into the educational programs that are offered. The common experience of presenter and participants has created a sense of solidarity and community. Some participants have connected in ongoing online forums after formal seminars to share new tips and experiences implementing the material presented. At the regular networking events members have connected with each other to identify new clients and share skills and tactics for excelling in freelance life.

Entities like mediabistro.com and Fractured Atlas also offer opportunities for freelancers to meet, exchange resources, and take courses, but they tend to focus on smaller segments of the workforce than Freelancers Union, and their charges are significantly higher.

Freelancers Union efforts, however, are still at an early and uncomplicated stage and have met with relatively little pressure at the boundaries—around economic, political, or value issues. The problems that lie ahead are the same as those we examined in health insurance: the need to maximize the benefits of member solidarity and commitment while balancing with the needs for effectiveness and economic self-sufficiency.

On the political front, the organization has not yet been involved with state-sponsored programs for job upgrading or retraining. However, Freelancers Union has a vision for how those programs should be restructured to accommodate the industries that are driving today's economy. With more tangible goods being created overseas, there are fewer needs for apprenticeship programs in upholstering and glass blowing and a greater need in fields like technology. In addition, government training programs could focus more on the skills necessary to succeed in the mobile economy, such as bookkeeping, marketing, and accounting. With the independent workforce continuing to grow due to mass layoffs, Freelancers Union will advocate for more government programs that help dislocated workers smoothly transition to this type of work.

On the economic front, charges for these sessions so far have generally covered instructor and administrative expenses, but there has been no effort to make a profit, nor has the organization decided yet whether profit is appropriate for this activity. On the value front, programs have so far addressed only concrete individuals' needs rather than potentially controversial issues of organizing and developing a freelancer agenda. Some or all of these problems lie on the road ahead, as the health care experience has already indicated, and they are likely to require in time a similar differentiation of the organization and the development of specialized member relations focused on the training area.

Aspirations

Freelancers Union aspires to provide comprehensive education and training options for freelancers. Like CSOs in general, it is well positioned for this, as it can act as intermediary between members and traditional educational institutions, government programs, and other CSOs.

A formalized program could create a bundle of courses, ranging from basic to advanced, for which freelancers could receive certification. This program could be tailored, leveraging Freelancers Union's offerings, industry-specific providers, and community colleges as well as government services. Independent workers with such certification would be viewed as more desirable than their competitors and may land more gigs from clients.

In its role as a "hub," the organization could bring together groups of members who share a common need and negotiate with potential providers—from community colleges to commercial training centers—to address them. This would be a far more flexible mechanism than the political one, which involves creating new programs and battling for broad public support. It would enable providers to connect rapidly with new clients and enable freelancers to quickly address emerging needs by connecting existing resources to members in interactive planning.

There is also an opportunity to build on the principles of mutual aid to create an alternative, do-it-yourself, or network-based approach to education and training. Entrepreneurs have long had to rely on themselves to network to obtain the right sets of skills; Freelancers Union hopes to reinforce communal linkages to create an alternate means of skill building by providing platforms to enable independent workers to exchange knowledge and skills with their peers. For instance, a web developer can provide services and/or training to an accountant who needs a website. The accountant in turn could help the web developer file quarterly taxes by either doing it directly or by training the web developer to do so. Freelancers Union has already put in place the technological infrastructure for such a web of exchange. Such initiatives could foster not only skill attainment and learning but also a sense of community that might mitigate the alienation often felt by these "solopreneurs."

Conclusion

In the provision of services such as health insurance or training, civil society organizations offer distinctive advantages, especially in their ability to build trust and dialogue with members of particular groups and thus to understand emerging needs rapidly and accurately. But the persistent weakness of many existing CSOs suggests that these benefits are not sufficient without also solving problems of money, structure, and values. At the same time, each of these challenges threatens to undermine CSOs' distinctive capabilities—leading them to undermine trust through emphasis on financial return, or to subordinate solidarity to political influence, to overemphasize internal discipline at the expense of involvement, or to demand value conformity at the expense of dialogue.

The experience of Freelancers Union in the health care arena indicates the difficulty of learning to balance these imperatives as the membership grows larger and the mission more complex. For training, the organization is still at a simpler stage of drawing heavily on associational enthusiasm, with minimal attention to financing and few connections to government programs or other outside forces.

One thing that is clear from the early efforts of Freelancers Union is that the members do have important training needs that are not being met by traditional providers. This is partly a delivery problem—freelancers are often unable to take traditional courses, especially in universities using semester systems—but more importantly a problem of content: Existing programs rarely address the particular needs of freelancers faced with independently navigating the complexities of business organization, taxation, planning, and so on in a highly fluctuating and uncertain environment.

It is also apparent that freelancers are enthusiastic about a vision that builds on their distinctive identity and needs. The simple act of getting together with others who face similar problems is often a powerful "educational" experience where they can both learn new techniques and strengthen their motivations. The challenge ahead is to develop that essential strength into a model that can be scaled to larger groups and more complex topics and that can become self-sustaining without losing its associational character.

Endnotes

[1] De Tocqueville was not the first to use the concept; Hegel had notably developed it in *Elements of a Philosophy of Right* (1827); Locke and Hobbes had used it earlier, and it is also traceable in Aristotle and other Greek philosophers. But all these saw civil society as a subordinate or incomplete form of organization—either subordinated to the state, or (in Hegel's case) a transitional phase on the way to a full moral state-centered community. De Tocqueville was, we believe, the first to present it as an alternative.

[2] In the world of work, our own research suggests that longevity is low: Of 30 employee association websites we surveyed in 2001, 26 were no longer operating five years later, and the rest had largely lost their associational character (Heckscher and Carré 2006).

[3] We are using the "sociological perspective" as a shorthand; of course there are many sociological views. What we mean is the "classic" tradition centered on Weber, Durkheim, and Parsons, with some aspects of Marx as well. We take from this tradition two core orienting perspectives: Societies are normatively integrated systems, and they develop through stages of increasing complexity. (See Heckscher 2009.)

[4] This was in part a response to a requirement for the establishment of the insurance company, though it had been under discussion for several years before that.

[5] A third of Americans receive health insurance through a government program, such as Medicaid or Medicare (http://wiki.answers.com/Q/How_many_people_receive_medicare_and_medicaid, accessed February 4, 2010). Over half receive health insurance through an employer (http://www.ahrq.gov/research/empspria/empspria.htm, accessed February 4, 2010).

[6] 2006 Employment Arrangements, United States Government Accountability Office. The difference is more apparent when looking at specific areas. In New York City, for instance, 63% of the U.S.-born self-employed have four years of college or more, while only 44% of U.S.-born wage and salary workers do, and 30% have graduate or professional degrees, while just 18% of employees do (2007 Economic Notes, Office of the New York City Comptroller).

References

Adler, Paul S. 2001. "Market, Hierarchy, and Trust: The Knowledge Economy and the Future of Capitalism." *Organization Science,* Vol. 12, no. 2, pp. 214–34.

Anheier, Helmut K., Mary Kaldor, and Marlies Glasius. 2005. *Global Civil Society 2005/6.* Beverly Hills, CA: Sage Publications.

Beloe, S., J. Elkington, K. F. Hester, and S. Newell. 2003. *The 21st Century NGO: In the Market for Change.* London: SustainAbility.

Benson, Herman. 2009. "Hybrid Unionism: Dead End or Fertile Future?" *Dissent,* Winter.

Castells, M. 2000. *The Rise of the Network Society.* Oxford, England: Blackwell Publishing.

Chaddad, F.R., and M.L. Cook. 2004. "The Economics of Organization Structure Changes: A US Perspective on Demutualization." *Annals of Public and Cooperative Economics,* Vol. 75, no. 4, pp. 575–94.

Clark, John. 2008. "The UN and Civil Society: 3 Years After the Cardoso Report." *Journal of Civil Society,* Vol. 4, no. 2, pp. 153–60.

Conference Board. 2010. *U.S. Job Satisfaction at Lowest Level in Two Decades.* Conference Board reports. January 6.

De Tocqueville, A. 1839. *Democracy in America.* New York: G. Adlard.

Durand-Zaleski, Isabelle. 2008. *The French Health Care System.* <http://www.commonwealthfund.org/~/media/Files/Resources/2008/Health%20Care%20System%20Profiles/France_Country_Profile_2008%20pdf.pdf>. [June 24, 2010].

258 TRANSFORMING THE U.S. WORKFORCE DEVELOPMENT SYSTEM

Durkheim, E. 1893/1933. *The Division of Labor in Society*. Trans. G Simpson. Glencoe, IL: Free Press.

Farber, H.S. 2007. "Is the Company Man an Anachronism? Trends in Long-Term Employment in the US, 1973–2006." In Sheldon Danziger and Cecilia Elena Rouse, eds., *The Price of Independence: The Economics of Early Adulthood*. New York: Russell Sage Foundation Publications, pp. 56–83.

Gamson, J. 1995. "Must Identity Movements Self-Destruct? A Queer Dilemma." *Social Problems*, Vol. 42, no. 3, pp. 390–407.

Ghimire, K.B. 2005. *The Contemporary Global Social Movements: Emergent Proposals, Connectivity and Development Implications*. Geneva: United Nations Research Institute for Social Development.

Giddens, A. 1998. *The Third Way: The Renewal of Social Democracy*. Cambridge, UK: Polity Press.

Gittell, M., and B. Hoffacker. 1980. *Limits to Citizen Participation: The Decline of Community Organizations*. Beverly Hills, CA: Sage Publications.

Heckscher, Charles. 2009. "Parsons as an Organization Theorist." In Paul S. Adler, ed., *The Oxford Handbook of Sociology and Organization Studies: Classical Foundations*. Oxford: Oxford University Press, pp. 607–32.

Heckscher, Charles, and Francoise Carré. 2006. "Strength in Networks: Employment Rights Organizations and the Problem of Co-Ordination." *British Journal of Industrial Relations*, Vol. 44, no. 4, pp. 605–28.

Jennings, Simon. 2006. "Innovating to Deliver Humanitarian Relief." October 24. <http://www.zdnet.com/blog/btl/oxfam-innovating-to-deliver-humanitarian-relief/3819>. [June 24, 2010].

Moynihan, D.P. 1969. *Maximum Feasible Misunderstanding: Community Action in the War on Poverty*. New York: Free Press.

New York Times. 2009. "Variations in Government Aid Across the Nation," May 9, sec. US. <http://www.nytimes.com/interactive/2009/05/09/us/0509-safety-net.html>. [May 10, 2009].

Newell, Peter. 2005. "Climate for Change? Civil Society and the Politics of Global Warming." In Helmut K. Anheier, Mary Kaldor, and Marlies Glasius, eds., *Global Civil Society 2005/6*. Beverly Hills, CA: Sage Publications, pp. 2–30.

O'Leonard, Karen. 2009. *The Corporate Learning Factbook 2009*. Oakland, CA: Bersin & Associates.

Osterman, P., and D. Burton. 2005. *Ports and Ladders: The Nature and Relevance of Internal Labor Markets in a Changing World*. Oxford: Oxford University Press.

Parsons, Talcott. 1971. *The System of Modern Societies*. Englewood Cliffs, NJ: Prentice-Hall.

Powell, W. 1990. "Neither Market Nor Hierarchy: Network Forms of Organization." *Research in Organizational Behavior*, Vol. 12, pp. 295–336.

Reisman, D., N. Glazer, and R. Denney. 1950. *The Lonely Crowd*. New Haven, CT: Yale University Press.

Sacks, Danielle. 2007. "Working with the Enemy." *Fast Company*, December. <http://www.fastcompany.com/magazine/118/working-with-the-enemy.html>. [December 9, 2009].

Shellenberger, M., and T. Nordhaus. 2004. *The Death of Environmentalism*. New York: Environmental Grantmakers Association.

Skjelsbaek, K. 1971. "The Growth of International Nongovernmental Organization in the Twentieth Century." *International Organization*, Vol. 25, no. 3, pp. 420–42.

Smith, A.; K. Haakonssen, ed. 1759/2002. *The Theory of Moral Sentiments*. Cambridge, UK: Cambridge University Press.

Tagle, Yovana Reyes, and Sehm Patomäk. 2007. *The Rise and Development of the Global Debt Movement: A North–South Dialogue*. Geneva: United Nations Research Institute for Social Development.

U.S. Government Accountability Office. 2006. *Employment Arrangements: Improved Outreach Could Help Ensure Proper Worker Classification*. <www.gao.gov/new.items/d06656.pdf>. [May 8, 2009].

U.S. Treasury. 2008. *Community Development Financial Institutions Fund—Overview of What We Do*. <http://www.cdfifund.gov/what_we_do/overview.asp>. [May 8, 2009].

Van Gelder, Sarah. 2008. *Sarah van Gelder: Italy's Co-ops Form a Different Sort of Economy*. <http://www.yesmagazine.org/svgblog/2008/09/italys-co-ops-form-different-sort-of.html>. [February 7, 2010].

Wapner, Paul. 1995. "Politics Beyond the State: Environmental Activism and World Civic Politics." *World Politics*, Vol. 47, no. 3 (April), pp. 311–40.

Wikipedia. 2010. "Mutual Insurance." <http://en.wikipedia.org/wiki/Mutual_insurance>. [March 10, 2010].

CHAPTER 11

Women, Welfare, and Workforce Development: An Agenda for the 21st Century

MARY GATTA
Rutgers University

LUISA S. DEPREZ
University of Southern Maine

The onset of the Industrial Revolution and the dominance of the capitalist mode of production brought forth significant features of a labor market that were forever changed from those of preindustrial times. As production moved from the home (the private sphere) to the factory (the public sphere), individuals were required to leave their homes and enter the paid labor market, where capitalists paid them wages in exchange for their labor. For most citizens, the route to economic independence and self-sufficiency was to be achieved solely through waged work. Because wages were tied to work in the paid labor market, one needed to be part of that labor market with a paid job. Success could then be measured by the receipt of wages, made possible in part by accumulated experience, upward job mobility, increased job status, advanced education, and accelerated training. Through this path, individuals and their families were expected to attain economic self-sufficiency and independence.

The goal, then, of many initiatives from the New Deal to the Great Society and beyond has been to make work pay, to enable workers and their families to achieve and sustain economic independence. This also translated into attempts to improve workforce preparedness and encourage low-wage workforce mobility, including moving up career ladders and fostering job retention as well as promoting practices that demonstrated care for workers, preempted worker difficulties, and encouraged access to higher education and to training—in essence, initiatives designed to help individuals achieve and secure jobs that would enable them to provide themselves and/or their families with the security necessary for day-to-day living.

We are mindful, however, that this model of work and workforce preparedness, with, importantly, the expectation of engaging in waged work that could support oneself and one's family is, in fact, gendered— premised on a model that assumes a male breadwinner and a female caregiver. Currently, 50% of the workforce is women (a number projected to grow), and substantial numbers of those workers are integral contributors to the family's self-sufficiency. In the typical married-couple family where both spouses work, the wife contributes just over a third— 35.6%—of the family's income, and 15.6% of working wives have a husband who is not working (Boushey 2009). A recent Pew Research study by Fry and Cohn (2010), however, reveals that 20% of women are currently out-earning their husbands. Additionally, 76% of single mothers are in the labor force; these women, raising their children on their own, are the family's only earner (U.S. Department of Labor 2008).

In the current economic recession, women have been reported to be disproportionately less affected than men, a conclusion often reached by comparing unemployment rates: currently 10.5% for men and 8.1% for women. Indeed, the unemployment rate for men has increased more steeply since 2001 than has the rate for women (Hartmann 2009). Hence, as women's labor force participation and economic contribution to the household income have increased, families rely on women's incomes to survive. As men experience greater job losses in the current recession, women can then be the only earners in their families. While comparing these rates is important and draws attention to the changing nature of breadwinner roles in families, we are also mindful that women's increased participation in the labor market and reduced rates of unemployment do not necessarily indicate greater equity for women in occupational groups in the various employment sectors.

In light of this, however, serious reconsideration needs to be given to the relevancy of these historically entrenched conventional and essentially normative work models if we are to focus on central questions facing the United States today: What jobs will Americans hold in the global economy of the 21st century, and how will they develop the skills needed to be competitive in these positions? These questions, the focus of this book, are essential ones, yet they cannot, as now framed, form the basis of a response to the myriad of complexities within American society— especially, we will argue, the complex intersection of gender, race, and class.

This chapter provides a conceptual framework through which to rethink workforce policy in ways that take the diverse lived experiences of women into account. One particular group that we will highlight is single mother–headed households, which have been, and continue to be, significantly disadvantaged by workforce policies and their corresponding conventions as well as by welfare policy, a significant institution providing minimal support for many women raising families on their own. This focus is important to consider here because at present, especially among African American families, households headed by single mothers have the highest probability of living in poverty. And while these women often work, they are too often unable to achieve or even come close to achieving economic independence. This paradoxical "disconnectedness" can, however, guide us toward a fuller understanding of the reality that "the importance of employment in the context of poverty stems from the fact that poor people rely mainly on the use of their labour power . . . to earn their livelihood. How much labour power they are able to use . . . is an important determinant of their income" (Osmani 2008:2).

Central here are the distinctive challenges faced by advantaged and disadvantaged workers in workforce preparation. This concern is evident in Harry Holzer's recent analysis (2008), in which he concludes that "in a labor market which places a greater premium on skill development than ever before, we now spend dramatically fewer resources on the training of disadvantaged workers than we did in the 1970's" (p. 27). This, he says, is the "basic paradox of workforce policy: that in an era in which skills are more important than ever as determinants of labor market earnings, we spend fewer and fewer public (federal) dollars on workforce development over time" (p. 1).

The analytic perspective we employ here acknowledges the importance of the gender–race–class intersection to more fully explore the complexity of both workforce and welfare policy—two avenues through which poor women can obtain support for themselves and their families—and details and assesses the ability of each to provide job access, mobility, training, and education to low-income women and single mothers in a holistic way. We argue that public workforce development systems, working in concert with public social welfare, care, and education and training systems and focused on economically disadvantaged groups, will strengthen not only individuals but society as a whole.

We begin by reviewing universally accepted indicators of economic independence and self-sufficiency in the United States to lay the foundation of how they are understood and valued in this country. We then explore these indicators a bit more deeply from an intersectional perspective, taking into account the long-standing notion of marriage— rather than work outside the home—as convention for women, and consider how this perspective has impacted women's abilities to achieve economic self-sufficiency. Central to this is a clear understanding of the ways that the convention of marriage has infiltrated not only how we think about women's lives in the private sphere, but also how it significantly shapes women's opportunities for economic self-sufficiency through waged work in the public sphere.

Economic Independence: Normative Constructions, Gender Perspectives

Employment—waged work—is the main source of income for most individuals and families. In the United States, 66% of eligible individuals are in the labor market—about 144 million people (Borbely 2009); 85% of wage and salary workers are members of a family and have day-to-day family responsibilities (Padavic and Reskin 2002).[1] Individuals work not just because it is vital to individual and family support but also because it is essential to the integrity and well-being of human beings: It affirms one's sense of self-respect and fulfillment (Sen 1999) and promotes human development (Osmani 2008). The common assumption in the United States is that earning an income through waged labor—in other words, working for pay—enables people to provide for themselves and their families. Hence, wages from work provide security—most importantly, the ability to provide and sustain the provision of that security: food, shelter, clothing, and other fundamental necessities of daily living.

While work is fundamental to achieving economic independence, among the keys to this achievement is ensuring one's employment sustainability. Significant here are level of education achievement, degree of specialized training, the ability to be mobile—to go where and when the work is without restrictions—the capacity to accumulate experience so as to take advantage of upward job mobility opportunities, and the quality of job matches, including the sector or status of the position.

While all these factors are essential for upward mobility and earnings increases, it is a "fundamental fact in labor economics . . . that, on average, wages tend to rise rapidly early in a worker's career" (Blank, Danziger, and Schoeni 2006:141). Hence, it is those prevailing components in an individual's early career stages—education, training, mobility, lack of restrictions—that will determine career wage growth. Of considerable importance, however, is a worker's ability to accumulate work experience (Blank, Danziger, and Schoeni 2006). In the instance of less-skilled or (often) involuntarily mobile workers, this connection between early career wages and later career wages presents a considerable challenge, especially since "much depends on the correspondence between the structure of opportunities that are opened up and the structure of capabilities possessed" by them (Osmani 2008:2). This is a particular challenge for lower-skilled, often poor, frequently female workers.

The converse of this understanding of the essentiality of wage work is also commonly assumed: that people who are unable to provide for themselves and/or their family must be not employed, not working hard enough, or just plain lazy. A 2004 U.S. Census Bureau report, however, revealed that for the greatest percentage of people who are not working, it is because of lack of jobs, child care responsibilities, and chronic health problems (Dalirazar 2007). The assumption regarding nonproviders, however, albeit an old one, has been a part of conventional "understanding" for centuries, and it is itself quite gendered. Women have borne and continue to bear the brunt of the caring labor, preventing them from reaching what Joan Williams (2001) refers to as the "ideal worker status"—one who takes no time off for childbearing, childrearing, or any caring labor and who works full-time and is available for overtime.

So how does economic independence—particularly its construction and attainment—get altered when gender comes into play? If we look forward from the 1970s, it is evident that women's participation in the workforce has dramatically changed, as have other indicators important in achieving economic independence: Educational gaps between men and women have been closed, women's college-graduation rates have surpassed men's, and women have entered formerly male-dominated professions at rates more quickly than before—though women still move into only about 20 of the available 426 Department of Labor established job categories, remaining overly concentrated in traditionally female work (see http://www.dol.gov/wb/factsheets/20lead2008.htm). Indeed, in order for the U.S. labor market to not be segregated by sex, 52.1% of the female labor force (the equivalent of about 39 million women) would have to change jobs (Padavic and Reskin 2002). "With respect to advancing in the workplace, women have been doing everything right for close to four decades now: getting educated, working more and more continuously, and moving out of dead-end, low-paying 'pink-collar' jobs. That's the good news. The bad news is that despite women's best and sustained efforts, progress toward gender equality is uneven and appears to be stalling" (Stone 2009:3).

Clearly, cultural, political, and ideological stances and traditions have significantly impacted the image of women in the workplace as well as their ability to ensure that their work—waged work—sustained them and their families. Under the well-entrenched shadow of the male breadwinner–female caregiver model, women have moved into a labor market not well-suited to them. Recently changed expectations in the workplace, for example, that stress the "combination of rising hours (the

US now has the world's longest work week), 24-7 accountability, insufficient and inadequate part-time and flex-time options . . . [and] lack of affordable child care" (Stone 2009:5) among others, have created what Pamela Stone calls the "motherhood bar." These changed expectations in work conventions have further challenged women in their quest for a secure economic position that entitles them and their families to economic independence and self-sufficiency. The challenge is particularly onerous for women with relatively low skills, as the jobs they are able to secure do not help them attain self-sufficiency, nor do they provide opportunities for growth. And during recessions, these jobs are the most likely to eliminated.

The differences among women are also important to take note of here, as most of the acceleration attributed to women has been among middle-class, college-educated, predominantly white women (Stone 2009). Low-skilled women continue to be among the most fragile and vulnerable. And despite the acclaim given to the movement of women off welfare and into jobs under welfare reform, the greatest percentage of those jobs are unstable, lack benefits, pay poorly, and afford few opportunities for advancement, if any. Central to this is that the opportunities for low-skilled workers to reach economic security are strongly correlated to the ability to stay in a job for a long period to develop the experience that affords greater opportunity for upward advancement and increased earnings. French, Mazumber, and Taber (2008) analyzed changing patterns of early career growth for low-skilled workers over the past 20 years and found experience accumulation to be the key to someone's moving out of poverty. Holzer and LaLonde (2000) also note that "difficulties in holding jobs and in moving to better ones retard wage growth for low-skill workers" (referenced by Blank, Danziger, and Schoeni 2006:142). French, Mazumber, and Taber (2008:188) then conclude that "experience is much more important than job matching."

This path toward higher wages, however, is very gendered. Women are known to be in and out of the labor market with greater regularity, due mostly to caring labor, and hence are not as able to develop significant job experience that might lead to increased wages. A 2004 U.S. Census Bureau Report titled *Reasons People Do Not Work: 2004* reports that "for non-workers 25–44 years of age, taking care of children or others was the main reason for not working at a paid job (44 percent), reflecting the importance of this reason among women, who make up nearly three-fourths (71 percent) of the non-workers in this age group" (Dalirazar 2007).

While it is undeniable that "despite the general trend of increasing equality between men and women . . . many economic, political, and cultural inequities remain," it is "women's economic dependence/ independence [that] is central in shaping gender inequality in society" (Huber et al. 2009:2). Importantly, however, women's earnings and abilities to earn are "profoundly shaped by welfare state and labor market configurations" (Huber et al. 2009:3).

But before we turn to a more detailed look at these systems, it is necessary to address and acknowledge the construction of marriage as the conventional route for women. Marriage has long been considered the proper route to economic security, and of late it is regaining popularity among some groups. Padavic and Reskin (2002) note quite clearly that "because social norms and job discrimination curtailed [women's] participation in the labor force, women's path to economic security and respectability was through a husband and domestic work, whereas unpaid home work denied women the esteem that society grants those who are economically productive" (p. 28). Indeed, much research has demonstrated that marriage and motherhood impact women's abilities to accrue human capital necessary to support them. Experiencing what is referred to as the marriage and motherhood penalty, women see their wages, opportunities for advancement and training, and status in the workplace decrease when they become wives and mothers. Such thinking continues to support the notion that it is marriage, not work, from which women attain economic success.

Yet this ideal of male breadwinner–female caretaker is often just that—an ideal. According to the National Women's Law Center (2008), 71% of American women with children under age 18 are in the labor force: 77% of women with children ages 6 to 17, 64% with children under age 6, and 56% with infants under age 1. Of married women with children under age 18, 68% are also in the labor force: 60% of those with children ages 6 to 17 and 75% of those with children under age 6. A majority of married mothers with infants—55% in 2006—are also in the labor force. These women are in the labor force out of economic necessity, and their incomes significantly contribute to their families' economic security.

In addition, the convention of marriage for economic security has been outside the experience or norm of many nonwhite and poor women. These women have always worked in both the paid and unpaid labor markets. For instance, in 1920 only 7% of European American married women worked in the labor market, while 33% of married African American women were employed (Padavic and Reskin 2002). African American women also sought ways to earn money at home throughout the 20th century, doing piecework or laundry, sewing, or taking in boarders. Even when they were married, some women had to work because their male partners, often confronted by race and class discrimination, were frequently unable to support their families without women's support. For these women, marriage did not automatically equate to the path toward economic security.

Not only did the convention of marriage fall short of its gendered ideals for some women, there were also women who had to support themselves. Women raising families on their own, especially at the lower income levels, face even greater challenges in reaching economic security. As the National Women's Law Center (2008) reports, "single mothers must earn a living in order to feed, clothe, house and otherwise sustain themselves and the children who are in their care. The average amount of child support, for custodial parents who receive it, is $4,700 annually, a boost to family income. But 39% of custodial mothers do not have a child support award, and 23% of custodial mothers owed child support receive nothing" (p. 2). As a result, many women—poor, and single heads of household—are pushed into the welfare system in order to support themselves and their families, while the workforce system remains typically on the periphery. As we indicated earlier, it is the integration of these two systems—welfare and work—that is essential to the well-being of women working in the United States, especially women with fewer advantages and skills and women heading households.

Over the past decade, considerable scholarly discourse has focused on the impact of welfare reform via the passage of the Personal Responsibility Work Opportunity and Reconciliation Act (PRWORA) on single mothers' chances of escaping poverty even though reducing poverty was not a goal of the act. And while this emphasis is important and appropriate, much less attention has been paid to the Workforce Investment Act (WIA), the federal employment and training legislation that provides the framework for the current public workforce training system and whose mandate is the co-location of services.

While both systems focus on labor force attachment, the "work first" approach of welfare reform differs significantly from the skills development orientation of workforce delivery systems, and so countless welfare recipients remain stuck in low-wage work, without access to the resources necessary to secure education and skills training needed to advance into higher-paid jobs. Further, investigations into systems around the country find countless examples of practices that severely limit women's ability to work.

Welfare and Workforce Development Policies in the United States

Welfare legislation in the United States has historically ensured the dependency of poor women, not only because it assumed them to be dependent, but because it needed them to be dependent to care for young children and remain out of contention for jobs in the competitive labor market. When the modern welfare state began, with the enactment of the Social Security Act of 1935, the section of the act that created Aid to Dependent Families (ADC) did so "for the purpose of encouraging the care of dependent children in their own homes or in the homes of relatives . . . to help maintain and strengthen family life and to help such parents (usually mothers) or relatives to attain or retain capability for the maximum self-support and personal independence" (42 U.S.C.{601}). ADC was widely understood to be an extension of the "mothers' pensions" or "widows' pensions" of the early 1900s, which had provided financial assistance to women so that they would not need to enter the paid labor market but could stay at home and care for their children (Deprez 2002; Gatta 2005; Grogger and Karoly 2005). There was little discussion of promoting work for women or of decreasing women's dependency on the state; the program was designed to raise the living standards of families who had become poor through no fault of their own (namely, the death of a husband). Distinguishing among women—the "deserving" from the "undeserving"—became a critical part of this, and subsequent, policy discussions. Widowed women were considered to be deserving; they had not "chosen" to bear children outside of marriage, nor were they divorced or deserted, while women bearing children outside of marriage faced the stigma of being labeled undeserving.

Amendments in 1939 to the Social Security Act changed the status of women who had been married to men covered by Old Age and Survivors Insurance (now Supplemental Security Income, or SSI). They and their children would now receive coverage in a nationalized program with standardized benefits, albeit at a reduced rate. At the same time, ADC—which was now comprised mostly of divorced, separated, unmarried poor and nonwhite women—was altered to require documentation of extreme poverty as a condition of eligibility and required means testing of beneficiaries. The provision of benefits to the child only rendered mothers invisible. As a result, the program became increasingly stigmatized and its beneficiaries referred to as welfare recipients. The vestiges of motherhood as service had been removed along with the support for it.

For most of the next 30 years, recipients—98% of whom were women, and disproportionately black—were forced to comply with local and regional conventions and norms as well as with workforce requirements. States enacted "suitable home" rules and "man in the house" rules and denied assistance to "employable mothers" (women with children who were no longer infants), and because each state could set its benefits level, inequities both within and between states were accentuated. And as the population of what became known as "welfare recipients" grew and the ethnic and racial composition and marital status of recipients changed, welfare policy grew more stringent, restrictive, and prescriptive.

This two-tiered system of family support was institutionalized by the middle of the 20th century, and key ideological beliefs became codified in policy. The initial aim of keeping women in their homes to care for their children gave way to requirements forcing poor women to work outside the home, handing over to others the care of their children. At the same time, white middle-class women were encouraged to remain at home and not engage in paid labor because doing so could presumably lead to the destruction of their families and communities.

By the 1980s the "new morality" focus of neoconservatives sought a return to "traditional" families that supported women's participation in marriage, childbearing, and at-home work but not their movement into the labor market—unless they were poor and in need of financial support from the state. By the late 1990s, the funneling of poor women into work became law. In 1996, President Clinton signed the Personal Responsibility and Work Opportunities Reconciliation Act (PRWORA), which "codified the view that welfare policy should reward and punish the intimate decisions and behaviors of poor single mothers" (Mink and Solinger 2003:536). This newly designed "work-first" model of welfare removed any notion that welfare was a social entitlement and severely restricted access to education and skills training. PRWORA's assistance program, Temporary Aid to Needy Families (TANF), set a two-year limit to find paid work and a five-year lifetime limit on the receipt of federally funded cash benefits by individuals: TANF was based on the idea that paid work was better than welfare, education, or motherhood for this group of women. Its requirements forced welfare recipients into low-wage work and kept women streaming into traditionally female low-paying service jobs without the opportunity to improve their lives.

The 1996 welfare reform promised to do three things: *reduce the rate of dependency* on welfare by *moving recipients into work* and, as a result, *establishing their self-sufficiency*. What it actually did was to flood the low-wage labor market with poor women, many of whom were women of color. The forced time limits and the "work or lose your benefits" ideology provided women little choice but to accept low-wage work. Frances Fox Piven and Richard Cloward (1993) argued that welfare is a labor market institution that systematically alters the wage terms of the lowest levels of the labor market, creating the floor of wages: As women "roll off" welfare and welfare itself becomes more stigmatized, poor women will move from "welfare recipients" to "working poor," joining the ranks of the millions of women already in that category who are not surviving economically.

PRWORA's promise of increased self-sufficiency remains significantly underdocumented in welfare research. There is no clear consensus on how women are really faring (Edin and Lein 1997; O'Connor 2001; Schram and Soss 2001; Hayes 2003; Gatta 2005; Blank 2006; Gatta and Deprez 2008; Pomeroy 2008). "We do not yet understand the short- and long-term consequences for women and children who have exhausted their TANF eligibility or been sanctioned. We know little about the circumstances of families who have been denied TANF benefits through state diversion programs. . . . We do not know whether work—even at low pay—translates into positive outcomes in the longer term. . . . We do not know whether TANF will ultimately attenuate the intergenerational transmission of poverty and welfare dependence. . . . We do not know" (Licter and Jayakody 2002:133).

At least one million single mothers—and two million children— are, in an average month, "both jobless and without income assistance from TANF, other cash aid programs, or other household members" (Parrott and Sherman 2007:381). "All evidence continues to show that a substantial minority of single mothers are not on welfare and not reporting employment" (Blank 2006:72), raising questions of concern about how they are managing to survive and how they and their families are faring.

A common theme in much of the critical analysis of welfare reform is that while it is true that women are working postwelfare, they remain stuck in low-wage work, and their earnings are not enough to raise them out of poverty. The 2003 Institute for Women's Policy Research report, *Before and After Welfare Reform: The Work and Well-Being of Low-Income Single Parents*, examined the employment characteristics, income sources, poverty status, and demographic characteristics of low-income single-parent families before and after the implementation of the 1996 welfare reform. It revealed that while more low-income single mothers were working, their earnings were low, and most single parents— particularly single mothers—remained concentrated in low-wage occupations. So while single mothers' income postwelfare is significantly more likely to come from employment, overall they and their children have seen little improvement in their economic well-being. Jane Henrici's ethnographic compilation of a three-city study—Chicago, Boston, and San Antonio—found quite simply that "welfare reform has not changed life for low income families" (Henrici 2006:194). Instead, families continued to face a series of destabilizing problems, whether they are on welfare or employed in the low-wage work that they moved into.

Women now comprise a large and growing portion of the working poor—individuals who work in the paid labor force, yet do not earn enough money to economically survive. Recent poverty rates reveal that among working men, 4.4% are poor, while among working women, 5.5% are poor. Importantly though, not all women share an equal probability of being among the ranks of the working poor: The poverty rate of working African American women is 12.0% and working Hispanic women 9.8%, compared to 4.8% for working white women (U.S. Department of Labor 2008). Moreover, when we look at family composition, families maintained by women with children under 18 years old have the highest probability of living in poverty—a rate of 21.9%, more than double that of families maintained by men with children under 18 (10.1%) and four times greater than the rate of married couple families with children (4.9%; U.S. Department of Labor 2000).

What can we conclude about welfare reform? Welfare as we used to know it does not exist. In its place is a haphazard array of programs that provide occasional but minimal support to low-wage, mostly female workers raising families, leaving countless numbers behind. Attacks on the welfare state, and specifically on single mothers, launched from a platform grounded in the individualist perspective have reinforced notions of individually engineered social problems, limited and conditional government intervention, and work-based entitlements. Many welfare reform advocates embraced the debatable premise that women who receive public assistance to support their families can become independent through work: Presumptions prevailed that work requirements were fair and constructive for welfare recipients and that the exchange—of welfare assistance for work—would both reduce welfare rolls and enhance individual self-sufficiency. Little, however, in the debates addressed the complexity and difficulty of upholding the dual roles of breadwinner and caregiver/nurturer that single women raising families are forced to do; offering marriage as the preferable option is not an acceptable resolution.

While the overall welfare policy discourse treats women as an undifferentiated category, the reality is that this is not the case. Alejandra Marchevsky and Jeanne Theoharis (2008) share a powerful ethnographic case study of Mexican immigrant women in Los Angeles County. Central to their analysis is how race, gender, and nationality intersect to impact the treatment and experiences of women in the welfare system. In contrast to welfare evaluations that demonstrate the success of moving women off welfare, theirs demonstrates not only that moving women off welfare does not equate with success, but also that it also ignores discrimination and structural inequality within the system. Older women in rural Appalachia were also deeply affected by welfare reform, especially by the mandates that required work and restricted benefits to five years, according to Debra Henderson and Ann Tickamyer (2008). Age, as well as location, did not allow older women to weather these changes well: The multiplicity of problems that these women faced, intensified not only by age but by isolated living conditions, exacerbated their numerous encounters with periods of extreme hardship. Their classification as "able-bodied" and "capable of working," for example, put them face to face with ageism in the marketplace and was especially acute in the rural area where they resided because of the severe lack of employment opportunities. Circumstances that added to their difficulties included the fact that over 50% of the women were providing in-home care for an uninsured, nonrecipient spouse with health problems, 43% had less than a high school education, and 68% were unemployed.

Using employment as the only success marker of welfare reform cannot fully capture how former welfare recipients are really faring, and in reality it is a problematic indicator of success. This sentiment is shared by Diana Pearce, who writes that "measuring success in welfare reform has been narrowly framed as simply mothers entering the work-force" (2000:135). It is a singular focus on entrance into the workforce, regardless of situation, condition, or availability of jobs. While employment is the means to an end that most women with children—and families with children—seek, for it to actually translate into economic security requires more than simply obtaining a job. Most importantly, it requires access to jobs that pay enough for women to support their families and access to services, including child care and health care, that will enable them to work (Pearce 2000). This was recently quite power-fully acknowledged by Katherine Newman: "We seem to feel that as long as we've taken people off public assistance, our job is done. But it isn't done—it isn't good enough in a country as wealthy as this to replace welfare-dependent poverty with working poverty"(Press 2007:22). Quite simply, the employment focus of welfare reform, with-out more holistic supports to sustain women and their families, basically ensures that women will neither have long-term success in the labor market nor raise themselves and their children out of poverty.

Alongside welfare policies are lesser known, but significantly impor-tant, workforce development policies. While these policies are not new—many date back to the Great Depression—their iterations in the late 1990s were profoundly impacted by the ideological underpinnings of welfare reform. Indeed, with the passage of the Workforce Invest-ment Act (WIA) in 1998, national policy on employment and training found itself inextricability tied to welfare policy. Central to this was a profound ideological policy change during the 20th century that shifted public workforce programs from job creation to job training to the eventual job placement in WIA. In the WIA, workforce policy, like welfare reform, became a work-first system where the unemployed and the underemployed are placed in private sector jobs.

Yet this was not always the case. During the 1930s, President Roosevelt created a series of employment and training programs as part of the New Deal. Through programs including the Works Progress Administration, the Civilian Conservation Corps, the National Youth Authority, and the Civil Works Administration, hundreds of thousands of unemployed workers received targeted training to qualify for subsidized employment in the public sector. And while there was much that was good about the progressive nature of these New Deal programs, clear and obvious racial and gender biases and discrimination prevailed. As Nancy Rose (1993) notes, these programs were designed for white males, leaving women and people of color excluded and marginalized. Women's participation in New Deal workforce programs, for example, was restricted to a maximum of one sixth of the program openings. In addition, only "heads of households" could be eligible for New Deal programs, and if a male was present in the home, he received services. "Works Progress Administration (WPA) reports justified these restrictions, citing 'a desire to put some brake upon women's eagerness to be the family breadwinner, wage recipient, and controller of the family pocketbook' and 'a desire to protect the WPA program against possible public criticism from employing too many women'" (Rose 1993:324).

Not only was discrimination written into New Deal workforce programs, labor market discrimination and segregation also made placement in training programs nearly impossible for women (a trend that unfortunately continues today). If a woman was provided access to training programs, she often experienced problems in obtaining a placement, as she was only considered for appropriate "women's work." Further, low pay rates for women and people of color were reinforced in the New Deal. As Rose writes, "Reflecting women's inferior labor market status and lower wage rates in the rest of the economy, lower wage scales were set for women. This female/male wage differential was institutionalized not only in the work programs but also in the National Industrial Recovery Administration (NIRA), the cornerstone of industrial policy during the first years of the New Deal" (Rose 1993:325).

As the country entered World War II, the focus on the public workforce system diminished, but it quickly reemerged after the war by way of one of the country's most significant training programs—the GI Bill of 1944. This legislation provided returning veterans with tuition assistance and supportive services to attend college. As noted by Shaw, Mazzeo, Rab, and Jacobs (2006), "this was perhaps the federal government's biggest intervention into education ever, and it opened doors to college for millions of men who otherwise would never have been able to afford it" (p. 22). What motivated such a generous education program at the federal level was the assurance that returning service*men* would remain out of the labor market: There were just not enough jobs to support them. The GI Bill, credited with keeping millions of *men* out of poverty and unemployment lines, also cemented a gendered human capital approach to poverty—strengthening the traditional male breadwinner–female caretaker family model.

The focus on education and training continued into the late 1960s, when the federal government passed the Manpower Demonstration Training Act, the goal of which was to reduce unemployment by providing short-term training. "Manpower" emerged out of the War on Poverty, and like several programs included in this "war," it was designed to provide education and training to the poor. Yet even as this piece of legislation was advanced, significant changes were occurring in our nation's welfare policy, in particular an increased attention to "work-first" strategies.

By the 1980s, "Manpower" and its successor, the Comprehensive Employment and Training Act (CETA), were criticized by both Republicans and conservative Democrats for a job creation focus. The lack of viable political support for public job creation led to the passing in 1982 of the Job Training Partnership Act (JTPA), signaling "a new approach to employment policy: Eschewing public jobs, JTPA sought to enhance skills building through a greater focus on improved training outcomes and stronger involvement of the private sector to meet the needs of local employers" (Shaw, Mazzeo, Rab, and Jacobs 2006:25).

Yet as ideological winds moved throughout the 1990s to a work-first approach, JTPA was eventually replaced with the Workforce Investment Act (WIA), representing a significant convergence of welfare and workforce policy. In 1998, WIA, with the institutionalization of One-Stop Career Centers, organized delivery of the workforce development system into state and local Workforce Investment Boards (WIBs) that would coordinate and oversee education and job training. WIA includes five titles[2] that prescribe individual programs or goals. Title I, the Workforce Investment System, has the goal

> to provide workforce investment activities that increase the employment, retention, and earnings of participants, and increase occupational skill attainment by participants, which will improve the quality of the workforce, reduce welfare

dependency, and enhance productivity and competitiveness of the Nation's economy. The goals are achieved through the workforce investment system (Chicago Jobs Council 2003:4).[3]

To achieve the five goals, One-Stop Career Centers were established in local neighborhoods where individuals could access core services and be directly referred to job training, education, and/or other services. Significant in WIA is that unlike its predecessor, the JTPA, all individuals 18 years and older have access to services. JTPA participation was limited to individuals who met a stringent eligibility requirement—at least 65% of clients had to be "hard to serve"[4]—which made it difficult to provide resources for upgrading low-wage workers' skills, as most resources had to be directed to placing unemployed individuals in jobs. In contrast, WIA was predicated on the concept of universal access, so that all adults can use the services without regard to income eligibility or employment status. And, unlike JTPA, WIA employed a work-first philosophy, putting limited emphasis on job training and education and focusing instead on job placement.

To accomplish its intent, WIA employs a three-tiered system of core, intensive, and training services. Core services, the most basic, include informational resources, self-services, job search, and job research assistance; these are available to all workers regardless of income, job, or educational level. The next level, intensive services, includes short-term assistance to provide individuals with job opportunities given their existing skills and is reserved for unemployed or underemployed people: The One-Stop Career Center operators are authorized to determine if clients need more services to obtain or retain employment that would lead to self-sufficiency. The highest level, training services, includes on-the-job training and classroom skills development that lead to a credential and/or occupation-specific skills. To access training, participants are given an Individualized Training Account (ITA) that serves as a voucher they can use to "purchase" training from an eligible provider. As with intensive services, eligibility for training services is determined by career center operators. Advancement through the tiers requires demonstrating that one's employment objectives cannot be met at the lower tier. This provides a venue, at least in theory, for the public workforce system to meet a diverse set of workers' needs.

In 2000, approximately 50,000 adults received training under WIA, compared with 150,000 annually in the final years of JTPA[5] (Chicago Jobs Council 2003), trends that continued over subsequent years. Single parents in particular have experienced a decline of training services under WIA. In 1998, for example, the last program year of JTPA, 43.7% of those exiting adult training were single parents. But by 2000, the first full year of WIA data, that proportion had fallen to 34.5% and continued to decline each year thereafter, falling to 24.6% in 2003 (Frank and Minoff 2005).

This decline in the numbers of individuals who receive training is directly related to the three-tiered levels of service. Indeed, WIA appears to be much more of an employment policy (particularly for private sector jobs) than a training policy, as individuals must pass through core and intensive services before they can access new training on occupation-specific skills. The tiered services have the effect of creating a barrier to skills training for many single, poor working mothers, who were only able to secure entry-level low-wage work. Further, within the sequential series of services, eligibility in training programs is often subjective, despite the evidence that education and job training have demonstrated success in increasing the wages of women workers and in securing their job stability. In addition, a prescribed menu of options does not often fit individuals' preferences, as it is the mandate to meet performance measures that determines the services they will receive.

These performance-driven practices often focus on targeted occupations needed for a state's economic benefit without consideration of the client's educational and career goals. The focus on short-term job training quite simply discourages long-term educational and advanced training investments. The focus on short-term job needs not only limits women's occupational and educational choices but also hinders their long-term prospects to attain economic self-sufficiency. Even when WIA does provide access to higher education, it is limited to community college courses, and the training is typically short-term, non-degree-bearing, and highly job-specific, despite the clear evidence that there are higher long-term economic returns for degree- and credential-granting programs. A recent New Jersey study looking at the impact of online training for single, poor working mothers found that of the 92% who completed the program, 15% continued on to college; a year out, women experienced an annual wage increase of over 14% (Gatta 2005).

It is also hard to know exactly who is being served by WIA; many Workforce Investment Boards do not collect data on the individuals they serve. Findings from the Wider Opportunities for Women/National Association of Workforce Investment Boards report (2003), for example, found that 35% of WIBs do not analyze demographic data—race, sex, ethnicity, age—of program participants. In addition, 58% said they did not know if women were placed in nontraditional occupations (occupations that are less than 25% female) or whether their agency even had those data available to analyze. Not surprisingly then, only 2.9% of women adult exiters were employed in nontraditional jobs after WIA

(Women Work! 2008). This is particularly problematic because nontraditional occupations often offer women opportunities for high wages, health benefits, and pensions not typically available in traditionally female fields.

Also problematic is the lack of attention to gender in these implementing policies. This has been particularly evident when looking at the sector of "displaced homemakers," a group of women for whom such services might be essential. While census data estimates that over 7.3 million women are displaced homemakers (through divorce, separation, or widowhood), two thirds of workforce boards report serving fewer than 25% of women who annually fit this category. In 2003, only 1.5% of the dislocated workers who were provided intensive or training services were displaced homemakers. Seventy-three percent of WIBs did not even collect data on how displaced homemakers are served and did not disaggregate this information from how dislocated workers in general are served. The disparity between the numbers of displaced homemakers in the United States and the number of those displaced homemakers served by WIA is clearly evident, and it is these inequities in services that often contribute to the earnings disparity for women exiting WIA relative to comparable men, with women earning about $1,000 less per quarter (Women Work! 2008).

These inextricable links to the gender wage gap and to occupation sex segregation require that attention be given to the lack of consideration to gender, race, and class issues both in policy formulation and in development and implementation.

Ensuring Economic Independence and Sustainability for Women

Throughout this paper we have shown that the U.S. welfare and workforce policy framework is predicated on a firmly entrenched gendered breadwinner–caretaker model. This model has skewed women's participation in the labor market and women's images in the workforce. Hence, women's economic independence has not occurred, and large groups of women, particularly those raising children on their own, and especially those in low-wage work, remain working and in poverty, with no assurance of self-sufficiency. Their situation has been exacerbated by the ways that welfare and workforce systems have not only not met these women's needs, but also have not converged—as they might—to form a seamless pathway from poverty to welfare to meaningful work that provides economic self-sufficiency. Policy remedies, premised on the notion that "one size fits all," have failed to work for anyone.

In addition, the increased attention to the gendered implications of the current recession sheds additional light on women's economic role.

As women's earnings become more of a significant, and sometimes the sole, support of their families, the traditional, gendered model of the family no longer applies. Indeed, if women lose their jobs or lack access to meaningful work that can support them and their families, their families do suffer. Even more important is recent research demonstrating that despite the increase among women as primary and equal economic providers for the family, women continue to bear the burden of the unpaid domestic work to support that family. Hartmann (2009) notes that "men's time spent on housework or family care does not increase when they become unemployed" (p. 46).

Knowing this, what elements need to be incorporated into a 21st-century workforce policy to provide real pathways to economic self-sufficiency for women and other marginalized groups? We believe that the breadwinner–caretaker model clearly does not represent the lived experiences of women or models of work that exist today (or may ever have existed for many groups). We need, then, to develop policy that reflects the reality of work and honors the work–family responsibilities that workers must deal with. As Huber et al. (2009) note, "If the goal is to gain a broad and policy-relevant picture of the determinants of women's capacity to maintain autonomous households above the poverty line and to make significant contributions to family income, the way in which welfare state, labor market and care policies shape employment opportunities and the availability of transfers for women become highly relevant" (p. 32). Indeed, the goal needs to be an "earned income independence for the family unit" (Kahne 2004:58). Workforce development policy is a pivotal route through which this can occur. For it to happen, however, workforce policy must experience a convergence of welfare, labor market, and care policy. Transcending these components is a dedicated focus on education and training, as it is through this route that worker productivity can be raised and movement to high-wage, high-skill jobs can be achieved (Kahne 2004).

People need the assurance of a meaningful job that pays a living wage with benefits. In the modern industrial world, exclusion from the marketplace carries an increasingly heavy price. In order to provide greater access to all those who want to work, institutional interventions must be undertaken that seek to alter both the structure and the number of jobs. This requires serious and deliberate collaboration between public and private sectors.

In addition, the importance of care work—raising children, taking care of sick and elderly family members—must be established as a legitimate job valued and rewarded in the same way as jobs in the conventional labor market.[6] Care work is as much a societal function as it is a familial one, and it needs to be addressed and integrated into our workforce policies and our workplaces.

A system of social protection—a new social contract—must be created that will serve and protect those who are working and not achieving economic independence. William Greider (2009) suggests putting forward a "platform of essential needs, which will give everyone more security and confidence." Food, shelter, clothing, health care, and a viable education must be entitlements of all American citizens regardless of personal income levels, circumstances, or individual choices.

> Such reforms, however, can only occur within a changed framework, one that would necessarily recognize class, gender, and race as legitimate "units of analysis"—not simply as demographic variables that can be isolated and controlled for, but as dimensions of social and economic stratification in their own right (O'Connor 2001:293).

Perhaps most significant is that the lived experiences of women, across race and class categories, will be the central driver of an integrated workforce policy coupled with welfare, care, and educational systems. In this way, policy will not be developed and implemented so that women simply fit into it, but instead it will be crafted around the complexity of the lives of women, the differences among women, and the differences in the social systems of which they are a part.

Endnotes

[1] The current economic crisis has seen a significant reduction in the number of employed persons in the United States. For example, in 2007 2.2 million more individuals were in the labor market than in 2008 (Borbely 2009).

[2] Title I, Workforce Investment Systems; Title II, Adult Education and Family Literacy; Title III, Workforce Investment Related Activities; Title IV, Vocational Rehabilitation; Title V, General Provisions.

[3] The law is available at http://www.doleta.gov.

[4] "Hard-to-serve" refers to individuals who possess at least one barrier to employment, such as physical, mental health, or substance abuse problems; domestic violence; language barrier; and/or lack of education, work experience, or skills.

[5] Many reasons account for this, including a work-first approach to WIA implementation, restrictive eligibility requirements for use of ITAs, and too little funding appropriated to infrastructure support.

[6] See Pamela Herd's (2005a, 2005b, 2006) work on allocating women a wage that is the equivalent of one half the median income during the time that she is bearing/raising children. This scheme would ensure that women's work in this area has value and is registered as such, especially with Social Security, where the current process is to allocate a woman zeroes for the time that she is out of the labor market.

References

Blank, Rebecca. 2006. "What Did the 1990s Welfare Reforms Accomplish?" In Alan J. Auerbach, David Card, and John M. Quigley, eds., *Public Policy and the Income Distribution*. New York: Russell Sage Foundation, pp. 33–79.

Blank, Rebecca, Sheldon Danziger, and Robert Schoeni. 2006. *Working and Poor: How Economic and Policy Changes are Affecting Low-Wage Workers*. New York: Russell Sage Foundation.

Borbely, James Marschall. 2009, March. "US Labor Market in 2008: Economy in Recession." *Monthly Labor Review*. <http://146.142.4.22/opub/mlr/2009/03/art1full.pdf>. [December 14, 2009].

Boushey, Heather. 2009. "Women Breadwinners, Men Unemployed." Washington, DC: Center for American Progress. <http://www.americanprogress.org/issues/2009/07/breadwin_women.html>. [January 15, 2010].

Frank, Abbey, and Elisa Minoff. 2005. *Declining Share of Adults Receiving Training Under WIA Are Low-income or Disadvantaged*. Washington, DC: Center for Law and Social Policy.<http://clasp.org/publications/decline_in_wia_training.pdf>. [January 15, 2010].

Chicago Jobs Council. 2003. *Improving Our Response to Work Needs: Recommendations for Reauthorization of the Workforce Investment Act of 1998*. <http://www.cjc.net/publications/files/2_Workforce_Investment_Act_PDFs/wia_improving_response_rpt.pdf>. [January 15, 2010].

Dalirazar, Nasrin. 2007. *Reasons People Do Not Work: 2004*. Current Population Reports. Washington, DC: U.S. Census Bureau, U.S. Department of Commerce, Economics and Statistics Administration.

Deprez, Luisa S. 2002. *The Family Support Act of 1988: A Case Study of Welfare Policy in the 1980s*. Lewiston, NY: Edwin Mellen Press.

Edin, Kathryn, and Laura Lein. 1997. *Making Ends Meet: How Single Mothers Survive Welfare and Low-Wage Work*. New York: Russell Sage Foundation Press.

Fox Piven, Frances, and Richard Cloward. 1993. *Regulating the Poor: The Functions of Public Welfare*. New York: Vintage Press.

French, Eri, Bhashkar Mazumber, and Christopher Taber. 2008. "The Changing Pattern of Wage Growth for Low-Skilled Workers." In Roberta M. Blank, Sheldon H. Danziger, and Robert F. Schoeni (eds.), *Working and Poor: How Economic and Policy Changes are Affecting Low-Wage Workers*. New York: Russell Sage Foundation, pp. 141–72.

Fry, Richard, and D'Vera Cohn. 2010. *New Economics of Marriage: The Rise of Wives*. Washington, DC: Pew Research Center.

Gatta, Mary. 2005. *Not Just Getting By: The New Era of Flexible Workforce Development*. Lanham, MD: Lexington Books.

Gatta, Mary, and Luisa S. Deprez. 2008. "Women's Lives and Poverty: Developing a Framework of Real Reform for Welfare." *Journal of Sociology and Social Welfare*, Vol. 35, no. 3, pp. 21–48.

Greider, William. 2009. "The Future of the American Dream." *The Nation*. May 25. <http://www.thenation.com/doc/20090525/greider>. [January 14, 2010].

Grogger, J., and L.A. Karoly. 2005. *Welfare Reform: Effects of a Decade of Change*. Cambridge, MA: Harvard University Press.

Hartmann, Heidi. 2009. "Women, Recession and the Stimulus Package." *Dissent*, Vol. 56, no. 4 (Fall), pp. 42–7.

Hays, Sharon. 2003. *Flat Broke With Children: Women in the Age of Welfare Reform.* New York: Oxford University Press.

Henderson, Debra, and Ann Tickamyer. 2008. "Lost in Appalachia: The Unexpected Impact of Welfare Reform on Older Women in Rural Communities." *Journal of Sociology and Social Welfare,* Vol 35, no. 3, pp. 153–72.

Henrici, Jane. 2006. *Doing Without: Women and Work After Welfare Reform.* Tucson: University of Arizona Press.

Herd, Pamela. 2005a. "Ensuring a Minimum: Social Security Reform and Women." *The Gerontologist,* Vol. 45, no. 1 (February), pp. 12–25.

Herd, Pamela. 2005b. "Reforming a Breadwinner Welfare State: Gender, Race, Class and Social Security Reform." *Social Forces,* Vol. 83, no. 4 (June), pp. 1365–93.

Herd, Pamela. 2006. "Crediting Care? Gender, Race, Class and Social Security Reform." *Journals of Gerontology: Social Sciences,* Vol. 61, no. 1 (January), pp. 524–34.

Holzer, Harry. 2008. *Workforce Development as an Antipoverty Strategy: What Do We Know? What Should We Do?* Working Paper #08-17. Ann Arbor, MI: National Poverty Center.

Holzer, Harry J., and Robert J. LaLonde. 2000. "Employment and Job Stability among Less-Skilled Workers." In David Card and Rebecca Blank, eds., *Finding Jobs: Work and Welfare Reform.* New York: Russell Sage Foundation, pp. 125–59.

Huber, Evelyne, John D. Stephens, David Bradley, Stephanie Moller, and Francois Nielsen. 2009. "The Politics of Women's Economic Independence." *Social Politics,* Vol. 16, no. 1, pp. 1–39.

Institute for Women's Policy Research. 2003. "Life After Welfare Reform: Low-Income Single Parent Families, Pre- and Post-TANF." *Research-in-Brief,* May 22. Washington, DC: Institute for Women's Policy Research.

Kahne, Hilda. 2004. "Low-Wage Single Mother Families in This Jobless Recovery: Can Social Policies Help?" *Analyses of Social Issues and Public Policy,* Vol. 4, no. 1, pp. 47–68.

Licter, Daniel, and Rukamalie Jayakody. 2002. "Welfare Reform: How Do We Measure Success?" *Annual Review of Sociology,* Vol. 28, pp. 117–41.

Marchevsky, Alejandra, and Jeanne Theoharis. 2008. "Dropped from the Rolls: Mexican Immigrants, Race, and Rights in an Era of Welfare Reform." *Journal of Sociology and Social Welfare,* Vol. 35, no. 3, pp. 71–96.

Mink, Gwendolyn, and Rickie Solinger. 2003. *Welfare: A Documentary History of U.S. Policy and Politics.* New York: New York University Press.

National Women's Law Center. 2008. *The Reality of the Workforce: Mothers Are Working Outside the Home.* <http://www.nwlc.org/pdf/WorkingMothers-March2008.pdf>. [December 16, 2009].

O'Connor, Alice. 2001. *Poverty Knowledge: Social Science, Social Policy, and the Poor in Twentieth Century U.S. History.* Princeton, NJ: Princeton University Press.

Osmani, Siddiq. 2008. "The Role of Employment in Promoting Human Development." *Maitreyee,* Vol. 10 (February), pp. 2–5.

Padavic, Irene, and Barbara Reskin. 2002. *Women and Men at Work* (2nd ed.). Newbury Park, CA: Pine Forge Press.

Parrott, Sharon, and Arloc Sherman. 2007. "TANF's Results Are More Mixed Than Is Often Understood." *Journal of Policy Analysis and Management,* Vol. 26, no. 2 (Spring), pp. 374–85.

Pearce, Diana. 2000. "Rights and Wrongs of Welfare Reform: A Feminist Approach." *Affilia*, Vol. 15, no. 2, pp. 133–52.

Pomeroy, Ann. 2008. "Welfare-to-Work: A Work in Progress." *HR Magazine*, Vol. 53, no. 2 (February 1). <http://www.shrm.org/Publications/hrmagazine/Editorial-Content/Pages/0208pomeroy2.aspx>. [Month date, year].

Press, Eyal. 2007. "The Missing Class." *The Nation*, pp. 22–3, July 26.

Rose, Nancy. 1993. "Gender, Race, and the Welfare State: Government Work Programs from the 1930s to the Present." *Feminist Studies*, Vol. 19, no. 2, pp. 319–42.

Schram, Sanford F., and Joe Soss. 2001. "Success Stories: Welfare Reform, Policy Discourse, and the Politics of Research." *Annals of the American Academy of Political and Social Science*, Vol. 577 (September), pp. 49–65.

Sen, Amartya. 1999. *Development as Freedom*. Oxford: Oxford University Press.

Shaw, Kathleen, Christopher Mazzeo, Sara Rab, and Jerry A. Jacobs. 2006. *Putting Poor People to Work: How the Work-first Idea Eroded College Access for the Poor*. New York City: Russell Sage Foundation.

Stone, Pamela, 2009. "Getting to Equal: Progress, Pitfalls and Policy Solutions on the Way to Gender Parity in the Workplace." *Pathways* (Spring), pp. 3–7. <http://www.stanford.edu/group/scspi/pdfs/pathways/spring_2009/Stone.pdf>. [January 20, 2010].

U.S. Department of Labor, 2000. *A Profile of the Working Poor*. <http://www.bls.gov/cps/cpswp2000.htm>. [December 15, 2009].

U.S. Department of Labor. 2008. *Women in the Labor Force: A Data Book*. <http://www.bls.gov/cps/wlf-databook-2008.pdf>. [December 15, 2009].

Wider Opportunities for Women/National Association of Workforce Investment Boards. 2003. *Reality Check: Promoting Self-Sufficiency in the Public Workforce System. A Promising Practices Guide for Workforce Boards*. Washington, DC: Wider Opportunities for Women. <http://www.wowonline.org/resources/documents/WOWRealityCheck.pdf>. [October 19, 2010].

Williams, Joan. 2001. *Unbending Gender: Why Work and Family Conflict and What to Do About It*. New York: Oxford University Press.

Women Work! Congressional Testimony. 2008, November 24. <http://www.womenwork.org/policy/WIArecommendations112408.pdf>. [December 15, 2009].

CHAPTER 12

Creating a 21st-Century Workforce Development System

F. RAY MARSHALL
University of Texas at Austin

HENRY A. PLOTKIN
New Jersey State Employment and Training Commission (retired)

This volume's intent is to provide a comprehensive understanding of the current workforce development system in the United States as well as a vision of a future 21st-century system. Translating a new vision into actual policy is a complicated affair, requiring that businesses, workers, potential workers, political leaders, and the public recognize human resource development as essential to economic growth and shared prosperity. They must demand that workforce development lie at the center, not the periphery, of the national agenda. The workforce development system itself must dramatically change to ensure that America's workforce can meet the needs of our economy as it struggles to recover and redefine itself in the face of rapid technological innovation and unforgiving global competition.

The research presented in this book provides a basis for an informed policy discussion of the various issues that must be addressed as we move to modernize the present system. What emerges is the complexity involved in creating a seamless workforce development system. Yet underlying that complexity is a common theme: The diverse set of institutions that deliver employment, training, and workforce education services must act as if they are part of a single system designed to improve labor market performance and maximize the skills of our fellow citizens. Primary and secondary schools, higher education, vocational schools, and literacy providers—especially those teaching English as a Second Language—as well as the welfare system, nonprofit organizations, the faith-based community, and public sector workforce development practitioners and policy makers must all be partners in this common endeavor. Business-driven needs, that is, the skill sets demanded by long-term secular changes in the

285

labor market, must be the touchstone for shaping workforce development programs and services.

For too many years, at least since the authorization of the GI Bill over half a century ago, the education and training needs of adults have been a residual priority, an afterthought in the U.S. workforce development system. Perhaps the most useful artifact of the current approach to workforce development is to offer public officials a cover, an easy answer to this question: What is being done to soften the impact of economic disruptions on workers' lives? Rarely acknowledged is the truth that, as a nation, we have neither devoted the resources nor demonstrated the will to make a meaningful difference to the prospects of many adults whose jobs have disappeared. The present workforce development system is mired in bureaucratic and policy confusion, lacks a clear vision of the direction of the economy, fails to explain the skill sets workers need to prosper, and is not valued by the business community. More, it is viewed as a "poverty" program rather than as part of economic development and employment opportunity.

The current system often focuses more on the vendors who deliver employment and training services than the "customers" for these services. This reversal of "ends" and "means" has helped create a system where the needs of students, workers and those seeking work, and the employer community are often ignored. Worse, this system is dramatically underfunded, nowhere matching resources to the educational needs of adults experiencing the trauma of a rapidly changing labor market.

The implementation of a 21st-century workforce development system faces significant barriers, not the least of which is the high wall that separates "academic" from "vocational" learning and separates school-based learning from the world of work. As the nature of work continues to evolve, with a higher premium placed on the mastery of 21st-century skills, the separation of the vocational and academic becomes untenable. Schurman and Soares (Chapter 6, this volume) point out that vocational education now demands competencies historically reserved for college graduates, including skills such as critical thinking, effective communication, and the application of knowledge, while academic education must engage students in experiential and applied learning.

The resistance of the K–12 system to the federal "School to Work" initiative bears testament to this "high wall" that limits the vision of many educators to the belief that college is the sole desired outcome for secondary school students. Few teachers are taught to understand the labor market and are as a result limited in their ability to advise students about the career opportunities in apprenticeship programs and other vocational options. Nor are teachers trained to help students make the contextual connections between their learning and its real-world application. A new initiative in New Jersey, NJ PLACE (New Jersey Pathways Leading Apprentices to a College Education, http://www.njplace.com) attempts to bridge this gap by offering college credit for apprenticeship programs (Schurman and Soares, Chapter 6, this volume). Yet such examples are rare as the traditional separation of the academic and vocational continues to cast its shadow on our educational system.

This is especially troubling in an economy that richly rewards the skilled and equally punishes the unskilled. Individuals who lack the appropriate workforce training will be relegated to the ranks of the working poor or, worse, the unemployed. Ironically, even during the depths of the recession, when unemployment reached 10%, some jobs were hard to fill because the mismatch between labor market demands and workforce skills remained.

It is our hope to give voice to ideas and policies that will meet the challenges of a global economy where a premium is paid to those nations with the most highly skilled workforces. Unless the needs of the workforce and the employer community are met, we will never achieve the level of economic growth of which we are capable, nor will we provide our fellow citizens the opportunities to which they are entitled. Our vision of a 21st-century workforce development system is not made from whole cloth. T.S. Eliot reminds us: "Time past and time future what might have been and what has been point to one end, which is always present." This reminds us that much of the future is found in both the present and the past. We can glimpse many of the ideas we offer in this essay, much like green shoots, sprouting across the American workforce landscape. Even during a time as difficult as this, creative and innovative solutions to our workforce dilemma continue to surface.

Principles for a 21st-Century Workforce Development System

Make Workforce Development a National Priority

America needs to develop an employment strategy to ensure that workforce development becomes a national priority. Elected officials, the media, and the public must be educated about the centrality of workforce development to economic growth and the employment aspirations of individuals. It is no small matter that the United States lacks a national employment strategy. While the nation episodically responds to crises—the Civilian Conservation Corps and Works Progress Administration of the New Deal, the National Defense Education Act after Sputnik in the 1950s, and the Comprehensive Employment and Training Act in the 1970s—we have never produced a clear strategy that would anticipate and respond to the workforce needs of a rapidly changing economy. The computer revolution of the late 1980s and 1990s, for instance, caught the nation unaware as firms embraced the new technology, flattening their organizational structures and making many workers redundant, thereby leading to massive worker dislocations.

In the recent economic maelstrom, it was clear we had not learned the lessons of the past by developing a national vision that will provide training opportunities for the "emerging" economy. For all the talk about America's "green future," we have not yet defined clearly what is meant by "green jobs," nor put the needed resources behind the massive infrastructure and training investments needed to transform the American economy with the potential to reverse the downward spiral in employment (Friedman 2008). While the U.S. Department of Labor has begun to fund green training initiatives, this appears isolated from any clear long-term national strategy that will endure after the current stimulus funding is exhausted. Ironically, the aftermath of the British Petroleum oil spill in the Gulf of Mexico may encourage the development such a strategy.

As the recent national debate on health care reform demonstrated, the United States is reluctant to create systemic federal programs. This is especially true for economic policy, where there exists a belief that employment problems can be addressed through the natural workings of competitive markets. Other industrialized nations, less reluctant to use state power, have developed stronger publicly supported employment and training systems to prepare their populations for the world of work. While none of those efforts is ideal, they represent attempts to move beyond "the invisible hand" by ensuring employment security and economic expansion.

The resistance to creating a national employment policy is not new; it is clearly illustrated in the debates concerning passage of the Employment Act of 1946. Originally called the "Full Employment Act," the law as conceived by its author, Wright Patman, aimed to make full employment a national goal and guarantee a job to all Americans. After the ordeal of high unemployment during the Depression, this act institutionalized Keynesian economics into the fabric of the federal budget. The law mandated that, as aggregate demand fluctuated due to a downturn in the business cycle, the federal government would intervene by investing directly in the economy to compensate for the shortfall in employment. The debate about this legislation serves as a case study illustrating the U.S. reluctance to have the public sector intervene decisively in the economy. Hence, the final legislation stripped the act of its authority to create jobs, calling instead for the government to "promote" employment. By reducing the mandate of the original legislation, government was effectively sidelined when it came to providing the necessary resources for an authentic jobs strategy (Santoni 1986).

Indeed, the intent of the original legislation went against the grain of the American job-creation experience. Historically the United States, with the expansion westward and rapid industrialization in the 19th century, had a scarcity of labor, a scarcity often addressed by attracting new immigrants willing to work at low wages. This resulted in a pattern of indifference to workforce development policy that was reinforced by the prosperity of the post–World War II world, where the American economy was a colossus that stood astride the devastated economies of Europe and Asia. It is no coincidence that the debate about workforce development policy began to intensify as the economies of Europe and Asia, especially Japan, recovered in the 1970s and began competing with the United States. As the world continued to "globalize," the issue of workforce preparedness became more pressing. In the midst of the current recession with the rise of China and India looming, the policy discussion has taken on a special urgency.

Still, it is worth remembering that much of our understanding of education's purpose is Jeffersonian. Education in America is seen as preparation for citizenship. In the "first new nation," absent the legacy of class and caste, of aristocrat and peasant, the equalizing impact of education was seen as a way to ensure opportunity and create a meritocracy. It would be an anathema to Americans, for instance, to import a European system that sorts students early on by "ability," reinforcing a class system. Hence, emphasizing "work" in primary and secondary schools is seen as limiting, not expanding, students' choices. The end of high school is college—students not college bound become part of what some critics have called "the forgotten half" (Halperin 1998). Because of our changing demographics, educational equity is a high priority, which means educating all students to high standards, not only those who aspire to attend elite colleges and universities. Experience shows that all students can learn to high standards.

We must also abandon the view that education ends with high school or college. One way to facilitate this change is to help political leaders and the public understand that learning is lifelong. There are compelling reasons why this understanding must take hold. First, given the rapid changes in the labor market, new skills are at a premium. This is why education at the workplace and online must be the rule, not the exception. This is a lesson that more in the employer community need to learn as they struggle to compete in an increasingly unforgiving marketplace, although it is noteworthy that some professions—law, accounting, and airlines, among others—have already learned this lesson, mandating continuing education requirements. Second, the old compact between workers and their employers has been broken—people will change jobs five to seven times or more during their work lives, and spending one's whole career at a single company has become increasingly less common. This will necessitate ongoing training that prepares individuals for new jobs and, indeed, new careers. Third, we are living longer, which means, among other things, that those who work physically demanding jobs will need training for less taxing forms of work as they age. And even those in less physically demanding jobs will likely need to plan for new careers to support themselves in "semiretirement." Finally, America's urgent adult learning needs are highlighted by the relatively low literacy of adults, especially among growing numbers of immigrants, at a time when the skill requirements for family-supporting jobs are rising.

While space does not allow us to address the overall direction of the American economy, some issues need to be examined to understand future skill requirements. Even before the current economic meltdown, substantial dislocations had roiled the labor market. We have witnessed a "hollowing out" of the middle class—fewer jobs will support a traditional middle-class lifestyle (Warren and Tyagi 2004). This is particularly true for the hemorrhaging of manufacturing over the past 30 years.

The decline of manufacturing not only affected those already employed, but it also denied blacks and other minorities the opportunity for jobs that had lifted previous generations of ethnic minorities into the middle or working class. Just as African Americans were achieving civil rights in the 1960s and antidiscrimination regulations offered more equal opportunity for real careers, those jobs began to vanish. Moreover, while there has been a great deal of discussion about the negative economic impact of the loss of manufacturing jobs, it is surely the case that the social impact—the externalities—has been just as devastating. Urban areas, once great centers for manufacturing, have been transformed into decaying brick deserts where the inhabitants live with little hope of escaping. Few events have done more than the loss of manufacturing jobs to make real the famous conclusion of the Kerner Commission report (1968): "Our nation is moving toward two societies, one black, one white—separate and unequal."

Thus, it is hard to imagine a 21st-century workforce development system that would not influence both the "demand side" (the question of job creation) as well as the "supply side" (the preparedness of the workforce). While public investment in economic development and job creation is woven into the fabric of American economic history, from the railroads of the 19th century to the "invention" of the Internet in the 20th, it has not been an essential part of the political debate until the recent economic collapse. A national workforce and public investment strategy can support high-value added job growth in several specific ways.

First, by upgrading workers' skills, economic developers can upgrade the quality of industries and jobs available. This is so because industry tends to adapt to the qualifications of workforces. Communities like Austin, Texas, for example, have used this strategy to promote high-value-added economic development, both by attracting outside companies like IBM, 3M, and Texas Instruments and by facilitating the development of indigenous companies like Dell. There also is abundant evidence that sector workforce development techniques can simultaneously create high-wage jobs and promote emerging growth sectors (Finegold and McCarthy, Chapter 8, this volume; Glover and King 2010).

Second, labor market policies can enhance the performance of macroeconomic policies by improving the functioning of labor markets. This would help overcome frictional unemployment, remove bottlenecks, and better match workers' skills with emerging labor market demand, thus reducing structural unemployment. Labor market policies complement macroeconomic policies by reducing inflationary pressures at any given level of employment, thus shifting the Phillips curve, which posits the inverse relationship between the rate of unemployment and the rate of inflation. Labor market policies likewise can maintain aggregate demand by providing unemployment compensation (an automatic stabilizer) and expenditures on direct job creation, which can, because they are targeted, create jobs at a lower cost and less inflationary pressure than tax cuts or other forms of government spending. Despite these advantages, since World War II we have rarely effectively coordinated labor market and macroeconomic policies. This coordination is particularly important in the present deep recession, when targeted labor market policies could help ease the pain of the recession, stimulate recovery, and moderate inflationary pressures.

One of the most promising components of public job creation during recessions is an investment that will create jobs immediately that also meet long-term national needs. Indeed, direct employment in economically important projects should be an essential feature of an authentic 21st-century workforce policy. We know, for instance, that painting roofs white would help reduce global warming by both conserving energy and reflecting sunlight back into space. Dr. Steven Chu, the U.S. Secretary of Energy and a Nobel Prize–winning scientist, has argued that making roofs and pavements white or light-colored would be the equivalent of taking all the world's cars off the road for 11 years (Connor 2009). Despite this, we have yet to begin such an undertaking on a national scale. Assuming that Chu's science is correct, why has no national program been implemented that could employ tens of thousands of the unemployed, including urban youth, in such an endeavor? Priority should be given to an initiative that would train those working in such projects to become competent in other, more sophisticated ways of making buildings energy efficient.

Another idea that has been on the back burner for years is the creation of a National Infrastructure Bank. As envisioned, the bank would be independent and nonpartisan, allowing it to fund projects based on merit and avoid the pitfalls of pork-barrel politics. Estimates are that, over a ten-year period, the bank could leverage a $60-billion contribution into over $500 billion in infrastructure investments, resulting in the creation of two million new jobs. A significant federal commitment to projects of national significance, including transportation, the environment, energy, education, and telecommunications, is critical to America's future. Although Barack Obama while president-elect entertained this idea during the transition, it never took root in the stimulus package. However, as massive job losses continue, there is renewed interest in efforts to counter underinvestment in the infrastructure and spur job growth. One legislative initiative, the Jobs for Main Street Act of 2010, redirects $75 billion from the Troubled Asset Relief Program (TARP) to investments in highways, bridges, transit, airports, clean water, energy, and schools, among others. The act also calls for funds to stabilize public jobs in education and law enforcement. For our purposes, however, it is enough to say that a 21st-century workforce development system should address areas of the economy where there is underinvestment, which serves to enhance both economic efficiency and job creation.

The nation's imagination should be captured by the sight of thousands of people working in ventures clearly designed for the public good. Such a workforce development system, where government programs serve as an essential bridge between labor supply and demand, would deserve widespread public support. In the end, a workforce development system is perceived as valuable to the extent that it leads directly to good jobs at good wages and facilitates economic progress. Moreover, Americans would be supportive of job creation in projects with visible and tangible benefits, such as high-speed rail, modernized airports, improved mass transit, and a host of others. Stimulating new industries and technologies, as well as enhancing the nation's critical manufacturing base through public investment, is an idea whose time has come.

Focus on Lifelong Learning

We must create the opportunity for adults to participate in a lifelong learning system finely attuned to changing labor market needs. This means ensuring that sufficient resources and programs are available to meet the needs of adults who wish to improve their skills. Americans understand the ineluctable connection between levels of education and wages. As Figure 1 demonstrates, this understanding is overwhelmingly supported by the data. Yet the public has not been convinced that this connection is also relevant beyond college and people in their early twenties. The correlation between education and wages applies with equal force to a lifelong system of education that nurtures the skills of adults, encompassing workers, the underemployed, and those seeking employment.

A productive 21st-century economy demands a workforce capable of learning new technologies and organizational structures and working cooperatively in a culturally diverse workplace. The breakneck pace of change means that education cannot end with a certificate of proficiency or even a college degree, but rather must be integrated into the work lives of individuals. Workforce development programs must be available throughout a person's life, in the school, at home, and in the workplace; providers must equip workers with the skills to be effective, self-directed learners. While job- and task-specific learning is appropriate for certain situations, the overall workforce system must offer broad-based education to meet the needs of the workplace or create entrepreneurial opportunities. This is consistent with a labor market that demands skills that are not routine and repetitive, but rather flexible and adaptive. The skills required by a 21st-century workforce center on collaboration:

FIGURE 1
Relationship Between Education Level and Earnings.

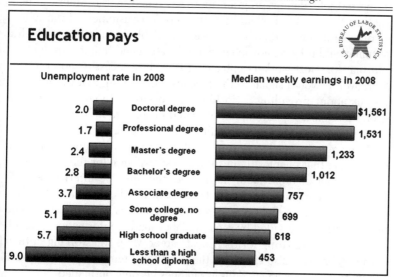

Source: Bureau of Labor Statistics. Current Population Survey.

Teamwork, project management, and effective communication with heterogeneous co-workers are among these core competencies (Finegold and Notabartolo, Chapter 2, this volume).

Quality research also plays an important role in ensuring that workforce development programs adapt to the future. Frequently, employers cannot read the tea leaves for the skills their employees need as their industry evolves and the economic context changes. Academic research should be used to help the workforce development system stay at the cutting edge of change. Researchers need to be fully engaged in helping both the employer and workforce communities understand the skill sets required during the ongoing secular changes in the economy and the organizational impacts of these changes. At a minimum, universities can help document and share best practices and lessons learned with the workforce system and employers.

Empower the Individual

To effectively develop a lifelong learning system, we must change the way the system is funded. There have been many ideas offered on this issue, including training vouchers, individual learning accounts, expanded Pell Grants, tax credits, increased support for community colleges, and simply adding more money to the current system. However, more resources will not achieve the desired aims if the system benefits vendors more than the clients. Therefore, creating the equivalent of a universal GI Bill has great appeal. There is probably no other publicly supported job training program more esteemed by the American people than the GI Bill. It would greatly empower customers of the system if some variation of that benefit were available to all citizens. Such a system would fully acknowledge that education and training are lifelong and that for most workers enhancing skills is a necessity, not a luxury. Moreover, it would signal to the business community that the nation is serious about providing a world-class workforce to compete against strong foreign competition, and it would encourage individual workers to continually assess their own skill sets and prepare for the future.

Implementing such a system involves creating an employment plan for workers that enables them to take responsibility for their own work life. The fact of rapid labor market change must be internalized and anticipated, encouraging people to prepare for the certainty that they will not only change jobs, but careers as well. This means that, assisted by the foresight provided by accurate labor market information, individuals will start preparing for their next career while still working in their current jobs. This also speaks to the need for a nimble adult education system that can teach new skills as old ones become outmoded.

Yet the creation of a new individualized training system has hazards of its own. Procedures are needed that will enable individuals to make reasonable and achievable choices and obtain appropriate training at a sensible cost for a realistic career, including these:

- Reliable labor market information that anticipates the evolution of the labor market
- Accurate assessment tools that help customers understand their interests and abilities
- Training for jobs in demand based on industry standards that lead to acknowledged certifications, credentials, or degrees
- Publicly available assessments that measure vendors' historic performance in job training, placement, and retention
- Specific educational requirements for training program instructors
- Well-trained, certified counselors who can offer guidance as well as approve final training decisions

An effective workforce development system provides customers with the best guidance possible while simultaneously protecting them from potential fraud and unrealistic expectations. Although we are proposing that individuals have "training accounts," safeguards, including due diligence with regard to the appropriateness of training and attainment of recognized qualifications from accredited providers, are critical. Hence, people would have a right to enhance their skills only if there is a high probability that they will succeed. In too many instances, people trained for jobs that do not exist or careers for which they are not prepared. A 21st-century workforce development system would have the assessment tools, training quality, labor market information, and counseling necessary to ensure that individuals obtain valuable and appropriate skills.

Create a System Through Partnerships

A transformed workforce development system will ensure "no wrong door" access for services, with strong, open partnerships among providers and strong connections to the labor market. These partnerships' major goal should be creating transparent career paths that will empower incumbent and potential workers to enhance their skills to both meet labor market demand and satisfy their career objectives.

The unfortunate truth is that the current workforce system is a patchwork of siloed and disconnected programs with a Rube Goldberg quality. The major federal job-training program, the Workforce Investment Act (WIA), created business-dominated Workforce Investment Boards (WIBs) that are responsible for local workforce planning. These boards are not currently aligned to regional labor markets, but to a narrower political geography (often counties), subjecting them to the vicissitudes of local politics. The political constraints on the workforce system all too frequently include the indifference or ignorance of local elected officials about their own role in promoting the workforce system. Staffing of One-Stop Career Centers, the major bodies responsible for delivering services, is often treated as merely opportunities for political favoritism, including patronage. The 1970s television program *Hill Street Blues* portrayed this problem in a particularly dramatic manner. In one episode, Captain Furillo is meeting with a bunch of youth gang members to try to establish peace among them. After reaching a tentative agreement, the gang members file out of Furillo's office, and one of them says to the captain, "Okay, I will keep the peace, but when that job training money comes down the pike I expect my share." Unfortunately, this story is not apocryphal: In too many cases, workforce funds are not used for training so much as for supporting politically connected supporters and vendors. And while it is always hazardous to generalize about all WIBs in all parts of the country, it is a glaring weakness of the current system that elected officials often do not grasp the centrality of workforce development or even the importance of connecting it to economic development.

The WIBs lack the authority to determine the training policies or economic development priorities of local education, income support, and training and economic planning institutions. WIBs stand at the margins and in many cases have only limited control of the WIA funding itself, which is usually allocated to local government entities and, ultimately, to One-Stop Career Centers. In the end, One-Stop "partners" see WIBs and WIA as a source of funding, not as a source of policy planning and guidance.

The numerous employment and training institutions should operate under the planning umbrella created by WIBs, defined not by political geography but by a regional labor market. Fashioning a WIB system that is immune from debilitating political interference, broadly representative of the regional labor market, and populated by members dedicated to the advancement of the workforce and the economy is not a simple undertaking. Clearly, WIBs need to be fiscally autonomous—they must have their own budgets and authority to hire highly qualified staff. There is a potential model for this transformation: Workforce Innovation in Regional Economic Development (WIRED), developed by the U.S. Department of Labor. WIRED created initiatives designed to integrate economic and workforce activities on a regional basis (see Finegold and McCarthy, Chapter 8, this volume). Despite facing significant obstacles, the best of the 39 WIRED regions achieved remarkable things in a short time with limited resources. These regional partnerships could serve as the template for the new labor market–oriented regional WIBs. A key feature of this initiative is that it explicitly links workforce and economic development, therefore making its value more evident. The federal government should overturn current WIB geography, mandate the creation of regional boards, and provide strict guidelines for their membership working closely with the business community. In order to give them greater financial independence, consideration should be given to providing these boards with bonding authority and renaming them "Regional Development Authorities" (RDAs), as recommended by the New Commission on the Skills of the American Workforce (NCSAW).

It should be noted that the fragmented process for formulating federal policy accounts for many of the problems faced by state and local actors. The divisions among congressional committees and government departments separate issues that require consolidation. The inability of Congress to develop a coordinated economic and workforce development policy framework makes it difficult to implement policy. And as one would expect in a democracy, politics, with the corresponding demands of various constituencies, plays a not-always-helpful role in shaping workforce policy. Frequently compromises are made between, say, the perceived needs of governors and mayors, each of whom wants a share of the resources and authority over how those resources are allocated. This and other accommodations to political reality create a system with divided authority where it is difficult to get anything accomplished. Even with its undemocratic implications, one can understand Thomas Friedman's desire for America to be "China for a day."

Federal agencies also play a role in limiting the workforce system's effectiveness. The Departments of Labor, Education, Health and Human Services, Homeland Security, and Commerce—the departments most interested in workforce issues—lack a history of cooperation, although it is noteworthy that leaders of the Obama administration's Departments of Education and Labor, among others, are making good-faith efforts to develop a collaborative ethos. The history of those relations and the congressional and bureaucratic barriers to genuine collaboration are formidable and not easily bridged. There is a substantial cost to the system in the incoherence of federal policy. Funds are allocated in a hodgepodge manner: some by formula, others through competitive grants, with some administered by states and others by localities. Often, agencies at the state level fail to coordinate programs, while at the local level disorder frequently rules. Federal agencies responsible for grants rarely consult with each other.

For instance, Housing and Urban Development (HUD) will award a literacy grant to a housing authority with no reference to similar grants administered by states or One-Stops. All these issues are compounded by the system's notorious lack of even the most elemental transparency.

As funds and programs filter down through the layers of government, a public policy "law of entropy" comes into play—disorder and complexity increase at the expense of coherence. It is no small cost to the system that, at the service delivery level, inordinate time is devoted to simply trying to put "Humpty Dumpty" back together again—trying to reconcile programs designed for similar constituencies but subject to the differing requirements of various departments. Solving this problem must be a major goal of newly formed RDAs. This is not a simple task, but it would be made immensely more achievable if such plans were mandated as a condition for local workforce agencies receiving federal funding. Those that submitted good plans and then demonstrated they could meet them would in turn be given much greater autonomy, similar to charter schools in K–12 education but in this case working within the system rather than separate from it.

RDAs with their expanded authority would be made even more effective if states and localities, as a condition of their funding, would require the same behavior. Duplication of services, insufficient leveraging of resources, and lack of common standards are among the issues that make accessing workforce services more difficult for those seeking to improve their skills and more daunting for the employer community. There is little justification for the lack of cooperation among institutions with similar workforce education goals when the economy is strong; it becomes a tragedy when the economy is weak and scarce resources are not being used to their fullest potential.

RDAs can accomplish this goal by creating a common forum where overall workforce policies are developed to transcend the narrow interests of individual agencies. Through its inclusive membership, RDAs would reflect the expertise of all workforce agencies, not a separate process or institution. It is the agencies' expertise in concert with the labor market's needs that will enable RDAs to develop comprehensive plans for the entire region. These plans will augment the work of the respective governing bodies by meshing them with the policies and priorities of other agencies and programs. This process would also provide local elected officials with the framework needed to engage effectively in economic planning, as well as assist them in making resource allocation decisions. Additionally, RDAs' plans could guide state agencies in the allocation of state and federal resources to the high-growth areas of the regional labor market. Synthesizing these plans at the state level, even the multistate level, would provide a rational basis for workforce development and economic planning.

In the end, RDAs would establish the context of workforce planning for their regions, and this shared process will greatly assist in guiding partner institutions and their governing bodies in more effectively discharging their responsibilities. Operating from a common "playbook" would free agencies from reinventing the wheel—they would be able to maximize their strengths, share expertise, and achieve economies of scale that would enhance performance and use of resources. Clearly, the interests of the clients of the various workforce institutions would be improved by such a collaborative approach to workforce development policies.

RDAs could specify the way workforce education and training institutions interact through the priorities and programs they establish in their plans. As these employment and training institutions are encouraged to adopt a "culture of cooperation," revitalized One-Stop Career Centers can become the effective point of entry for those seeking services. With the use of technology, different workforce agencies should be able to communicate easily with one another and their common customers. Videoconferencing, for instance, can be used to ensure that there is really "no wrong door"—that no matter which agency a customer visits, communication with all agencies can be effectively provided. Seamless transition among disparate programs, career ladders, and bridges to employers is essential to a 21st-century workforce system.

Foster Transparency

For a workforce system worthy of the demands of the 21st century to be created, its outcomes must be transparent. Historically, the workforce system has failed to create a simple and publicly available way to measure program performance. Indeed, a major advance would be a modern accountability system, simply and clearly displayed on the Internet, where citizens and leaders could assess both the performance of the system as a whole and the individual partners of that system. It is an unnerving fact that we have, at best, an uneven system for measuring results or, even worse, no systematic data to make any real judgment. This state of affairs is recognized by the K–12 system as it attempts at both state and federal levels to develop school report cards and for the nation as a whole in the StateoftheUSA.org initiative that went live in the summer of 2010. Yet there is no real equivalent attempt for the workforce system.

The WIA system's accountability standards lack the comprehensiveness to give an accurate understanding of how the system is actually performing. Those who have been involved in evaluating the WIA system know that the standards themselves are often arbitrary. Negotiated between the states and the federal government, these standards, in effect, offer only symbolic reassurance that the system is accountable rather than creating real accountability replete with potential sanctions. Indeed, it is a paradox of the present system that while poor outcomes rarely affect future funding, the fear of sanctions by program administrators makes them risk averse. We have created, in effect, the worst of both worlds. Worse yet, we create perverse disincentives to offer effective long-term training by overemphasizing per-capita costs and short-term placements versus career advancement and wage sustainability.

Ironically, tools currently exist to assess the workforce system. Matching accurate student data with wage records for unemployment insurance would provide a reasonable approximation of system outcomes. This same process can be used to evaluate incumbent worker training programs. In the end, if we do not have a way to measure performance and hold programs accountable, we wind up with a system that operates in the dark. When the value of the workforce system is not provable, why would we expect to find any public support? Indeed, when the workforce system is not valued for the outcomes it produces, it becomes a natural prey for those who seek to use it for patronage or as a way of creating fly-by-night training programs that cheat their customers. The system also becomes vulnerable to political attacks from those interested in cutting public programs that cannot clearly demonstrate their value. Hence, accountability is not simply about making programs behave responsibly; it is also essential to obtaining public support.

Emphasize Adult Literacy

The National Commission on Adult Literacy (2008) has argued that basic skills education (adult literacy) must become a special priority for the workforce development system. Lack of literacy among adults, including those for whom English is not their first language, is the *major* reason why even in good economic times many workers are unable to reach their full potential. Creating a universally available literacy education system that emphasizes the use of online learning must be a core value for workforce development.

The National Adult Literacy Survey (NALS) of 1994 dramatically revealed the skeleton in America's workforce closet: *Nearly one half of adults (age 16 to 64) function at the lowest levels of literacy,* as defined by the survey. Despite these dramatic results, there was barely any public outrage or a policy response by the federal government. Adult education professionals who had expected a *Time* magazine cover story with the headline "Johnny Can't Read and Neither Can His Parents" were mystified by the lack of interest in the report. Indeed, in the midst of the economic boom of the 1990s, it was common knowledge that low literacy skills robbed individuals of good jobs at good wages and undermined the economic development of the nation.

Subsequent adult literacy studies, including The National Assessment of Adult Literacy of 2003, substantially replicated these findings. Adding to the troubling nature of these results is the lower levels of literacy among African Americans, Latinos, and immigrants who will account for most U.S. workforce growth in the coming decades. This reinforces and partially explains the economic inequality that exists among the races. The inescapable conclusion is that the K–12 system has failed to address the most fundamental literacy needs of far too many Americans. A full discussion of the problems of the primary and secondary schools system is beyond the scope of this chapter. However, it is appalling that after over 40 years of policy debate there has been little overall improvement in educational outcomes and that the educational attainment of African Americans and Latinos still lags substantially behind whites, with the concomitant result of pronounced inequality among adult workers. While there are some positive ideas for educational reform emerging from the Obama administration, sadly the history of such reform has been "full of sound and fury, signifying nothing."

Addressing the problem of adult literacy must be a preeminent goal of a 21st-century workforce system. Simply put, unless we address this issue, economic inequality will be exacerbated, there will be a lack of skilled workers, and the social costs of a large underemployed and unemployed population will increase. Hence, the lack of literacy not only deeply affects the individuals who are bereft of fundamental skills, but also harms the very nature of our society. The Jeffersonian ideal of republican self-government will also suffer, as citizens will be less able to understand those public issues that most affect their lives. One cannot look at the subprime mortgage crisis or credit card indebtedness without despairing about the ability of the American public to understand economic reality.

One limitation on meeting the educational needs of adults, at least in the short run, is the shortage of classrooms and teachers. And while we discuss the role of distance learning in more depth later, it has a special role in adult education. A "ubiquitous" literacy website should be established where individuals could have their level of literacy assessed and be offered online education programs to improve those skills. The advantage of such an approach is that the program could be self-paced, allowing adults to enhance their skills in a manner suitable to their background. Moreover, the extent to which online offerings connect to specific job categories serves to motivate individuals to study in order to advance their careers.

An Adult Education Framework

A 21st-century literacy system requires a framework that meets the needs of adults. Equipped for the Future (EFF) offers a promising adult literacy content standards approach. These standards, originally developed by the National Institute of Literacy, are currently managed at the University of Tennessee's Center for Literacy Studies. The EFF "wheel" portrays the comprehensive series of literacy-related skills adults need to succeed, not only in the workplace, but as parents and citizens as well.

The great utility of the EFF approach is that it can be translated into standards that employers want for entry-level workers. An essential element that should characterize the 21st-century workforce system is the

FIGURE 2
The EFF Wheel.

Source: Stein, Sondra. 2000. From *Equipped for the Future: Content Standards—What Adults Need to Know and Be Able to Do in the 21st Century* (National Institute for Literacy). Reprinted with the permission of the copyright holder, The Center for Literacy, Knoxville, TN.

availability of portable credentials that can assure employers that a new hire is, in fact, work-ready. This is particularly important for welfare recipients, immigrants, and new entrants to the labor market. A 2001 National Association of Manufacturers survey explored the "most common reasons companies reject applicants as hourly production workers"; it found that 69% are rejected because of "inadequate basic employability skills," which included, among other deficiencies, attendance, timeliness, and work ethic. Notably, lack of reading skills (32%) and math skills (21%) were also identified as barriers to employment. (National Association of Manufacturers 2001).

One recent attempt to address this issue is the National Work Readiness Credential (WRC, http://www.workreadiness.com), which applies the standards created by EFF to the employers' requirement for entry-level hires. The WRC is the first national standards-based assessment for entry-level workers to provide a universal, transferable, national standard for work readiness. It assesses the knowledge, skills, and abilities that supervisors, managers, and other workforce experts agree are most important when looking for people who can successfully perform entry-level work as follows:

• Complete work accurately, on time, and to a high standard of quality
• Work in teams to achieve mutual goals and objectives
• Follow work-related rules and regulations
• Demonstrate willingness to work and show initiative
• Display responsible behaviors at work, including avoiding absenteeism and demonstrating promptness

As the research underlying the WRC indicates, it has the potential to provide the following benefits for employers:

• Reduced recruitment costs
• Improved productivity
• Minimized turnover
• Maximized effectiveness of on-the-job-training

The WRC represents an important collaboration between the workforce system and the employer community. The original source for many of the insights gleaned from employers is a distinguished U.S. Department of Labor report issued in 1991 by the Secretary's Commission on Achieving Necessary Skills (SCANS). This report, aside from its excellent substance, also represents a template for how a modern workforce development system ought to function; unfortunately, almost two decades later, the template still has not been followed. SCANS used extensive employer input to determine what firms' actual needs were rather than simply assuming these were well known. Indeed, this interaction with employers is precisely the kind of partnership we need to improve our current system. The adoption of such a standard, one that links levels of literacy to the requirement for entry-level workers, is a critical component of a 21st-century workforce system.

Distance Learning

Distance learning must be universally available as an option for adults to improve their work skills. Distance learning provides ways to meet the needs of adults through the rapid adoption of "real-time" labor market information to educational offerings. Online learning is cost efficient and more convenient for the users—both job holders and job seekers. And the quality is improving rapidly, as new technologies and broader bandwidth enable greater interaction and student engagement.

Distance learning is crucial to ensure that the workforce system keeps current with the ever-changing skill demands of the labor market. There are significant advantages in distance learning, especially for adult learners. First, there is the obvious benefit of learning from home, thereby saving time and transportation and childcare costs. For many, especially single parents, there is an obvious desire to maximize the time spent with their families. Second, the availability of asynchronous courses allows learners to participate when they have free time. Thus, the Internet has the potential to provide virtually unlimited access to courses in distant sites; one is not restricted to the course offerings of the local community college or adult learning center. Third, the very act of learning online increases the student's computer skills, which are transferrable to the workplace. Fourth, education is self-paced; one can learn in an unhurried, relaxed fashion or accelerate to quickly meet a goal. Fifth, for those with disabilities, especially any involving mobility, distance learning is of obvious value. Sixth, for those who feel insecure in a classroom, the opportunity to learn in private is a great relief from the fear of embarrassment.

Last, and maybe most important, computer-generated courseware can create educational building blocks that are continually assembled and disassembled in innovative ways to address different people with different learning styles. This is in sharp contrast to rigidly structured courses or sequences of courses that treat all learners the same. The pedagogy behind computer-based learning allows "customizing" curriculum to the particular needs of the student. The extent to which computer-based education can improve the skills of the workforce cannot be overstated. As McCain points out (Chapter 5, this volume), the benefits of distance learning extend to individuals regardless of their skill level. From those who need to learn about new, cutting-edge technologies to those who need to master English, their needs are met by distance learning. Moreover, while computer-based curricula lie at the heart of distance learning, the role of an actual teacher can be accommodated, where appropriate.

It is almost axiomatic to say that a 21st-century workforce system should fully embrace 21st-century technology. One of the puzzles of America is why the world's leading technology nation has not fully implemented technology into its educational system. For both the K–12 and adult education systems, the influence of technology has been far less apparent than the computer and broadband revolution that has fundamentally changed the private sector. Particularly ironic is that while the education system itself has failed to adopt this new technology, students in their private lives have enthusiastically adopted MySpace, Facebook, and Twitter. They freely text each other, share photographs, use Google Maps, and otherwise immerse themselves in the digital age. This immersion becomes ubiquitous as wired connectivity is recast into the realm of wireless continuous communication. Computer games themselves have become so compelling that young people forsake television time to play "Call to Duty: Modern Warfare" or "Guitar Hero."

Arguably, the seduction of both social networking and computer games has made the largely "analog" world of adult education appear less enticing. A digital transformation of education would include the ways material is both presented and delivered. With respect to presentation, it is an uncomfortable fact that much of what passes for "computer education" courseware is mere "shovelware"—that is, the porting over of analog material to the computer with little regard to the difference in the media. Simply put, the best programmers, the best minds in computing, do not gravitate to the educational market. That market, state- and locally based as it is, does not provide the customer base to justify large expenditures in creating top-flight educational software. The near invisibility of the federal government pushing for such a change is also noteworthy. And while there are many examples of innovative attempts to "digitize" education, the overall education system remains mostly enmeshed in an earlier era.

The use of the Internet for workforce education can put individuals in charge of their education by providing user-friendly websites containing comprehensive services and information that can be customized to specific needs. These services should include self-assessment tools and career inventories that help individuals build development plans.

To access all this information and coursework, a freely available website must be created. Most critically, this website would allow users to search for training programs, both online and in traditional brick-and-mortar locations, that meet their career aspirations as well as provide labor market information. Additionally, the website should serve as a *Consumer Reports* for training providers. Individuals could obtain information on the various programs offered by each training provider and compare programs and providers. One could compare and contrast programs based on location and length of training, cost, employment outcomes, and starting salary after graduation. Further, by emulating Amazon's customer review feature, students and employers would be able offer their assessments of individual programs. There is nothing like public exposure to encourage responsible behavior, especially when reinforced by real performance measures with sanctions against providers failing to meet the aforementioned objective standards.

While some websites have been introduced with many of these features, rarely are they populated with data comprehensive enough to make meaningful assessments concerning quality of program performance. The federal government ought to mandate, as a condition of funding, that educational institutions submit all relevant data to such a website. It should also establish a national website populated by the most sophisticated tools available; it is wasteful to ask states and localities to invest in similar projects. What would make sense is the adoption of a vetted "open source" approach that would permit others to contribute their best ideas. Making dynamic, multimedia, and employment-relevant materials freely available through a federally supported website would result in a dramatic increase in the skill level of the nation. An innovative idea may be a prize competition for the development of a whole set of applications that would be free and/or low-cost to download for the adult literacy market; perhaps Apple could be enticed to donate one iPad for literacy for every 100 it sells.

The potential for online learning for the incumbent workforce is that it can transform the modern firm into a learning environment where workers can not only keep abreast of current technologies, but also become conversant in new ones. There are also reasons to believe that the education of workers can be vastly enhanced by integrating social networking into the education process. An obvious use for social networking, for instance, is the creation of educational wikis and sharing of information. It could also create learning communities within the firm that can become professional expert groups sharing information ranging from solving problems to marketing new products.

If one envisions education broadly, beyond the ken of classrooms and courses, engaging in a virtual world where sharing knowledge and applying that knowledge is the norm, then mastering new skills and techniques becomes the centerpiece of work activities. The sharing of such stories or narratives will increase both productivity and knowledge. A less obvious virtue of social networking is that it is a wonderful forum for telling stories. Social networking fosters narratives about experiences in undertaking a task or trying to solve problems. Thus, in some ways social networking is just an electronic extension of the apprenticeship programs, where individuals learn by observing the journeyman or the master. Social networking allows the sharing of these experiences across a much broader landscape. It is worth noting that Pope Benedict XVI, who blogs, recently urged priests to use all available multimedia tools to teach the Gospel. Clearly, the Pope understands the power of the web as a way to teach and communicate.

Recommendations for Creating a World-Class Workforce Development System

The following recommendations offer a comprehensive framework for a revitalized 21st-century workforce development system. This framework contains labor market polices that will strengthen the capacity of the employers to respond to rapid changes in the economy while also providing new opportunities for student workers and those seeking employment.

1. Adopt a shared-prosperity strategy for improving productivity, quality, flexibility, and innovation as a way to maintain and improve American incomes in a globally competitive, knowledge-intensive economy. In addition to promoting high-performance work organizations and learning systems, a shared-prosperity strategy would adopt family-oriented social safety nets and regulations to limit wage competition. It also would strengthen workers' ability to form organizations to represent their interests in the workplace and in the formulation of public policies.

   Shared prosperity policies would require the coordination of education and workforce development with economic development and macroeconomic policies, including restoring the balance between policies to combat unemployment as well as inflation. This inflation–unemployment policy balance is mandated by the Humphrey-Hawkins (Full Employment and Balanced Growth) Act, but in practice policy decisions have been dominated by financial and macro economists who place far greater emphasis on inflation. This imbalance is a significant reason why the United States was unprepared to address the rising unemployment (structural and cyclical) resulting from the deep recession that started in 2007.

European countries like Norway, Denmark, and the Netherlands had a much more balanced array of policy instruments to prevent rising unemployment (Cohen 2009).

2. Establish a highly professional and independent commission on foreign worker adjustments to provide reliable and timely data and analyses to assist Congress and the president in making better and more flexible decisions in adjusting immigration and temporary foreign workers to labor market shortages while protecting the interests of foreign and domestic workers. Immigration has become far too important to the American economy—and has far too opaque, rigid, and inefficient administrative processes—to occupy such a low status on the national policy agenda (Marshall 2009).

3. Make educational equity and quality the foundation for a world-class workforce development system. There is strong evidence that our public schools and higher education systems do not meet either of these objectives very well, causing the United States to have greater disparities in educational attainment and mediocre performance relative to both our strongest international competitors and the requirements for shared prosperity. The components of world-class school systems include the following (New Commission on the Skills of the American Workforce 2008):

a. High standards for teachers should never be waived, just as we would not waive qualifications for doctors or other professionals. Teachers should be offered overall rewards, respect, and a quality of life that attracts the top third of college graduates into the profession, including bonuses for the superior qualifications needed for high-performance schools, student learners, and service in struggling schools or other challenging teaching situations. The experience of Teach for America suggests it is possible to recruit the top college graduates into inner city schools without offering very high salaries, but retaining them will require major reforms in the work environment, as outlined below.

b. Low-quality accountability tests geared to minimum standards should be replaced with high-quality diagnostic performance exams geared to internationally benchmarked standards. These assessments should be closely linked to high-quality curricular materials, syllabi, and instruction systems based on what we know about learning rather than such myths as "learning is mainly due to innate ability."

c. Schools and teachers should have much more autonomy, governed by professional standards for teachers and guided by high-quality standards for students, not detailed regulations and top-down management systems. School systems should collect and distribute a wide range of data on the performance of schools and students to be used for continuous improvement as well as for accountability purposes.

d. Schools should be held accountable for student performance and rewarded for superior achievements. Teachers and administrators should jointly decide how those rewards are distributed. It is not a good idea to hold individual teachers accountable for student scores on low-quality standardized tests.

e. Much more equitable financing processes should be provided for schools.

   i. Replace local property taxes with state financing for K–12 education.

   ii. Distribute resources to schools on the basis of students' learning needs, with relatively more resources going to schools with more disadvantaged students. With student-weighted budgeting, students and parents should have districtwide school choice.

   iii. Provide technical assistance and the best teachers and principals to low-performing schools.

   iv. Improve the access to postsecondary education for all students, especially those from low-income backgrounds.

f. High-quality, externally administered board exams (modeled after Advanced Placement and International Baccalaureate exams) should be administered to students at the end of their high school careers. Students should be allowed to take these board exams when they are ready and to take them as many times as needed to pass. Assistance should be provided for struggling students to help them pass the exams. Students who pass should be allowed to attend college for at least two years without going into significant debt or requiring remediation. Successful experiments to combine an associate's degree with the final two years of high school should be extended.

g. Youth apprenticeships, career academies, and other processes that provide high-quality academic and work experience should be available to all students. Local elected officials, educators, and businesses should form compacts, modeled after the Boston Compact, to bridge the gaps between schools, higher education, and work. Experience shows such compacts to be mutually advantageous to all participants, especially disadvantaged students.

4. Include the following elements:

a. An effective workforce development infrastructure coordinated with related functions at the national, state, and local labor market areas. At the local labor market level, Workforce Investment Boards (WIBs) should be replaced with Regional Development Authorities (RDAs) with the authority and resources to perform strategic planning for the whole labor market area and to coordinate appropriate training, education, labor market, economic development, and support services. RDAs would coordinate what are now WIBs, Economic Development Districts (EDDs), community colleges, adult education, and such support services as childcare and income supports for workers. Unlike existing WIBs and EDDs, RDAs would be able to plan and coordinate the delivery of an array of services across labor markets. In addition to existing funding streams, the RDAs should have bonding authority to ensure greater financial stability and independence. Labor market participants should be able to receive information about funding (Pell Grants, Individual Development Accounts, and other services) from One-Stop Career Centers.

b. Replacement of the present adjustment programs for trade and other purposes with an effective general adjustment system for all displaced workers. The present programs are too narrow, require too many administrative resources to determine eligibility, and are unfair because some employees are not eligible, even when working beside other employees who are. Trade adjustment assistance, for instance, covers only goods-producing employees displaced by trade agreements, which excludes over 80% of service workers. Labor markets would be more efficient with a general adjustment program, which experience in other countries demonstrates also causes much less resistance to change.

c. Because of greater labor force participation by women, provision of much more family-friendly workforce and support services. The Family and Medical Leave Act, for example, should be amended to make paid leave available for workers to care for their families during sickness and emergencies. And high-quality childcare and preschool services should be available to all families.

d. More effective and equitable worker supports, which could strengthen shared-prosperity programs by increasing human resource development and limiting low-wage competition. The unemployment insurance system has been an effective automatic stabilizer for cyclical unemployment, but it is much less effective for addressing rising structural unemployment. It is no longer "automatic" when Congress has to go through the lengthy and often contentious process to enact legislation for extended unemployment compensation during periods of rising long-term unemployment. Unemployment compensation would therefore be a much more effective strategy if there were automatic triggers like the level of unemployment or the percentage of workers who had exhausted their benefits. Unemployment compensation also does not cover many contingent, part-time, and temporary workers. The system should be based on hours of work, not the obsolete notion of tenure with a particular employer. The United States also should consider allowing greater use of unemployment compensation funds to support worker training and shorter hours as alternatives to layoffs. These processes give greater flexibility to labor markets in the Netherlands, Denmark, Germany, and Norway. Indeed, these countries' labor markets are as flexible as ours with the added advantage of minimizing the problems associated with large-scale unemployment.

e. Contingency plans for public employment and public works programs as effective ways to employ workers who are unable to readily find private sector jobs. Such jobs are particularly useful for employing young and disadvantaged workers in useful work that otherwise would go undone.

f. More specialized training and labor market research, evaluation, and development services, which characterized labor market programs before the 1980s. These services made better data and information available to evaluate and improve labor market programs and provided information to practitioners about the kinds of interventions that could be effective for different employers and workers. The federal government should create a strong network of research, training, and technical assistance to providers, modeled after the Agricultural Experiment Stations and Department of Commerce's National Institute of Standards and Technology programs to strengthen labor market institutions and programs. It is particularly important to involve more private employers and unions in sector and industry training processes, which experience suggests can yield high returns. Workforce development professionals could provide technical assistance to unions and employers working to establish joint education and training programs (Glover and King 2010).

g. Training obligations or tax incentives, like those used effectively in Singapore, to counteract the market failures that cause individual employers to underinvest in incumbent worker training.

Final Thoughts

As the chapters in this volume reflect, systemic change in workforce development is as daunting as it is critical. While our focus is on workforce development, it is a mistake to ignore the political and social context of America that makes change so difficult. Lack of faith in most institutions permeates public opinion, with particular loss of trust in political institutions. The recent economic meltdown and the failure of both public and private institutions to protect the public reinforce the national predisposition to doubt the capacity of either to meet their obligations. A restless public whose economic and social lives have been uprooted by the massive changes in the global economy and the attendant labor market are deeply skeptical of any national effort to address their needs. It is not only the health care debate that illustrated this phenomenon, but a host of policies including immigration, climate change, and financial reform. How, then, in this environment can we expect widespread support for fundamentally changing the nation's workforce development system?

The answer lies in the nature of workforce development itself. Systemic reforms of workforce development must be based on the principle of providing workers with more control over their economic lives. By protecting them from the worst uncertainties in the labor market and offering them a safe harbor of income support and training as they move to enter new careers, support would be forthcoming—even from a skeptical public. This is especially true for a public seeking to escape from the indignity of dependence and helplessness as they experience forces they cannot foresee or control battering their lives. In the end, the promise of real reform of the workforce development system under the framework of a vision of "shared prosperity" offers the public the chance to regain a semblance of autonomy required by citizens in a democracy. Indeed, a new and vital workforce development system offers workers the opportunity to fulfill not only their own promise but also the promise of American life.

References

Cohen, Adam. 2009. "A Dutch Formula Holds Down Joblessness." *Wall Street Journal*, December 29, Page A5.

Connor, Steve. 2009. "Obama's Climate Guru: Paint Your Roof White!" *The Independent*, May 27. <http://www.independent.co.uk/environment/climate-change/obamas-climate-guru-paint-your-roof-white-1691209.html>. [May 15, 2010].

Friedman, Thomas L. 2008. *Hot, Flat, and Crowded: Why We Need a Green Revolution—And How It Can Renew America.* New York: Farrar, Straus and Giroux.

Glover, Robert W., and Christopher T. King. 2010. "Sectoral Approaches to Workforce Development: Toward an Effective U.S. Labor Market Policy." In Charles Whalen, ed., *Human Resource Economics and Public Policy: Essays in Honor of Vernon M. Briggs, Jr.* Kalamazoo, MI: Upjohn Institute, pp. 215–52.

Halperin, S. 1998. *The Forgotten Half Revisited: American Youth and Young Families, 1988–2008.* Washington, DC: American Youth Policy Forum.

Kerner Commission. 1968. *Report of the National Advisory Commission on Civil Disorders.* Washington, DC: U.S. Government Printing Office.

Marshall, Ray. 2009. *Immigration for Shared Prosperity: A Framework for Comprehensive Reform.* Washington, DC: Economic Policy Institute.

National Association of Manufacturers. 2001. *The Skills Gap.* Los Angeles, CA: Center for Workforce Success.

National Commission on Adult Literacy. 2008. *Reach Higher America: Overcoming Crisis in the U.S. Workforce.*

New Commission on the Skills of the American Workforce. 2008. *Tough Choices or Tough Times: The Report of the New Commission on the Skills of the American Workforce.* Washington, DC: National Center on Education and the Economy.

Santoni, G.J. 1986. *The Employment Act of 1946: Some History Notes.* <http://research.stlouisfed.org/publications/review/86/11/Employment_Nov1986.pdf>. [May 15, 2010].

Secretary's Commission on Achieving Necessary Skills. 1991. *What Work Requires of Schools: A SCANS Report for America 2000.* Washington, DC: U.S. Department of Labor.

Warren, Elizabeth, and Amelia Warren Tyagi. 2004. *The Two-Income Trap: Why Middle-Class Parents Are Going Broke.* New York: Basic Books.

ABOUT THE CONTRIBUTORS

George S. Benson is an associate professor at the University of Texas at Arlington and an affiliated researcher with the Center for Effective Organizations. George earned his Ph.D. from the University of Southern California in the Marshall School of Business. George also holds degrees from Washington and Lee University and Georgetown University. He previously worked as a research analyst at the American Society for Training and Development in Alexandria, Virginia.

Luisa S. Deprez is professor of sociology and women and gender studies at the University of Southern Maine. She has authored *The Family Support Act of 1988: A Case Study of Welfare Policy in the 1980s* (2002) and co-edited *Shut-Out: Low Income Mothers and Higher Education in Post-Welfare America* (2004). Numerous of her writings about current welfare policy restrictions on low-income women seeking access to higher education appear in national and international journals and books. Her recent work centers on women and workforce development and the application of Amartya Sen's "capability approach" to promote and situate deliberative democracy knowledge and practice in higher education.

Althea Erickson is the associate director of advocacy and policy at Freelancers Union, where she led its successful 2009 campaign to repeal the Unincorporated Business Tax, saving New York City freelancers up to $3,400 a year. She also launched the union's political action committee and recently introduced a bill in the New York State legislature to protect freelancers from unpaid wages. Prior to joining Freelancers Union, Althea worked as a research associate at the Rockefeller Foundation, where she focused on strategies to build economic security in the U.S. workforce. Althea also has extensive organizing and campaign experience.

David Finegold is the dean of Rutgers University's School of Management and Labor Relations. Prior to joining Rutgers he was a professor at the Keck Graduate Institute of Applied Life Sciences in Claremont, California. David is the author of more than 80 journal articles and book chapters and has written or edited six books, including *Are Skills the Answer?* (with Colin Crouch and Mari Sako). He graduated *summa cum laude* with a B.A. in social studies from Harvard University in 1985 and was a Rhodes Scholar at Oxford University, where he completed his Ph.D. in politics in 1992.

Mary Gatta is the director of gender and workforce policy at the Center for Women and Work and on the faculty in the Department of Labor Studies and Employment Relations of Rutgers University. She holds a Ph.D. and an M.A. in sociology from Rutgers and a B.A. from Providence College. Mary's areas of expertise include gender and public policy, low-wage work, and evaluation research. She has published books, articles, and policy papers. Her latest book, *Not Just Getting By: The New Era of Flexible Workforce Development*, chronicles groundbreaking thinking and research on workforce development initiatives delivering training to single, working poor mothers.

Charles Heckscher is a professor at Rutgers University and director of the Center for Workplace Transformation. His research focuses on organization change and the changing nature of employee representation. He has also worked as a practitioner and consultant on processes of organizational development, primarily in the telecommunications industry. Before coming to Rutgers, Heckscher worked for the Communications Workers' union; he has taught human resources management at the Harvard Business School and the Wharton School. His books include *The New Unionism, White-Collar Blues, Agents of Change*, and *The Collaborative Enterprise*.

Sara Horowitz is the founder and executive director of Freelancers Union. She has been widely recognized for her entrepreneurial efforts to create a new labor institution for independent workers. In 1999 Sara was honored with a John D. and Catherine T. MacArthur Foundation Fellowship, and the Schwab Foundation selected her as one of its 100 Global Leaders for Tomorrow at the 2002 World Economic Forum. In 2010, *Crain's* named her one of "25 People to Watch." Before founding Freelancers Union, Sara was a labor attorney in private practice and a union organizer with 1199, the National Health and Human Service Employees Union. She has a master's degree from Harvard University's Kennedy School of Government, a law degree *cum laude* from the SUNY Buffalo Law School, and a B.S. from Cornell University's School of Industrial and Labor Relations.

Edward E. Lawler III is distinguished professor of business and director of the Center for Effective Organizations in the Marshall School of Business at the University of Southern California. He has been honored as a top contributor to the fields of organizational development, human resources management, organizational behavior, and compensation. Author of over 350 articles and 43 books, his most recent books include *Achieving Strategic Excellence: An Assessment of Human Resource Organizations* (2006), *Built to Change* (2006), *The New American Workplace* (2006), *America at Work* (2006), *Talent: Making People Your*

Competitive Advantage (2008), and *Achieving Excellence in Human Resource Management* (2009). For more information, visit http://www.edwardlawler.com and http://ceo.usc.edu.

Robert I. Lerman is an institute fellow at Urban Institute, professor of economics at American University, and research fellow at the Institute for the Study of Labor in Bonn, Germany. He has published widely on employment, income support, and youth employment issues. In the 1970s, he served as staff economist for the Congressional Joint Economic Committee and U.S. Department of Labor. He was one of the first scholars to examine the economic determinants of unwed fatherhood and to propose a U.S. youth apprenticeship strategy. He earned his A.B. at Brandeis University and Ph.D. in economics at MIT.

Leonard Lynn's earlier work concentrated on comparative U.S.–Japanese studies of technology policy and management. He is now working with Hal Salzman and other colleagues around the world on studies of the globalization of technology development. Lynn has published three books (with another forthcoming) as well as articles in *Science, IEEE Transactions on Engineering Management, Research Policy, Asian Business and Management, Organization Studies, Change,* and *Issues in Science and Technology.* He joined the faculty at Case Western Reserve University in 1987, where he became a full professor in 1995. He was previously on the faculty at Carnegie Mellon University.

Daniel Marschall is a professorial lecturer in sociology at George Washington University. He works for the AFL-CIO as their policy specialist for workforce issues. Recent publications have appeared in the *Journal of Applied Linguistics; Information, Communication and Society; The Annals of the American Academy of Political and Social Science;* and the *Journal of Computer-Mediated Communication.* Marschall has edited books on urban political conflict, office automation, and high-performance work systems. He is currently completing a book based on his ethnographic research among Internet technologists at a small software development firm. He has a Ph.D. in sociology from Lancaster University, UK.

F. Ray Marshall holds the Audre and Bernard Rapoport Centennial Chair in Economics and Public Affairs at the University of Texas-Austin. He co-chairs the National Center on Education and the Economy, is a trustee and founder of the Economic Policy Institute, and is a member of the State Department's Advisory Committee on International Economic Policy. His former positions include U.S. Secretary of Labor (1977–81), national president of the Industrial Relations Research Association (1977), and member of the State Department's Advisory Committee on Labor Diplomacy (1994–2005). Ray is the author most recently of *Immigration for Shared Prosperity* (2009).

Mary McCain is senior vice president of TechVision21, a Washington, DC, consulting group specializing in technology's impact on economic and workforce development in the public and private sectors. Her clients include the Microsoft Corporation, the American Association of Community Colleges, and the Council for Advancement of Adult Literacy. She holds Ph.D. in European labor and economic history from Georgetown University and is an affiliate fellow of Rutgers University's Center for Women and Work. Her publications include *The Power of Technology to Transform Adult Learning: Expanding Access to Adult Education and Workforce Skills through Distance Learning* (2009) and *E-Learning: Challenges and Opportunities for Business* (2008).

John McCarthy is a third-year doctoral student at the Rutgers University School of Management and Labor Relations. His research centers on the antecedents to successful knowledge transfer and combination within and between organizations. John is also interested in the differential interpretations that employees form regarding group-level network structures and how these interpretations help to frame a broader range of attitudes, including perceptions of climate.

Alexis Spencer Notabartolo is the public policy coordinator at the Writers Guild of America, West (WGAW). She received her B.A. in political studies (honors) from Pitzer College in Claremont, California. Prior to her work with the WGAW, Alexis worked with the Department for Professional Employees, AFL-CIO and conducted research on civil society development in the Republic of Georgia on a Fulbright research scholarship. While in Georgia, Alexis served as an election monitor with the AFL-CIO's Solidarity Center and taught courses at several universities in Tbilisi. In August 2008, she returned from Georgia to work as a field organizer with the Obama campaign in central Florida.

Henry A. Plotkin was the executive director of the New Jersey State Employment and Training Commission from March 1997 until his retirement in November 2008. He was the principal author of *New Jersey in Transition: The Crisis of the Workforce*, a white paper that resulted in the reorganization of the state's workforce development system. He helped establish the Council on Gender Parity, the State Council for Adult Literacy, and Workforce Investment Boards. The New Jersey American Society for Public Administration honored Henry with the Public Administrator of the Year Award. He received his Ph.D. and M.A. from Rutgers University and his B.A. from Queens College.

Hal Salzman is a sociologist and professor of public policy at the Bloustein School and Heldrich Center for Workforce Development, Rutgers University. His research focuses on globalization of science and engineering, S&E workforce education and development, workplace restructuring, skill requirements, and technology. Recent articles include analysis of international educational performance (in *Nature*) and new science and technology policy approaches. With colleagues he is studying the globalization of engineering, and he has conducted a number of studies of the IT industry and of corporate restructuring and the impact on jobs and training. Current projects include a National Science Foundation/International Polar Year study of employment, subsistence, and sustainability in the Arctic.

Louis Soares is the director of the Postsecondary Education Program at the Center for American Progress. He has held leadership positions in state economic and workforce development and has expertise in adult literacy, worker training, and postsecondary education. A thought leader on human capital issues, Soares has published articles and op-eds on workforce and innovation. Featured publications include *College-Ready Students, Student-Ready Colleges: A Federal Agenda for Postsecondary Completion* and *Working Learners: Educating America's Entire Workforce for the 21st Century*. He holds a master's degree in public administration from Harvard University and a bachelor's degree in business economics from Brown University.

Susan J. Schurman is dean of the Rutgers University College Community—serving nontraditional students—and professor of labor studies and employment relations in the School of Management and Labor Relations. From 1997 to 2007 she served as founding president of the National Labor College, an independent degree-completion college in Maryland supported by the AFL-CIO. Schurman received B.A. and M.A. degrees from Michigan State University and a Ph.D. in higher, adult, and continuing education from the University of Michigan. She was recently elected to the LERA board.

Ellen Scully-Russ is an assistant professor of human and organizational learning at The George Washington University. Her scholarship and practice focus on the role of adult education in meeting the individual and the political–economic challenges of the emerging knowledge society. Ellen has more than 25 years' experience working with union–management partnerships at firm, regional, and industrial levels to develop policies and programs that both support individual learning and development and improve industry and firm performance.